W9-CZL-250

Elementary Theory of Structures

Elementary Theory of Structures

Fourth Edition

YUAN-YU HSIEH

S.T. MAU

PRENTICE HALL, *Englewood Cliffs, New Jersey 07632*

Library of Congress Cataloging-in-Publication Data

Hsieh, Yuan-yu, (date)
    Elementary theory of structures / Yuan-yu Hsieh, S.T. Mau. — 4th
ed.
      p.   cm.
    Includes index.
    ISBN 0–13–301201–8
    1. Structural analysis (Engineering)   I. Mau, S. T.   II. Title.
TA645.H75   1995
624.1'73—dc20   94-26975
                                                    CIP

Editorial/production supervision and
   interior design: *TKM Productions*
Cover design: Maureen Eide
Manufacturing buyer: Bill Scazzero

 © 1995, 1988, 1982 and 1970 by Prentice-Hall, Inc.
A Simon & Schuster Company
Englewood Cliffs, New Jersey 07632

Printed in the United States of America
10 9 8 7 6 5 4

ISBN 0-13-301201-8

PRENTICE-HALL INTERNATIONAL (UK) Limited, *London*
PRENTICE-HALL OF AUSTRALIA PTY. Limited, *Sydney*
PRENTICE-HALL CANADA INC., *Toronto*
PRENTICE-HALL HISPANOAMERICANA, S.A., *Mexico*
PRENTICE-HALL OF INDIA PRIVATE LIMITED, *New Delhi*
PRENTICE-HALL OF JAPAN, INC., *Tokyo*
SIMON & SCHUSTER ASIA PTE. LTD., *Singapore*
EDITORA PRENTICE-HALL DO BRASIL, LTDA., *Rio de Janeiro*

Contents

Theme I

3   Structural Statics   35

4   Elastic Deformations   81

5   Method of Consistent Deformations   122

6   Matrix Force Method   161

Appendixes

Answers to Selected Problems   373

Index   379

Preface to the Fourth Edition

A quarter-century has elapsed since the publication of the first edition of this book. During the period the world of structural analysis has been changing continuously due to the increasing use of computers. The second and the third editions of the book more or less reflected the change. Today the use of computers in structural analysis is no longer a point of debate but a fact of life. This fact is amply reflected in this new edition by the omnipresence of the matrix method and the reference to computer programs.

It is our belief, however, that the prevalent utilization of computers only underscores the importance of understanding the basic theories and behavior of structures. Thus, a considerable portion of the book is still devoted to the classical methods of structural analysis. What sets the new edition apart from the previous editions is twofold: the reorganization of the materials in a more logical order and a diskette supplement containing computer programs for solving structural problems. The book centers on the two major methods of analysis: the force method and the displacement method. The classical force method—the analysis of force and deflection of statically determinate structures and the method of consistent deformation for statically indeterminate structures—is immediately followed by the matrix force method. Similarly, the classical displacement methods—the moment distribution method and slope-deflection method—are immediately followed by the matrix displacement method. In both cases, the matrix methods are presented as a natural extension and a generalization of the classical methods. After all, the matrix methods are integral parts of the general structural theory, made prominent only by the application of computers. The presentation of the matrix methods is guided by current engineering practice, rather than theoretical completeness. Thus, the coverage of the matrix displacement method is much simplified. Also, the coverage of the moment distribution method is shortened for the same reason. Several computer programs are provided as learning tools not for the matrix methods, but for the demonstration of the behavior of structures.

Despite the reorganization of the book, care has been taken to keep each chapter more or less self-sufficient so that each teacher may develop his or her own sequence of classroom deliberation. The coverage of the classical methods is sufficient for a single semester if all topics are treated in detail. On the other hand, experience indicates that both the classical methods and the matrix methods may be covered in a single semester also. During the revision process for the current edition, every effort has been made to achieve the original goals of the previous editions: the treatment is kept simple but comprehensive, and the text is readable and teachable.

The authors wish to express their sincere appreciation to many university professors and students in various parts of the world, who have read, used, and supported this book. Special thanks are due to Dr. Y. C. Fung of the University of California at San Diego and the editors at Prentice Hall for their encouragement and editorial guidance. Finally, the authors are indebted to their respective lifelong partners, Nelly Hsieh and Gerry Mau, to whom this book is dedicated.

Y. Y. Hsieh
S. T. Mau

Preface to the First Edition

This book is intended for elementary courses in the structural theory of civil engineering. In preparing material for it, the author has assumed that the reader is not familiar with the subject. The first seven chapters contain the basic concepts of structure and an analysis of statically determinate structures. Chapter 8 deals with elastic deformations. Chapters 9 through 15 are concerned with statically indeterminate structures, including the method of consistent deformations, least work, slope deflection, and moment distribution. Chapter 16 is devoted to an introductory discussion of matrix algebra. The scope is wide enough to provide adequate background for reading the remainder of the book. Finally, the last two chapters present a unified treatment of structures by matrix methods based on the finite-element approach. Since this is an elementary treatment, emphasis is on the development of general theory in terms of matrix operations rather than on the particular details of computer programs.

The elementary theory of structures is not difficult, involving as it does only a limited amount of higher mathematics. For most of the book, the only preparation needed is a knowledge of arithmetic and high school algebra. We may also say, however, that this theory is difficult, in that it generally requires careful study in order to achieve a thorough understanding of its basic philosophy. The author has endeavored to present clearly and lucidly the fundamentals of structural theory. These fundamentals are arranged in a systematic order and are supplemented by examples illustrating their application in some of the common structures—namely, beams, trusses, and rigid frames.

While written primarily for use as a textbook in the classroom, this book can also be of help to structural and architectural engineers in their independent study.

The author wishes to express his appreciation to those who have assisted in the preparation of this book. He is especially grateful to Dr. Y. C. Fung, professor at the University of California, San Diego, for his enthusiastic encouragement throughout the writing of this volume and for his constructive criticism of the manuscript. Particular acknowledgment is also due Dr. Z. A. Lu of the University of California, Berkeley, who made many valuable suggestions for improving the contents, and Dr. John Yao, who read part of the manuscript. Thanks also are due Pamela Fischer and Cordelia Thomas of Prentice-Hall, who offered their competent knowledge in producing and editing this book. Finally, the author is indebted to his wife, Nelly, who typed all of the manuscript.

Y.Y.H.

Chapter 1

Introduction

1-1 ENGINEERING STRUCTURES

The word *structure* has various meanings. By an *engineering structure* we mean roughly something constructed or built. The principal structures of concern to civil engineers are bridges, buildings, walls, dams, towers, shells, and cable structures. Such structures are composed of one or more solid elements so arranged that the whole structures as well as their components are capable of holding themselves without appreciable geometric change during loading and unloading.

The design of a structure involves many considerations, among which are four major objectives that must be satisfied:

1. The structure must meet the performance requirement (utility).
2. The structure must carry loads safely (safety).
3. The structure should be economical in material, construction, and overall cost (economy).
4. The structure should have a good appearance (beauty).

Consider, for example, the roof truss resting on columns shown in Fig. 1-1. The purposes of the roof truss and of the columns are, on the one hand, to hold in equilibrium their own weights, the load of roof covering, and the wind and snow (if any) and, on the other hand, to provide rooms for housing a family, for a manufacturing plant, or for other uses. During its development the design is generally optimized to achieve minimum expenditure for materials and construction. Proper attention is also given to the truss formation so that it is both practical and esthetic. In this book, however, we are concerned only with the load-carrying function of structures.

1

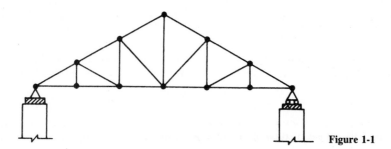

Figure 1-1

1-2 PROCESS OF STRUCTURAL DESIGN

The complete design of a structure is outlined in the following stages:

1. *Developing a general layout.* The general layout of a structure is selected from many possible alternatives. The primary concern is the purpose for which the structure is to be built. This stage involves the choice of structural type, the selection of material, and a tentative estimation of cost based on a reasonable analysis of a preliminary structural design. It may also involve selecting the best location or adapting the structure to a site that has not been predetermined. There are many other considerations, including the legal, financial, sociological, cultural, esthetic, and environmental aspects. It is clear that this stage of design calls for an engineer with a high order of experience, skill, general knowledge, and imagination.

2. *Investigating the loads.* Before a refined structural analysis can be carried out, it is necessary to determine the loads for which a given structure should be designed. General information about the loads imposed on a structure is usually given in the specifications and codes. However, it is part of the designer's responsibility to specify the load conditions and to take care of exceptional cases.

The weight of the structure itself together with the material permanently attached to it is called *dead load* and is regarded as fixed in magnitude and location. Since the dead load must be approximated before the structure is designed, the preliminary data are only tentative. Revision must be made if the initial estimation is not satisfactory.

All loads other than dead load may be called *live loads*. Live loads are generally classified as movable loads and moving loads. *Movable loads* are loads that may be transported from one location to another on a structure without dynamic impact; for example, people, furniture, and goods on a building floor, or snow or ice on a roof. *Moving loads* are loads that move continuously over the structure, such as railway trains or tracks on a bridge, wind on a roof or wall, or hydrostatic pressure on an abutment. Moving loads may also be applied suddenly to the structure, for example, the centrifugal and longitudinal forces induced by the acceleration of vehicles and the dynamic forces generated by earthquakes.

In an ordinary structural design all loads are treated as static loads in order to simplify the analysis. In this way the impact due to a moving live load is expressed as a percentage of the live load, and the earthquake force is commonly considered to be a horizontal force equal to a fraction of the weight of a structure.

Other load considerations may include thermal effects and resistance to bomb blasting.

3. *Preliminary stress analysis*. Once the basic form of the structure and the external loads are defined, a structural analysis can be made to determine the internal forces in various members of the structure and the displacements at some controlling points. When live loads are involved, it is important to determine the maximum possible stresses in each member being considered. The principles governing this phase of design are usually discussed in the theory of structures.

4. *Selection of elements*. The selection of suitable sizes and shapes of members and their connections depends on the results of the stress analysis together with the design provisions of the specifications or codes. A trial-and-error approach may be used in the search for a proportioning of elements that will be both economical and adequate. A sound knowledge of strength of materials and process of fabrication is also essential.

5. *Reanalysis*. In many cases, the selected member sizes and shapes may deviate from those assumed in the preliminary analysis to the extent that the accuracy of the preliminary analysis may be in question. The design engineer needs to make a judgment as to whether a reanalysis is warranted. A great advantage of a computerized structural analysis is the ease with which a reanalysis is performed comparing to the tedious repetition associated with hand calculation. The process of analysis and design is clearly an iterative one, to be repeated to the satisfaction of the design engineer. It should also be emphasized that an experienced engineer is often able to proportion the structure such that the need for reanalysis is minimized or eliminated altogether.

6. *Drawing and detailing*. Once the makeup of each part of the structure has been determined, the last stage of design can begin. This final stage includes the preparation of contract drawing, detailing, job specification, and final cost; this information is necessary for construction to proceed.

These six stages are interrelated and may be subdivided and modified. In many cases they must be carried out more or less simultaneously. The subject matter of the theory of structures is stress analysis with occasional reference to loadings. The emphasis of structural theory is usually on the fundamentals, rather than on the details of design.

1-3 CLASSIFICATION OF STRUCTURAL THEORIES

Structural theories may be classified from various points of view. For convenience of study, we shall characterize them by the following aspects:

1. *Statics versus dynamics*. Ordinary structures are usually designed under static loads. Dead load and snow load are static loads that cause no dynamic effect on structures. Some live loads, such as trucks and locomotives moving on bridges, are also assumed to be concentrated static load systems. They do cause impact on structures; however, the dynamic effects are treated as a fraction of the moving loads to simplify the design.

The specialized branch that deals with the dynamic effects on structures of accelerated moving loads, earthquake loads, wind gusts, or bomb blasts is *structural dynamics*.

2. *Plane versus space.* No structure is really planar, that is, two-dimensional. However, structural analyses for beams, trussed bridges, or rigid frame buildings are usually treated as plane problems. On the other hand, in some structures, such as towers and framing for domes, the stresses between members not lying in a plane are interrelated in such a way that the analysis cannot be simplified in terms of component planar structures. Such structures must be considered as space frameworks under a noncoplanar force system.

3. *Linear versus nonlinear structures.* Linear structure means that a linear relationship is assumed to exist between the applied loads and the resulting displacements in a structure. This assumption is based on the following conditions:

a. The material of the structure is elastic and obeys Hooke's law at all points and throughout the range of loading considered.

b. The changes in the geometry of the structure are so small that they can be neglected when the stresses are calculated.

Note that, if the principle of superposition is to apply, a linear relationship must exist, or be assumed to exist, between loads and displacements. The principle of superposition states that the total effect at some point in a structure due to a number of causes (forces or displacements) acting simultaneously is equal to the sum of the effects for the causes acting separately.

A nonlinear relationship between the applied actions and the resulting displacements exists under either of two conditions:

a. The material of the structure is inelastic.

b. The material is within the elastic range, but the geometry of the structure changes significantly during the application of loads.

The study of nonlinear behavior of structures includes *plastic analysis of structures* and *buckling of structures*.

4. *Statically determinate versus statically indeterminate structures.* The term *statically determinate structure* means that structural analysis can be carried out by statics alone. If this is not so, the structure is statically indeterminate.

A statically indeterminate structure is solved by the equations of statics together with the equations furnished by the geometry of the elastic curve of the structure in linear analysis. We note that the elastic deformations of the structure are affected not only by the applied loads on the structure, but also by the material properties (e.g., the modulus of elasticity E) and by the geometric properties of the member section (e.g., the cross-sectional area A or the moment of inertia I). Thus, loads, material properties, and geometric properties are all involved in solving a statically indeterminate structure, while load factor alone dominates in a statically determinate problem.

5. *Force versus displacement*. Force and displacement are two categories of events that affect a structure. The objective of a structural analysis is to determine the forces and displacements pertaining to the structure and to analyze their relationships as specified by the geometric and material properties of structural elements. Structural analysis in a broader sense can then be divided into two categories: the force method and the displacement method. In the *force method*, we treat the forces as the basic unknowns and express the displacements in terms of forces, whereas in the *displacement method*, we regard the displacements as the fundamental unknowns and express the forces in terms of displacements. In matrix analysis of linear structures, the force method is often referred to as the *flexibility method*, and the displacement method is called the *stiffness method*.

1-4 ACTUAL AND IDEAL STRUCTURES

In subsequent chapters, we will deal with structures with clearly and simply defined geometry, material properties, connection and support conditions, and loadings. These are ideal structures that serve as the model of the actual or real structures. Because structural analysis is performed on ideal structures, whereas the design and construction are for real structures, it is imperative that the results obtained on ideal structures be reasonably close to those of the real structures.

The process of defining an ideal structure from a real structure is called *modeling*. It usually involves the imposition of simplifying assumptions. A nontrivial example is that of defining the length of a member in a multimember frame. The length of the girder in Fig. 1-2 can alternatively be defined as the face-to-face clear span length *a–b* or the center-to-center length *a'–b'*, depending on the relative stiffness of the girder and the column.

Another example of modeling is the definition of connection. Referring to Fig. 1-2 again, we see that the connection between the girder and the column can be defined in different ways depending on how they are put together. The various idealized connections are described in Section 2-5.

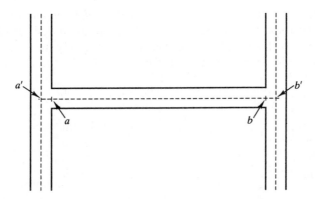

Figure 1-2

In addition to the geometry and material properties of the structure, we often have to make assumptions on the response of structures under loads, such as the material will follow a linear stress–strain law and the deflected geometry will not deviate significantly from the undeflected geometry. These assumptions affect the method of analysis, as described in Section 1-3.

It is obvious, then, that the validity of the structural analysis performed on an ideal structure is bounded by the assumptions we make in carrying out the analysis. How well these assumptions describe the real structure behavior is a matter of engineering judgment, which should be based on experience and the in-depth understanding of real structure behavior.

1-5 SCOPE OF THIS BOOK

Three major types of basic structures are thoroughly discussed in this book:

1. Beam
2. Truss
3. Rigid frame

A *beam*, in its narrow sense, is a straight member subjected only to transverse loads. A beam is completely analyzed when the values of bending moment and shear are determined.

A *truss* is composed of members connected by frictionless hinges or pins. The loads on a truss are assumed to be concentrated at the joints. Each member of a truss is considered as a two-force member subjected to axial forces only.

A *rigid frame* is built of members connected by rigid joints capable of resisting moment. Members of a rigid frame, in general, are subjected to bending moment, shear, and axial forces.

This book is confined exclusively to the planar aspect of structures. The main content is conveniently divided into four parts. The two chapters in *Prelude* are devoted to the introduction of fundamental concepts and methodology of structural analysis. The four chapters in *Theme I* contain the first major theme of the book: the *force method* of structural analysis. Chapter 3 deals with the analysis of statically determinate structures for force. Chapter 4 follows with the analysis of statically determinate structures for deformation. The classical force method of consistent deformations is then introduced in Chapter 5 for statically indeterminate structures. The systematic application of the classical method of consistent deformations in a matrix formulation results in the matrix force method described in Chapter 6. The second major theme of the book, the displacement method, is unveiled in *Theme II* in three chapters. The concept of using joint rotation and member translation as controlling factors in beam and frame analysis is introduced through the classical moment distribution method in Chapter 7. The formulation of the equilibrium conditions leads to the explicit equations in terms of the joint rotations and member translation. This is known as the classical slope-deflection method and is given in Chapter 8. The generalization of the slope-deflection method results in the matrix displacement method of Chapter 9. The remaining two chapters of the book are contained in *Coda*. The classical subject of influence lines is covered in Chapter 10. The treatment of nonprismatic members is given in Chapter 11. The four appendixes, covering mathematics, computer programs, theoretical derivations, and useful tables, are very much integral parts of the book.

Chapter 2

Fundamentals

2-1 GENERAL

The fundamental concepts and ingredients of structural analysis are described in this chapter. Of foremost importance is the concept of equilibrium and the equations of equilibrium. A brief review of the equations of equilibrium for a coplanar force system is given in Sec. 2-2. Human-made structures on earth are always connected to their foundations through supports. The various types of supports and their reactions and constraints are discussed in Sec. 2-3. Structures considered in this book are composed of individual members. Each member is associated with a certain number of internal member forces. Section 2-4 contains an account of member forces based on member equilibrium. To make up a structure, the members are linked together through connections. A description of connections, the forces they transmit, and the motions that they allow are contained in Sec. 2-5. How a structure is supported and its members are connected determine whether the structure is statically stable and whether the member forces can be solved by the equations of statics alone. These matters of stability and determinacy are discussed in Secs. 2-6 and 2-7. To conclude this chapter, the two different methods of structural analysis, the force method and the displacement method, are illustrated through two simple examples in Sec. 2-8.

2-2 EQUATIONS OF EQUILIBRIUM

The first and major function of a structure is to carry loads. Beams, trusses, and rigid frames all have one element in common: Each sustains the burden of certain loads without showing appreciable distortions. In structural statics all force systems are assumed to act on rigid bodies. Actually, there are always some small deformations that may cause some small change of dimension in structure and a shifting of the action lines of the forces. However, such deviations are neglected in stress analysis.

A structure is said to be *in equilibrium* if, under the action of external forces, it remains at rest relative to the earth. Also, each part of the structure, if taken as a free body isolated from the whole, must be at rest relative to the earth under the action of the internal forces at the cut sections and of the external forces thereabout. If such is the case, the force system is balanced, or in equilibrium, which implies that the resultant of the force system (either a resultant force or a resultant couple) imposed on the structure, or segment thereof, must be zero.

Since this book is confined to planar structures, all the force systems are coplanar. The generally balanced coplanar force system must then satisfy the following three simultaneous equations:

$$\sum F_x = 0, \qquad \sum F_y = 0, \qquad \sum M_a = 0 \qquad (2\text{-}1)$$

where $\sum F_x$ = summation of the x components of each force in the system
$\sum F_y$ = summation of the y components of each force in the system

The subscripts x and y indicate two mutually perpendicular directions in the Cartesian coordinate system:

$\sum M_a$ = summation of moments about any point a in the plane due to each force in the system

Note that $\sum F_x$ also represents the x component of the resultant of the force system, $\sum F_y$ the y component of the resultant of the force system, and $\sum M_a$ the moment about a of the resultant of the force system.

The alternative to Eq. 2-1 may be given by

$$\sum F_y = 0, \qquad \sum M_a = 0, \qquad \sum M_b = 0 \qquad (2\text{-}2)$$

provided that the line through points a and b is not perpendicular to the y axis, a and b being two arbitrarily chosen points and the y axis being an arbitrarily chosen axis in the plane. Or

$$\sum M_a = 0, \qquad \sum M_b = 0, \qquad \sum M_c = 0 \qquad (2\text{-}3)$$

provided that points a, b, and c are not collinear, a, b, and c being three arbitrarily chosen points in the plane.

The explanation of Eq. 2-2 is as follows:

1. Let R denote the resultant of the force system. Assume that $R \neq 0$. Since $\sum M_a = 0$ and $\sum M_b = 0$, the resultant R cannot be a couple. It must be a force through a and b and by assumption is not perpendicular to the y axis.
2. By $\sum F_y = 0$, we mean that the resultant has no y-axis component and must therefore be perpendicular to the y axis.

The foregoing contradictory statements lead to the conclusion that the force is also zero. Therefore, Eq. 2-2 is the condition for $R = 0$.

A similar explanation is given here for Eq. 2-3:

1. Assume that $R \neq 0$. Since $\Sigma M_a = 0$, $\Sigma M_b = 0$, and $\Sigma M_c = 0$, the resultant R cannot be a couple. It must be a force through a, b, and c.
2. But by assumption a, b, and c are not collinear.

These statements lead us to conclude that the force is also zero. Therefore, Eq. 2-3 is the condition for $R = 0$.

Two special cases of the coplanar force system in equilibrium are worth noting:

1. *Concurrent forces*. If a system of coplanar, concurrent forces is in equilibrium, then the forces of the system must satisfy the following equations:

$$\Sigma F_x = 0, \qquad \Sigma F_y = 0 \tag{2-4}$$

Another set of independent equations necessary and sufficient for the equilibrium of the forces of a coplanar, concurrent force system is

$$\Sigma F_y = 0, \qquad \Sigma M_a = 0 \tag{2-5}$$

provided that point a is not on the line through the concurrent point of forces and perpendicular to the y axis.

A third set of equations of equilibrium for a coplanar, concurrent force system is

$$\Sigma M_a = 0, \qquad \Sigma M_b = 0 \tag{2-6}$$

where a and b are any two points in the plane of the forces, provided that the line through a and b does not pass through the concurrent point of forces.

2. *Parallel forces*. If a coplanar, parallel force system is in equilibrium, the forces of the system must satisfy the equations

$$\Sigma F_y = 0, \qquad \Sigma M_a = 0 \tag{2-7}$$

where the y axis is in the direction of the force system and a is any point in the plane.

Another set of independent equations of equilibrium for a system of coplanar, parallel forces may be given as

$$\Sigma M_a = 0, \qquad \Sigma M_b = 0 \tag{2-8}$$

where a and b are any two points in the plane, provided that the line through a and b is not parallel to the forces of system.

There are two simple, special cases of equilibrium that deserve explicit mention:

1. *Two-force member*. Figure 2-1 shows a body subjected to two external forces applied at a and b. If the body is in equilibrium, then the two forces cannot

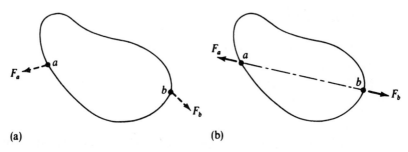

Figure 2-1

be in random orientation, as shown in Fig. 2-1(a), but must be directed along ab, as shown in Fig. 2-1(b). Furthermore, they must be equal in magnitude and opposite in sense. This can be proved by using first the equations $\Sigma M_a = 0$ and $\Sigma M_b = 0$. In order for the moment a to vanish, the force F_b must pass through a. Similarly, the force F_a must pass through b. Next, since $\Sigma F = 0$, it is readily seen that $F_a = -F_b$.

    2. *Three-force member.* Figure 2-2 shows a body subjected to the action of three external forces applied at a, b, and c. If the body is in equilibrium, then the three cannot be in random orientation, as shown in Fig. 2-2(a). They must be concurrent at a common point O, as shown in Fig. 2-2(b); otherwise, the total moment about the intersection of any two forces could not vanish. A limiting case occurs when point O moves off at infinite distance from a, b, and c, in which case the forces F_a, F_b, and F_c are parallel.

2-3 SUPPORTS

Structures are either partially or completely restrained so that they cannot move freely in space. Such restraints are provided by supports that connect the structure to some stationary body, such as the ground or another structure. The first step in structural analysis is to take the structure without the supports and calculate the forces, known as *reactions*, exerted on the structure by the supports. The reactions

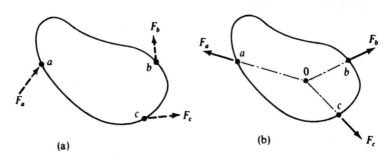

Figure 2-2

are considered part of the external forces other than the loads on the structure and
are to balance the other external loads in a state of equilibrium.

Certain symbols used to designate supports must first be described. There are
generally three different types of support: the *hinge*, the *roller*, and the *fixed
support*. Some intermediate models of support between the idealized three can be
made to respond to the reality. The distribution of the reactive forces of a support
may be very complicated, but in an idealized state the resultant of the forces may
be represented by a single force completely specified by three elements: the *point
of application*, the *direction*, and the *magnitude*. It may be noted that, in analysis,
the direction simply means the slope of the action line, while the magnitude of force
may be positive or negative, thus indicating not only its numerical size but also the
sense of the action line.

Hinge support.   A hinge support is represented by the symbol ⟁ or
⟁. It can resist a general force P in any direction, but cannot resist the moment
of the force about the connecting point, as illustrated in Fig. 2-3. From the figure,
it is also clear that the effect of a hinge support is to restrain the member from any
translational movements at the support.

The reaction of a hinge support is assumed to be through the center of the
connecting pin; its magnitude and slope of action line are yet to be determined. It
is therefore a reaction with two unknown elements, which could equivalently be
represented by the unknown magnitudes of its horizontal and vertical components,
both acting through the center of the hinge pin. This representation is justified by
the following equations from statics:

$$|R| = \sqrt{R_x^2 + R_y^2}, \qquad \theta_x = \tan^{-1}\frac{R_y}{R_x} \qquad (2\text{-}9)$$

where $|R|$ = magnitude of the reaction R
$\quad\quad R_x$ = x component of R
$\quad\quad R_y$ = y component of R
$\quad\quad \theta_x$ = angle that R makes with the x direction

The magnitude and direction of R can be determined if the unknown magnitudes
of R_x and R_y are found.

Thus, a hinge support can also be replaced by two links along the horizontal
and vertical directions through the center of the connecting pin, as shown in Fig.

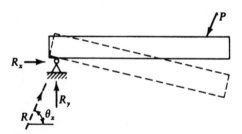

Figure 2-3

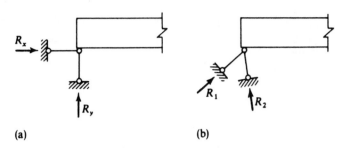

(a)   (b)

Figure 2-4

2-4(a). Each link is a two-force member, the axial force of which represents an element of reaction (R_x or R_y). In general, a hinge support is equivalent to two supporting links provided in any two different directions, which are not necessarily an orthogonal set, through the connecting point, as shown in Fig. 2-4(b), where R_1 and R_2 indicate the axial forces in two links. The reaction R at the pin can always be determined if the magnitudes of R_1 and R_2 are obtained.

Roller support.   A roller support is represented by either the symbol ⩘

or ⩘ . The support mechanism used is such that the reaction acts normal to the supporting surface through the center of the connecting pin, as shown in Fig. 2-5(a) to (c). The reaction may be either away from or toward the supporting surface. As such, the roller support is incapable of resisting moment and lateral force along the surface of support.

A roller support supplies a reactive force, fixed at a known point and in a known direction, the magnitude of which is unknown. It is therefore a reaction with one unknown element. It also restrains the member from any translational movement normal to the supporting surface.

A link support, shown in Fig. 2-5(d), is also of this type since the link is a two-force member and the reaction must be along the link.

Fixed support.   A fixed support is designated by the symbol ⊣ . It is capable of resisting force in any direction and moment of force about the connecting end, thus preventing the end of the member from both translation and rotation. The reaction supplied by a fixed support may be represented by the unknown

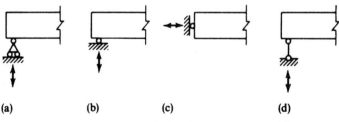

(a)   (b)   (c)   (d)

Figure 2-5

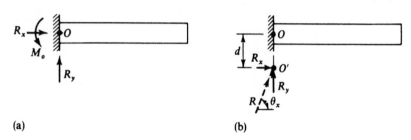

(a)   (b)

Figure 2-6

magnitudes of a moment called M_o, a horizontal force R_x, and a vertical force R_y acting through the centroid of the end cross section O, as shown in Fig. 2-6(a). These three unknown elements can be expressed as equal to a single force R with its three elements—the magnitude, direction, and point of application—yet to be determined, as shown in Fig. 2-6(b). Now the magnitude and direction of R can be related to its components R_x and R_y by Eq. 2-9,

$$|R| = \sqrt{R_x^2 + R_y^2}, \qquad \theta_x = \tan^{-1}\frac{R_y}{R_x}$$

and the point of application O' can be located by the distance d from O, which, in turn, is related to M_o by

$$d = \frac{M_o}{R_x}$$

Since fixed support provides moment resistance, it is one step beyond the hinge support in rigidity.

Two devices equivalent to the fixed support are shown in Fig. 2-7. Each is composed of a hinge and a roller and represents three elements of reaction capable of resisting both force and moment.

2-4 MEMBER FORCES

A truss structure is composed of pin-connected members and is assumed to be pin-loaded, as shown in Fig. 2-8(a). Now, if any one of the members is taken from its connecting pins as a free body, the forces exerted on the member must be

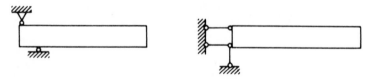

Figure 2-7

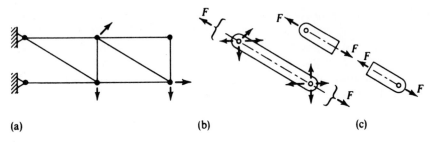

Figure 2-8

concentrated at the two ends of the member through the centers of pins. Furthermore, these two systems of concurrent forces can be combined into two resultant forces that must be equal, opposite, and collinear, as indicated in Fig. 2-8(b). In other words, each member of a truss is a *two-force* member. Hence, the internal forces existing in any cut section of a truss member (assumed straight and uniform) must be a pair of equal and opposite axial forces to balance the axial forces exerted on the ends, as shown in Fig. 2-8(c). This internal force pair is called the *member force* of the truss member.

The fact that each member of a truss represents an unknown element of internal force enables us to obtain the total number of unknown elements of internal force by counting the total number of members of which the truss is composed.

Members of structures, such as beams and rigid frames, are acted on by more than two forces. Let us investigate the elements of internal force in any cut section *A–A* of the beam in Fig. 2-9(a) or of the rigid frame in Fig. 2-9(b).

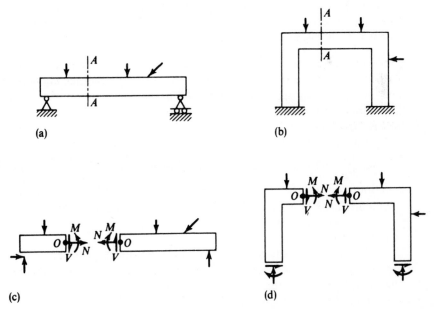

Figure 2-9

We begin by taking the free bodies of the portions to the left and right of section *A–A*, as shown in Fig. 2-9(c) and (d). It is obvious that forces of internal constraint must exist between these two portions in order to hold them together. Such internal forces, of course, always occur in pairs of equal and opposite forces. The actual distribution of these internal forces cannot be easily discovered. To maintain the equilibrium of the free body, however, the internal forces must be statically equal and opposite to the system of forces acting externally on the portion considered, and the internal forces can always be represented by a force applied at the centroid *O* of the cross section together with a couple of moment *M*. Furthermore, the force can, in turn, be resolved into a normal component *N* and a tangential component *V*. Thus, in Fig. 2-9(c) and (d) we represent the stress resultant on any section *A–A* by the three unknown magnitudes of *N*, *V*, and *M*, called, respectively, the *normal force*, the *shearing force*, and the *resisting moment* at that section.

From the foregoing discussion, we remember that to take a free body from a beam or rigid frame we must assume three unknown elements of internal force generally existing in the cut section. The three elements of the internal force at any cut section may be called the *member forces*, because the internal forces at any other sections are related to them through equilibrium conditions.

2-5 CONNECTIONS

Whereas supports link a structure to its foundation, connections link structural members to each other. The counterpart of a fixed support is a *rigid* connection. A rigid connection does not allow any relative movement, translation, or rotation between members. It is used in rigid frames and is capable of transmitting normal force, shear force, and moment from one member to another. Since a rigid connection is usually assumed for rigid frames, it is often not even explicitly marked at the joints of two or more members. Occasionally, it may appear as $\ulcorner\,$ In steel structures, a connection between a beam and a column may allow partial rotation and is called a *semirigid* connection. The amount of rotation of a semirigid connection is related to the moment it transmits.

A *hinge* connection is similar to a hinge support. It prevents relative translation, but allows relative rotation between members. It is implicitly assumed for all truss member connections. It will transmit force, but not moment. When a hinge connection is used to connect two or more frame members, it creates one or more conditions on the force system, thus providing additional equations of statics to supplement the equations of equilibrium. These equations are called *equations of condition* or *construction*. We discuss these further in Sec. 2-7. A hinge connection is represented by the symbol —O—.

A *roller* connection is used occasionally in steel structures to provide the freedom to expand between two members. It usually prevents translation only in the direction normal to the member axis, thus transmitting only shear force. It is represented by the symbol ⌐O⌐ .

2-6 STABILITY AND DETERMINACY OF A STRUCTURE WITH RESPECT TO SUPPORTS

When we consider the design of a structure, we must give careful thought to the number and arrangement of the supports directly related to the stability and determinacy of the structure. In the following discussions we shall treat the structures as a monolithic rigid body mounted on a number of supports. Thus, no internal condition will be involved, and the stability and determinacy of the structure will be judged solely by the stability and determinacy of supports.

  1. Two elements of reaction supplied by supports, such as two forces each with a definite point of application and direction, are not sufficient to ensure the stability of a rigid body, because the two are either collinear, parallel, or concurrent. In each of these cases, the condition of equilibrium is violated, not because of the lack of strength of supports, but because of the insufficient number of support elements. This situation is referred to as *statical instability*.

  If two reactive forces are collinear [see Fig. 2-10(a)], they cannot resist an external load that has a component normal to the line of reactions. If they are parallel [see Fig. 2-10(b)], they cannot prevent the body from lateral sliding. If they are concurrent [see Fig. 2-10(c) or (d)], they cannot resist the moment about the concurrent point O due to any force not through O.

  Algebraically, in each of the cases above, one equilibrium condition is not satisfied. For instance, in Fig. 2-10(a) or (b) the condition $\Sigma F_x = 0$ is violated (x indicates the direction normal to the line of reaction, whereas in Fig. 2-10(c) or (d)

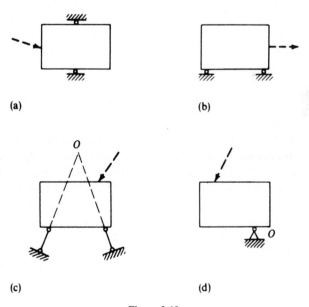

(a)   (b)

(c)   (d)

Figure 2-10

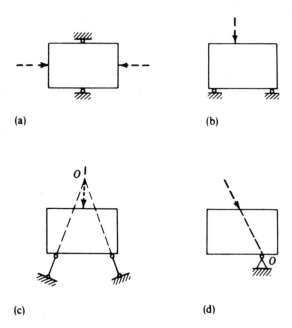

Figure 2-11

the condition $\Sigma M_o = 0$ is not fulfilled. The body is, therefore, not in equilibrium; it is unstable.

Only under some very special conditions of loading can the body be stable, such as those shown in Fig. 2-11. In Fig. 2-11(a) the applied loads acting on the body are themselves in equilibrium; therefore, no reaction is required. In Fig. 2-11(b) the applied load is in the same direction as the reactions, so equilibrium can be maintained for the parallel force system; and in Fig. 2-11(c) or (d) the applied load is through the concurrent point O; therefore, equilibrium can also be established.

Structures stable under special conditions of loading but unstable under general conditions of loading are said to be in a state of *unstable equilibrium* and are classified as unstable structures.

2. At least three elements of reaction are necessary to restrain a body in stable equilibrium. Consider each case shown in Fig. 2-12. The rigid body is subjected to restraints by three elements of reaction, and the restraints can be solved by the three available equilibrium equations. The satisfaction of all three equilibrium equations,

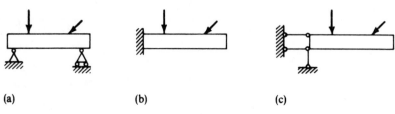

Figure 2-12

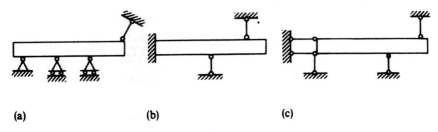

(a)   (b)   (c)

Figure 2-13

$\Sigma F_x = 0$, $\Sigma F_y = 0$, and $\Sigma M = 0$, for loads and reactions acting on the body guarantees, respectively, that the body will neither move horizontally or vertically nor rotate. The system is said to be *statically stable and determinate*.

3. If there are more than three elements of reaction, as in each case shown in Fig. 2-13, the body is necessarily more stable, because of the additional restraints. Since the number of unknown elements of reaction is greater than the number of equations for static equilibrium, the system is said to be *statically indeterminate* with regard to the reactions of support.

4. That the number of elements of reaction should be at least three is a necessary but not a sufficient condition for an externally stable structure. There are many cases that are obviously not stable with respect to the support system even though three or more than three elements of reaction are supplied. When, for example, the lines of reaction are all parallel, as in Fig. 2-14(a), the body is unstable, because it is vulnerable to lateral sliding. Another case is shown in Fig. 2-14(b), where the lines of the three reaction elements are originally concurrent at point O. The system is also unstable because, even though complete collapse probably will not result, a small initial rotation about O because of the moment caused by any force not through O will certainly occur until the three reaction lines form the triangle indicated by the crosshatched lines.

The above-mentioned instability, which results from the inadequacy of arrangement of supports, is referred to as *external geometric instability*.

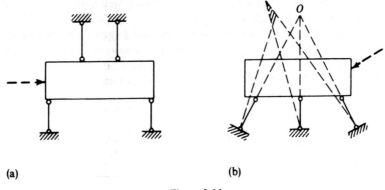

(a)   (b)

Figure 2-14

5. A monolithic rigid body is rigid by definition; hence, it will have no problem of internal instability. Furthermore, at any cut section of a monolithic rigid body, the elements of internal force, which are no more than three in number, can always be determined by the equations of equilibrium once the reactions are completely defined. Therefore, the stability and determinacy of the entire system mentioned in this section are solely determined by the stability and determinacy of supports and reactions.

Let us sum up the main points of the foregoing discussions as follows:

1. If the number of unknown elements of reaction is fewer than three, the equations of equilibrium are generally not satisfied, and the system is said to be statically unstable.
2. If the number of unknown elements of reaction is equal to three and if no external geometric instability is involved, then the system is statically stable and determinate.
3. If the number of unknown elements of reaction is greater than three, then the system is statically indeterminate; it is statically stable provided that no external geometric instability is involved. The excess number n of unknown elements designates the nth degree of statical indeterminacy. For example, in each case of Fig. 2-13 there are five unknown elements of reaction. Thus, $5 - 3 = 2$, which indicates a statical indeterminacy of second degree.

2-7 GENERAL STABILITY AND DETERMINACY OF STRUCTURES

Structural stability and determinacy must be judged by the number and arrangement of the supports as well as the number and arrangement of the members and the connections of the structure. They are determined by inspection or by formula. For convenience, we shall deal with the general stability and determinacy of beams, trusses, and rigid frames in separate sections.

2-7a General Stability and Determinacy of Beams

If a beam is built up without any internal connections (internal hinge, roller, or link), the entire beam may be considered as a single monolithic rigid body placed on a number of supports, and the question of the stability and of the determinacy of the beam is settled solely by the number and arrangement of supports, as discussed in Sec. 2-6.

Now let us investigate what will happen if a certain connecting device is inserted in a beam. Let us suppose that a hinge is introduced into the statically stable and determinate beam of Fig. 2-15(a) or (b). The beam in each case will obviously become unstable under general loading as the result of a relative rotation between the left and the right portions of the beam at the internal hinge, as indicated in

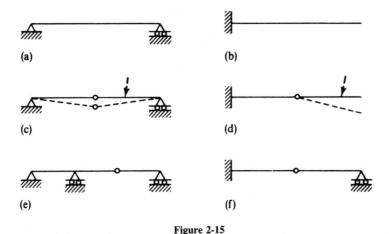

Figure 2-15

Fig. 2-15(c) or (d). That the hinge has no capacity to resist moment constitutes a restriction on the external forces acting on the structure; that is,

$$M = 0$$

about the hinge. In other words, the moment about the hinge calculated from the external forces on either side of the hinge must be zero in order to guarantee that these portions will not rotate about the hinge.

Referring to Fig. 2-15(c) or (d), we see in each case that three elements of reaction are supplied by supports, whereas there are four conditions of statics to restrict the external forces—three from equilibrium plus one from construction. This means that the number of unknown elements of reaction is one fewer than the independent equations of statics available for their solution. Therefore, the equations of statics for the force system are generally not satisfied. The beam is statically unstable unless we provide at least one additional element of reaction, such as the additional roller support shown in Fig. 2-15(e) or (f), which makes the total number of unknown elements of reaction equal to the total number of independent equations of statics needed to determine the elements. If this is done, the beam will be restored to a statically stable and determinate state.

Next, let us suppose that a link (or a roller) is introduced into a section of the statically stable and determinate beam of Fig. 2-15(a) or (b). We expect that this beam will be less stable than one with a hinged connection, because the link (roller) cannot resist both moments about the link pin and forces normal to the link. The beam will collapse under general types of loading as a result of the relative rotation and the lateral translation of the left and right portions of the beam at the link, as indicated in Fig. 2-16(a) or (b).

That a link (or roller) has no capacity to resist lateral forces and moments constitutes two restrictions to the external forces acting on the structure,

$$H = 0 \quad \text{and} \quad M = 0$$

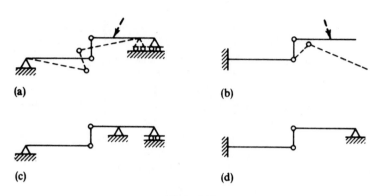

Figure 2-16

about the link (either of two pins). *H* is the sum of forces on either side of the link in the direction normal to the link. The satisfaction of condition *H* = 0 for the portion of the structure on either side of the link prevents the movement of one portion of the structure relative to the other in the direction normal to the link. Satisfying condition *M* = 0 for the portion of the structure on either side of the link ensures that these portions will not rotate about the pins of the link.

Referring to Fig. 2-16(a) or (b), we find that in each case there are three elements of reaction supplied by the support system, while there are five conditions of statics to restrict them—three from equilibrium and two from construction. Since the number of elements in reaction is two fewer than the number of statical equations to determine them, the beam is, therefore, quite unstable unless we supply at least two more elements of reaction, such as the hinged support shown in Fig. 2-16(c) or (d), to balance the situation. This done, the beam will be restored to its statically stable and determinate state.

There are beams for which the number of reaction elements is greater than the total number of independent equations of statics available. The beams are then classified as *statically indeterminate*, and the excess number of unknown elements indicates the degree of statical indeterminacy.

Geometric instability is most likely to occur whenever internal connections are introduced into an originally stable structure. Consider, for example, Fig. 2-17(a). The beam is statically indeterminate to the first degree. Now, if a hinge is inserted into the beam, as shown in Fig. 2-17(b), it seems to be statically determinate. However, when a load is applied, a small initial displacement will result and will not

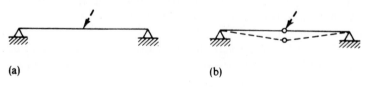

Figure 2-17

be resisted elastically by the structure. In such a case, the beam is unstable not because of the inadequacy of the supports, but because of the inadequacy of the arrangement of members. This situation is referred to as *internal geometric instability*. Very often, when this occurs, the structure will collapse. In the present case collapse will not occur; the beam will come to rest in a position such as that marked by the dashed lines shown in Fig. 2-17(b).

From the foregoing discussions, a criterion may be established for the statical stability and determinacy of beams. Let r denote the number of reaction elements and c the number of equations of condition ($c = 1$ for a hinge; $c = 2$ for a roller; $c = 0$ for a beam without internal connection).

1. If $r < c + 3$, the beam is statically unstable.
2. If $r = c + 3$, the beam is statically determinate provided that no geometric instability (internal and external) is involved.
3. If $r > c + 3$, the beam is statically indeterminate.

Further illustrations are given in Table 2-1.

TABLE 2-1

Beam	r	c	$r \lesseqqgtr c + 3$	Classification
	5	2	$5 = 5$	Stable and determinate
	6	2	$6 > 5$	Stable and indeterminate to the first degree
	5	2	$5 = 5$	Unstable[a]
	4	3	$4 < 6$	Unstable
	6	3	$6 = 6$	Stable and determinate
	7	2	$7 > 5$	Unstable[a]

[a] Internal geometric instability; a possible form of displacement is indicated by the dashed lines.

2-7b General Stability and Determinacy of Trusses

A truss is composed of a number of bars connected at their ends by a number of pinned joints so as to form a network, usually a series of triangles, and mounted on a number of supports, such as the one shown in Fig. 2-18(a). Each bar of a truss is a two-force member; hence, each represents one unknown element of internal force (see Sec. 2-4). The total number of unknown elements for the entire system is counted by the number of bars (internal) plus the number of independent reaction elements (external). Thus, if we let b denote the number of bars and r the number of reaction components, the total number of unknown elements of the entire system is $b + r$. Now, if the truss is in equilibrium, every isolated portion must likewise be in equilibrium. For a truss having j joints, the entire system may be separated into j free bodies, as illustrated in Fig. 2-18(b), in which each joint yields two equilibrium equations, $\Sigma F_x = 0$ and $\Sigma F_y = 0$, for the concurrent force system acting on it. From this a total of $2j$ independent equations, involving $(b + r)$ unknowns, is obtained. We may thus establish criteria for the statical stability and the determinacy of a truss by counting the total unknowns and the total equations.

1. If $b + r < 2j$, the system is statically unstable.
2. If $b + r = 2j$, the system is statically determinate provided that it is also stable.
3. If $b + r > 2j$, the system is statically indeterminate.

The satisfaction of condition $b + r \geqslant 2j$ does not ensure a stable truss. For the truss to be stable requires fulfillment of further conditions. First, the value of r must be equal to or greater than the three required for statical stability of supports. Next, there must be no inadequacy in the arrangement of supports and bars so as to avoid both external and internal geometric instability.

Basically, a stable truss can usually be obtained by starting with three bars pinned together at their ends in the form of a triangle and then by extending from it by adding two new bars for each new joint, as shown in Fig. 2-18(a). Since this truss satisfies $b + r = 2j$ ($b = 13, r = 3, j = 8$), it is statically determinate.

Suppose that this truss form is changed, as shown in Fig. 2-19. The number of bars and joints remains the same; the criterion equation is still satisfied. But it is geometrically unstable, since there is no bar to carry the vertical force (shear) in the panel where the diagonal is omitted. Other examples are given in Table 2-2.

Figure 2-20 shows a long span trussed bridge, which we may consider to be composed of three rigid trusses connected by a hinge A and a link BC and mounted

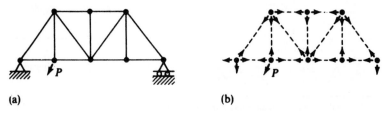

(a)   (b)

Figure 2-18

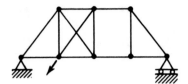

Figure 2-19

TABLE 2-2

Truss	b	r	j	$b + r \lesseqgtr 2j$	Classification
	7	3	5	$10 = 10$	Stable and determinate
	7	3	5	$10 = 10$	Unstable[a]
	7	3	5	$10 = 10$	Unstable[b]
	6	3	5	$9 < 10$	Unstable
	6	4	5	$10 = 10$	Stable and determinate
	8	4	5	$12 > 10$	Stable and indeterminate to the second degree
	6	4	5	$10 = 10$	Unstable[c]

[a] Internal geometric instability due to three pins a, b, c on a line; possible displacement as indicated by dashed lines.

[b] External geometric instability due to parallel lines of reaction.

[c] Internal geometric instability due to lack of lateral resistance in panel $abcd$.

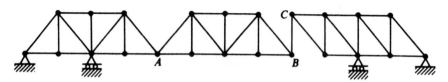

Figure 2-20

on a number of supports. These connections are not completely rigid, so certain equations of condition are introduced to restrict the external forces acting on the structure. In this case the hinge at A provides one condition equation, $M_A = 0$, which means that the moment about A of the forces on either side of A must be zero. The hanger BC provides two condition equations, $M_B = 0$ (or $M_C = 0$) and $H = 0$, which means that the moment about B (or C) of the forces on either side of B (or C) must be zero and also that the sum of the horizontal forces on either side of the hanger must be zero, since the vertical hanger is incapable of resisting horizontal forces.

The stability and determinacy of the truss may be investigated by first counting the number of bars, joints, and reaction elements. It is found that the equation $b + r = 2j$ is satisfied by the truss since $b = 40$, $r = 6$, and $j = 23$. Thus, the necessary condition for the system to be statically determinate is fulfilled. Next, there is no obvious instability either in the formation of the truss or in the supports. Both the portions to the left of A and to the right of BC are rigidly formed and adequately supported. The portion in the center span is also rigidly formed. Its connection to the side portions by a hinge and a hanger constitutes three elements of support. In regard to reactions, there is a total of six elements that can just be determined by six statical equations, three from equilibrium and three from construction. Thus, the entire system is stable and statically determinate; furthermore, it is stable and statically determinate as regards support reactions.

In certain cases the stability or instability of a truss is not obvious. One way of determining stability is to attempt a stress analysis and to discover whether the results are consistent or not. An inconsistent result indicates that the answer is not unique, but infinite and indeterminate. If such is the case, the truss is said to be *unstable*. We discuss this further in Sec. 3-5.

2-7c General Stability and Determinacy of Rigid Frames

A rigid frame is built of beams and columns connected rigidly, such as the one shown in Fig. 2-21(a). The stability and determinacy of a rigid frame may also be investigated by comparing the number of unknowns (internal unknowns and reaction unknowns) with the number of equations of statics available for their solution. Like a truss, a rigid frame may be separated into a number of free bodies of joints, as shown in Fig. 2-21(b), which requires that every member of the frame be taken apart. As discussed in Sec. 2-4, usually three unknown magnitudes (N, V, M) exist in a cut section of a member. However, if these quantities are known at one section of a member, similar quantities for any other section of the same member can be determined. Hence, there are only three independent, internal, unknown elements

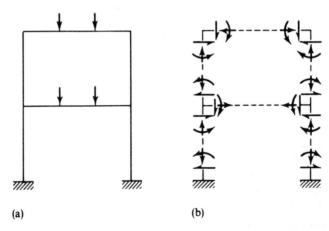

Figure 2-21

for each member in a frame. If we let b denote the total number of members and r the reaction elements, the total number of independent unknowns in a rigid frame is $(3b + r)$.

Next, a rigid joint isolated as a free body will generally be acted on by a system of forces and couples, as indicated in Fig. 2-21(b), since a rigid joint is capable of resisting moments. For equilibrium of such a joint, this system, therefore, must satisfy three equilibrium equations, $\Sigma F_x = 0$, $\Sigma F_y = 0$, and $\Sigma M = 0$. Thus, if the total number of rigid joints is j, then $3j$ independent equilibrium equations may be written for the entire system.

It may happen that hinges or other devices of construction are introduced into the structure so as to provide additional equations of statics, say a total of c. Then the total number of equations of statics available for the solution of the $(3b + r)$ unknowns is $(3j + c)$. The criteria for the statical stability and determinacy of the rigid frame are thus established by comparing the number of unknowns $(3b + r)$ with the number of independent equations $(3j + c)$:

1. If $3b + r < 3j + c$, the frame is statically unstable.
2. If $3b + r = 3j + c$, the frame is statically determinate provided that it is also stable.
3. If $3b + r > 3j + c$, the frame is statically indeterminate.

Recall from the similar discussion dealing with the criteria for trusses that satisfaction of the condition $3b + r \geqslant 3j + c$ does not warrant a stable frame unless $r \geqslant 3$ and, also, that no geometric instability is involved in the system.

Consider the frame in Fig. 2-21(a). There are six joints (including those at supports), six members, and six reaction elements, but no condition of construction. Thus, $3b + r = 18 + 6 > 3j + c = 18 + 0$. The excess number six in unknowns indicates that the frame is statically indeterminate to the sixth degree. Further examples for classifying frame stability and determinacy are given in Table 2-3.

Criteria such as the above are general and useful; but many problems, which

TABLE 2-3

Frame	h	r	j	c	$3b + r \gtreqless 3j + c$	Classification
	10	9	9	0	$39 > 27$	Indeterminate to the twelfth degree
	10	9	9	4	$39 > 31$	Indeterminate to the eighth degree
	10	9	9	1	$39 > 28$	Indeterminate to the eleventh degree
	10	9	9	3^{a}	$39 > 30$	Indeterminate to the ninth degree
	10^{b}	6	9	0	$36 > 27$	Indeterminate to the ninth degree

[a] If a pin is inserted in a rigid frame, generally, c = the number of members meeting at the pin minus one. In this case $c = 4 - 1 = 3$.

[b] The overhanging portions, such as ab and cd on the right side of the frame, should not be counted in the number of members.

may be investigated by a formula, can readily be settled by inspection through cutting frame members and reducing the structure to several simple parts.

Suppose that we wish to analyze the degree of indeterminacy of the frame shown in Fig. 2-22(a). The best approach is to cut members, as indicated in Fig. 2-22(b), so that the structure is separated into three statically determinate and stable parts. The number of restraints removed to accomplish this result gives the degree of indeterminacy of the frame. Since each cut involves three internal unknown elements, the total number of restraints removed by four cuts is $(4)(3) = 12$; the frame is statically indeterminate to the twelfth degree.

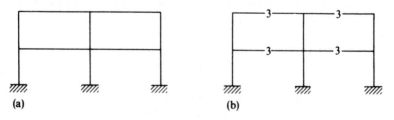

(a)   (b)

Figure 2-22

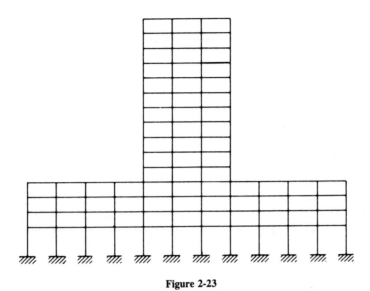

Figure 2-23

The advantage of this approach over counting the number of bars and joints and reaction elements will easily be seen when we come to determine the degree of indeterminacy of the frame of a tall building, such as the one shown in Fig. 2-23. Since the building can be separated into 12 stable and determinate parts by 77 cuts in the beams, it is statically indeterminate to the 231st degree.

2-8 METHODS OF ANALYSIS

Basically, there are two methods of structural analysis: the force method and the displacement method. They are illustrated through the following simple examples.

2-8a Force Method

Consider the one-dimensional structure shown in Fig. 2-24(a), which is composed of two bars connected together and supported at one end. An axial force is applied at the connection. Movement and stability in the transverse direction are not concerned. The structure has three unknown forces: one from each of the two members and one reaction force at joint a. The structure also has three equilibrium equations: one at each joint. Thus, it is a statically determinate structure. The following procedure typifies the force method of analysis.

1. *Joint equilibrium:* As shown in Fig. 2-24(b), the equilibrium of joint c leads to a zero member force for member 2. The equilibrium of joint b leads to a tensile member force P for member 1 and, finally, the equilibrium of joint a produces the reaction force $R_a = P$. Thus, all the internal and reaction forces are determined. The generalization of this part of the force method for more complex problems is given in Chapter 3.

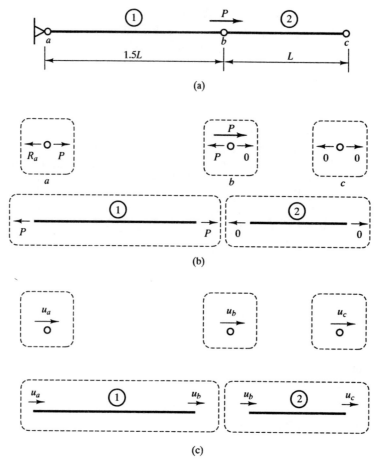

Figure 2-24

2. *Member flexibility:* Let us assume that the two members have the same cross-sectional area A and the same Young's modulus E. The elongations of members 1 and 2 are then $1.5PL/EA$ and 0, respectively. The $1/EA$ is the cross-sectional flexibility and the $1.5L/EA$ is the member flexibility of member 1. From the member flexibility, the member elongation is determined.

3. *Joint displacement:* Now let us examine Fig. 2-24(c). The fact that the members are connected and the structure is supported is reflected by the common joint displacements u_a, u_b, and u_c. Thus, *compatibility* conditions are implicitly satisfied. The support condition at joint a dictates $u_a = 0$. This, in turn, leads to $u_b = u_a + 1.5PL/EA = 1.5PL/EA$, and $u_c = u_b + 0 = 1.5PL/EA$. The generalization of this part of the force method to find structural deformation from member flexibility is given in Chapter 4.

Now, let us solve the problem in Fig. 2-25(a). The problem is similar to that of Fig. 2-24(a) except that joint c is supported. This introduces one additional force unknown: R_c, the reaction at c. Thus, the problem is statically indeterminate to the first degree. We may follow the same procedure as before.

1. *Joint equilibrium:* Since we know that the three joint equilibrium equations are not sufficient to solve for the two member forces P_1 and P_2 and the two reaction forces R_a and R_c, we may select R_c as a *redundant force* and express the other three unknowns in terms of the applied load P and R_c. Thus, from equilibrium conditions at c, b, and a, we obtain $P_2 = R_c$, $P_1 = P + R_c$, and $R_a = P + R_c$, respectively.

2. *Member flexibility:* The elongations of members 1 and 2 are $1.5(P + R_c)L/EA$ and $R_c L/EA$, respectively.

3. *Joint displacement:* From $u_a = 0$, we obtain $u_b = 1.5(P + R_c)L/EA$, and $u_c = 1.5(P + R_c)L/EA + R_c L/EA$. The support condition at c dictates $u_c = 0$. Thus, $1.5(P + R_c)L/EA + R_c L/EA = 0$, from which $R_c = -0.6P$. Thus, the force unknown R_c is solved only when the *compatibility* condition $u_c = 0$ is applied. Once the redundant force R_c is obtained, the other unknowns are all solved: $P_1 = 0.4P$, $P_2 = -0.6P$, and $u_b = 0.6PL/EA$. This procedure of the force method is called the *method of consistent deformations* in the classical content and is described in detail in Chapter 5.

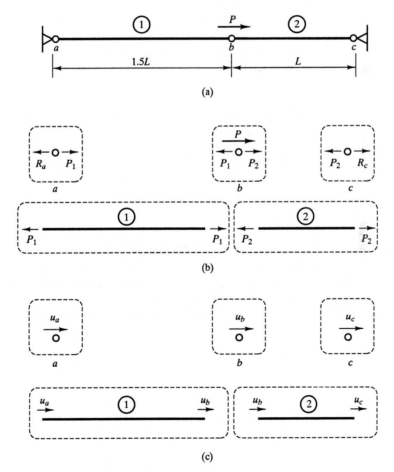

(a)

(b)

(c)

Figure 2-25

The systematic presentation of the force method using matrix notations is given in Chapter 6.

2-8b Displacement Method

Let us consider the problem shown in Fig. 2-25(a) again. The following procedure typifies the displacement method of analysis.

1. *Joint displacement:* There are three joint displacement unknowns, u_a, u_b, and u_c, but $u_a = u_c = 0$, due to support conditions. Thus, the only displacement unknown is u_b.

2. *Member stiffness:* The elongations of members 1 and 2 are $u_b - u_a$ ($= u_b$) and $u_c - u_b$ ($= -u_b$), respectively. The member forces needed to produce such elongations are $P_1 = EAu_b/(1.5L)$ and $P_2 = -EAu_b/L$ for members 1 and 2, respectively. The expressions $EA/(1.5L)$ and EA/L are the member stiffnesses and are the reciprocals of the member flexibility described before.

3. *Joint equilibrium:* At joint b, equilibrium condition yields $P_1 - P_2 = P$. Upon substitution of the member forces in terms of the joint displacement u_b, we obtain $EAu_b/(1.5L) + EAu_b/L = P$, from which $u_b = 0.6PL/EA$, the same as obtained by the force method. Once the displacement unknown is obtained, other unknowns are all solved by simple substitution.

Should the displacement method be applied to the problem shown in Fig. 2-24(a), it would involve two equilibrium equations (one for joint b and one for joint c) in terms of the joint displacements u_b and u_c (Problem 2-4). Thus, the number of equations to be solved is equal to the number of displacement unknowns.

The concept of using joint displacement as unknowns is further explored in Chapters 7 and 8 for beam and frame analysis. The general procedure of the displacement method in a matrix form is presented in Chapter 9.

PROBLEMS

2-1. Discuss the stability and determinacy of the beams shown in Fig. 2-26.

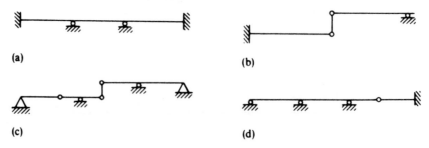

(a)

(b)

(c)

(d)

Figure 2-26

2-2. Discuss the stability and determinacy of the trusses shown in Fig. 2-27.

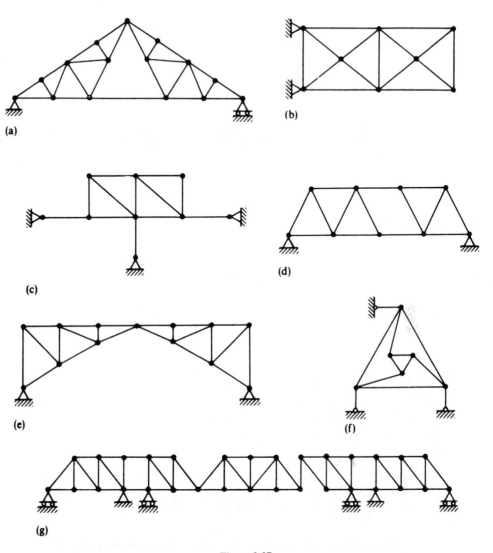

(a)

(b)

(c)

(d)

(e)

(f)

(g)

Figure 2-27

2-3. Discuss the stability and determinacy of the rigid frames shown in Fig. 2-28.

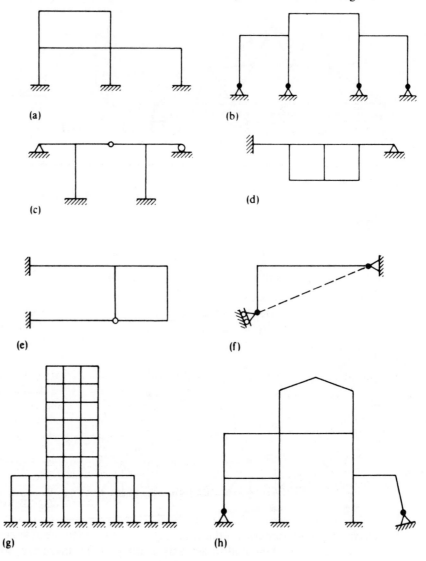

Figure 2-28

2-4. Solve the axial member problem of Fig. 2-24(a) by the displacement method.

Chapter 3

Structural Statics

3-1 GENERAL

In this chapter we analyze planar statically determinate structures, including beams, trusses, and rigid frames.

A *beam* is defined as a structural member predominantly subjected to bending moment. We limit our discussions to beams of symmetrical section, in which the centroidal axis is a straight line. Furthermore, we assume that the beam is acted on by only transverse loading and moment loading and that all the loads and reactions lie in the plane of symmetry. It thus follows that such a beam will be subjected to bending and shear in the plane of loading without axial stretching and twisting.

The basic types of statically determinate beams are *simple beams* and *cantilever beams*. A beam that is supported at its two ends with a hinge and a roller is called a *simply supported beam*, or *simple beam*. A cantilever beam is fixed or built in at one end and free at the other end. The end portion (or portions) of a simple beam may extend beyond the support to form a simple beam with overhang. Several beams of different types may be connected by internal hinges or rollers to form a *compound beam*. These are illustrated in Fig. 3-1.

A *truss*, such as the one shown in Fig. 3-2, may be defined as a plane structure composed of a number of members joined together at their ends by smooth pins so as to form a rigid framework, the external forces and reactions of which are assumed to lie in the same plane and to act only at the pins. Furthermore, we assume that the centroidal axis of each member coincides with the line connecting the joint centers at the ends of member and that the weight of each member is negligible in comparison to the other external forces acting on the truss. From these conditions it follows that each member in a truss is a *two-force* member and is subjected only to direct axial forces (tension or compression).

A modern truss made of bolted or welded joints is not really a truss by a strict interpretation of this definition. However, since a satisfactory stress analysis may usually be worked out by assuming that such a structure acts as if it were pin-connected, it may still be called a truss.

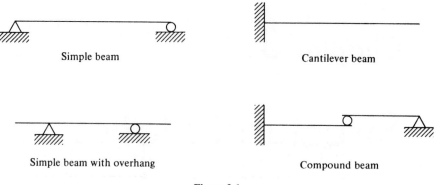

Simple beam

Cantilever beam

Simple beam with overhang

Compound beam

Figure 3-1

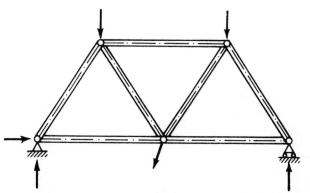

Figure 3-2

   Common trusses may be classified according to their formations as *simple*, *compound*, and *complex*. A rigid plane truss can always be formed by beginning with three bars pinned together at their ends in the form of a triangle and then extending from this two new bars for each new joint, as explained in Sec. 2-6. Of course, the new joint and the two joints to which it is connected should never lie along the same straight line, to avoid geometric instability. Trusses whose members have been so arranged are called *simple trusses*, for they are the simplest type of bar arrangement encountered in practice.

   The trusses shown in Fig. 3-3 are all simple trusses. The shaded triangle *abc* in each truss diagram is the base figure from which we extended the form by using two additional bars to connect each of the new joints in alphabetical order.

   It can easily be shown that there exists a very definite relationship between the number of bars b and the number of joints j in a simple truss. Since the base triangle of a simple truss consists of three bars and three joints, the additional bars and joints required to complete the truss are $(b - 3)$ and $(j - 3)$, respectively. These two numbers should be in a $2:1$ ratio. Thus,

$$b - 3 = 2(j - 3)$$

or

$$b + 3 = 2j$$

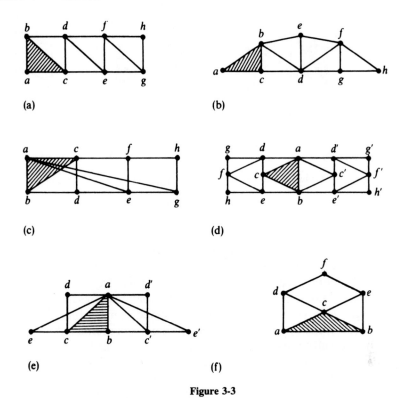

Figure 3-3

Comparing the above equation with the necessary condition for a statically determinate truss (see Sec. 2-6) given by

$$b + r = 2j$$

we find that if the supports of a simple truss are so arranged that they are composed of three elements of reaction neither parallel nor concurrent, then the structure is stable and statically determinate under general conditions of loading.

If two or more simple trusses are connected together to form one rigid framework, the composite truss is called a *compound truss*. One simple truss can be rigidly connected to another simple truss at certain joints by three links neither parallel nor concurrent or by the equivalent of this type of connection. Additional simple trusses can be joined in a similar manner to the framework already constructed to obtain a more elaborate compound truss.

Trusses that cannot be classified as either simple or compound are called *complex trusses*.

Figure 3-4(a) shows a simple truss. Rearranging the bars results in a compound truss such as the one shown in Fig. 3-4(b). However, the truss shown in Fig. 3-4(c), made of the same number of bars and joints, does not belong to either of the above categories and may be termed a complex truss. Similarly, we find that the truss

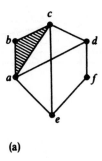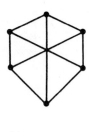

(a)   (b)   (c)

Figure 3-4

shown in Fig. 3-5(a) is a simple truss, that in Fig. 3-5(b) a compound truss, and that in Fig. 3-5(c) a complex truss.

A *rigid frame* may be defined as a structure composed of a number of members connected together by joints some or all of which are rigid, that is, capable of resisting both force and moment as distinguished from a pin-connected joint, which offers no moment resistance. In steel structures, rigid joints may be formed by certain types of riveted, bolted, or welded connections. In reinforced concrete structures, the materials in the joined members are mixed together in one unit so as to be substantially rigid. In the analysis of rigid frames, we assume that the centroidal axis of each member coincides with the line connecting the joint centers of the ends of the member. The joint center is therefore the concurrent point of all centroidal axes of members meeting at the joint. With the joint rigid, the ends of all connected members must not only translate but also rotate identical amounts at the joint. Rigid frames are usually built to be highly statically indeterminate. The discussion of statically determinate rigid frames in this chapter is primarily of academic interest, rather than of practical use, and serves as a prelude to the analysis of statically indeterminate frames.

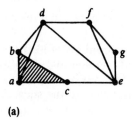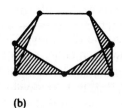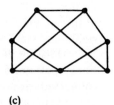

(a)   (b)   (c)

Figure 3-5

3-2 ANALYSIS OF STATICALLY DETERMINATE BEAMS

To illustrate the general procedure in analyzing a statically determinate beam, let us consider the loaded beam in Fig. 3-6(a).

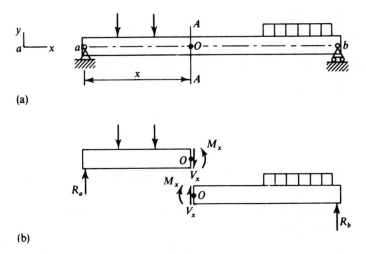

(a)

(b)

Figure 3-6

The first step in the analysis is to find the reactions at ends a and b, denoted by R_a and R_b, respectively. This can readily be accomplished by applying the equilibrium equations:

$$\sum M_a = 0, \qquad \sum M_b = 0$$

or

$$\sum M_b = 0, \qquad \sum F_y = 0$$

Next we investigate the shear force and bending moment at each transverse cross section of the beam. The *shear force* at any transverse cross section of the beam, say section A–A, at a distance x from the left end [see Fig. 3-6(a)], is the algebraic sum of the external forces (including those of reaction) applied to the portion of the beam on either side of A–A. The *bending moment* at section A–A of the beam is the algebraic sum of the moments taken about an axis through O (the centroid of section A–A) and normal to the plane of loading of all the external forces applied to the portion of the beam on either side of A–A. By considering either the left or the right portion as the free body, as shown in Fig. 3-6(b), we readily see that the *shear resisting force* at section V_x is equal and opposite to the shear force for that section just defined; and the *resisting moment* at section M_x is equal and opposite to the bending moment for the section just defined. The values of V_x and M_x can be found from the two equations of equilibrium

$$\sum F_y = 0 \quad \text{and} \quad \sum M_o = 0$$

for the portion considered.

Since the shear and bending moment in a transversely loaded beam will, in general, vary with the distance x defining the location of the cross section on which they occur, both are therefore functions of x. It is advisable to plot curves or diagrams from which the value of functions (V_x and M_x) at any cross section may readily be obtained. To do this, we let one axis, the x axis, coincide with the centroidal axis of the beam, indicating the position of the beam section, and the other axis, the y axis, indicate the value of function V_x or M_x. The graphic representation is called *shear* or *moment curve*.

Our sign conventions for beam shear and moment are as follows:

1. Shear is considered positive at a section when it tends to rotate the portion of the beam in the clockwise direction about an axis through a point inside the free body and normal to the plane of loading; otherwise, it is negative [see Fig. 3-7(a)].
2. Bending moment is considered positive at a section when it tends to bend the member concave upward; otherwise, it is negative [see Fig. 3-7(b)].

Such sign conventions, although arbitrary, must be carefully observed to avoid confusion.

The analysis of statically determinate beams is illustrated in the following examples.

Example 3-1

Figure 3-8(a) shows a simple beam under a concentrated load P acting at C. The reactions R_A and R_B are readily found to be

$$R_A = \frac{Pb}{l}, \qquad R_B = \frac{Pa}{l}$$

from $\Sigma M_B = 0$ and $\Sigma M_A = 0$.

The shear at any section to the left of P is equal to R_A; that is,

$$V_x = \frac{Pb}{l}, \qquad 0 < x < a$$

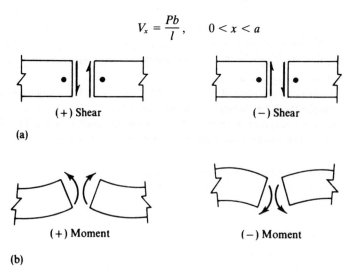

(+) Shear   (−) Shear

(a)

(+) Moment   (−) Moment

(b)

Figure 3-7

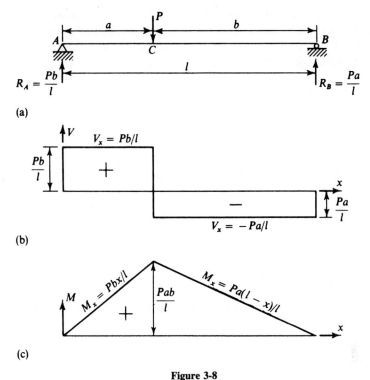

Figure 3-8

The shear at any section to the right of P is found to be equal to R_B but with negative sign, according to our sign convention. Thus,

$$V_x = -\frac{Pa}{l}, \qquad a < x < l$$

A change process of shear occurs at section C, the total change being $-P$ (from Pb/l to $-Pa/l$). In this connection, we note that at a concentrated load (including reaction) there is, in general, an abrupt change in the shear equal to the load. Consider the shear in the immediate vicinity of each support. The shear on a section an infinitesimal distance to the right of point A is Pb/l; therefore, the shear curve rises abruptly from zero to Pb/l at A. Similarly, the shear goes to zero from the value $-Pa/l$ at B. In general, *the shear curve always starts at zero and ends at zero* [see Fig. 3-8(b) for the shear curve].

The bending moment at any section distance x from A is given by

$$M_x = \frac{Pb}{l}x, \qquad 0 \leqslant x \leqslant a$$

$$M_x = \frac{Pa}{l}(l - x), \qquad a \leqslant x \leqslant l$$

Both are of linear variation and are plotted in Fig. 3-8(c).

If there are several concentrated loads on the beam, we need as many linear equations to represent the shear or moment as the number of segments involved. The shear or moment diagram is then composed of a series of line segments.

It is customary to drop the coordinate axes in the diagram unless the origin of the coordinate system is otherwise specified.

Example 3-2

Figure 3-9(a) shows a simple beam subjected to a uniform load of intensity w. Because of symmetry, the reactions are each equal to $wl/2$, as shown. Then, at any section distance x from the left end A, we have

$$V_x = \frac{wl}{2} - wx$$

$$M_x = \frac{wl}{2}x - \frac{wx^2}{2}$$

These are shown in Fig. 3-9(b) and (c), respectively.

Example 3-3

Figure 3-10(a) shows a simple beam subjected to an external couple of M applied at C. The reactions R_A and R_B must be such as to form a couple to balance M. They must be equal to M/l and opposite in sense, as indicated in Fig. 3-10(a).

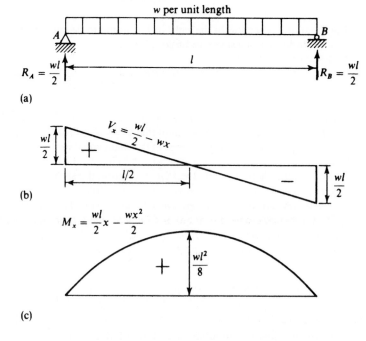

(a)

(b)

(c)

Figure 3-9

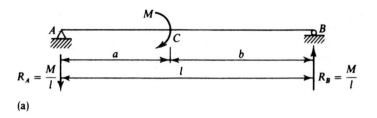

(a)

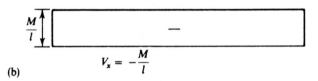

(b)

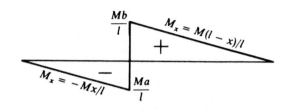

(c)

Figure 3-10

In this case the shear is of constant value equal to $-M/l$ in the range $0 < x < l$, as shown in Fig. 3-10(b).

The moments vary linearly from A to C and from C to B and are given by

$$M_x = -\frac{M}{l}x, \qquad 0 \leq x < a$$

$$M_x = \frac{M}{l}(l - x), \qquad a < x \leq l$$

The process of moment changes at $C(x = a)$, the total change being M (from $-Ma/l$ to Mb/l). The moment diagram is shown in Fig. 3-10(c), and the point of inflection (zero moment) is at C where the moment curve passes the x axis.

If the beam is subjected to several loads (or several groups of loads), the shear or the moment diagram may be plotted separately for each load (or each group of loads) and then combined into one diagram by the principle of superposition.

Table 3-1 shows the application of this principle in drawing a qualitative moment diagram for a simple beam (or a general member) restrained by end

TABLE 3-1

Case	Separate Moment Diagram	Combined Moment Diagram[a]

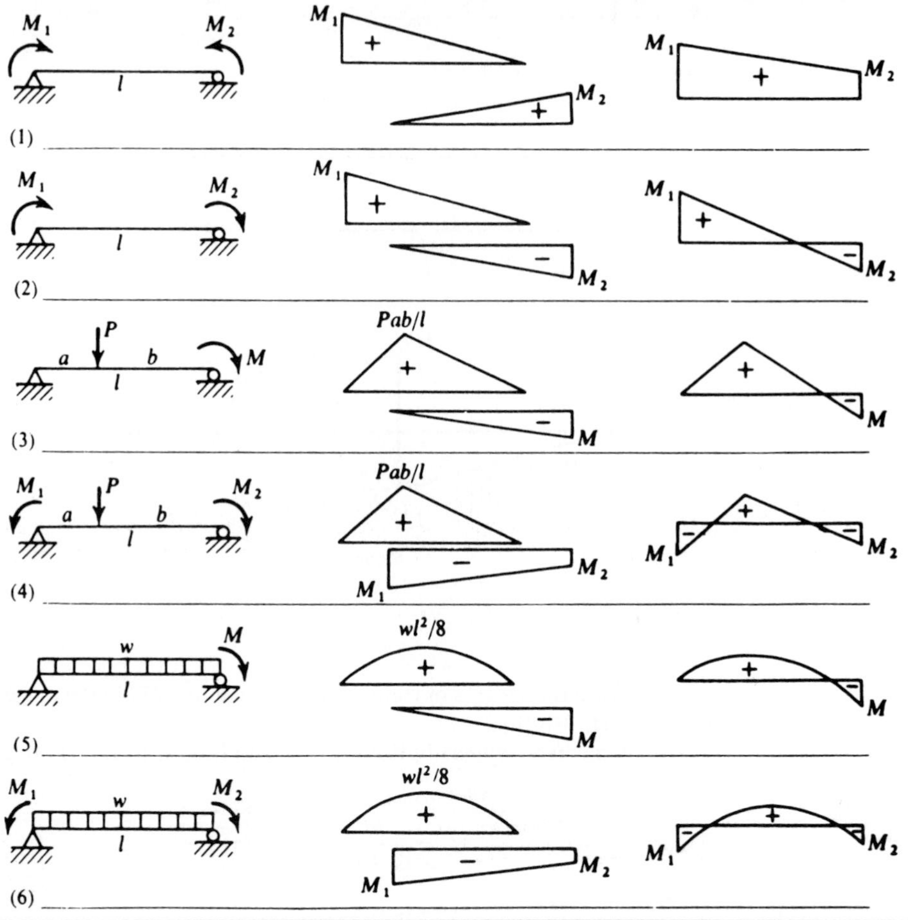

(1)

(2)

(3)

(4)

(5)

(6)

[a] With large end moment (or moments) the combined moment diagrams for cases (3), (4), (5), or (6) could be all negative without point of inflection.

moments. From the table we see that, if the beam carries no load but end moments, the moment curve is a straight line with one point of inflection or no point of inflection. If the beam carries a concentrated load or a uniform load together with the end moment on one end or both ends, the moment curve may pass zero at one, or two, or no point on the beam axis.

It may be worth mentioning here that, if the beam is made of elastic material, the beam will be deformed under load; the elastic deformations of beams are primarily caused by bending. With reference to the moment diagram and points of zero moment, we can easily sketch the deflected elastic curve.

Example 3-4

Figure 3-11(a) shows a cantilever carrying a distributed load the intensity of which varies linearly from w per unit length at the fixed end to zero at the free end. At any section distance x from the free end a,

$$V_x = -\left(\frac{wx}{l}\right)\left(\frac{x}{2}\right) = -\frac{wx^2}{2l}$$

$$M_x = -\left(\frac{wx^2}{2l}\right)\left(\frac{x}{3}\right) = -\frac{wx^3}{6l}$$

These are plotted in Fig. 3-11(b) and (c), respectively.

Example 3-5

For the loaded compound beam of Fig. 3-12(a), draw the shear and moment diagrams.

Theoretically, we can use two equilibrium equations and a condition equation ($M = 0$ at hinge b) to find the three reaction elements and then determine the shear and moment of the beam. But in the present case, we can conveniently separate the beam from the connecting hinge into two portions, a simple beam and a cantilever, as shown in Fig. 3-12(b). The shear and moment diagrams are easily drawn for each of the separated portions and then combined, as shown in Fig. 3-12(c) and (d), respectively.

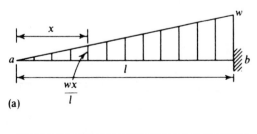

(a)

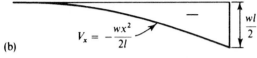

(b)

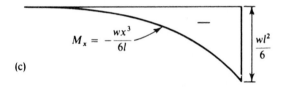

(c)

Figure 3-11

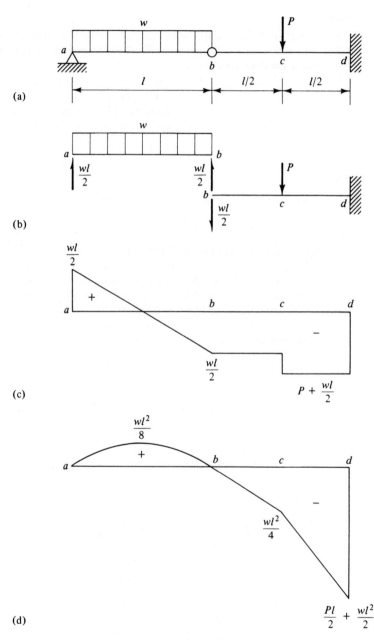

(a)

(b)

(c)

(d)

Figure 3-12

3-3 RELATIONSHIPS AMONG LOAD, SHEAR, AND BENDING MOMENT

There exist at any cross section of a loaded beam certain relationships among load, shear, and bending moment that are tremendously helpful in constructing the shear and bending moment curves.

Consider a portion of a beam of any type subjected to transverse loading and moment loading, such as the one shown in Fig. 3-13(a). To investigate the relationships among load, shear, and bending moment in a beam, we may classify the beam segments in the following way [as partly illustrated in Fig. 3-13(a)]:

1. Segment under no load
2. Segment under distributed load

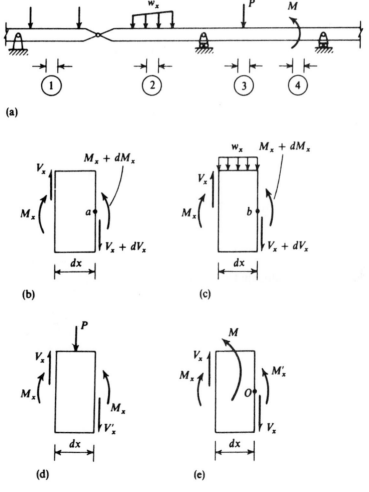

Figure 3-13

3. Segment under concentrated load

4. Segment under moment load

We shall deal with each of these four cases as follows:

1. *Segment under no load.* As indicated in Fig. 3-13(a), a segment between two concentrated loads is an example of a segment under no load. Let us take an element cut out by two adjacent cross sections at a distance dx apart, as shown in Fig. 3-13(b). On the left-hand face of this element, we represent the shear force and bending moment by V_x and M_x and on the right-hand face of the element, by $V_x + dV_x$ and $M_x + dM_x$, in which dV_x and dM_x are changes of shear and moment in dx. We assume that x increases from left to right. Since the element is in equilibrium, we have from $\Sigma F_y = 0$

$$V_x - (V_x + dV_x) = 0$$

That is,

$$dV_x = 0$$

or

$$V_x = \text{constant} \tag{3-1}$$

Also, from $\Sigma M_a = 0$,

$$M_x + V_x\,dx - (M_x + dM_x) = 0$$

Reducing and using Eq. 3-1, we arrive at

$$\frac{dM_x}{dx} = \text{constant} \tag{3-2}$$

Equation 3-1 states that no change of shear takes place, and Eq. 3-2 states that the rate of change of bending moment at any point with respect to x is constant.

2. *Segment under distributed load.* Let us take an element subjected to a distributed load cut out by two adjacent cross sections distance dx apart, as shown in Fig. 3-13(c). Assume a downward distributed load in a positive direction. From $\Sigma F_y = 0$,

$$V_x - (V_x + dV_x) - w_x\,dx = 0$$

$$dV_x = -w_x\,dx$$

or

$$\frac{dV_x}{dx} = -w_x \tag{3-3}$$

From $\Sigma M_b = 0$,

$$M_x + V_x \, dx - w_x \, dx \frac{dx}{2} - (M_x + dM_x) = 0$$

Neglecting the small term $w_x(dx)^2/2$ and reducing, we find that

$$\frac{dM_x}{dx} = V_x \qquad\qquad (3\text{-}4)$$

Equation 3-3 states that the rate of change of shear with respect to x at any point is equal to the intensity of the load at that point, but with the opposite sign. Equation 3-4 states that the rate of change of bending moment with respect to x at any point is equal to the shear force at that point.

   3. *Segment under concentrated load.* Figure 3-13(d) shows an element subjected to a concentrated load P. Now P is assumed to be acting at a point. As the distance between two adjacent sections becomes infinitesimal, there will be no moment difference between the sections to the immediate left of P and to the immediate right of P. However, an abrupt change in the shear force equal to P between the two sections takes place, since from $\Sigma F_y = 0$,

$$V_x - P - V'_x = 0$$

or

$$V'_x = V_x - P \qquad\qquad (3\text{-}5)$$

as indicated in Fig. 3-13(d). Accordingly, there will be an abrupt change in the derivative dM_x/dx at the point of application of concentrated force.

   4. *Segment under moment load.* Figure 3-13(e) shows an element subjected to a couple of M. Now M is assumed to be acting at a point. As the distance between the two adjacent sections becomes infinitesimal, there will be no shear difference between the sections to the immediate left of M and to the immediate right of M. However, there will be an abrupt change of moment equal to M between the two sections, for from $\Sigma M_o = 0$, we have

$$M_x - M - M'_x = 0$$

or

$$M'_x = M_x - M \qquad\qquad (3\text{-}6)$$

as indicated in Fig. 3-13(e).

   Construction of the shear and moment diagrams is facilitated by the relationships previously stated. For instance, the equation

$$\frac{dV_x}{dx} = -w_x$$

implies that the slope of the shear curve at any point is equal to the negative value of the ordinate of load diagram applied to the beam at that point. There are cases worth noting:

1. For a segment under no load, the slope of the shear curve is zero (i.e., parallel to the beam axis). The shear curve is therefore a line parallel to the beam axis.
2. For a segment under a uniform load of intensity w, the slope of the shear curve is constant. The shear curve is therefore a sloping line.
3. At a point of concentrated load, the intensity of the load is infinite, and the slope of the shear curve will thus be infinite (i.e., vertical to the beam axis). There will be a discontinuity in the shear curve, and a change process of shear equal to the applied force occurs between the two sides of the loaded point.
4. Under distributed load the change in shear between two cross sections a differential distance dx apart is

$$dV_x = -w_x \, dx$$

Thus, the difference in the ordinates of the shear curve between any two points a and b is given by

$$V_b - V_a = -\int_{x_a}^{x_b} w_x \, dx \tag{3-7}$$

$$= -(\text{area of load diagram between } a \text{ and } b)$$

Suppose that there are additional concentrated forces ΣP acting between a and b. The result of the shear difference between the two points must include the effect due to ΣP:

$$V_b - V_a = -\int_{x_a}^{x_b} w_x \, dx - \Sigma P \tag{3-8}$$

$$= -\left(\text{area of load diagram between } a \text{ and } b + \Sigma P\right)$$

in which ΣP has been assumed to act downward.

Similarly, from the equation

$$\frac{dM_x}{dx} = V_x$$

the slope of the bending moment curve at any point equals the ordinate of the shear curve at that point. We note the following:

1. If the shear is constant in a portion of the beam, the bending moment curve will be a straight line in that portion.
2. If the shear varies in any manner in a portion of the beam, the bending moment curve will be a curved line.
3. At a point where a concentrated force acts, there will be an abrupt change in the ordinate of shear curve and, therefore, an abrupt change in the slope of the bending moment curve at the point. In fact, the moment curve will have two different slopes at that point.
4. Maximum and minimum bending moments occur at the points where a shear curve goes through the x axis: the maximum where shear changes from positive (at the left) to negative (at the right); the minimum in the reverse manner.
5. For a concentrated force system the maximum bending moment must occur under a certain concentrated force, since change of shear from positive to negative must occur at a certain point where a concentrated force is applied.
6. Referring to the equation $dM_x/dx = V_x$, we find that under transverse loading the change in bending moment between two cross sections a differential distance dx apart is given by

$$dM_x = V_x \, dx$$

Therefore, the difference in the ordinates of the bending moment curve between any two points a and b is given by

$$M_b - M_a = \int_{x_a}^{x_b} V_x \, dx \tag{3-9}$$

$$= \text{area of shear diagram between } a \text{ and } b$$

If there are external moments ΣM acting between a and b, then the result of the moment difference between the two points must include the effect due to these moments:

$$M_b - M_a = \int_{x_a}^{x_b} V_x \, dx - \Sigma M \tag{3-10}$$

$$= (\text{area of shear diagram between } a \text{ and } b) - \Sigma M$$

in which ΣM has been assumed to act in a counterclockwise direction.

Example 3-6

Consider the beam shown in Fig. 3-14(a). From $\Sigma M_b = 0$ and $\Sigma M_d = 0$, the support reactions are found to be

$$R_b = 22 \text{ kN}, \qquad R_d = 14 \text{ kN}$$

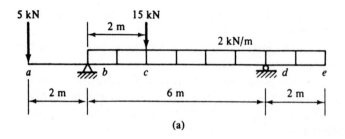

(a)

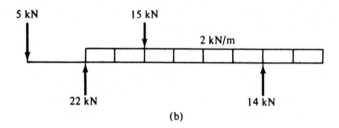

(b)

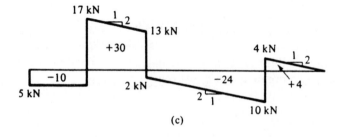

(c)

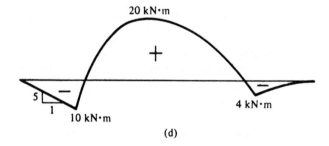

(d)

Figure 3-14

We may now regard the beam as being in equilibrium under the balanced system of applied loads and reactions and present the load diagram as shown in Fig. 3-14(b).

A freehand sketch of the shear diagram can then be drawn, as in Fig. 3-14(c). In connection with this diagram, we note the following facts:

1. The shear at *a* goes from 0 dropping to −5 kN; also, the shear at *e* is 0. Recall that the shear curve always starts at zero and ends up at zero.
2. There will be constant shear in portion *ab* since it is not loaded. As a result, the shear curve in this portion is a horizontal line parallel to the beam axis.
3. Except abrupt changes in shear at *b*, *c*, and *d* corresponding to the concentrated

forces acting at these points, the shear curves from b to e are sloping lines, the slope being given by

$$\frac{dV}{dx} = -w = -2$$

that is, $2:1$ downward to the right, as indicated in Fig. 3-14(c).

A freehand sketch of a bending moment diagram can be drawn, as in Fig. 3-14(d). In connection with it, we note the following:

1. Moments at a and e are null. The moment curve from a to b is a sloping line with the slope given by

$$\frac{dM}{dx} = V = -5$$

that is, $5:1$ downward to the right, as indicated in Fig. 3-14(d).

2. There are extreme values of moment at points b, c, and d where the shear curve goes through the x axis. Minimum bending moments occur at b and d since abrupt changes in the slope of moment curve from negative to positive take place at these points, corresponding to the abrupt changes in shear from negative to positive. Maximum bending moment occurs at c, where an abrupt change in the slope of the moment curve from positive to negative takes place, corresponding to the shear change from positive to negative at c.

3. Since the shear curve between bc or cd or de decreases from left to the right, the slope of the moment curve in each portion also decreases from left to right. This means that the moment curve in each portion is concave downward.

4. One way to obtain the ordinates of the moment diagram at b, c, and d is to compute the areas of the shear diagram [see the values indicated in Fig. 3-14(c)], from which we may find the moment difference between any two points:

$$M_b - M_a = -10 \text{ kN} \cdot \text{m}, \qquad M_c - M_b = 30 \text{ kN} \cdot \text{m}$$

$$M_d - M_c = -24 \text{ kN} \cdot \text{m}, \qquad M_e - M_d = 4 \text{ kN} \cdot \text{m}$$

From the above and using $M_a = M_e = 0$, we find that

$$M_b = -10 \text{ kN} \cdot \text{m}, \qquad M_c = 20 \text{ kN} \cdot \text{m}, \qquad M_d = -4 \text{ kN} \cdot \text{m}$$

as indicated in Fig. 3-14(d).

The algebraic sum of the total area of the shear diagram for the beam is zero in this example, since $M_a = M_e = 0$ and there is no moment force acting between a and e.

3-4 ANALYSIS OF STATICALLY DETERMINATE TRUSSES

The method of joint and the method of section are the most fundamental tools in the analysis of trusses. These procedures may be explained by considering a specific example, such as the simple truss shown in Fig. 3-15.

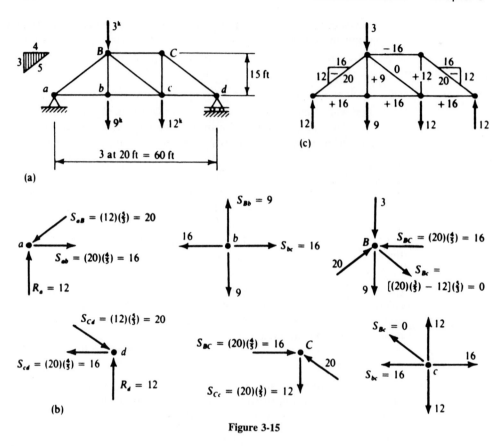

Figure 3-15

Method of joint. The reactions

$$R_a = R_d = 12 \text{ kips}$$

are first obtained by taking the whole truss as a free body.

The two equations of equilibrium $\Sigma F_x = 0$ and $\Sigma F_y = 0$ are then applied to the *free body of each joint* in such an order that not more than two unknown forces are involved in each free body. This can always be done for a simple truss. In this example we start with joint a at the left end and proceed in succession to joints b and B; then we turn to joint d at the right end and proceed to joints C and c. We thus provide three checks for the analysis by obtaining the internal forces in members BC, Bc, and bc from two directions.

The analysis for each joint is given briefly in Fig. 3-15(b). Usually, when the slopes of the members are in simple ratios, the solution for unknown forces can readily be obtained by inspection, rather than by using equations. The arrows in each free body of the joint indicate the directions of the member forces acting on the joint, not the actions of the joint on the member. Note that the internal force in the member is a tensile force if it acts outward, such as S_{ab}, and that the internal force in the member is a compressive force if it acts toward the joint, such as S_{aB}.

The *answer diagram* [Fig. 3-15(c)] gives the results obtained from the preceding analysis together with the horizontal and vertical components. A plus sign indicates a tensile force, and a minus sign indicates a compressive force.

Method of section.   Sometimes, when only the forces in certain members are desired or when the method of joint is less convenient for solving forces, it is expedient to use the method of section, which involves isolating a portion of the truss by cutting certain members and then solving the forces on these members with the equilibrium equations. Consider the truss in Fig. 3-15(a). Let us determine the internal forces in the members BC, Bc, and bc.

We start by passing a section *m–m* through these members and treating either side of the truss as a free body (see Fig. 3-16). Note that the sense of the unknown force in each cut member is assumed to be tensile, and if this is done, a plus sign in the answer indicates that the assumed sense is correct, and therefore tension, whereas a minus sign indicates that the assumed sense is incorrect, and therefore compression.

Since in each free body only three unknown forces are involved, the unknowns can be solved by three equilibrium equations. In this example, it is convenient to solve S_{BC} by $\Sigma M_c = 0$, S_{bc} by $\Sigma M_B = 0$, and S_{Bc} by $\Sigma F_y = 0$. Thus, if we consider the left portion of Fig. 3-16 as a free body, we have

$$\Sigma M_c = 0, \qquad (12)(40) - (9 + 3)(20) + 15S_{BC} = 0$$

$$S_{BC} = -16 \text{ kips} \quad \text{(compression)}$$

$$\Sigma M_B = 0 \qquad (12)(20) - 15S_{bc} = 0$$

$$S_{bc} = +16 \text{ kips} \quad \text{(tension)}$$

$$\Sigma F_y = 0 \qquad 12 - (9 + 3) - V_{Bc} = 0$$

$$V_{Bc} = 0 \quad \text{or} \quad S_{Bc} = 0$$

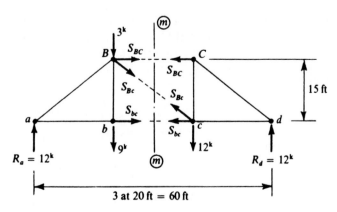

Figure 3-16

in which V_{Bc} represents the vertical component of S_{Bc}. Since $S_{Bc} = (5/3)V_{Bc}$, the zero value of V_{Bc} evidently implies the nonexistence of S_{Bc}.

In applying the method of section, we note that by proper choice of moment centers we can often determine the forces on certain members, such as the members BC and bc of Fig. 3-16, directly from the moment equations and avoid solving simultaneous equations. This technique is called the *method of moment* and can best be illustrated in the following example.

Example 3-7

In Fig. 3-17(a) is shown a simple nonparallel chord truss. Find the forces in chord members cd and CD and in the diagonal Cd.

First, from $\Sigma M_i = 0$ for the entire structure, the reaction at a is found to be

$$R_a = \frac{(5)(60) + (4 + 3 + 2 + 1)(90)}{8} = 150 \text{ kips}$$

Next, to find the internal force in member cd, we pass a section $m\text{–}m$ through members CD, Cd, and cd, as indicated by the broken line in Fig. 3-17(a), and take the left portion of the truss as a free body, as shown in Fig. 3-17(b).

From $\Sigma M_C = 0$,

$$S_{cd} = \frac{(150)(50)}{30} = 250 \text{ kips} \quad \text{(tension)}$$

To find the internal force in member CD, we use the same free body and resolve

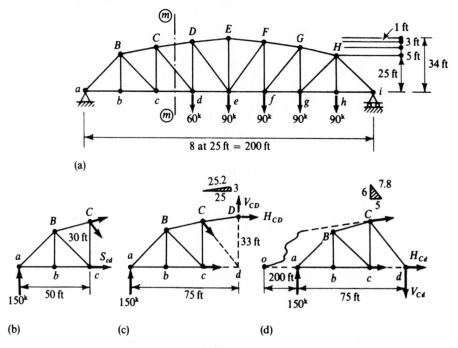

(a)

(b)   (c)   (d)

Figure 3-17

S_{CD} into a vertical component V_{CD} and a horizontal component H_{CD} at D, as shown in Fig. 3-17(c).

From $\Sigma M_d = 0$,

$$H_{CD} = -\frac{(150)(75)}{33} = -341 \text{ kips} \quad \text{(compression)}$$

Thus,

$$S_{CD} = (-341)\left(\frac{25.2}{25}\right) = -344 \text{ kips} \quad \text{(compression)}$$

Similarly, to find the internal force in member Cd, we resolve S_{Cd} into a vertical component V_{Cd} and a horizontal component H_{Cd} at d, as shown in Fig. 3-17(d). Note that the moment center is chosen at o, where the extending lines of members CD and cd intersect. The distance oa is found to be 200 ft.

From $\Sigma M_o = 0$,

$$V_{Cd} = \frac{(150)(200)}{275} = 109 \text{ kips} \quad \text{(tension)}$$

Thus,

$$S_{Cd} = (109)\left(\frac{7.8}{6}\right) = 142 \text{ kips} \quad \text{(tension)}$$

In general, no truss is analyzed by one method alone. Instead, it is often analyzed by a mixed method based on knowledge from both the joint and section methods combined, as illustrated in the following example.

Example 3-8

In Fig. 3-18(a) we have a compound truss consisting of two simple trusses (shaded) connected by three bars, BC, EF, and GH. The truss is subjected to a vertical load of 90 kN at joint D.

The first step in the analysis is to obtain the reactions at A and E by considering the entire truss as a free body. Thus,

$$H_A = 120 \text{ kN}, \qquad H_E = 120 \text{ kN}, \qquad V_E = 90 \text{ kN}$$

as indicated.

After this the method of joint fails, since each remaining joint involves more than two unknowns. It also appears at first glance that it is not possible to apply the method of section, since we cannot take any section that cuts only three bars that are not concurrent. However, if we pass section m–m through five bars, as indicated in Fig. 3-18(a), we can easily obtain from $\Sigma M_C = 0$ that

$$S_{AF} = -\frac{(120)(3)}{12} = -30 \text{ kN}$$

by taking either portion of the truss as a free body and by assuming that S_{AF} acts in a

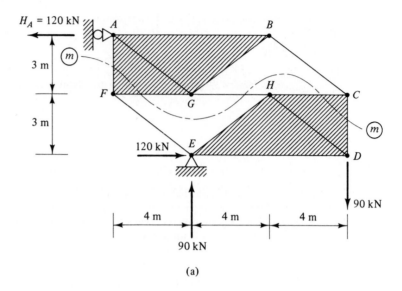

(a)

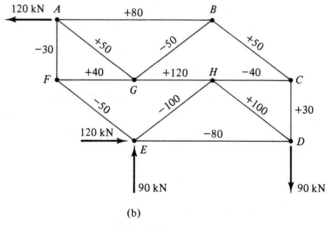

(b)

Figure 3-18

positive direction. Similarly, from $\Sigma M_F = 0$ or $\Sigma F_y = 0$, we obtain that

$$S_{CD} = 30 \text{ kN}$$

Having done this, we can solve the forces for the remaining bars by the method of joint without difficulty. An answer diagram for the analysis is given in Fig. 3-18(b).

In analyzing a complex truss, we frequently find that the method of joint and the method of section, described in previous sections, are not directly applicable. For example, let us consider the loaded complex truss shown in Fig. 3-19(a). After the reactions at A and E are found, we observe that no further progress can be made by either the method of joint or the method of section. One way to handle this is

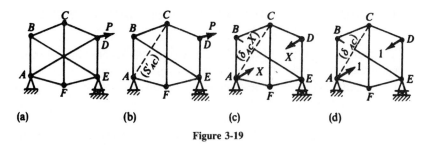

(a)   (b)   (c)   (d)

Figure 3-19

to substitute for the bar AD a bar AC and thus obtain a stable simple truss, as in Fig. 3-19(b), which can be completely analyzed by the method of joint for the given loading. Next, let the same simple truss be loaded with two equal and opposite forces X at A and D representing the internal force in bar AD, as shown in Fig. 3-19(c). Again a complete analysis can be carried out by the method of joint such that the internal force for each member will be expressed in terms of the unknown X. Or, for convenience, we put a pair of unit forces in place of the X's, as given in Fig. 3-19(d). It is apparent that the bar forces obtained from Fig. 3-19(d) times X will give those of Fig. 3-19(c).

Now the analysis of Fig. 3-19(a) can be made equivalent to the superposing effects of Fig. 3-19(b) and (c) if we let the bar force of AC obtained from (b) and (c), or from (b) and (d) times X, be equal to zero. Thus, if we let S'_i denote the force in any bar of (b) and δ_i the corresponding bar force of (d), then the corresponding internal force S_i in any bar of (a) is expressed by

$$S_i = S'_i + \delta_i X$$

in which X is solved by

$$S_{AC} = S'_{AC} + \delta_{AC} X = 0$$

or

$$X = -\frac{S'_{AC}}{\delta_{AC}}$$

With the value of X determined, the force in any other bar of the given truss can be obtained without difficulty.

It should be noted that complex trusses may often be arranged so as to be geometrically unstable. However, it is not always possible to see a critical form just by inspection. Detection is based on the principle that, if the analysis for the truss yields a unique solution, then the truss is stable and statically determinate; on the other hand, if the analysis fails to yield a unique solution, the truss has a critical form.

It is further noted that the method just described is practical for complex trusses with only a few members when it is easy to determine which member is to be substituted. A more practical method, applicable to all trusses, is the matrix analysis based on the method of joints described in the next section.

3-5 MATRIX ANALYSIS OF STATICALLY DETERMINATE TRUSSES

Theoretically, we can always solve any statically stable and determinate truss by $2j$ simultaneous equilibrium equations for j joints of the system. The method is perfectly general but must be done with the aid of a modern computer.

As a simple illustration of this process, let us consider the three-hinged truss shown in Fig. 3-20. The unknown elements involved in this truss are the reaction components H_A and V_A at joint A, H_B and V_B at joint B, and the bar forces S_a and S_b. The six unknowns can be solved by six equilibrium equations, two for each of three discrete joints. Thus,

$$\text{Joint } A: \quad \sum F_x = 0, \quad -H_A - 0.6S_a = 0$$
$$\sum F_y = 0, \quad -V_A - 0.8S_a = 0$$

$$\text{Joint } B: \quad \sum F_x = 0, \quad -H_B + 0.8S_b = 0$$
$$\sum F_y = 0, \quad -V_B - 0.6S_b = 0$$

$$\text{Joint } C: \quad \sum F_x = 0, \quad 0.6S_a - 0.8S_b = 0$$
$$\sum F_y = 0, \quad 0.8S_a + 0.6S_b = -10$$

Collecting the preceding six equations in matrix form gives

$$
\begin{bmatrix}
-1 & 0 & 0 & 0 & -0.6 & 0 \\
0 & -1 & 0 & 0 & -0.8 & 0 \\
0 & 0 & -1 & 0 & 0 & 0.8 \\
0 & 0 & 0 & -1 & 0 & -0.6 \\
0 & 0 & 0 & 0 & 0.6 & -0.8 \\
0 & 0 & 0 & 0 & 0.8 & 0.6
\end{bmatrix}
\begin{Bmatrix}
H_A \\ V_A \\ H_b \\ V_B \\ S_a \\ S_b
\end{Bmatrix}
=
\begin{Bmatrix}
0 \\ 0 \\ 0 \\ 0 \\ 0 \\ -10
\end{Bmatrix}
$$

$$A \qquad\qquad\qquad Q \qquad\qquad R$$

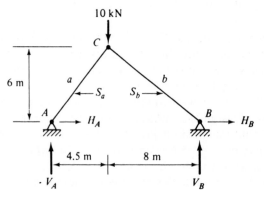

Figure 3-20

or

$$AQ = R$$

The unknown values are found by solving this matrix equation using the Gaussian elimination method as described in Appendix A.

$$Q = \begin{Bmatrix} H_A \\ V_A \\ H_b \\ V_B \\ S_a \\ S_b \end{Bmatrix} = \begin{Bmatrix} 4.8 \\ 6.4 \\ -4.8 \\ 3.6 \\ -8 \\ -6 \end{Bmatrix} \text{ kN}$$

Symbolically, the force vector Q may be represented by

$$Q = A^{-1} R$$

where A^{-1} is the inverse of A. Although using Gaussian elimination, A^{-1} is not needed in finding Q, it has a special meaning in this case. Let us denote $b = A^{-1}$. Then

$$Q = bR$$

This is a *force transformation equation*, and the matrix b is called the *force transfer matrix* because it relates the applied load vector R to the internal member force and reaction force vector Q. Matrix b can also be found by Gaussian elimination (Appendix A).

$$b = \begin{bmatrix} -1 & 0 & 0 & 0 & -0.36 & -0.48 \\ 0 & -1 & 0 & 0 & -0.48 & -0.64 \\ 0 & 0 & -1 & 0 & -0.64 & 0.48 \\ 0 & 0 & 0 & -1 & 0.48 & -0.36 \\ 0 & 0 & 0 & 0 & 0.6 & 0.8 \\ 0 & 0 & 0 & 0 & -0.8 & 0.6 \end{bmatrix}$$

It is clear that each column of b is the solution of internal member force and reaction force due to a unit load applied in a specific direction at one of the three joints. This force transfer matrix is useful in finding joint displacements (Chapter 4) and solving statically indeterminate problems (Chapter 5).

It should be noted that the unknowns Q are to be uniquely determined by $Q = A^{-1} R$ under the condition of the nonsingularity of the square matrix A; that is, the determinant containing the same elements as A is not zero. This principle provides a general way of detecting the stability of a structural system; that is, if

$$|A| \neq 0$$

then the system has a unique solution, which indicates that the system is stable; on the other hand, if

$$|A| = 0$$

then the system is unstable, since many solutions are possible. Refer to Fig. 3-20. If we replace the hinge support at B with a roller ($H_B = 0$), then

$$A = \begin{bmatrix} -1 & 0 & 0 & 0 & -0.6 & 0 \\ 0 & -1 & 0 & 0 & -0.8 & 0 \\ 0 & 0 & 0 & 0 & 0 & 0.8 \\ 0 & 0 & 0 & -1 & 0 & -0.6 \\ 0 & 0 & 0 & 0 & 0.6 & -0.8 \\ 0 & 0 & 0 & 0 & 0.8 & 0.6 \end{bmatrix}$$

Apparently,

$$|A| = 0$$

implying that the truss is unstable.

Although the illustration we have considered concerns a simple truss, the principle and the method of detecting a critical form described above can be applied to other types of structures, such as beams and rigid frames.

3-6 DESCRIPTION OF BRIDGE AND ROOF TRUSS FRAMEWORKS

Figure 3-21 shows a typical *through trussed bridge*. The word *through* indicates that the trains (or vehicles) actually travel through the bridge. If the bridge is installed under the floor or deck, then the bridge is called a *deck bridge*. If the trains pass between trusses, but the depth is insufficient to allow the use of a top chord bracing system, the bridge is called *half-through*.

Referring to Fig. 3-21, we place the road surface (or the rail and tie system in railways) on the short longitudinal beams called *stringers*, assumed simply supported on the *floor beams*, which in turn are supported by the two *main trusses*. The moving loads on bridge are transmitted to the main trusses through the system of the connection of road surface (or rail and tie), stringer, and floor beam.

The top series of truss members parallel to the stringer are called *top chords*, while the corresponding bottom series of members are called *bottom chords*. The members connecting the top and bottom chords form the web system and are referred to as *diagonals* and *verticals*. The end diagonals are called *end posts*, and the side verticals are called *hip verticals*. The point at which web members connect to a chord is called a *panel point*, and the length between two adjacent panel points on the same chord is called the *panel length*.

The cross struts at corresponding top-chord panel points, together with the top diagonals connecting the adjacent struts, make up the top-chord lateral system. The

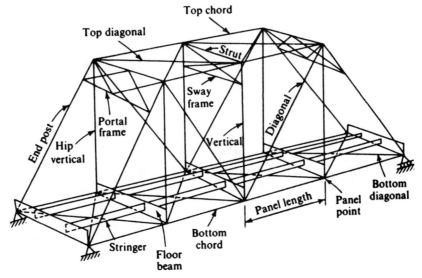

Figure 3-21

bottom-chord lateral system is composed of the floor beams and the bottom diagonals connecting the adjacent floor beams.

The two main trusses are also cross braced at each top-chord panel point by *sway frames*. The frame in the plane of each pair of end posts is called a *portal frame*.

The members of a main truss may be arranged in many different ways. However, the principal types of trusses encountered in bridges are shown in Fig. 3-22. Among these types, the Pratt, Howe, and Warren trusses are more commonly used. We may note that in the Pratt truss the diagonals, except the end posts, are stressed in tension and that the verticals, except the hip verticals, are stressed in compression under dead load. On the other hand, in a Howe truss the diagonals are in compression and the verticals are in tension. Note also that, of all the trusses shown in Fig. 3-22 under dead load, the upper chords are in compression and bottom chords in tension.

A typical roof truss framework supported by columns is shown in Fig. 3-23. A roof truss with its supporting columns is called a *bent*. The space between adjacent bents is called a *bay*. *Purlins* are longitudinal beams that rest on the top chord and preferably at the joints of the truss, in accordance with the definition of truss. The *roof covering* may be laid directly on the purlins for very short bay lengths, but usually is laid on the wood *sheathings* that, in turn, rest either on the purlins or on the *rafters* (if provided). Rafters are the sloping beams extending from the *ridge* to the *eaves* and are supported by the purlins.

For a symmetrical roof truss the ratio of its *rise*, center height, to its *span*, the horizontal distance between the center lines of the supports, is called *pitch*.

The truss consists of top-chord, bottom-chord, and *web members*. Although the purlins act to strengthen the longitudinal stability, additional bracing is always necessary. The *bracing members* may run from truss to truss longitudinally or diagonally and may be installed in the plane of the bottom chord, the top chord, or

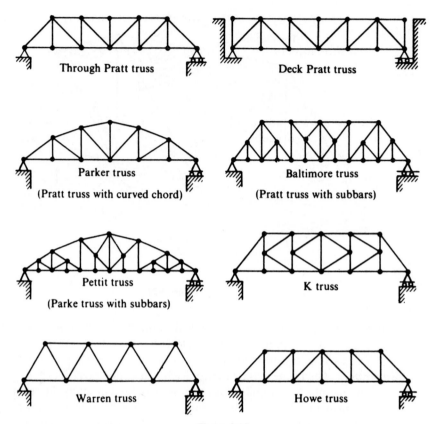

Through Pratt truss

Deck Pratt truss

Parker truss

(Pratt truss with curved chord)

Baltimore truss

(Pratt truss with subbars)

Pettit truss

(Parke truss with subbars)

K truss

Warren truss

Howe truss

Figure 3-22

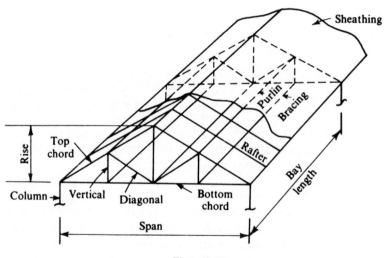

Sheathing

Rise

Top chord

Purlin

Bracing

Rafter

Column

Vertical

Diagonal

Bottom chord

Bay length

Span

Figure 3-23

both. Surface loads are transmitted from covering, sheathing, rafter, and purlin and distributed to adjacent trusses.

The common types of roof trusses are shown in Fig. 3-24.

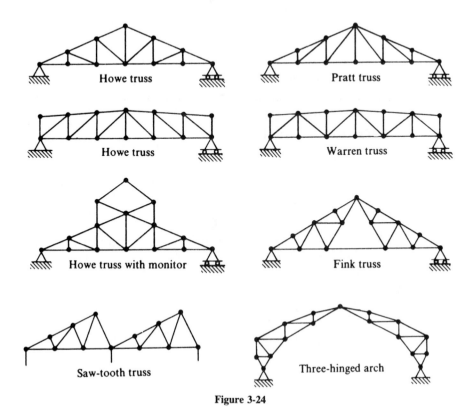

Howe truss   Pratt truss

Howe truss   Warren truss

Howe truss with monitor   Fink truss

Saw-tooth truss   Three-hinged arch

Figure 3-24

3-7 ANALYSIS OF STATICALLY DETERMINATE RIGID FRAMES

To analyze a statically determinate rigid frame, we start by finding the reaction components from statical equations for the entire structure. This done, we are able to determine the shear, moment, and axial force at any cross section of the frame by taking a free-body cut through that section and by using the equilibrium equations. Based on the centroidal axis of each member, we can plot the shear, bending moment, and the direct force diagrams for the rigid frame. However, it is the bending moment diagram with which we are mainly concerned in the analysis of a rigid frame.

The following numerical examples will serve to illustrate the procedure.

Example 3-9

Analyze the rigid frame in Fig. 3-25(a). Let H_a, V_a, and M_a denote the horizontal, vertical, and rotational reaction components, respectively, at support a, and let V_e be the vertical reaction at support e.

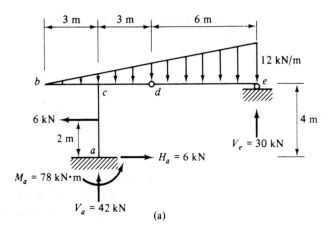

(a)

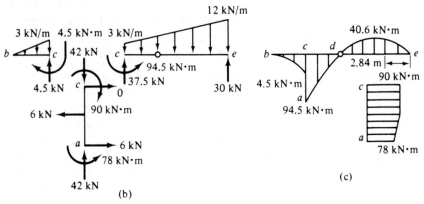

(b)

(c)

Figure 3-25

From the condition equation $M_d = 0$, we find that $V_e = 30$ kN; from $\Sigma F_x = 0$, $H_a = 6$ kN; from $\Sigma F_y = 0$, $V_a = 42$ kN; and from $\Sigma M_a = 0$, $M_a = 78$ kN · m, as indicated in Fig. 3-25(a).

After all the external forces acting on the rigid frames are determined, the internal forces at each end of the members can easily be obtained by taking each member as a free body [Fig. 3-25(b)]. Take member ac, for instance. At end c of ac, we find the shear force equal to zero by applying $\Sigma F_x = 0$, axial force equal to 42 kN (down) from $\Sigma F_y = 0$, and the resisting moment equal to 90 kN · m (clockwise) from $\Sigma M_c = 0$. By inspection, we see that the shear and moment at end c of the overhanging portion ac are 4.5 kN (up) and 4.5 kN · m (clockwise), respectively. Finally, we use the equilibrium of joint c to obtain the end forces at c of member ce as

$$\text{shear} = 37.5 \text{ kN} \quad (\text{up}), \qquad \text{moment} = 94.5 \text{ kN} \cdot \text{m} \quad (\text{counterclockwise})$$

With all the end forces for each member found, the shear, bending moment, and axial force in any section of the frame can be obtained by simple statics.

The moment diagrams for beam be and column ac are shown separately in Fig. 3-25(c).

Example 3-10

Analyze the simply supported gable frame shown in Fig. 3-26(a), which is composed of two columns and two sloping members.

From $\Sigma F_x = 0$, $\Sigma M_e = 0$, and $\Sigma F_y = 0$ for the entire frame, the reaction elements are found to be

$$H_a = 8 \text{ kips}, \qquad V_a = 11 \text{ kips}, \qquad V_e = 21 \text{ kips}$$

as shown in Fig. 3-26(a).

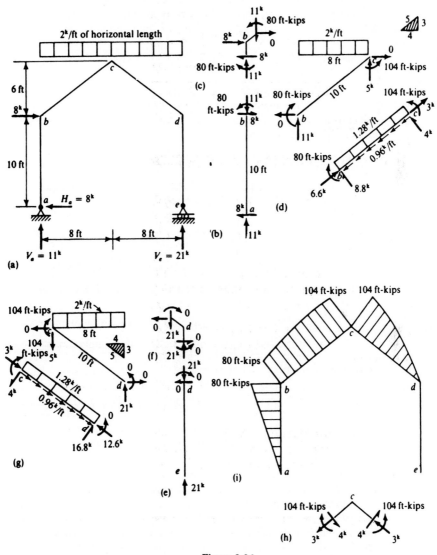

Figure 3-26

Next, we take member ab as a free body. With the end forces known at a, we can readily obtain those at the other end b from the equilibrium conditions:

shear = 8 kips,   moment = 80 ft-kips,   axial force = 11 kips

acting as indicated in Fig. 3-26(b).

Following this, we sketch the free-body diagram for joint b, as shown in Fig. 3-26(c). Note that the joint is shown in an exaggerated manner, since theoretically it should be represented by a point, and all forces acting on the joint should be concurrent at this point.

Next, let us take member bc as a free body subjected to the external load of 2 kips per horizontal unit length. With the internal forces known at end b, we can apply $\Sigma F_x = 0$, $\Sigma F_y = 0$, and $\Sigma M_c = 0$ to obtain the internal forces at end c as

horizontal force = 0,   vertical force = 5 kips,   moment = 104 ft-kips

These act as indicated in the upper sketch of Fig. 3-26(d). To determine the forces in each section of the member, we resolve all the indicated forces into components normal and tangential to the member section, as shown in the lower sketch of Fig. 3-26(d). For instance, at end b we have

$$\text{normal force (axial force)} = (11)(\tfrac{3}{5}) = 6.6 \text{ kips}$$

$$\text{tangential force (shear)} = (11)(\tfrac{4}{5}) = 8.8 \text{ kips}$$

Similarly, at end c we have

$$\text{normal force (axial force)} = (5)(\tfrac{3}{5}) = 3 \text{ kips}$$

$$\text{tangential force (shear)} = (5)(\tfrac{4}{5}) = 4 \text{ kips}$$

The total uniform load on member bc is 16 kips, of which there are

$$(16)(\tfrac{4}{5}) = 12.8 \text{ kips acting transversely to the member axis}$$

$$(16)(\tfrac{3}{5}) = 9.6 \text{ kips acting axially to the member axis}$$

thus giving a uniform load of intensity:

$$\frac{12.8}{10} = 1.28 \text{ kips/ft acting transversely to the member axis}$$

$$\frac{9.6}{10} = 0.96 \text{ kip/ft acting axially to the member axis}$$

With these determined, the shear, bending moment, and direct force in any section of member bc can readily be obtained, as shown in Fig. 3-27.

In this manner we may proceed from member bc to joint c, then to member cd and joint d, and finally to member de. However, it seems more convenient to analyze de now and then to turn to joint d and member cd, and to leave the joint c as a final check, as shown in Fig. 3-26(e), (f), (g), and (h), respectively. The bending moment diagram for the whole frame is plotted in Fig. 3-26(i).

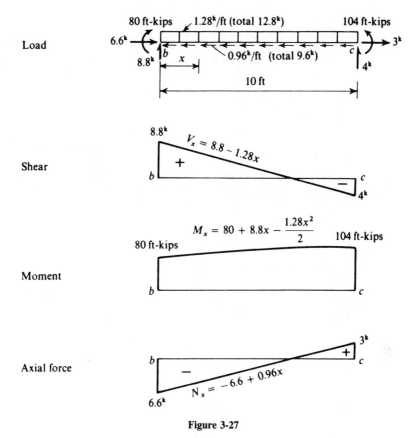

Figure 3-27

Example 3-11

Consider the three-hinged frame loaded as in Fig. 3-28(a). The four reaction elements at supports a and e are first obtained by solving simultaneous equations, three from equilibrium and one from construction.

$$\sum F_x = 0, \qquad H_a - H_e = 0$$

$$\sum F_y = 0, \qquad V_a + V_e - 12 = 0$$

$$\sum M_e = 0, \qquad 12V_a - (12)(10) = 0$$

$$M_c = 0, \qquad 6V_e - 8H_e = 0$$

which give

$$V_a = 10 \text{ kips}, \qquad V_e = 2 \text{ kips}, \qquad H_a = H_e = 1.5 \text{ kips}$$

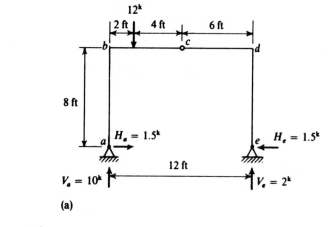

(a)

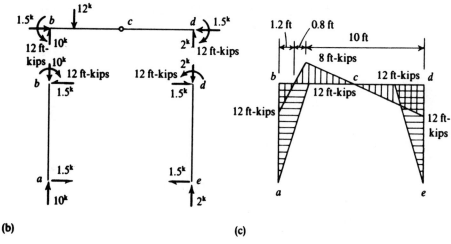

(b)   (c)

Figure 3-28

The free-body diagrams for members ab, bd, and de are then drawn as in Fig.
3-28(b). From these we plot the moment diagram for the frame, as shown in Fig. 3-28(c).

It is interesting to note that in this particular case the portion to the right of hinge
c (i.e., cde) carries no external load and is therefore a two-force member if isolated.
The line of reaction at support e, called R_e, must be through points e and c and must
meet the action line of the applied load at some point o, as shown in Fig. 3-29(a). Now,
if we take the whole frame as a free body, we see that the system constitutes a three-force
member subjected to the applied load and support reactions. Thus, the line of reaction
at support a, called R_a, must be through points a and o, so the three forces are
concurrent at point o as required by equilibrium. The vectors R_a and R_e can then be
easily determined by the equilibrium triangle, as shown in Fig. 3-29(b).

In the case where loads are placed both to the left and to the right of the
connecting hinge of a three-hinged frame, one way to analyze this is to use the method
of superposition. This is illustrated in Fig. 3-30, in which the case shown in part (a) can
be made equivalent to the sum of effects of (b) nd (c), each analyzed by the method
discussed previously.

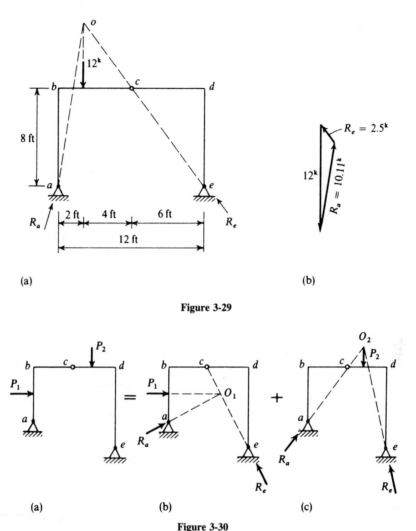

Figure 3-29

Figure 3-30

3-8 APPROXIMATE ANALYSIS FOR STATICALLY INDETERMINATE
RIGID FRAMES

As previously mentioned, the rigid frames of present-day construction are highly indeterminate. It will be seen in the later chapters, which deal with statically indeterminate structures, that to obtain the solution for a building frame based on more exact analyses is often tedious and time consuming. In many cases, we cannot obtain the solution without the aid of modern electronic computers. For this reason empirical rules and approximate methods were often used in the past by structural and architectural engineers in designing various kinds of indeterminate structures. To do this, as many independent equations of statics as there are independent unknowns must be available. The additional equations of statics are worked out by reasonable assumptions based on experience and knowledge of the more exact analyses. Even today the approximate methods are still useful in a preliminary design and cost estimation.

To illustrate, consider a frame subjected to uniform floor loads, such as the one shown in Fig. 3-31(a). The frame is indeterminate to the 24th degree, since eight cuts in the girders would render the frame into three stable and determinate parts and since each cut involves the removal of three elements of restraint (i.e., bending moment, shear, and axial force). A preliminary survey of stresses may be performed by assuming the following so that the indeterminate frame can be solved by a determinate approach, that is, by equations of statics alone:

1. The axial force in each girder is small and can be neglected.
2. A point of inflection (zero moment) occurs in each girder at a point one-tenth of the span length from the left end of the girder.
3. A point of inflection occurs in each girder at a point one-tenth span length from the right end of the girder.

This would render the frame equivalent to the one shown in Fig. 3-31(b), which is statically determinate.

Another case that may also be worth brief mention, without going into details, is the approximate analysis for wind or earthquake stresses in building frames. Consider a frame subjected to lateral forces (equivalent wind or earthquake) acting at the joints such as the one shown in Fig. 3-32(a). The frame is statically indeterminate to the 27th degree. Several methods are available for dealing with the

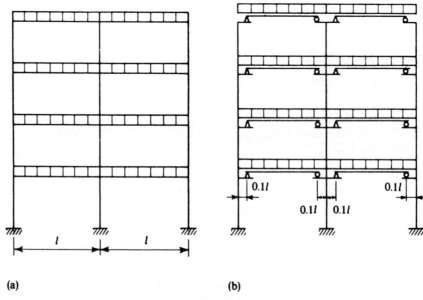

(a)   (b)

Figure 3-31

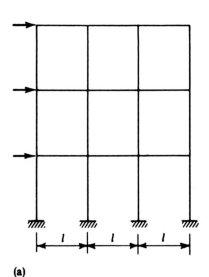

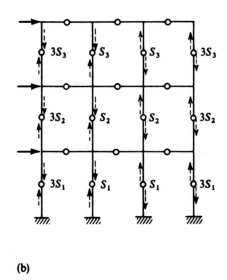

(a)   (b)

Figure 3-32

problem. The method chosen to illustrate this is called the *cantilever method* and is based on the following assumptions:

1. A point of inflection exists at the center of each girder.
2. A point of inflection exists at the center of each column.
3. The unit axial stresses in the columns of a story vary as the horizontal distances of the columns from the center of gravity of the bent. It is usually further assumed that all columns are identical in a story, so the axial forces of the columns in a story will vary in proportion to the distances from the center gravity of the bent.

   This would lead the frame to appear as the form shown in Fig. 3-32(b). Note that the last assumption virtually puts the column axial forces in one story in terms of a single unknown [see the dashed arrows in Fig. 3-32(b)]. It is therefore equivalent to making $(n - 1)$ additional assumptions for each story, n being the number of columns in one story. In this case, there are three for each story, or nine in total regarding column axial forces. As a result, the total number of additional equations is 30 (9 from column axial forces and 21 from inserting pins), which is 3 more than are necessary. However, it happens that a statical analysis for the frame can be carried out without inconsistency on the basis of the foregoing assumptions. The following example illustrates this method.

   Consider the frame shown in Fig. 3-33(a) under lateral loads. Using the cantilever method, zero-moment inflection points are assumed at the center of each girder and each column. The free-body diagram of Fig. 3-33(b) exposes the column forces at the top story. If the axial forces in the interior columns are denoted by S, then the axial force in the exterior columns is $27.5S/7.5 = 3.67S$. By equating the sum of moments about a point at the lower left end of Fig. 3-33(b), we obtain

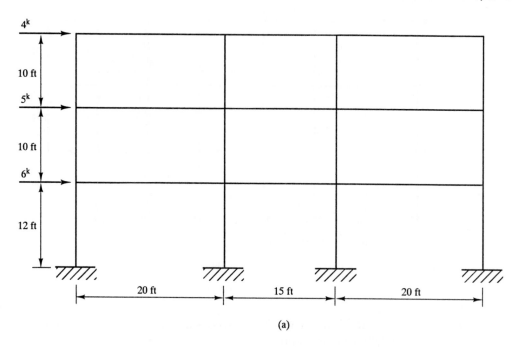

(a)

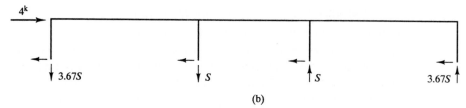

(b)

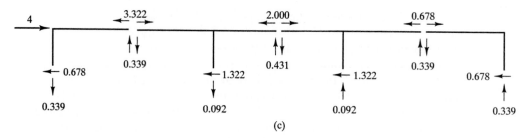

(c)

Figure 3-33

$S = 0.092$. Thus, all the axial forces in the columns of the top story become known. Next, we draw four free-body diagrams from the top half of the top story by cutting through the girder center points [Fig. 3-33(c)]. Working from left to right, we find that each diagram contains only three unknowns; therefore, they can be solved by statics alone. The resulting axial and shear forces are shown in Fig. 3-33(c). This procedure may be repeated for lower stories (Problem 3-10).

PROBLEMS

3-1. In each part of Fig. 3-34, qualitative loadings are shown. Draw the shear and moment diagrams consistent with these loadings; give the equations for each curve.

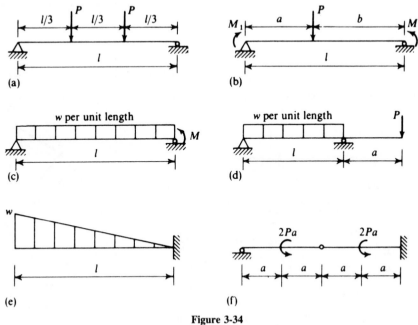

Figure 3-34

3-2. Sketch the shear and moment diagrams for each of the loaded beams shown in Fig. 3-35. Use the relationships among load, shear, and moment.

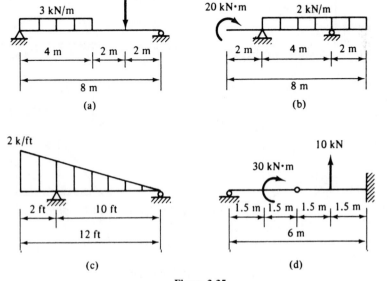

Figure 3-35

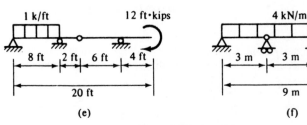

Figure 3-35 (cont'd)

3-3. Determine the bar force in each member of the trusses shown in Fig. 3-36 by the method of joint.

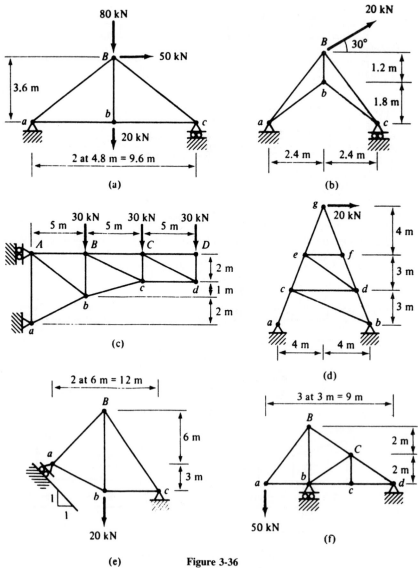

Figure 3-36

3-4. By the method of section, compute the bar forces in the letter bars of the trusses shown in Fig. 3-37.

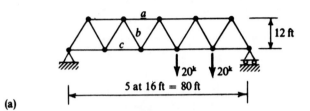

(a)

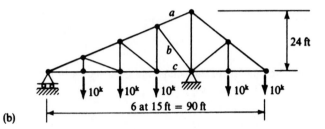

(b)

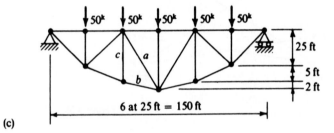

(c)

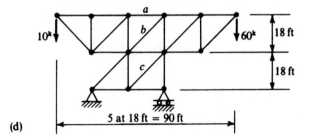

(d)

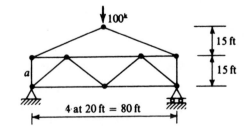

(e)

Figure 3-37

3-5. By the mixed method of joint and section, determine the bar forces in the lettered bars of the K truss shown in Fig. 3-38.

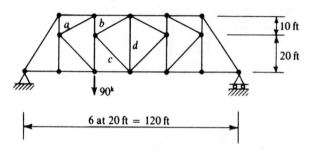

Figure 3-38

3-6. Make a complete analysis of the compound truss shown in Fig. 3-39.

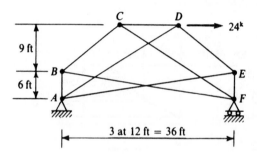

Figure 3-39

3-7. Use the substitute member method to make a complete analysis of the complex truss shown in Fig. 3-40. Repeat it by solving 12 joint equations if a digital computer is available.

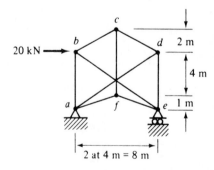

Figure 3-40

3-8. Analyze each frame shown in Fig. 3-41, and draw the bending moment diagram.

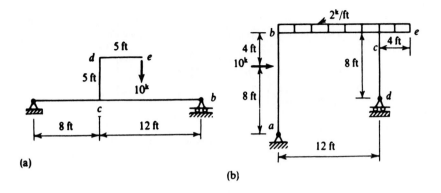

(a)

(b)

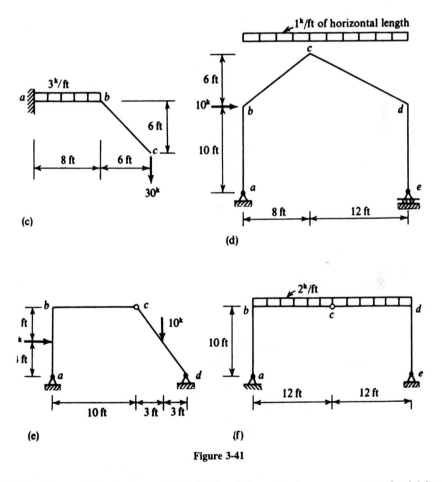

(c)

(d)

(e)

(f)

Figure 3-41

3-9. Analyze each frame shown in Fig. 3-42 and draw the shear, moment, and axial force diagrams for member *bc*.

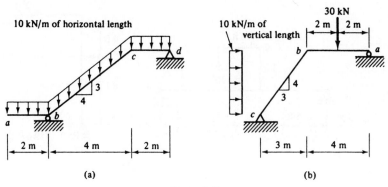

(a)   (b)

Figure 3-42

3-10. Complete the analysis of the frame shown in Fig. 3-33(a) by the cantilever method and draw the axial force, shear, and moment diagrams of the frame. Assume constant EI for all members.

Chapter 4

Elastic Deformations

4-1 GENERAL

The calculation of elastic deformations of structures, both the linear displacements of points and the rotational displacements of lines (slopes) from their original positions, is of great importance in the analysis, design, and construction of structures. For instance, in the erection of a bridge structure, especially when the cantilever method is used, the theoretical elevations of some or all joints must be computed for each stage of the work. In building design the sizes of beams and girders are sometimes governed by the allowable deflections. Most important, the stress analysis for statically indeterminate structures is based largely on an evaluation of their elastic deformations under load. By a statically indeterminate structure we mean a structure in which the number of unknown forces involved is greater than the number of equations of statics available for their solution. If such is the case, there will be an infinite number of solutions that can satisfy the statical equations. To reach a *unique* correct solution, the conditions of the *continuity* of structure, which are associated with the geometric and elastic properties of structure, are a necessary supplement.

Numerous methods of computing elastic deformation have been developed. Only the most significant ones in structural analysis are discussed in this chapter. For beam deformation, the governing differential equation is derived first. The *conjugate beam method* is then presented as a special technique of solving the differential equation using the concept of mathematical analogy.

More general methods applicable to all structures can be derived from energy theorems. Two are presented herein: the *method of virtual force* (*unit load method*) and *Castigliano's second theorem*.

For structures such as trusses, the deformation of a structure may be represented by its joint, or nodal, displacements. These nodal displacements can be found systematically using a *matrix method*, which is also based on energy considerations.

4-2 CURVATURE OF AN ELASTIC LINE

The mathematical definition for curvature is *the rate at which a curve is changing direction*. To derive the expression for curvature, we shall consider a curve such as the one shown in Fig. 4-1. The average rate of change of direction between points P_1 and P_2 is $\Delta\phi/\Delta s$. The limiting value of this ratio as Δs approaches zero is called *curvature*, and the *radius of curvature* is the reciprocal of the curvature. Thus, if we let κ denote the curvature and ρ the radius of curvature, we have

$$\kappa = \frac{1}{\rho} = \lim_{\Delta s \to 0} \frac{\Delta\phi}{\Delta s} = \frac{d\phi}{ds}$$

Now since $\tan\phi = dy/dx$,

$$\frac{d}{dx}\tan\phi = \frac{d^2 y}{dx^2}$$

or

$$(1 + \tan^2\phi)\frac{d\phi}{dx} = \frac{d^2 y}{dx^2}$$

This gives

$$\frac{d^2 y}{dx^2} = \left[1 + \left(\frac{dy}{dx}\right)^2\right]\frac{d\phi}{dx}$$

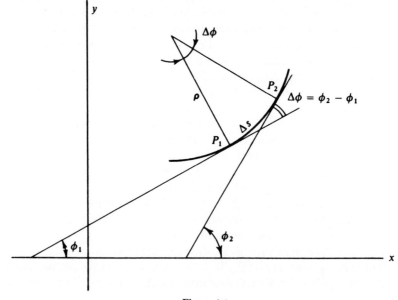

Figure 4-1

whereby

$$\frac{d\phi}{dx} = \frac{d^2y/dx^2}{1 + (dy/dx)^2}$$

Also,

$$\frac{dx}{ds} = \frac{1}{ds/dx} = \frac{1}{[(dx^2 + dy^2)/dx^2]^{1/2}} = \frac{1}{[1 + (dy/dx)^2]^{1/2}}$$

Hence,

$$\kappa = \frac{d\phi}{ds} = \frac{d\phi}{dx}\frac{dx}{ds} = \frac{d^2y/dx^2}{[1 + (dy/dx)^2]^{3/2}} \qquad (4\text{-}1)$$

For a loaded beam with its longitudinal axis taken as the x axis, we may set dy/dx in formula 4-1 equal to zero if the deflection of the beam is small. Thus, we obtain

$$\kappa = \frac{d\phi}{ds} \approx \frac{d^2y}{dx^2} \qquad (4\text{-}2)$$

In general, except for very deep beams with a short span, the deflection due to the shearing force is negligible and only that due to the bending moment is considered. To develop a formula for the curvature due to elastic bending, let us consider a small element of a beam shown in Fig. 4-2. Owing to the action of bending moment M, the two originally parallel sections AB and $A'B'$ will change directions. This angle change is denoted by $d\phi$. If the length of the element is ds and the maximum bending stress, which occurs at the extreme fibers, is called f, the total elongation at the top or bottom fiber is $c\,d\phi$ (see Fig. 4-2), which equals $f\,ds/E$, E being the modulus of elasticity. Thus,

$$c\,d\phi = \frac{f\,ds}{E}$$

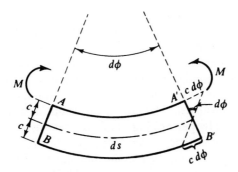

Figure 4-2

or

$$\frac{d\phi}{ds} = \frac{f}{Ec}$$

Replacing f with Mc/I, I being the moment of inertia of the cross-sectional area of the beam about the axis of bending, gives

$$\frac{d\phi}{ds} = \frac{M}{EI} \tag{4-3}$$

which expresses the relationship between the curvature and the bending moment. Now, equating Eqs. 4-2 and 4-3, we obtain the approximate curvature for a loaded beam:

$$\frac{d^2y}{dx^2} = \frac{M}{EI} \tag{4-4}$$

Note that Eq. 4-4 involves four major assumptions:

1. Small deflection of beam
2. Elastic material
3. Only bending moment considered significant
4. Plane section remaining plane after bending

The curvature, established in the coordinate axes of Fig. 4-1, clearly has the same sign as M, but the sign may be reversed if the direction of the y axis is reversed. In that case, we have

$$\frac{d^2y}{dx^2} = -\frac{M}{EI} \tag{4-4a}$$

4-3 CONJUGATE BEAM METHOD

It is clear that the beam slope and deflection may be obtained by integrating Eq. 4-4a once and twice, respectively, after the expression of $M(x)$ is properly derived. The integration may have to be performed over more than one segment of the beam due to support and connection conditions, and the integration constants are to be determined from these conditions and the condition of continuity. These procedures are tedious and prone to mistakes. The conjugate beam method offers a way of accomplishing the same goal by performing simple operations of drawing shear and moment diagrams from an imaginary beam (conjugate beam).

Consider a typical loaded beam, such as the one shown in Fig. 4-3(a), for which we may plot the moment diagram and, therefore, the M/EI diagram as in Fig. 4-3(b).

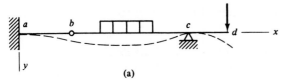

(a)

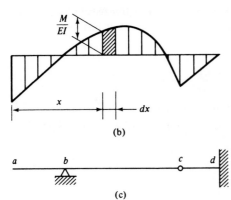

(b)

(c)

Figure 4-3

We recall that the curvature at any point of the beam of Fig. 4.3(a) is given by Eq. 4-4a:

$$\frac{d^2 y}{dx^2} = -\frac{M}{EI}$$

Now, since the slope at any point of the beam is expressed by

$$\frac{dy}{dx} = \tan\theta \approx \theta$$

for small deformation, we have

$$\frac{d\theta}{dx} = -\frac{M}{EI}$$

or

$$d\theta = -\frac{M\,dx}{EI}$$

Integrate.

$$\theta = -\int \frac{M}{EI} dx \tag{4-5}$$

Substituting for θ by dy/dx and integrating again gives

$$y = \int \theta \, dx = -\iint \frac{M}{EI} dx \, dx \qquad (4\text{-}6)$$

Next, for a beam under a distributed load of intensity $w(x)$, the relationships among the load, the shear, and the bending moment at any point are given by (see Sec. 3-3)

$$\frac{dV}{dx} = -w$$

and

$$\frac{dM}{dx} = V$$

Thus, over a portion of the beam

$$V = -\int w \, dx \qquad (4\text{-}7)$$

and

$$M = \int V \, dx = -\iint w \, dx \, dx \qquad (4\text{-}8)$$

Now suppose that we have a beam, called a *conjugate beam*, whose length equals that of the actual beam in Fig. 4-3(a). Let this beam be subjected to the *elastic load* of intensity M/EI given in Fig. 4-3(b). [Elastic load is sometimes referred to as the *angle load*, a term obviously associated with $d\theta = M(dx/EI)$.] The integral expressions for the shear and moment over a portion of the conjugate beam, denoted by $\overline{V}$ and $\overline{M}$, respectively, can be obtained by replacing w in Eqs. 4-7 and 4-8 with M/EI:

$$\overline{V} = -\int \frac{M}{EI} dx \qquad (4\text{-}9)$$

and

$$\overline{M} = -\iint \frac{M}{EI} dx \, dx \qquad (4\text{-}10)$$

When we compare Eqs. 4-5 and 4-6 with Eqs. 4-9 and 4-10, it follows logically that, with properly prescribed boundary conditions for the conjugate beam, we may reach the following results:

1. The slope at a given section of a loaded beam (actual beam) equals the shear in the corresponding section of the conjugate beam subjected to the elastic load.

2. The deflection at a given section of a loaded beam equals the bending moment in the corresponding section of the conjugate beam subjected to the elastic load.

Thus far we have stated only that the conjugate beam is identical to the actual beam with regard to the length of the beam. In order that the above-stated identities be possible, the setup of the support and connection of the conjugate beam must be such as to induce shear and moment in the conjugate beam in conformity to the slope and deflection induced by the counterparts in the actual beam. These requirements are given in Table 4-1 and can be briefly summarized as follows:

$$\text{fixed end} \leftrightarrow \text{free end}$$

$$\text{simple end} \leftrightarrow \text{simple end}$$

$$\text{interior connection} \leftrightarrow \text{interior support}$$

The symbols between the two groups indicate conjugation.

Thus, the conjugate beam for the beam in Fig. 4-3(a) is the one shown in Fig. 4-3(c). If we use the M/EI diagram of Fig. 4-3(b) as the load to put on the beam in Fig. 4-3(c), the resulting shear and bending moment for any section of this beam will give the slope and deflection for the corresponding section of the original beam. Other examples of conjugate beams are shown in Fig. 4-4.

Unlike the actual beams, the conjugate beams may be unstable in themselves. For instance, the conjugate beams shown in Fig. 4-4(c) and (f) are unstable beams. However, they will maintain an unstable equilibrium under the action of an elastic load.

The same figure indicates that the conjugate beam method is not limited to the

TABLE 4-1

Actual Beam Subjected to Applied Load			Conjugate Beam Subjected to Elastic Load
Fixed end	$\begin{cases} \theta = 0 \\ y = 0 \end{cases}$	$\left.\begin{matrix} \bar{V} = 0 \\ \bar{M} = 0 \end{matrix}\right\}$	Free end
Free end	$\begin{cases} \theta \neq 0 \\ y \neq 0 \end{cases}$	$\left.\begin{matrix} \bar{V} \neq 0 \\ \bar{M} \neq 0 \end{matrix}\right\}$	Fixed end
Simple end (hinge or roller)	$\begin{cases} \theta \neq 0 \\ y = 0 \end{cases}$	$\left.\begin{matrix} \bar{V} \neq 0 \\ \bar{M} = 0 \end{matrix}\right\}$	Simple end (hinge or roller)
Interior support (hinge or roller)	$\begin{cases} \theta \neq 0 \\ y = 0 \end{cases}$	$\left.\begin{matrix} \bar{V} \neq 0 \\ \bar{M} = 0 \end{matrix}\right\}$	Interior connection (hinge or roller)
Interior connection (hinge or roller)	$\begin{cases} \theta \neq 0 \\ y \neq 0 \end{cases}$	$\left.\begin{matrix} \bar{V} \neq 0 \\ \bar{M} \neq 0 \end{matrix}\right\}$	Interior support (hinge or roller)

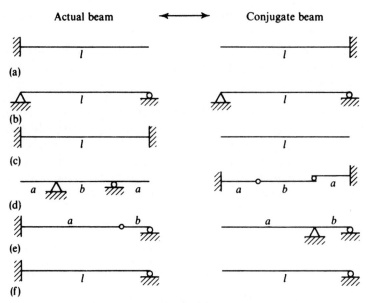

Figure 4-4

analysis of statically determinate beams; in fact, the conjugate beam method is also applicable to statically indeterminate beams.

The sign convention we use may be stated as follows. The origin of the loaded beam is taken at the left end of the beam with y positive downward and x positive to the right. As a result, a positive deflection means a downward deflection and a positive slope means a clockwise rotation of the beam section. Recall that the derivation from the relationships among load, shear, and bending moment is based on taking the downward load as positive. Therefore, a positive M/EI should be taken as a downward elastic load.

Having defined these, we readily see that a positive shear at a section of the conjugate beam corresponds to a clockwise rotation at the section of the actual beam. A positive moment at a section of the conjugate beam corresponds to a downward deflection at the section of the actual beam.

Example 4-1

Find, by the conjugate beam method, the vertical deflection at the free end c of the cantilever beam shown in Fig. 4-5(a). Assume constant EI.

To do this, we place an elastic load on the conjugate beam, as shown in Fig. 4-5(b). The vertical deflection at c of the actual beam is the moment at c of the conjugate beam. Thus,

$$\Delta_c = \frac{wk^3}{6EI}\left(l - \frac{1}{4}k\right) \quad \text{(down)}$$

Example 4-2

Find θ_A, θ_C, and Δ_C for the loaded beam shown in Fig. 4-6(a) by the conjugate beam method. Assume constant EI.

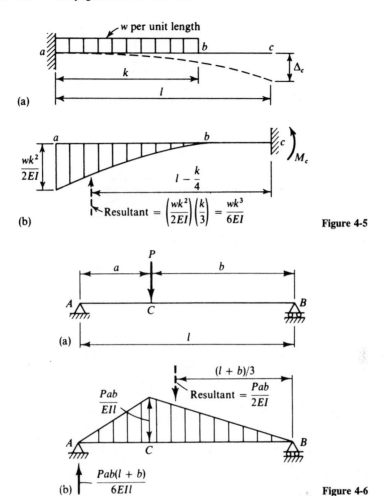

Figure 4-5

Figure 4-6

The conjugate beam together with the elastic load is shown in Fig. 4-6(b), in which the resultant of the loading is found to be $Pab/2EI$ acting at a distance $(l + b)/3$ from the right end as indicated. Thus,

$$\theta_A = \frac{Pab(l + b)}{6EIl} \qquad \text{(clockwise)}$$

$$\theta_C = \frac{Pab(l + b)}{6EIl} - \left(\frac{Pab}{EIl}\right)\left(\frac{a}{2}\right) = \frac{Pab(b - a)}{3EIl} \qquad \text{(clockwise, if } b > a)$$

$$\Delta_C = \frac{Pa^2 b(l + b)}{6EIl} - \left(\frac{Pab}{EIl}\right)\left(\frac{a}{2}\right)\left(\frac{a}{3}\right) = \frac{Pa^2 b^2}{3EIl} \qquad \text{(down)}$$

Example 4-3

Use the conjugate beam method to determine the deflection and rotation at point b in Fig. 4-7(a). $E = 20{,}000 \text{ kN/cm}^2$.

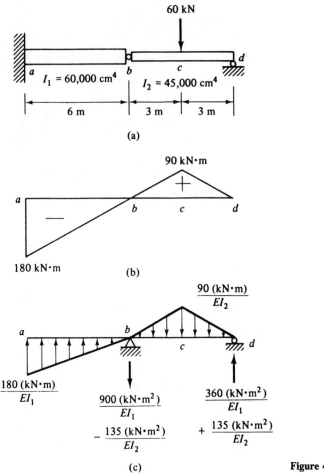

Figure 4-7

To do this, we first plot the moment diagram as shown in Fig. 4-7(b). The diagram for the elastic load and the conjugate beam is then given in Fig. 4-7(c).

The deflection at b of the original beam is the bending moment about b of the conjugate beam subjected to the elastic load. Using the overhanging portion of the conjugate beam, we obtain

$$\Delta_b = \frac{(180)(6)(4)}{2EI_1} = \frac{2,160}{EI_1}$$

$$= \frac{(2,160)(10)^6}{(20,000)(60,000)} = 1.8 \text{ cm} \quad (\text{down})$$

Because of the hinge connection provided at b, a change of slope takes place at that point. In fact, we have different slopes to the immediate left and right of b, corresponding to the shearing forces in the conjugate beam. Thus,

$$(\theta_b)_{\text{left}} = \frac{(180)(6)}{2EI_1} = \frac{540}{EI_1}$$

$$= \frac{(540)(10)^4}{(20,000)(60,000)} = 0.0045 \text{ rad} \quad (\text{clockwise})$$

$$(\theta_b)_{\text{right}} = \frac{270}{EI_2} - \left(\frac{360}{EI_1} + \frac{135}{EI_2}\right) = -\frac{360}{EI_1} + \frac{135}{EI_2}$$

$$= -\frac{(360)(10)^4}{(20,000)(60,000)} + \frac{(135)(10)^4}{(20,000)(45,000)}$$

$$= -0.0015 \text{ rad} \quad (\text{counterclockwise})$$

The relative rotation between the left and right sides of b is the reaction at support b of the conjugate beam:

$$\frac{900}{EI_1} - \frac{135}{EI_2} = \frac{(900)(10)^4}{(20,000)(60,000)} - \frac{(135)(10)^4}{(20,000)(45,000)} = 0.006 \text{ rad}$$

4-4 EXTERNAL WORK AND INTERNAL WORK

If a variable force F moves along its direction a distance ds, the work done is $F\,ds$. The total work done by F during a period of movement may be expressed by

$$W = \int_{s_1}^{s_2} F\,ds \tag{4-11}$$

where s_1 and s_2 are the initial and final values of the position.

Consider a load gradually applied to a structure. Its point of application deflects and reaches a value Δ as the load increases from 0 to P. As long as the principle of superposition holds, a linear relationship exists between the load and the deflection, as represented by the line oa in Fig. 4-8. The total work performed by the applied load during this period is given by

$$W = \int_0^\Delta F\,ds = \int_0^\Delta \left(\frac{Ps}{\Delta}\right)ds = \frac{1}{2}P\Delta \tag{4-12}$$

which equals the area of the shaded triangle oab in Fig. 4-8.

If further deflection $\delta\Delta$, caused by an agent other than P, occurs to the structure in the action line of P, then the additional amount of work done by the already existing load P will be $P\,\delta\Delta$, which equals the shaded rectangular area $abcd$ shown in Fig. 4-8.

Similarly, the work done by a couple M to turn an angular displacement $d\phi$ is $M\,d\phi$. The total work done by M is

$$W = \int_{\phi_1}^{\phi_2} M\,d\phi \tag{4-13}$$

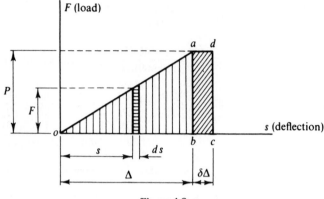

Figure 4-8

Also, the work performed by a gradually applied couple C accompanied by a rotation increasing from 0 to Θ is given by

$$W = \tfrac{1}{2}C\Theta \tag{4-14}$$

Now consider a beam subjected to gradually applied forces. As long as the linear relationship between the load and the deflection holds, all the external work will be converted into internal work or elastic strain energy. Let dW be the strain energy restored in an infinitesimal element of the beam (see Fig. 4-2). We have

$$dW = \tfrac{1}{2}M\,d\phi$$

if only the bending moment M produced by the forces on the element is considered significant. Using Eq. 4-3,

$$\frac{d\phi}{ds} = \frac{M}{EI}$$

or

$$d\phi = \frac{M\,ds}{EI}$$

we have

$$dW = \frac{M^2\,ds}{2EI}$$

For a loaded beam with its longitudinal axis taken as the x axis, we let $ds \approx dx$ and obtain

$$dW = \frac{M^2\,dx}{2EI}$$

The total strain energy restored in the beam of length l is, therefore, given by

$$W = \int_0^l \frac{M^2\, dx}{2EI} \tag{4-15}$$

For a truss subjected to gradually applied loads, the internal work performed by a member with constant cross-sectional area A, length L, and internal axial force S is $S^2 L/2AE$. The total internal work or elastic strain energy for the entire truss is

$$W = \sum \frac{S^2 L}{2AE} \tag{4-16}$$

In some special cases, deformations of structures can be found by equating external work W_E and internal work (strain energy) W_I:

$$W_E = W_I \tag{4-17}$$

For instance, to find the deflection at the free end of the loaded cantilever beam shown in Fig. 4-9, we have

$$W_E = \tfrac{1}{2} P\Delta_b$$

$$W_I = \int_0^l \frac{M^2\, dx}{2EI}$$

$$= \int_0^l \frac{(-Px)^2\, dx}{2EI} = \frac{P^2 l^3}{6EI}$$

Setting $W_E = W_I$ gives

$$\Delta_b = \frac{Pl^3}{3EI}$$

Note that the method illustrated is quite limited in application since it is applicable only to deflection at a point of concentrated force. Furthermore, if more than one force is applied simultaneously to a structure, then more than one unknown deformation will appear in one equation, and a solution becomes impossible. Thus, we do not consider this as a general method.

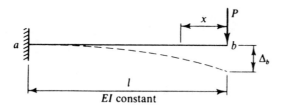

l

EI constant   **Figure 4-9**

4-5 METHOD OF VIRTUAL FORCE (UNIT LOAD METHOD)

Consider the two cases in Fig. 4-10. Figure 4-10(a) illustrates a deformed elastic structure (be it a beam, a rigid frame, or a truss) subjected to the gradually applied loads $P_1, P_2, \ldots$, which move their points of application the distances $\Delta_1, \Delta_2, \ldots$, respectively. To find an expression for the deformation at any point of the structure, say the vertical deflection component Δ at point C, we present the case of Fig. 4-10(b), which shows the same structure with all the actual loads removed, but a virtual load of unity being gradually applied at point C along the desired deflection. Let δ denote the distance the unit load moves its point of application. Note that the virtual load is supposed to be vanishingly small and so are the corresponding virtual deformations.

Also shown in Fig. 4-10(a) is one of the typical deformed elements (be it a fiber in a beam or a rigid frame or a bar in a truss) of length L subjected to internal forces, called S, with a corresponding change in length dL. In Fig. 4-10(b) the same element is subjected to internal forces, called u, with a corresponding change in length dL_1.

Since the external work done by the applied loads must equal the internal strain energy of all elements in the structure, we obtain, for Fig. 4-10(a),

$$\tfrac{1}{2}P_1\Delta_1 + \tfrac{1}{2}P_2\Delta_2 = \tfrac{1}{2}\sum S \cdot dL \tag{4-18}$$

and for Fig. 4-10(b),

$$\tfrac{1}{2}(1)(\delta) = \tfrac{1}{2}\sum u \cdot dL_1 \tag{4-19}$$

Now imagine that the case in Fig. 4-10(b) exists first; the actual loads P_1 and P_2 are then gradually applied to it. Equating the total work done and the total strain energy restored during this period, we have

$$\tfrac{1}{2}(1)(\delta) + \tfrac{1}{2}P_1\Delta_1 + \tfrac{1}{2}P_2\Delta_2 + 1 \cdot \Delta$$
$$= \tfrac{1}{2}\sum u \cdot dL_1 + \tfrac{1}{2}\sum S \cdot dL + \sum u \cdot dL \tag{4-20}$$

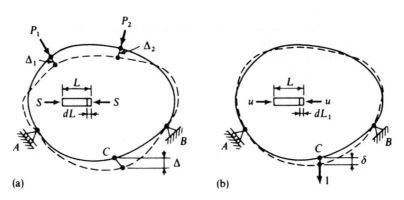

(a)   (b)

Figure 4-10

Since the strain energy and work done must be the same whether the loads are applied together or separately, we obtain, from subtracting the sum of Eqs. 4-18 and 4-19 from Eq. 4-20,

$$1 \cdot \overset{\text{virtual}}{\underset{\text{}}{\Delta}} = \sum \overset{\text{actual}}{u \cdot dL} \tag{4-21}$$

Note that Eq. 4-21 is the basic equation of the unit load method. When the rotation of tangent at any point in the structure is desired, we need only replace the unit virtual force with a *unit virtual couple* in the procedure described above, and we obtain

$$1 \cdot \overset{\text{virtual}}{\underset{\text{}}{\theta}} = \sum \overset{\text{actual}}{u \cdot dL} \tag{4-22}$$

where u is the internal force for a typical element caused by the unit couple and θ is the desired rotation angle.

To find a working formula for solving beam deformations, let us consider a statically determinate beam subjected to loads P_1 and P_2 as shown in Fig. 4-11(a); the longitudinal axis of the beam is taken as the x axis. To find the vertical deflection

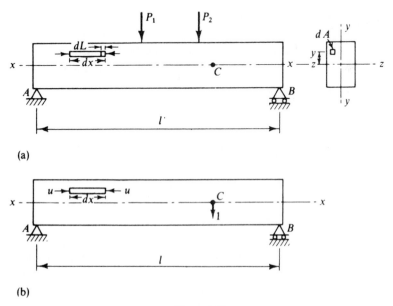

(a)

(b)

Figure 4-11

Δ at an arbitrary point C, we place a unit vertical force at C, as shown in Fig. 4-11(b), and apply Eq. 4-21:

$$1 \cdot \Delta = \sum u \cdot dL$$

To interpret the terms dL and u involved in the equation above, let us first refer to Fig. 4-11(a) and observe that in the present case dL is the change of length of any fiber having length dx and cross-sectional area dA caused by the actual loads P_1 and P_2. dL equals unit elongation times dx and can, therefore, be expressed by $My\,dx/EI$, in which M is the bending moment at the section considered resulting from the actual loads, I the moment of inertia of the cross-sectional area of the beam about the axis of bending, y the distance from the fiber to the axis of bending, and E the modulus of elasticity. Next, refer to Fig. 4-11(b) and observe that u in this case is the internal force of the same fiber resulting from a fictitious unit load applied at C; u equals the bending stress of the fiber times dA, that is, $u = my\,dA/I$, where m is the bending moment at the same section due to the unit load.

Substituting $dL = My\,dx/EI$ and $u = my\,dA/I$ in the basic equation gives

$$1 \cdot \Delta = \sum \left(\frac{my}{I}dA\right)\left(\frac{My}{EI}dx\right)$$

$$= \int_0^l \frac{Mm\,dx}{EI^2} \int_A y^2\,dA$$

Using $\int_A y^2\,dA = I$, we obtain

$$1 \cdot \Delta = \int_0^l \frac{Mm\,dx}{EI} \tag{4-23}$$

Equation 4-23 is the working formula for the determination of the deflection at any point of a beam. If rotation of the tangent at C is desired, we place a unit couple at C and apply the basic formula

$$1 \cdot \theta = \sum u \cdot dL$$

In a similar manner, we obtain

$$1 \cdot \theta = \int_0^l \frac{Mm\,dx}{EI} \tag{4-24}$$

where m is the bending moment at any section due to a unit couple at C.

The right-hand-side of Eq. 4-24 contains the integration of the product of two functions. The regular way of obtaining the integration is to actually express each function properly and carry out the integration as illustrated by the following examples. If the functions are linear, then much time is saved by using the easy-to-memorize formulas given in Appendix D.

Example 4-4

Find the deflection and slope at the free end of a cantilever beam subjected to a uniform load [Fig. 4-12(a)].

To find Δ_b, we place a unit vertical downward load at b [Fig. 4-12(b)].

$$\Delta_b = \int_0^l \frac{Mm\,dx}{EI} = \int_0^l \frac{(-wx^2/2)(-x)\,dx}{EI} = \frac{wl^4}{8EI}$$

To find θ_b, we place a unit clockwise couple at b [Fig. 4-12(c)].

$$\theta_b = \int_0^l \frac{Mm\,dx}{EI} = \int_0^l \frac{(-wx^2/2)(-1)\,dx}{EI} = \frac{wl^3}{6EI}$$

The positive results indicate that Δ_b and θ_b are in the directions assumed.

Example 4-5

Find θ_A, θ_C, and Δ_C of the loaded beam in Fig. 4-13(a). Assume constant EI.

To do this, we find it is advantageous to use double origins to perform the integration. That is,

$$\int_0^l \frac{Mm\,dx}{EI} = \int_0^a \frac{Mm\,dx}{EI} + \int_0^b \frac{Mm\,dx}{EI}$$

The terms of M and m in the expression above, solving for θ_A, θ_C, and Δ_C, are evaluated as shown in Table 4-2.

$$\theta_A = \int_0^a \frac{(Pbx/l)[1 - (x/l)]\,dx}{EI} + \int_0^b \frac{(Pax/l)(x/l)\,dx}{EI}$$

$$= \frac{1}{EI}\left(\frac{Pa^2 b}{2l} - \frac{Pa^3 b}{3l^2} + \frac{Pab^3}{3l^2}\right) = \frac{Pab}{6EIl}\left(3a - \frac{2a^2}{l} + \frac{2b^2}{l}\right) = \frac{Pab(l + b)}{6EIl}$$

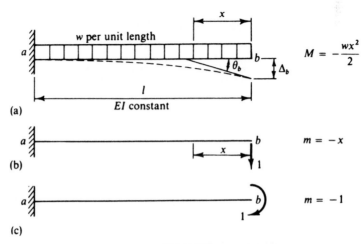

(a)

EI constant

$$M = -\frac{wx^2}{2}$$

(b) $m = -x$

(c) $m = -1$

Figure 4-12

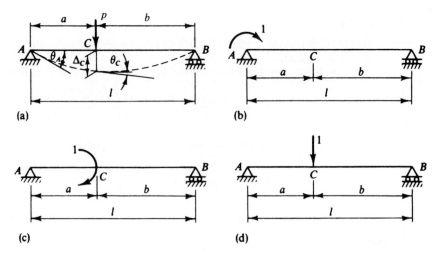

(a)   (b)   (c)   (d)

Figure 4-13

TABLE 4-2

Section	Origin	Limit	M Fig. 4-13(a)	m for θ_A Fig. 4-13(b)	m for θ_C Fig. 4-13(c)	m for Δ_C Fig. 4-13(d)
AC	A	0 to a	$\dfrac{Pb}{l}x$	$1 - \dfrac{x}{l}$	$-\dfrac{x}{l}$	$\dfrac{b}{l}x$
BC	B	0 to b	$\dfrac{Pa}{l}x$	$\dfrac{x}{l}$	$\dfrac{x}{l}$	$\dfrac{a}{l}x$

$$\theta_C = \int_0^a \frac{(Pbx/l)(-x/l)\,dx}{EI} + \int_0^b \frac{(Pax/l)(x/l)\,dx}{EI}$$

$$= \frac{1}{EI}\left(-\frac{Pa^3 b}{3l^2} + \frac{Pab^3}{3l^2}\right) = \frac{Pab(b-a)}{3EIl}$$

$$\Delta_C = \int_0^a \frac{(Pbx/l)(bx/l)\,dx}{EI} + \int_0^b \frac{(Pax/l)(ax/l)\,dx}{EI}$$

$$= \frac{1}{EI}\left(\frac{Pa^3 b^2}{3l^2} + \frac{Pa^2 b^3}{3l^2}\right) = \frac{Pa^2 b^2}{3EIl}$$

If $a = b = l/2$, then

$$\theta_C = 0, \qquad \theta_A = \frac{Pl^2}{16EI}, \qquad \Delta_C = \frac{Pl^3}{48EI}$$

Example 4-6

Find the deflection at the center of the beam in Fig. 4-14. Use $E = 30{,}000$ kips/in.[2].

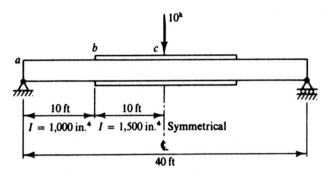

Figure 4-14

Refer to Table 4-3 and obtain

$$EΔ_C = \int_0^l \frac{Mm\,dx}{I}$$

$$= 2\left[\frac{1}{1,000}\int_0^{10}(5x)\left(\frac{x}{2}\right)dx + \frac{1}{1,500}\int_0^{10}\frac{5(10+x)^2}{2}\,dx\right]$$

$$= 2\left\{\frac{1}{1,000}\left[\frac{5}{6}x^3\right]_0^{10} + \frac{1}{1,500}\left(\frac{5}{2}\right)\left[100x + 10x^2 + \frac{x^3}{3}\right]_0^{10}\right\}$$

$$= 2\left(\frac{5}{6} + \frac{70}{18}\right) = 9.44$$

Now let us check the dimensions of both sides of the preceding expression. Note that a unit load of 1 kip must be included in the left side of the expression.

$$30,000\left(\frac{\text{kips}}{\text{in.}^2}\right)(1\text{ kip})(Δ_C) = 9.44\ \frac{\text{ft-kips ft-kips ft}}{\text{in.}^4}$$

Thus,

$$Δ_C = \frac{9.44}{30,000}\ \frac{\text{ft}^3}{\text{in.}^2}$$

or

$$Δ_C = \frac{(9.44)(1.728)\text{ in.}}{30,000} = 0.544\text{ in.}\quad\text{(down)}$$

TABLE 4-3

Section	Origin	Limit (ft)	M (ft-kips)	m (ft-kips)[a]	I (in.⁴)
ab	a	0 to 10	5x	$\frac{x}{2}$	1,000
bc	b	0 to 10	5(10 + x)	$\frac{1}{2}(10 + x)$	1,500

[a] We use a unit load of 1 kip.

In a rigid frame the strain energy due to axial forces and shearing forces is usually much smaller than that due to bending moment and can, therefore, be neglected. The formula

$$\int \frac{Mm\,dx}{EI}$$

previously derived for beam deformations is also good for finding the elastic deformations for a rigid frame, as illustrated in the following examples.

Example 4-7

Determine the horizontal, vertical, and rotational deflection components at end a of the rigid frame shown in Fig. 4-15(a). Assume that all members have the same value of EI.

To perform the integration for the entire frame denoted by

$$\int_{F}$$

we must consider each member as a unit, the centroidal axis of the member being taken as the x axis. Thus,

$$\int_{F} \frac{Mm\,dx}{EI} = \int_{ab} \frac{Mm\,dx}{EI} + \int_{bc} \frac{Mm\,dx}{EI} + \int_{cd} \frac{Mm\,dx}{EI}$$

The terms of M and m in this expression, when we solve for each deflection component at a, are listed in Table 4-4, in which we use m_1 to denote the bending moment at any

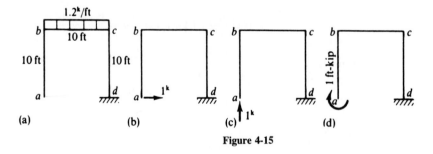

(a)   (b)   (c)   (d)

Figure 4-15

TABLE 4-4

Member	Origin	Limit (ft)	M (ft-kips) Fig. 4-15(a)	m_1 (ft-kips) Fig. 4-15(b)	m_2 (ft-kips) Fig. 4-15(c)	m_3 (ft-kips) Fig. 4-15(d)
ab	a	0 to 10	0	$-x$	0	1
bc	b	0 to 10	$-\dfrac{1.2x^2}{2}$	-10	x	1
cd	c	0 to 10	-60	$x-10$	10	1

section due to a unit horizontal force applied at a, m_2 that due to a unit vertical force at a, and m_3 that due to a unit couple at a. Note that the bending moment resulting in compression on the outside fibers of the frame is assumed to be positive.

To find the horizontal deflection at a, called Δ_1, we apply

$$\Delta_1 = \int_F \frac{Mm_1\,dx}{EI}$$

$$= \frac{1}{EI}\left[0 + \int_0^{10}\left(-\frac{1.2x^2}{2}\right)(-10)\,dx + \int_0^{10}(-60)(x-10)\,dx\right]$$

$$= 5{,}000\,\frac{\text{kips-ft}^3}{EI}\quad\text{(right)}$$

Similarly, we have the vertical deflection at a, called Δ_2,

$$\Delta_2 = \int_F \frac{Mm_2\,dx}{EI}$$

$$= \frac{1}{EI}\left[0 + \int_0^{10}\left(-\frac{1.2x^2}{2}\right)(x)\,dx + \int_0^{10}(-60)(10)\,dx\right]$$

$$= -7{,}500\,\frac{\text{kips-ft}^3}{EI}\quad\text{(down)}$$

and the rotational displacement at a, called Δ_3,

$$\Delta_3 = \int_F \frac{Mm_3\,dx}{EI}$$

$$= \frac{1}{EI}\left[0 + \int_0^{10}\left(-\frac{1.2x^2}{2}\right)(1)\,dx + \int_0^{10}(-60)(1)\,dx\right]$$

$$= -800\,\frac{\text{kips-ft}^2}{EI}\quad\text{(counterclockwise)}$$

Example 4-8

Find the deflection components at a of the same frame for each of three loading cases shown in Fig. 4-15(b) to (d). Let

δ_{11} = horizontal deflection at a due to a unit horizontal force at a

δ_{21} = vertical deflection at a due to a unit horizontal force at a

δ_{31} = rotational displacement at a due to a unit horizontal force at a

Then

$$\delta_{11} = \int_F \frac{(m_1)^2\,dx}{EI}, \qquad \delta_{21} = \int_F \frac{m_1 m_2\,dx}{EI}, \qquad \delta_{31} = \int_F \frac{m_1 m_3\,dx}{EI}$$

since in this case [see Fig. 4-15(b)] $M = m_1$.

Likewise, if the frame is subjected only to a unit vertical force at a [see Fig.

4-15(c)], the three deflection components at a are found to be

$$\delta_{12} = \int_F \frac{m_2\,m_1\,dx}{EI}, \qquad \delta_{22} = \int_F \frac{(m_2)^2\,dx}{EI}, \qquad \delta_{32} = \int_F \frac{m_2\,m_3\,dx}{EI}$$

And if the frame is subjected only to a unit couple at a [see Fig. 4-15(d)], the three deflection components at a are found to be

$$\delta_{13} = \int_F \frac{m_3\,m_1\,dx}{EI}, \qquad \delta_{23} = \int_F \frac{m_3\,m_2\,dx}{EI}, \qquad \delta_{33} = \int_F \frac{(m_3)^2\,dx}{EI}$$

Taking numerical values from Table 4-4 and substituting in each of the expressions above, we find

$$\delta_{11} = \frac{1}{EI}\left[\int_0^{10} x^2\,dx + \int_0^{10} (-10)(-10)\,dx + \int_0^{10} (x-10)^2\,dx\right]$$

$$= 1{,}667\,\frac{\text{kips-ft}^3}{EI} \quad (\text{right})$$

$$\delta_{21} = \frac{1}{EI}\left[0 + \int_0^{10} (-10)(x)\,dx + \int_0^{10} (x-10)(10)\,dx\right]$$

$$= -1{,}000\,\frac{\text{kips-ft}^3}{EI} \quad (\text{down})$$

$$\delta_{31} = \frac{1}{EI}\left[\int_0^{10} (-x)(1)\,dx + \int_0^{10} (-10)(1)\,dx + \int_0^{10} (x-10)(1)\,dx\right]$$

$$= -200\,\frac{\text{kips-ft}^2}{EI} \quad (\text{counterclockwise})$$

$$\delta_{12} = \delta_{21} = -1{,}000\,\frac{\text{kips-ft}^3}{EI} \quad (\text{left})$$

$$\delta_{22} = \frac{1}{EI}\left[0 + \int_0^{10} x^2\,dx + \int_0^{10} (10)^2\,dx\right] = 1{,}333\,\frac{\text{kips-ft}^3}{EI} \quad (\text{up})$$

$$\delta_{32} = \frac{1}{EI}\left[0 + \int_0^{10} (x)(1)\,dx + \int_0^{10} (10)(1)\,dx\right] = 150\,\frac{\text{kips-ft}^2}{EI} \quad (\text{clockwise})$$

$$\delta_{13} = -200\,\frac{\text{kips-ft}^3}{EI} \quad (\text{left})$$

$$\delta_{23} = 150\,\frac{\text{kips-ft}^3}{EI} \quad (\text{up})$$

$$\delta_{33} = \frac{1}{EI}\left[\int_0^{10} dx + \int_0^{10} dx + \int_0^{10} dx\right] = 30\,\frac{\text{kips-ft}^2}{EI} \quad (\text{clockwise})$$

Note that δ_{13} has the same values as δ_{31}, but they differ by one dimension of length. The same is true for δ_{23} and δ_{32}.

In matrix form the previous result is

$$
\begin{bmatrix} \delta_{11} & \delta_{12} & \delta_{13} \\ \delta_{21} & \delta_{22} & \delta_{23} \\ \delta_{31} & \delta_{32} & \delta_{33} \end{bmatrix} = \begin{bmatrix} \int_F \dfrac{(m_1)^2\,dx}{EI} & \int_F \dfrac{m_1 m_2\,dx}{EI} & \int_F \dfrac{m_1 m_3\,dx}{EI} \\[2ex] \int_F \dfrac{m_1 m_2\,dx}{EI} & \int_F \dfrac{(m_2)^2\,dx}{EI} & \int_F \dfrac{m_2 m_3\,dx}{EI} \\[2ex] \int_F \dfrac{m_1 m_3\,dx}{EI} & \int_F \dfrac{m_2 m_3\,dx}{EI} & \int_F \dfrac{(m_3)^2\,dx}{EI} \end{bmatrix}
$$

$$
= \begin{bmatrix} 1{,}667\ \text{ft} & -1{,}000\ \text{ft} & -200\ \text{ft} \\ -1{,}000\ \text{ft} & 1{,}333\ \text{ft} & 150\ \text{ft} \\ -200 & 150 & 30 \end{bmatrix} \dfrac{\text{kips-ft}^2}{EI}
$$

The working formula for the deflection of any joint of a loaded truss can be evaluated from the basic equation, Eq. 4-21,

$$
1 \cdot \Delta = \sum u \cdot dL
$$

by considering each member of the truss as an element. Thus, the term dL is the shortening or lengthening of a bar due to applied loads and can be expressed by SL/AE. The equation above becomes

$$
1 \cdot \Delta = \sum_1^m \frac{SuL}{AE} \tag{4-25}
$$

where S = internal force in any member due to actual loads
  u = internal force in the same member due to a fictitious unit load at the point where the deflection is sought, acting along the desired direction
  L = length of the member
  A = cross-sectional area of the member
  E = modulus of elasticity of the member
  m = total number of members

Equation 4-25 in matrix form is

$$
\Delta = \begin{bmatrix} u_1 & u_2 & \cdots & u_m \end{bmatrix} \begin{bmatrix} \dfrac{L_1}{A_1 E} & & & \\ & \dfrac{L_2}{A_2 E} & & \\ & & \ddots & \\ & & & \dfrac{L_m}{A_m E} \end{bmatrix} \begin{Bmatrix} S_1 \\ S_2 \\ \vdots \\ S_m \end{Bmatrix} \tag{4-25a}
$$

Sometimes the change of bar length dL is not caused by any external force but is due to the effect of temperature. If this is the case, we let $dL = \alpha t L$, and the working formula for finding deflection due to temperature change is given by

$$1 \cdot \Delta = \sum u \cdot \alpha t L \qquad (4\text{-}26)$$

where α = coefficient of linear thermal expansion
t = temperature rise in degrees

Example 4-9

Find the vertical deflection of joint b of the loaded truss shown in Fig. 4-16(a). Assume that L (ft)$/A$ (in.^{2}) = 1 and that E = 30,000 kips/in.^{2} for all members.

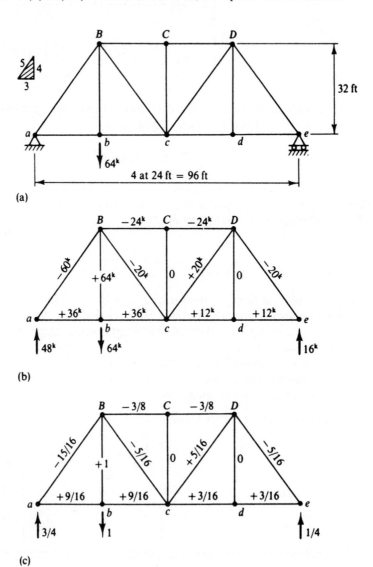

Figure 4-16

We begin with the evaluation of S and u. The answer diagrams for them are shown in Fig. 4-16(b) and (c), respectively. Next we apply Eq. 4-25. The complete solution is given in Table 4-5.

$$\Delta_v = \sum \frac{SuL}{AE} = \frac{+202}{30,000} = +0.00673 \text{ ft} \quad \text{(down)}$$

Example 4-10

For the loaded structure in Example 4-9, find the absolute deflection of joint b.

To do this, we have to obtain the horizontal deflection of joint b in addition to the vertical deflection of that joint already found. The vector sum of these two displacement components is the solution.

When a unit horizontal load is applied at joint b to the right, only the member ab is under the stress of tension (i.e., $u = 1$); all other members are unstressed. The horizontal movement, called Δ_h, at joint b is thus given by

$$\Delta_h = \left(\frac{SuL}{AE} \right)_{ab} = \frac{(36)(1)}{30,000} = +0.0012 \text{ ft} \quad \text{(right)}$$

and the absolute deflection of joint b is given by

$$\Delta = \sqrt{(\Delta_v)^2 + (\Delta_h)^2} = \sqrt{(0.00673)^2 + (0.0012)^2} = 0.00684 \text{ ft}$$

Moving down to the right and making an angle ϕ with the horizontal direction,

$$\phi = \tan^{-1} \frac{0.00673}{0.00120} = \tan^{-1} 5.72 \approx 80°$$

TABLE 4-5

Member	$\dfrac{L}{A} \left(\dfrac{\text{ft}}{\text{in.}^2} \right)$	S (kips)	u [a]	$\dfrac{SuL}{A} \left(\dfrac{\text{ft-kips}}{\text{in.}^2} \right)$
ab	1	+36	+9/16	+ 20.25
bc	1	+36	+9/16	+ 20.25
cd	1	+12	+3/16	+ 2.25
de	1	+12	+3/16	+ 2.25
BC	1	−24	−3/8	+ 9.0
CD	1	−24	−3/8	+ 9.0
aB	1	−60	−15/16	+ 56.25
Bb	1	+64	+1	+ 64.0
Bc	1	−20	−5/16	+ 6.25
Cc	1	0	0	0
cD	1	+20	+5/16	+ 6.25
Dd	1	0	0	0
De	1	−20	−5/16	+ 6.25
		Σ		+202.0

[a] We use a fictitious load of 1 (not 1 kip) for determining u values.

Example 4-11

For the same loaded truss [Fig. 4-16(a)], find the rotation of member bc.

   Finding the rotation of member bc is equivalent to finding the relative displacement between ends b and c (in the direction perpendicular to bc) divided by the length of bc. Assume counterclockwise rotation. We then apply a pair of unit fictitious loads to joints b and c and evaluate the u value for each member, as shown in Fig. 4-17. The computation leading to the solution of the relative displacement between joints b and c perpendicular to the original line of bc is contained in Table 4-6. The rotation of the member, denoted by θ, is then determined:

$$\theta = \frac{80}{24E} = \frac{80}{(24)(30,000)} = \frac{1}{9,000} \text{ rad}$$

The positive value of the angle indicates a counterclockwise rotation.

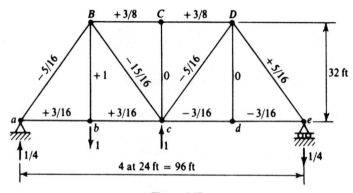

Figure 4-17

TABLE 4-6

Member	$\dfrac{L}{A}\left(\dfrac{\text{ft}}{\text{in.}^2}\right)$	S (kips)	u	$\dfrac{SuL}{A}\left(\dfrac{\text{ft-kips}}{\text{in.}^2}\right)$
ab	1	+36	+3/16	+27/4
bc	1	+36	+3/16	+27/4
cd	1	+12	−3/16	− 9/4
de	1	+12	−3/16	− 9/4
BC	1	−24	+3/8	− 9
CD	1	−24	+3/8	− 9
aB	1	−60	−5/16	+75/4
Bb	1	+64	+1	+64
Bc	1	−20	−15/16	+75/4
Cc	1	0	0	0
cD	1	+20	−5/16	−25/4
Dd	1	0	0	0
De	1	−20	+5/16	−25/4
			Σ	+80

Example 4-12

Find the vertical deflection at joint b resulting from a rise in temperature of 50°F in the top chords BC and CD (Fig. 4-18). $\alpha = 0.0000065$ in./in./1°F.

On a statically determinate truss, no reactions or internal forces can be developed because of a temperature rise or drop in truss members. However, certain changes of bar length will take place if the temperature rises or drops in a bar. This in turn will cause the distortion of the whole truss.

To find the vertical deflection of joint b, we apply Eq. 4-26,

$$\Delta_b = \sum u \cdot \alpha t L$$

Note that, in this problem, only bars BC and CD are involved in the computation since the rest of the members undergo no change of length. Now $u = -\frac{3}{8}$ [see Fig. 4-16(c)] and $\alpha t L = (0.0000065)(50)(24) = 0.0078$ for BC and CD. Thus,

$$\Delta_b = 2(-\tfrac{3}{8})(0.0078) = -0.00585 \text{ ft}$$

The negative sign indicates an upward movement of joint b.

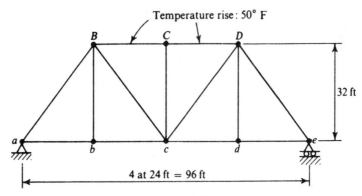

Figure 4-18

4-6 CASTIGLIANO'S SECOND THEOREM

In 1876, Alberto Castigliano published a notable paper in which he presented a general method for determining the deformations of linear structures: *the first partial derivative of the total strain energy of the structure with respect to one of the applied actions gives the displacement along that action.*

If we use P to denote the action (force or couple), Δ_p the corresponding displacement (deflection or rotation) along P, and W the total strain energy, the statement can be expressed by

$$\Delta_p = \frac{\partial W}{\partial P} \tag{4-27}$$

To demonstrate the theorem, consider the loaded beam in Fig. 4-19. The deflected position is represented by the dashed line. If we consider only the internal work resulting from the bending moment, we have the total strain energy of the beam (see Eq. 4-15):

$$W = \int_0^l \frac{M^2\,dx}{2EI}$$

Now let M_1 be the bending moment at any section due to the gradually applied load P_1, and let M_2 be the bending moment at the same section due to the gradually applied load P_2. The total bending moment at any section is given by

$$M = M_1 + M_2 = m_1\,P_1 + m_2\,P_2$$

where m_1 = bending moment at any section due to a unit load in place of P_1
$\quad\quad m_2$ = bending moment of the same section due to a unit load in place of P_2

Thus,

$$\frac{\partial W}{\partial P_1} = \frac{\partial}{\partial P_1}\int_0^l \frac{M^2\,dx}{2EI} = \int_0^l \frac{M(\partial M/\partial P_1)\,dx}{EI} = \int_0^l \frac{Mm_1\,dx}{EI} = \Delta_1$$

and

$$\frac{\partial W}{\partial P_2} = \frac{\partial}{\partial P_2}\int_0^l \frac{M^2\,dx}{2EI} = \int_0^l \frac{M(\partial M/\partial P_2)\,dx}{EI} = \int_0^l \frac{Mm_2\,dx}{EI} = \Delta_2$$

The last equality in each of the two expressions above is based on Eq. 4-23 from virtual work.

Let us now turn to the loaded truss in Fig. 4-20. The total strain energy (see Eq. 4-16) is

$$W = \sum \frac{S^2 L}{2AE}$$

If we let

$\quad\quad S_1$ = internal force in any bar due to the gradually applied load P_1
$\quad\quad S_2$ = internal force in the same bar due to the gradually applied load P_2

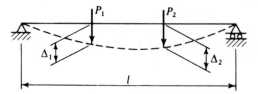

Figure 4-19

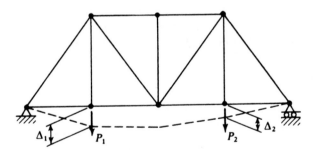

Figure 4-20

then the total internal force in any bar is given by

$$S = S_1 + S_2 = P_1 u_1 + P_2 u_2$$

where u_1 = internal force in any bar due to a unit load in place of P_1
       u_2 = internal force in the same bar due to a unit load in place of P_2

Thus,

$$\frac{\partial W}{\partial P_1} = \frac{\partial}{\partial P_1} \sum \frac{S^2 L}{2AE} = \sum \frac{S(\partial S/\partial P_1)L}{AE} = \sum \frac{Su_1 L}{AE} = \Delta_1$$

and

$$\frac{\partial W}{\partial P_2} = \frac{\partial}{\partial P_2} \sum \frac{S^2 L}{2AE} = \sum \frac{S(\partial S/\partial P_2)L}{AE} = \sum \frac{Su_2 L}{AE} = \Delta_2$$

The last equality in each expression above is based on Eq. 4-25 from virtual force.

It is interesting to point out that Castigliano's theorem basically does not differ from the method of virtual force for the analysis of linear structures subjected to external forces. The difference is only a matter of the arrangement of calculation. Using the method of virtual force, we have from Eqs. 4-23 and 4-25,

$$\Delta = \int \frac{Mm\,dx}{EI} \qquad \text{for a beam or rigid frame}$$

and

$$\Delta = \sum \frac{SuL}{AE} \qquad \text{for a truss}$$

while applying Castigliano's theorem, we have

$$\Delta = \int \frac{M(\partial M/\partial P)\,dx}{EI} \qquad \text{for a beam or rigid frame} \qquad (4\text{-}28)$$

and

$$\Delta = \sum \frac{S(\partial S/\partial P) L}{AE} \qquad \text{for a truss} \qquad (4\text{-}29)$$

Example 4-13

Find the vertical deflection at the free end b of a cantilever beam ab subjected to a concentrated load P at b (see Fig. 4-9).

$$\Delta_b = \frac{\partial W}{\partial P} = \int_0^l \frac{M(\partial M/\partial P)\, dx}{EI} = \frac{1}{EI} \int_0^l M \frac{\partial M}{\partial P} dx$$

Now

$$M = -Px, \qquad \frac{\partial M}{\partial P} = -x$$

Therefore,

$$\Delta_b = \frac{1}{EI} \int_0^l (-Px)(-x)\, dx = \frac{Pl^3}{3EI} \quad \text{(down)}$$

Example 4-14

For the beam and load shown in Fig. 4-21(a), find the vertical and rotational displacements at the free end a. Given $w = 15$ kN/m, $l = 5$ m, $E = 20{,}000$ kN/cm², and $I = 12{,}000$ cm⁴, determine the magnitude of the displacements.

To find the displacements at the free end, we note that in this case no vertical force or moment force actually acts at the free end; thus Castigliano's theorem cannot be directly applied. To carry out the partial derivative, we must first assume the imaginary forces Q_1, Q_2, corresponding respectively to the vertical deflection Δ_a and the rotation θ_a at the free end, and then set $Q_1 = Q_2 = 0$ in the final operation.

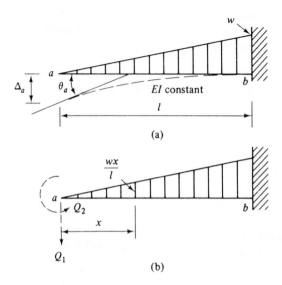

(a)

(b)   **Figure 4-21**

Refer to Fig. 4-21(b). The moment at any section is given by

$$M = -Q_1 x - Q_2 - \frac{wx^3}{6l}$$

It follows that

$$\frac{\partial M}{\partial Q_1} = -x \quad \text{and} \quad \frac{\partial M}{\partial Q_2} = -1$$

$$\Delta_a = \int_0^l \frac{M(\partial M/\partial Q_1)\, dx}{EI}$$

$$= \int_0^l \frac{(-wx^3/6l)(-x)\, dx}{EI} = \frac{wl^4}{30EI} \quad \text{(down)}$$

$$\theta_a = \int_0^l \frac{M(\partial M/\partial Q_2)\, dx}{EI}$$

$$= \int_0^l \frac{(-wx^3/6l)(-1)\, dx}{EI} = \frac{wl^3}{24EI} \quad \text{(counterclockwise)}$$

Substituting $w = 15\,\text{kN/m}$, $l = 5\,\text{m}$, $E = 20{,}000\,\text{kN/cm}^2$, and $I = 12{,}000\,\text{cm}^4$ into the foregoing expressions, we have

$$\Delta_a = \frac{(15)(5)^4(10)^6}{(30)(20{,}000)(12{,}000)} = 1.3\,\text{cm}$$

$$\theta_a = \frac{(15)(5)^3(10)^4}{(24)(20{,}000)(12{,}000)} = 0.003\,\text{rad}$$

Example 4-15

Find, by Castigliano's theorem, the horizontal displacement Δ_1 and the rotational displacement Δ_2 at support c for the rigid frame shown in Fig. 4-22(a). Consider the bending effect only.

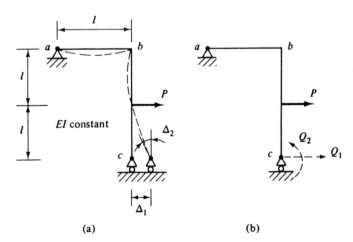

(a)   (b)

Figure 4-22

TABLE 4-7

Member	Origin	Limit	M	$\dfrac{\partial M}{\partial Q_1}$	$\dfrac{\partial M}{\partial Q_2}$	$\displaystyle\int \dfrac{M(\partial M/\partial Q_1)\,dx}{EI}$	$\displaystyle\int \dfrac{M(\partial M/\partial Q_2)\,dx}{EI}$
ab	a	0 to l	$\left(P + 2Q_1 + \dfrac{Q_2}{l}\right)x$	$2x$	$\dfrac{x}{l}$	$\displaystyle\int_0^l \dfrac{(Px)(2x)\,dx}{EI}$	$\displaystyle\int_0^l \dfrac{(Px)(x/l)\,dx}{EI}$
bc	c	l to $2l$	$P(x - l) + Q_1x + Q_2$	x	1	$\displaystyle\int_l^{2l} \dfrac{P(x - l)(x)\,dx}{EI}$	$\displaystyle\int_l^{2l} \dfrac{P(x - l)(1)\,dx}{EI}$
						$\Delta_1 = \dfrac{3Pl^3}{2EI}$	$\Delta_2 = \dfrac{5Pl^2}{6EI}$

Since no horizontal force or moment actually acts at support c, we must assume forces Q_1 and Q_2 of zero value, corresponding respectively to the desired displacements Δ_1 and Δ_2 at c [Fig. 4-22(b)], in order to carry out the partial derivatives such that

$$\Delta_1 = \int_F \frac{M(\partial M/\partial Q_1)\,dx}{EI}$$

$$\Delta_2 = \int_F \frac{M(\partial M/\partial Q_2)\,dx}{EI}$$

where $\int_F$ indicates the sign of integration carried through the entire frame. The complete solution is given in Table 4-7.

Example 4-16

Given the loaded truss in Fig. 4-16(a), find the horizontal deflection at D.

Assume that joint D will move to the right. To apply the theorem, we place an imaginary horizontal force Q acting at D, as shown in Fig. 4-23(a). The bar forces thus obtained are shown in Fig. 4-23(b). The complete solution is shown in Table 4-8.

$$\Delta = \sum \frac{S(\partial S/\partial Q)L}{AE} = +\frac{36}{30,000} = +0.0012 \text{ ft} \quad \text{(right)}$$

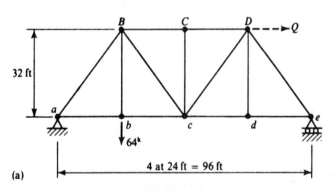

(a)

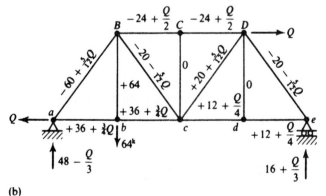

(b)

Figure 4-23

TABLE 4-8

Member	$\dfrac{L}{A}$ (ft/in.²)	S (kips)	$\dfrac{\partial S}{\partial Q}$	$\dfrac{S(\partial S/\partial Q)L}{A}$ (ft-kips/in.²)
ab	1	$+36 + 3/4Q$	$+3/4$	$+27$
bc	1	$+36 + 3/4Q$	$+3/4$	$+27$
cd	1	$+12 + 1/4Q$	$+1/4$	$+ 3$
de	1	$+12 + 1/4Q$	$+1/4$	$+ 3$
BC	1	$-24 + 1/2Q$	$+1/2$	-12
CD	1	$-24 + 1/2Q$	$+1/2$	-12
aB	1	$-60 + 5/12Q$	$+5/12$	-25
Bb	1	$+ 64$	0	0
Bc	1	$-20 - 5/12Q$	$-5/12$	$+ 8.33$
Cc	1	0	0	0
cD	1	$+20 + 5/12Q$	$+5/12$	$+ 8.33$
Dd	1	0	0	0
De	1	$-20 - 5/12Q$	$-5/12$	8.33
			Σ	$+36.0$

4-7 MAXWELL'S LAW OF RECIPROCAL DEFLECTIONS

Referring to Fig. 4-24, we note that Maxwell's law simply states that

$$\Delta_{21} = \Delta_{12} \tag{4-30}$$

where Δ_{21} = deflection at point 2 due to the load P applied at point 1

Δ_{12} = deflection at point 1 along the original line of action of P due to the same load applied at point 2 along the original deflection Δ_{21}

To prove this statement, both deflections are evaluated by the method of virtual force. Thus, from Fig. 4-24(a) we have

$$\Delta_{21} = \int_0^l \frac{M_1 m_2 \, dx}{EI}$$

where M_1 = moment at any section due to load P applied at point 1

m_2 = moment at the same section due to a unit load applied at point 2 along the desired deflection

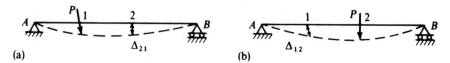

(a)   (b)

Figure 4-24

Similarly, from Fig. 4-24(b) we obtain

$$\Delta_{12} = \int_0^l \frac{M_2 m_1 \, dx}{EI}$$

but

$$M_1 = Pm_1 \quad \text{and} \quad M_2 = Pm_2$$

It is readily seen that

$$\Delta_{21} = \int_0^l \frac{(Pm_1)m_2 \, dx}{EI} = \int_0^l \frac{(Pm_2)m_1 \, dx}{EI} = \int_0^l \frac{M_2 m_1 \, dx}{EI} = \Delta_{12}$$

The special case is that $P = 1$, for which we can write

$$\delta_{21} = \delta_{12} \tag{4-31}$$

where δ_{21} = deflection at point 2 resulting from a unit load applied at point 1

   δ_{12} = deflection at point 1 along the original line of action due to a unit load applied at point 2 along the original deflection δ_{21}

We have hitherto demonstrated the law in regard to applied forces and their corresponding linear deflections. However, the reciprocity extends also to rotational displacement. For the case of two unit couples applied separately to any two points of a structure, the law is *the rotational deflection at point 2 on a structure caused by a unit couple at point 1 is equal to the rotational deflection at point 1 due to a unit couple at point 2.*

Because of virtual force we also observe that the *rotational deflection at point 2 due to a unit force at point 1 is equal in magnitude to the linear deflection at point 1 along the original force due to a unit couple at point 2.*

Maxwell's law is perfectly general and is applicable to any type of structure as long as the material of the structure is elastic and follows Hooke's law.

4-8 MATRIX METHOD FOR TRUSS DISPLACEMENTS

The matrix method offers a systematic way of computing displacements. It is best introduced through an example. Let us consider the problem solved in Sec. 3-5 and plot the loaded truss in Fig. 4-25(a). In a matrix formulation, it is convenient to treat the supports as equivalent truss members as shown in Fig. 4-25(b) and number all members from 1 to 6. The six member forces are denoted by $Q_1, Q_2, \ldots, Q_6$, instead of $H_A, \ldots, V_A, S_b$, and they constitute a member force vector Q. The relationship between the Q's and the original designation is $Q_1 = -H_A$, $Q_2 = -V_A$, $Q_3 = -H_B$, $Q_4 = -V_B$, $Q_5 = S_a$, and $Q_6 = S_b$. Note that the negative sign is due to the convention that tensile member forces are designated as positive. With this definition of

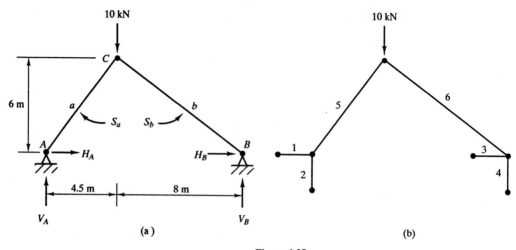

Figure 4-25

member force vector, the equilibrium equation, originally listed in Sec. 3-5, becomes

$$
\begin{bmatrix}
1 & 0 & 0 & 0 & 0.6 & 0 \\
0 & 1 & 0 & 0 & 0.8 & 0 \\
0 & 0 & 1 & 0 & 0 & -0.8 \\
0 & 0 & 0 & 1 & 0 & 0.6 \\
0 & 0 & 0 & 0 & 0.6 & -0.8 \\
0 & 0 & 0 & 0 & 0.8 & 0.6
\end{bmatrix}
\begin{Bmatrix}
Q_1 \\ Q_2 \\ Q_3 \\ Q_4 \\ Q_5 \\ Q_6
\end{Bmatrix}
=
\begin{Bmatrix}
0 \\ 0 \\ 0 \\ 0 \\ 0 \\ -10
\end{Bmatrix}
$$

$$ A \qquad\qquad Q \qquad R $$

or

$$ AQ = R \tag{4-32} $$

The solutions of member forces are

$$
Q =
\begin{Bmatrix}
Q_1 \\ Q_2 \\ Q_3 \\ Q_4 \\ Q_5 \\ Q_6
\end{Bmatrix}
=
\begin{Bmatrix}
-4.8 \\ -6.4 \\ 4.8 \\ -3.6 \\ -8 \\ -6
\end{Bmatrix}
\text{kN}
$$

Symbolically, the solution vector may be represented as

$$Q = bR \tag{4-33}$$

where the matrix b is the inverse of A.

$$b = \begin{bmatrix} 1 & 0 & 0 & 0 & 0.36 & 0.48 \\ 0 & 1 & 0 & 0 & 0.48 & 0.64 \\ 0 & 0 & 1 & 0 & 0.64 & -0.48 \\ 0 & 0 & 0 & 1 & -0.48 & 0.36 \\ 0 & 0 & 0 & 0 & 0.6 & 0.8 \\ 0 & 0 & 0 & 0 & -0.8 & 0.6 \end{bmatrix} \tag{4-34}$$

4-8a Member Deformation

Knowing the member forces, the elongation of each member, q_i, is obtained directly from multiplying the member force by the member flexibility coefficient f_i; that is, $q_i = f_i Q_i, i = 1, 2, \ldots, 6$. For both members 5 and 6, the flexibility coefficient is L/EA. We assume that $E = 200$ kN/mm^2, and the cross-sectional area is proportional to the member length L (mm)/A (mm^2) = 2. Thus, $f_5 = f_6 = 0.01$ mm/kN. For the four support elements, the flexibility is simply zero: $f_1 = f_2 = f_3 = f_4 = 0$. Define a *member flexibility matrix f* containing the member flexibility coefficients f_i on its diagonal. Then the member elongations are written as

$$\begin{Bmatrix} q_1 \\ q_2 \\ q_3 \\ q_4 \\ q_5 \\ q_6 \end{Bmatrix} = \begin{bmatrix} 0 & 0 & 0 & 0 & 0 & 0 \\ 0 & 0 & 0 & 0 & 0 & 0 \\ 0 & 0 & 0 & 0 & 0 & 0 \\ 0 & 0 & 0 & 0 & 0 & 0 \\ 0 & 0 & 0 & 0 & 0.01 & 0 \\ 0 & 0 & 0 & 0 & 0 & 0.01 \end{bmatrix} \begin{Bmatrix} -4.8 \\ -6.4 \\ 4.8 \\ -3.6 \\ -8 \\ -6 \end{Bmatrix} = \begin{Bmatrix} 0 \\ 0 \\ 0 \\ 0 \\ -0.08 \\ -0.06 \end{Bmatrix} \text{mm}$$

$$\quad q \qquad\qquad f \qquad\qquad Q$$

or

$$q = fQ \tag{4-35}$$

4-8b Nodal Displacements and Contragredient Transformation

Once the member elongations are known, the nodal displacements are completely determined from geometrical considerations. In fact, graphical methods may be devised to find the nodal displacements. Using the matrix formulation, however, a simple formula for nodal displacements can be derived from energy theorems (see Sec. 4-4).

Note that the vectors Q and q are a pair of vectors representing the internal member forces and the corresponding member elongations, respectively. The internal work of the whole structure is $Q^T q/2$. The vector R represents the applied nodal forces. Let the corresponding nodal displacements vector be denoted by r.

$$r = \begin{Bmatrix} r_1 \\ r_2 \\ r_3 \\ r_4 \\ r_5 \\ r_6 \end{Bmatrix}$$

For example, r_1 and r_2 are the horizontal and vertical nodal displacements at joint A, respectively. The external work is then $R^T r/2$. Equating the external work and the internal work and canceling the common factor $\frac{1}{2}$, we obtain

$$R^T r = Q^T q \tag{4-36}$$

We already know that $Q = bR$ from Eq. 4-33; thus, $Q^T = R^T b^T$. Substituting the Q^T in Eq. 4-36 by $R^T b^T$ leads to

$$R^T(r) = R^T(b^T)$$

Since this equation is valid for any value of vector R, we conclude that

$$r = b^T q \tag{4-37}$$

This is the nodal displacement formula we are looking for. Substituting the b matrix from Eq. 4-34 and the q vector from Eq. 4-35 into Eq. 4-37, we obtain

$$\begin{Bmatrix} r_1 \\ r_2 \\ r_3 \\ r_4 \\ r_5 \\ r_6 \end{Bmatrix} = \begin{Bmatrix} 0 \\ 0 \\ 0 \\ 0 \\ 0 \\ -0.01 \end{Bmatrix}$$

Note that $r_5 = 0$ is due to the geometry and member sizes and is purely incidental. The vertical displacement $r_6 = -0.01$ mm means that node C is pushed downward by 0.01 mm.

We observe that the derivation of Eq. 4-37, which is a displacement transformation relationship, is only based on Eq. 4-36 and the force transformation $Q = bR$. This pair of transformation relationships is called *contragredient transformation*, which states that *if four vectors are linked by $R^T r = Q^T q$, then one transformation $Q = bR$ will lead to another transformation $r = b^T q$*. This relationship is very general and does not require the length of the two vectors Q and R being equal. The contragredient transformation will be used in the derivation of useful formulas in Chapters 5 and 6.

PROBLEMS

4-1. Find the vertical deflection at center and the slope at left end of a simply supported beam subjected to a uniform load over the entire span using (a) the conjugate beam method, (b) the method of virtual force, and (c) Castigliano's second theorem. Assume constant EI.

4-2. Find the vertical deflections at the load point and at the center of the beam in Fig. 4-26 using (a) the conjugate beam method, (b) the method of virtual force, and (c) Castigliano's second theorem. Assume constant EI.

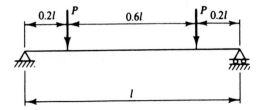

Figure 4-26

4-3. Find the slope and deflection at the load point of the beam in Fig. 4-27 using (a) the conjugate beam method, (b) the virtual force method, and (c) Castigliano's second theorem. $E = 30,000$ kips/in.^{2}.

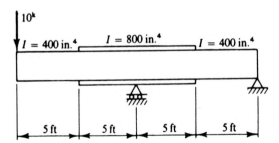

Figure 4-27

4-4. For the load and beam shown in Fig. 4-28, use the conjugate beam method to find the deflection at b and the rotation at c. $E = 20,000$ kN/cm^2 and $I = 5,000$ cm^4.

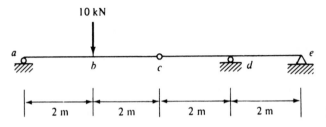

Figure 4-28

4-5. Determine the horizontal, vertical, and rotational displacement components at point a of the frame shown in Fig. 4-29 using (a) the virtual force method and (b) Castigliano's second theorem. Use $E = 30,000$ kips/in.^{2} and $I = 500$ in.^{4}.

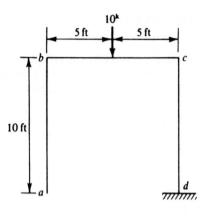

Figure 4-29

4-6. For the load and beam in Fig. 4-30, determine the slope and deflection at points b and c using (a) the method of virtual force and (b) Castigliano's second theorem.

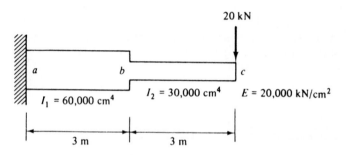

Figure 4-30

4-7. For the loads and frame in Fig. 4-31, find the horizontal, vertical, and rotational displacement components at point a using (a) the method of virtual force and (b) Castigliano's second theorem. $EI = 2 \times 10^8$ kN · cm².

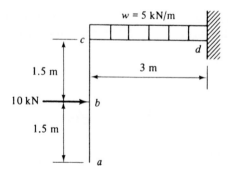

Figure 4-31

4-8. For the loads and truss in Fig. 4-32, find the displacement components corresponding to the applied loads at joint B using (a) the method of virtual force and (b) Castigliano's second theorem. $E = 20,000$ kN/cm² and $A = 20$ cm².

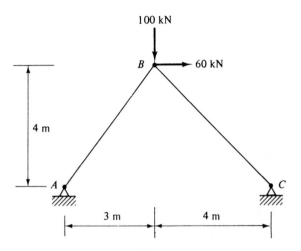

100 kN

B

60 kN

4 m

A

C

3 m   4 m

Figure 4-32

4-9. For the truss in Fig. 4-33, the area of each bar in square inches equals one-half its length in feet. $E = 30,000$ kips/in.^{2}. Compute (1) the vertical deflection at point B, (2) the horizontal deflection at point C, (3) the relative deflection between points b and C along the line joining them, and (4) the rotation of member bc using (a) the method of virtual force, (b) Castigliano's second theorem, and (c) the matrix method with the computer program described in Appendix B.

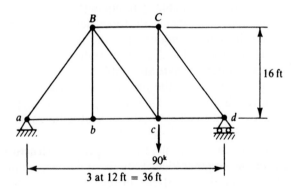

B   C

16 ft

a

b   c   d

90^k

3 at 12 ft = 36 ft   **Figure 4-33**

Chapter 5

Method of Consistent Deformations

5-1 GENERAL

Statically indeterminate structures can be analyzed by direct use of the theory of elastic deformations developed in Chapter 4. Any statically indeterminate structure can be made statically determinate and stable by removing the extra restraints called *redundant forces* or *statical redundants*, that is, the force elements that are more than the minimum necessary for the static equilibrium of the structure. The number of redundant forces therefore represents the degrees of statical indeterminacy of the original structure. The statically determinate and stable structure that remains after removal of the extra restraints is called the *primary*, or *released*, *structure*. The choice of the redundant forces is arbitrary. They may be external support reactions or internal member forces or both. In all cases, the statical redundants should be so chosen that the resulting primary structure is stable.

The original structure is then equivalent to the primary structure subjected to the combined action of the original loads plus the unknown redundants. The conditional equations for geometric consistence of the original structure at redundant points (releases), called the *compatibility equations*, are then obtained from the primary structure by superposition of the deformations caused separately by the original loads and redundants. There can be as many compatibility equations as the number of unknown redundants so that the redundants can be determined by solving these simultaneous equations. This method, known as *consistent deformations*, is generally applicable to the analysis of any structure, whether it is being analyzed for the effect of loads, support settlement, temperature change, or any other case. However, there is one restriction on the use of this method: the principle of superposition must hold.

As an illustration, consider the loaded continuous beam with nonyielding supports shown in Fig. 5-1(a). It is statically indeterminate to the second degree, that

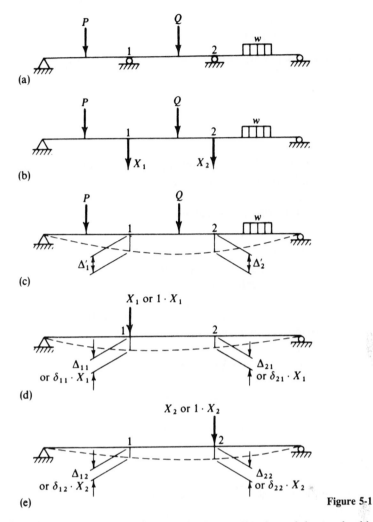

(a)

(b)

(c)

(d)

(e)

Figure 5-1

is, with two redundants. The first step in the application of the method is to remove, say, the two interior supports and to introduce in these releases the redundant actions called X_1 and X_2, respectively, and by so doing to reduce or cut back the structure to a condition of determinateness and stability. The original structure is now considered as a simple beam (the primary structure) subjected to the combined action of a number of external forces and two redundants X_1 and X_2, as shown in Fig. 5-1(b).

The resulting structure in Fig. 5-1(b) can be regarded as the superposition of those shown in Fig. 5-1(c) to (e). Consequently, any deformation of the structure can be obtained by the superposition of these effects.

Referring to Fig. 5-1(b), for unyielding supports we find that compatibility requires

$$\Delta_1 = 0 \tag{5-1}$$

$$\Delta_2 = 0 \tag{5-2}$$

where Δ_1 = deflection at redundant point 1 (in the line of redundant force X_1)
Δ_2 = deflection at redundant point 2 (in the line of redundant force X_2)

By the principle of superposition, we may expand Eqs. 5-1 and 5-2:

$$\Delta_1' + \Delta_{11} + \Delta_{12} = 0 \qquad (5\text{-}3)$$

$$\Delta_2' + \Delta_{21} + \Delta_{22} = 0 \qquad (5\text{-}4)$$

where Δ_1' = deflection at redundant point 1 due to external loads [see Fig. 5-1(c)]
Δ_{11} = deflection at redundant point 1 due to redundant force X_1 [see Fig. 5-1(d)]
Δ_{12} = deflection at redundant point 1 due to redundant force X_2 [see Fig. 5-1(e)]

The rest are similar.

Equations 5-3 and 5-4 may be expressed in terms of the *flexibility coefficients*. A typical flexibility coefficient δ_{ij} is defined by

δ_{ij} = displacement at point i due to a unit action at j, all other points being assumed unloaded

Thus, Eqs. 5-3 and 5-4 may be written as

$$\Delta_1' + \delta_{11} X_1 + \delta_{12} X_2 = 0 \qquad (5\text{-}5)$$

$$\Delta_2' + \delta_{21} X_1 + \delta_{22} X_2 = 0 \qquad (5\text{-}6)$$

Apparently,

δ_{11} = deflection at point 1 due to a unit force at point 1 [see Fig. 5-1(d)]

δ_{12} = deflection at point 1 due to a unit force at point 2 [see Fig. 5-1(e)]

and so on.

Both the deflections resulting from the original external loads and the flexibility coefficients for the primary structure can be obtained by any method described in Chapter 4. The remaining redundant unknowns are then solved by simultaneous equations. In general, for a structure with n redundants, we have

$$
\begin{aligned}
\Delta_1' + \delta_{11} X_1 + \delta_{12} X_2 + \cdots + \delta_{1n} X_n &= 0 \\
\Delta_2' + \delta_{21} X_1 + \delta_{22} X_2 + \cdots + \delta_{2n} X_n &= 0 \\
&\vdots \\
\Delta_n' + \delta_{n1} X_1 + \delta_{n2} X_2 + \cdots + \delta_{nn} X_n &= 0
\end{aligned}
\qquad (5\text{-}7)
$$

Equation 5-7 in matrix form is

$$\begin{Bmatrix} \Delta'_1 \\ \Delta'_2 \\ \vdots \\ \Delta'_n \end{Bmatrix} + \begin{bmatrix} \delta_{11} & \delta_{12} & \cdots & \delta_{1n} \\ \delta_{21} & \delta_{22} & \cdots & \delta_{2n} \\ \vdots & \vdots & \ddots & \vdots \\ \delta_{n1} & \delta_{n2} & \cdots & \delta_{nn} \end{bmatrix} \begin{Bmatrix} X_1 \\ X_2 \\ \vdots \\ X_n \end{Bmatrix} = \begin{Bmatrix} 0 \\ 0 \\ \vdots \\ 0 \end{Bmatrix} \tag{5-8}$$

or simply

$$\Delta' + F'X = 0 \tag{5-9}$$

In a more general form, we may include the prescribed displacements (other than zeros) occurring at the releases of the original structures. Then these values $\Delta_1, \Delta_2, \ldots$ must be substituted for the zeros on the right-hand side of Eq. 5-8. Thus,

$$\begin{Bmatrix} \Delta'_1 \\ \Delta'_2 \\ \vdots \\ \Delta'_n \end{Bmatrix} + \begin{bmatrix} \delta_{11} & \delta_{12} & \cdots & \delta_{1n} \\ \delta_{21} & \delta_{22} & \cdots & \delta_{2n} \\ \vdots & \vdots & \ddots & \vdots \\ \delta_{n1} & \delta_{n2} & \cdots & \delta_{nn} \end{bmatrix} \begin{Bmatrix} X_1 \\ X_2 \\ \vdots \\ X_n \end{Bmatrix} = \begin{Bmatrix} \Delta_1 \\ \Delta_2 \\ \vdots \\ \Delta_n \end{Bmatrix} \tag{5-10}$$

or simply

$$\Delta' + F'X = \Delta \tag{5-11}$$

in which the column matrix Δ' on the left-hand side represents the displacements at redundant points of the released structure due to the original loads; the square matrix F' represents the structure flexibility, each column of which gives various displacements at redundant points due to a certain unit redundant force; and the column matrix Δ on the right-hand side contains the actual displacements at redundant points of the original structure. Equation 5-11 expresses the compatibility at redundant points in terms of unknown redundant forces.

The remainder of this chapter is mostly devoted to the application of Eq. 5-11 to beam, truss, and frame problems using hand computation. At the end, it is shown that Eq. 5-11 can be generated automatically for truss problems through a matrix formulation, and the process is amenable to computer implementation. Further generalization to frame problems is given in Chapter 6.

5-2 ANALYSIS OF STATICALLY INDETERMINATE BEAMS BY THE METHOD OF CONSISTENT DEFORMATIONS

The method of consistent deformations is easy to understand and can be most effectively demonstrated by a series of illustrations. In all the following examples we assume that only the bending distortion is significant.

Example 5-1

Analyze the propped beam shown in Fig. 5-2(a), which is statically indeterminate to the first degree. Assume constant EI.

Solution 1   One reaction may be considered as being extra. In this case let us first choose the vertical reaction at b as the redundant assumed to be acting downward, as shown in Fig. 5-2(b). By the principle of superposition, we may consider the beam as being subjected to the sum of the effects of the original uniform loading and the unknown redundant X_b, as shown in Fig. 5-2(c) and (d), respectively.

Next, we find that the vertical deflection at b resulting from the uniform load [Fig. 5-2(c)] is given by

$$\Delta_b' = \frac{wl^4}{8EI}$$

and that the vertical deflection at b because of a unit load applied at b in place of X_b [Fig. 5-2(d)] is given by

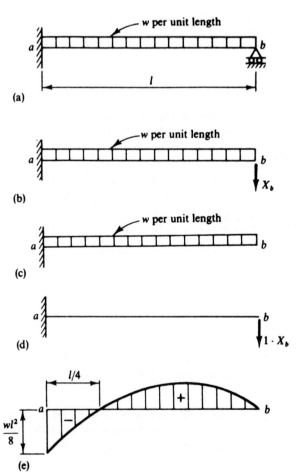

(a)

(b)

(c)

(d)

(e)   **Figure 5-2**

$$\delta_{bb} = \frac{l^3}{3EI}$$

Note that Δ_b' and the flexibility coefficient δ_{bb} may be found by any method described in Chapter 4.

Applying the compatibility equation

$$\Delta_b = \Delta_b' + \delta_{bb} X_b = 0$$

we obtain

$$\frac{wl^4}{8EI} + \left(\frac{l^3}{3EI}\right) X_b = 0$$

from which

$$X_b = -\frac{3wl}{8}$$

The minus sign indicates an upward reaction.

With reaction at b determined, we find that the beam reduces to a statically determinate one. We can readily obtain reaction components at a from the equilibrium equations:

$$\sum F_y = 0, \qquad V_a = wl - \tfrac{3}{8}wl = \tfrac{5}{8}wl \quad \text{(upward)}$$

$$\sum M_a = 0, \qquad M_a = \tfrac{1}{2}wl^2 - \tfrac{3}{8}wl^2 = \tfrac{1}{8}wl^2 \quad \text{(counterclockwise)}$$

The moment diagram for the beam is shown in Fig. 5-2(e).

Solution 2   The beam in Fig. 5-2(a) can be rendered statically determinate by removing the fixed support and replacing it with a hinged support. In addition to the original uniform loading, a redundant moment M_a is then applied to the primary structure, a simple beam, as shown in Fig. 5-3(a). The unknown M_a can be solved by the condition of compatibility that the rotation at end a must be zero.

The rotation at end a for the primary structure due to the uniform loading alone [Fig. 5-3(b)] is given by

$$\theta_a' = \frac{wl^3}{24EI}$$

and that due to a unit couple applied at end a [Fig. 5-3(c)] is given by

$$\delta_{aa} = \frac{l}{3EI}$$

Using the compatibility equation

$$\theta_a = \theta_a' + \delta_{aa} M_a = \frac{wl^3}{24EI} + \frac{M_a l}{3EI} = 0$$

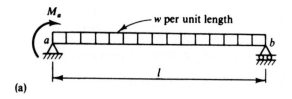

(a)

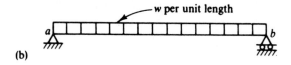

(b)

(c)   Figure 5-3

we solve for

$$M_a = -\tfrac{1}{8}wl^2$$

The minus sign indicates a counterclockwise moment. After M_a is determined, the rest of the analysis can be carried out without difficulty.

Solution 3   From the previous solutions we recognize that we are free to select redundants in analyzing a statically indeterminate structure, the only restriction being that the redundants should be so selected that a *stable* cut structure remains. Figure 5-4 will serve as an illustration. Let us cut the beam at midspan section c and introduce in its place a hinge so that the beam is stable and determinate. A pair of redundant couples, called M_c, together with the original loading are then applied to the primary structure, as shown in Fig. 5-4(a).

The redundant M_c is solved by the condition of compatibility that the rotation of the left side relative to the right side at section c must be zero.

Using the method of virtual force, we evaluate the relative rotation at c due to the external loading alone [Fig. 5-4(b)] as

$$\theta_c' = \int_0^l \frac{Mm\,dx}{EI} = \int_0^l \frac{[(wlx/4) - (wx^2/2)](2x/l)\,dx}{EI} = -\frac{wl^3}{12EI}$$

and that due to a pair of unit couples acting at c [Fig. 5-4(c)] as

$$\delta_{cc} = \int_0^l \frac{m^2\,dx}{EI} = \int_0^l \frac{(2x/l)^2\,dx}{EI} = \frac{4l}{3EI}$$

Setting the total relative angular displacement at c equal to zero, we have

$$-\frac{wl^3}{12EI} + M_c\left(\frac{4l}{3EI}\right) = 0$$

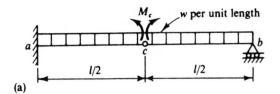

(a)

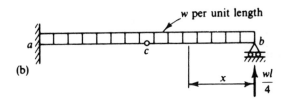

(b)

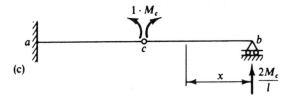

(c)

Figure 5-4

from which

$$M_c = +\frac{wl^2}{16}$$

After M_c is determined, the rest of the analysis can easily be carried out.

Example 5-2

Suppose that the support at b of Example 5-1 is elastic and the spring flexibility is f (displacement per unit force), as shown in Fig. 5-5. Determine the reaction at b (the spring force), denoted by X_b.

Assume downward X_b (i.e., tension in the spring) as positive. The compatibility is

$$\Delta_b' + \delta_{bb} X_b + fX_b = 0$$

This equation can be explained by putting it in the form

$$\Delta_b' - \delta_{bb}(-X_b) = f(-X_b)$$

Since $(-X_b)$ represents the compression in the spring, the equation indicates that the downward deflection at b caused by the beam load minus that caused by upward reaction should be equal to the spring contraction.

By substituting $\Delta_b' = wl^4/8EI$, $\delta_{bb} = l^3/3EI$ in the preceding equation, we obtain

$$\frac{wl^4}{8EI} + \frac{X_b l^3}{3EI} + fX_b = 0$$

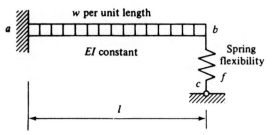

Figure 5-5

from which

$$X_b = -\frac{3}{8}wl\left[\frac{1}{1 + (3fEI/l^3)}\right]$$

The minus sign indicates an upward reaction.

For a nonyielding support, $f = 0$, the preceding equation gives

$$X_b = -\tfrac{3}{8}wl$$

as found previously.

If a beam is provided with n redundant elastic supports having spring flexibilities $f_1, f_2, \ldots, f_n$, respectively, then the general compatibility equation is

$$\begin{Bmatrix} \Delta_1' \\ \Delta_2' \\ \vdots \\ \Delta_n' \end{Bmatrix} + \begin{bmatrix} \delta_{11} + f_1 & \delta_{12} & \cdots & \delta_{1n} \\ \delta_{21} & \delta_{22} + f_2 & \cdots & \delta_{2n} \\ \vdots & \vdots & \ddots & \vdots \\ \delta_{n1} & \delta_{n2} & \cdots & \delta_{nn} + f_n \end{bmatrix} \begin{Bmatrix} X_1 \\ X_2 \\ \vdots \\ X_n \end{Bmatrix} = \begin{Bmatrix} 0 \\ 0 \\ \vdots \\ 0 \end{Bmatrix} \qquad (5\text{-}12)$$

Example 5-3

Find the reactions for the beam with two sections shown in Fig. 5-6(a).

In this problem it may be convenient to select the vertical reaction at support b as redundant. The beam is then considered as a simple beam subject to the original loading and the redundant R_b, as shown in Fig. 5-6(b) and (c), respectively.

The compatibility requires

$$\Delta_b = \Delta_b' + \delta_{bb}R_b = 0$$

Using the method of virtual force, we have

$$\int \frac{Mm_b\,dx}{EI} + R_b \int \frac{(m_b)^2\,dx}{EI} = 0$$

from which

$$R_b = -\frac{\displaystyle\int Mm_b\,dx/EI}{\displaystyle\int (m_b)^2\,dx/EI}$$

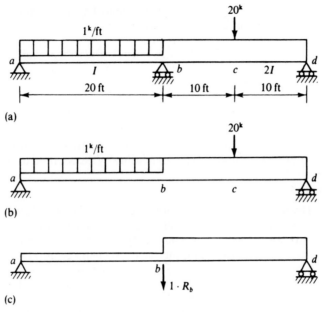

Figure 5-6

where M = bending moment at any section of the primary beam caused by the original
loading [Fig. 5-6(b)]

m_b = bending moment at the same section of the primary beam caused by a unit
load in place of the redundant R_b [Fig. 5-6(c)]

The solution is completely shown in Table 5-1.

$$R_b = -\frac{\displaystyle\int_0^{20} \frac{(20x - x^2/2)(x/2)\,dx}{EI} + \int_0^{10} \frac{(20x)(x/2)\,dx}{2EI} + \int_{10}^{20} \frac{(200)(x/2)\,dx}{2EI}}{\displaystyle\int_0^{20} \frac{(x/2)^2\,dx}{EI} + \int_0^{10} \frac{(x/2)^2\,dx}{2EI} + \int_{10}^{20} \frac{(x/2)^2\,dx}{2EI}}$$

$$= -25.84 \text{ kips}$$

The negative sign indicates an upward reaction at support b.

TABLE 5-1

Section	Origin	Limit (ft)	M (ft-kips)	m_b (ft-kips)	I
ab	a	0 to 20	$20x - \dfrac{(1)(x)^2}{2}$	$\dfrac{x}{2}$	I
dc	d	0 to 10	$20x$	$\dfrac{x}{2}$	$2I$
cb	d	10 to 20	$20x - 20(x - 10)$ or 200	$\dfrac{x}{2}$	$2I$

After R_b is obtained, we can readily find the reactions at the other two supports by statics. That is,

$$R_a = R_d = 20 - (\tfrac{1}{2})(25.84) = 7.08 \text{ kips}$$

acting upward.

The end moments for a fixed-end beam, called *fixed-end moments*, are important in the methods of slope-deflection and of moment distribution, which are discussed in later chapters. The following examples are attempts to solve fixed-end moments due to common types of loading by the method of consistent deformations.

Example 5-4

The fixed-end beam of uniform cross section subjected to a single concentrated load shown in Fig. 5-7(a) is statically indeterminate to the second degree since the horizontal force does not exist. End moments M_A and M_B are selected as redundants. The original beam is then considered as equivalent to a simple beam (not shown) under the combined action of a concentrated force P and redundant moments M_A and M_B. It is convenient to apply the conjugate beam method to determine M_A and M_B based on the condition that the slope and deflection at either end of the fixed-end beam must be zero. In other words, there will be no support reactions for the conjugate beam, and the positive and negative M/EI diagrams (elastic loads) given in Fig. 5-7(b) must form a balanced system. Thus, from $\Sigma F_y = 0$,

$$\frac{Pab}{2EI} - \frac{M_A l}{2EI} - \frac{M_B l}{2EI} = 0$$

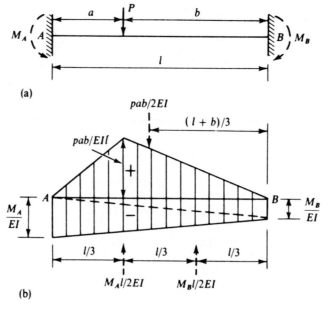

(a)

(b)

Figure 5-7

or

$$M_A + M_B = \frac{Pab}{l} \tag{5-13}$$

From $\Sigma M_B = 0$,

$$\left(\frac{Pab}{2EI}\right)\left(\frac{l+b}{3}\right) - \left(\frac{M_A l}{2EI}\right)\left(\frac{2l}{3}\right) - \left(\frac{M_B l}{2EI}\right)\left(\frac{l}{3}\right) = 0$$

or

$$2M_A + M_B = \frac{Pab}{l} + \frac{Pab^2}{l^2} \tag{5-14}$$

Solving Eqs. 5-13 and 5-14 simultaneously, we obtain

$$M_A = \frac{Pab^2}{l^2}, \qquad M_B = \frac{Pa^2 b}{l^2} \tag{5-15}$$

Example 5-5

Find the end moments of a fixed-end beam of constant EI caused by a uniform load, as shown in Fig. 5-8(a).

Because of symmetry, the beam is statically indeterminate to the first degree, since $M_A = M_B = M$, as indicated in Fig. 5-8(a). By the method of conjugate beam [Fig. 5-8(b)], $\Sigma F_y = 0$,

$$\left(\frac{wl^2}{8EI}\right)\left(\frac{2l}{3}\right) - \frac{Ml}{EI} = 0$$

from which

$$M = \tfrac{1}{12} wl^2 \tag{5-16}$$

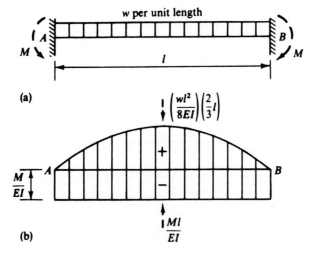

(a)

(b)

Figure 5-8

Example 5-6

If the fixed-end beam is loaded with an external couple M as shown in Fig. 5-9(a), the deflected elastic shape will be somewhat like that shown by the dashed line, which gives the sense of the end moments as indicated.

As before, end moments M_A and M_B are chosen as redundants. The elastic loads based on the moment diagrams divided by EI plotted for external moment M and redundants M_A and M_B, as given in Fig. 5-9(b) and (c), must be in equilibrium themselves. From $\Sigma F_y = 0$,

$$\frac{M_A l}{2EI} + \frac{Mb^2}{2EIl} - \frac{M_B l}{2EI} - \frac{Ma^2}{2EIl} = 0$$

or

$$M_A - M_B = \frac{M(a^2 - b^2)}{l^2} \tag{5-17}$$

From $\Sigma M_B = 0$,

$$\left(\frac{M_A l}{2EI}\right)\left(\frac{2l}{3}\right) + \left(\frac{Mb^2}{2EIl}\right)\left(\frac{2b}{3}\right) - \left(\frac{M_B l}{2EI}\right)\left(\frac{l}{3}\right) - \left(\frac{Ma^2}{2EIl}\right)\left(b + \frac{a}{3}\right) = 0$$

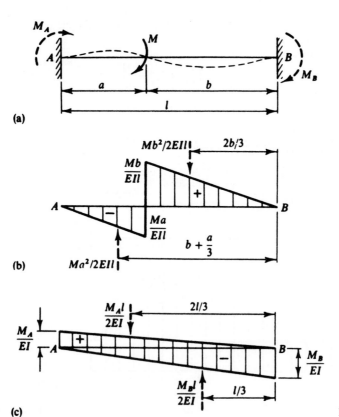

(a)

(b)

(c)   Figure 5-9

or

$$2M_A - M_B = \frac{M[a^2 + 2b(a - b)]}{l^2} \tag{5-18}$$

Solving Eqs. 5-17 and 5-18 simultaneously, we obtain

$$M_A = \frac{Mb}{l^2}(2a - b), \qquad M_B = \frac{Ma}{l^2}(2b - a) \tag{5-19}$$

Note that M_A and M_B bear the same sense as the externally applied M, as indicated in Fig. 5-9(a), if $a > l/3$ and $b > l/3$.

5-3 ANALYSIS OF STATICALLY INDETERMINATE RIGID FRAMES BY THE METHOD OF CONSISTENT DEFORMATIONS

The general procedure illustrated in Sec. 5-2 in solving statically indeterminate beams can be applied equally well to the analysis of statically indeterminate rigid frames, as in the following example.

Example 5-7

For the loaded rigid frame shown in Fig. 5-10(a), find the reaction components at the fixed end a, and plot the moment diagram for the entire frame. Assume the same EI for all members.

To do this, we start by removing support a and introducing in its place three redundant reaction components X_1, X_2, and X_3, as shown in Fig. 5-10(b). These can be taken as the superposition of four basic cases, as shown in Fig. 5-10(c), (d), (e), and (f), respectively. Since end a is fixed, compatibility requires that

$$\begin{Bmatrix} \Delta_1' \\ \Delta_2' \\ \Delta_3' \end{Bmatrix} + \begin{bmatrix} \delta_{11} & \delta_{12} & \delta_{13} \\ \delta_{21} & \delta_{22} & \delta_{23} \\ \delta_{31} & \delta_{32} & \delta_{33} \end{bmatrix} \begin{Bmatrix} X_1 \\ X_2 \\ X_3 \end{Bmatrix} = \begin{Bmatrix} 0 \\ 0 \\ 0 \end{Bmatrix} \tag{5-20}$$

Taking advantage of Examples 4-7 and 4-8, we note that

$$\begin{Bmatrix} \Delta_1' \\ \Delta_2' \\ \Delta_3' \end{Bmatrix} = \frac{1}{EI} \begin{Bmatrix} 5,000 \\ -7,500 \\ -800 \end{Bmatrix}$$

and

$$\begin{bmatrix} \delta_{11} & \delta_{12} & \delta_{13} \\ \delta_{21} & \delta_{22} & \delta_{23} \\ \delta_{31} & \delta_{32} & \delta_{33} \end{bmatrix} = \frac{1}{EI} \begin{bmatrix} 1,667 & -1,000 & -200 \\ -1,000 & 1,333 & 150 \\ -200 & 150 & 30 \end{bmatrix}$$

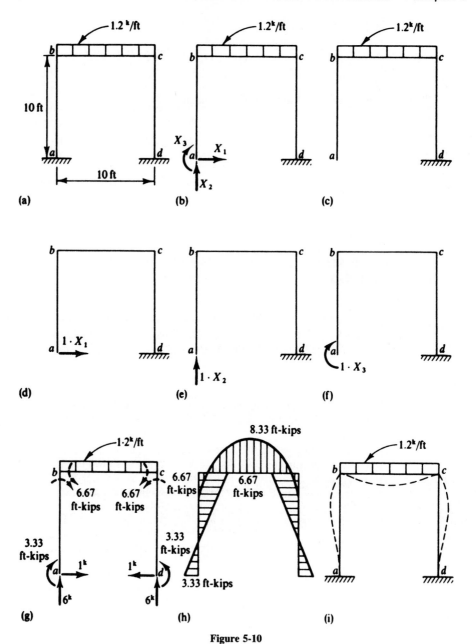

Figure 5-10

Substituting these values in Eq. 5-20, we obtain

$$\begin{Bmatrix} 5,000 \\ -7,500 \\ -800 \end{Bmatrix} + \begin{bmatrix} 1,667 & -1,000 & -200 \\ -1,000 & 1,333 & 150 \\ -200 & 150 & 30 \end{bmatrix} \begin{Bmatrix} X_1 \\ X_2 \\ X_3 \end{Bmatrix} = \begin{Bmatrix} 0 \\ 0 \\ 0 \end{Bmatrix} \tag{5-21}$$

Solving, we obtain

$$\begin{Bmatrix} X_1 \\ X_2 \\ X_3 \end{Bmatrix} = \begin{Bmatrix} 1 \\ 6 \\ 3.33 \text{ ft} \end{Bmatrix} \text{ kips}$$

Note that the solution of this problem could be simplified by setting $X_2 = 6$ kips in Eq. 5-20, since we know this value beforehand because of the symmetry of the loaded frame.

The final results are shown in Fig. 5-10(g); the moment diagram for the whole frame is shown in Fig. 5-10(h). A sketch of the elastic deformation of the frame due to bending distortion is shown by the dashed line in Fig. 5-10(i). Note that in this case there is one point of inflection in each column and two points of inflection in the beam.

By referring to Example 5-7, we see that by using the method of consistent deformations in analyzing a rigid frame, we encounter tedious calculations of the flexibility coefficients. The work, if done by hand, will become intolerable if the problem involves as many redundants as a rigid frame usually does. As a matter of fact, the method of consistent deformations is seldom used for analysis of rigid frames by hand calculation, since a solution can be much more easily obtained by the method of slope-deflection or of moment distribution. However, with the development of high-speed *electronic computers*, this method can be made amenable to computers through a matrix formulation, as shown in Sec. 5-6 and Chapter 6.

5-4 ANALYSIS OF STATICALLY INDETERMINATE TRUSSES BY THE METHOD OF CONSISTENT DEFORMATIONS

The indeterminateness of a truss may be due to redundant supports or redundant bars or both. If it results from redundant supports, the procedure for attack is the same as that described for a continuous beam. If the superfluous element is a bar, the bar is considered to be cut at a section and replaced by two equal and opposite axial redundant forces representing the internal action for that bar. The condition equation is such that the relative axial displacement between the two sides at the cut section caused by the combined effect of the original loading and the redundants should be zero.

Example 5-8

Analyze the continuous truss in Fig. 5-11(a). Assume that $E = 30,000$ kips/in.^{2} and L (ft)/A (in.^{2}) = 1 for all members.

In this problem it is convenient to select the central support as the redundant element. We begin by removing support c and introducing in its place a redundant reaction X_c, as shown in Fig. 5-11(b). The primary structure is then a simply supported truss subjected to an external load of 64 kips at joint b and a redundant X_c. The effects can be separated, respectively, as shown in Fig. 5-11(c) and (d).

Since support c is on a rigid foundation, the compatibility equation can be expressed by

$$\Delta_c = \Delta_c' + \delta_{cc} X_c = 0$$

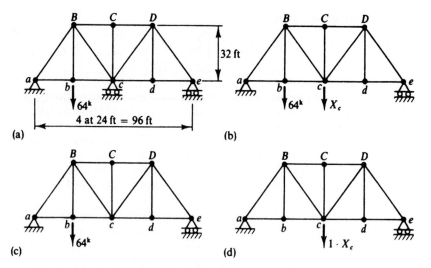

Figure 5-11

Using virtual force gives

$$\sum \frac{S'u_c L}{AE} + X_c \sum \frac{u_c^2 L}{AE} = 0$$

from which

$$X_c = -\frac{\sum(S'u_c L/AE)}{\sum(u_c^2 L/AE)}$$

where S' = internal force in any member of the primary truss due to the original loading [Fig. 5-11(c)]

u_c = internal force in the same member of the primary truss due to a unit force at c [Fig. 5-11(d)]

The solution is shown completely in Table 5-2.

$$X_c = -\frac{122}{3.25} = -37.5 \text{ kips}$$

The negative sign indicates an upward reaction at support c.

After X_c is determined, we can readily obtain each bar force S from

$$S = S' + u_c X_c$$

as given in the last column of Table 5-2.

Example 5-9

Analyze the truss in Fig. 5-12(a). Assume that E = 30,000 kips/in.^{2} and L (ft)/A (in.^{2}) = 1 for all members.

TABLE 5-2

Member	$\dfrac{L}{A}$ (ft/in.^{2})	S' (kips)	u_c	$\dfrac{S'u_c L}{A}$ (ft-kips/in.^{2})	$\dfrac{u_c^2 L}{A}$ (ft/in.^{2})	$S = S' + u_c X_c$ (kips)
ab	1	+36	+3/8	+13.5	+9/64	$36 - 14.1 = +21.9$
bc	1	+36	+3/8	+13.5	+9/64	$36 - 14.1 = +21.9$
cd	1	+12	+3/8	+ 4.5	+9/64	$12 - 14.1 = -2.1$
de	1	+12	+3/8	+ 4.5	+9/64	$12 - 14.1 = -2.1$
BC	1	−24	−3/4	+18	+36/64	$-24 + 28.2 = +4.2$
CD	1	−24	−3/4	+18	+36/64	$-24 + 28.2 = +4.2$
aB	1	−60	−5/8	+37.5	+25/64	$-60 + 23.4 = -36.6$
Bb	1	+64	0	0	0	$+64 + 0 = +64$
Bc	1	−20	+5/8	− 12.5	+25/64	$-20 - 23.4 = -43.4$
Cc	1	0	0	0	0	0
cD	1	+20	+5/8	+12.5	+25/64	$+20 - 23.4 = -3.4$
Dd	1	0	0	0	0	0
De	1	−20	−5/8	+12.5	+25/64	$-20 + 23.4 = +3.4$
			Σ	+122	+3.25	

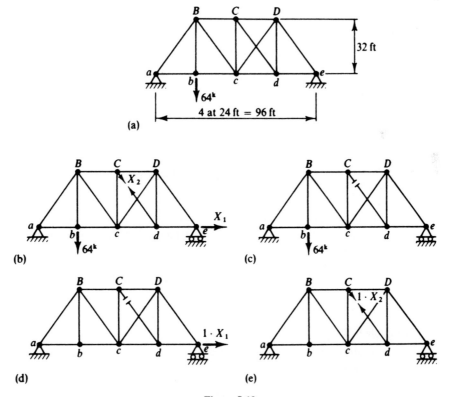

Figure 5-12

The truss in Fig. 5-12(a) has two redundant elements, one in the reaction component and the other in the bar. Let us select the horizontal component of reaction at the right-end hinge and the internal force in bar *Cd* as redundants. We then have a primary truss loaded, as shown in Fig. 5-12(b), in which the original hinged support *e* is replaced by a roller acted on by a redundant horizontal reaction X_1, and the bar *Cd* is cut and a pair of redundant forces X_2 applied to it. This may again be replaced by the three basic cases shown in Fig. 5-12(c) to (e). Since both the horizontal movement at support *e* and the relative axial displacement between the cut ends of bar *Cd* are zero, we have

$$\begin{Bmatrix} \Delta_1 \\ \Delta_2 \end{Bmatrix} = \begin{Bmatrix} \Delta_1' \\ \Delta_2' \end{Bmatrix} + \begin{bmatrix} \delta_{11} & \delta_{12} \\ \delta_{21} & \delta_{22} \end{bmatrix} \begin{Bmatrix} X_1 \\ X_2 \end{Bmatrix} = \begin{Bmatrix} 0 \\ 0 \end{Bmatrix} \tag{5-22}$$

or

$$\begin{Bmatrix} \sum \dfrac{S'u_1 L}{AE} \\ \sum \dfrac{S'u_2 L}{AE} \end{Bmatrix} + \begin{bmatrix} \sum \dfrac{u_1^2 L}{AE} & \sum \dfrac{u_1 u_2 L}{AE} \\ \sum \dfrac{u_1 u_2 L}{AE} & \sum \dfrac{u_2^2 L}{AE} \end{bmatrix} \begin{Bmatrix} X_1 \\ X_2 \end{Bmatrix} = \begin{Bmatrix} 0 \\ 0 \end{Bmatrix} \tag{5-23}$$

Note that

S' = internal force in any bar of the primary truss due to the original loading [Fig. 5-12(c)]

u_1 = internal force in the same bar of the primary truss due to a unit horizontal force acting at *e* [Fig. 5-12(d)]

u_2 = internal force in the same bar of the primary truss due to a pair of unit axial forces acting at the cut ends of bar *Cd* [Fig. 5-12(e)]

Using the values summed up in Table 5-3, we reduce Eq. 5-23 to

$$\begin{Bmatrix} 96 \\ 27.2 \end{Bmatrix} + \begin{bmatrix} 4 & -\tfrac{3}{5} \\ -\tfrac{3}{5} & 4 \end{bmatrix} \begin{Bmatrix} X_1 \\ X_2 \end{Bmatrix} = \begin{Bmatrix} 0 \\ 0 \end{Bmatrix} \tag{5-24}$$

Solving, we obtain

$$\begin{Bmatrix} X_1 \\ X_2 \end{Bmatrix} = \begin{Bmatrix} -25.6 \\ -10.6 \end{Bmatrix} \text{ kips}$$

The negative signs indicate that the horizontal reaction at hinge *e* acts to the left and that the axial force in member *Cd* is compressive. The rest of the member forces are obtained by

$$S = S' + u_1 X_1 + u_2 X_2$$

The complete solution is shown in Table 5-3.

Example 5-10

Analyze the truss in Fig. 5-13(a) subject to a rise of 50°F at the top chords *BC* and *CD*. Assume $\alpha = 0.0000065$ in./in./1°F, $E = 30,000$ kips/in.^{2}, and L (ft)/A (in.^{2}) = 1 for all members.

The truss is statically indeterminate to the first degree. Cut bar *Cd* and select its

TABLE 5-3

Member	$\frac{L}{A}$ (ft/in.²)	S' (kips)	u_1	u_2	$\frac{S'u_1 L}{A}$ (ft-kips/in.²)	$\frac{S'u_2 L}{A}$ (ft-kips/in.²)	$\frac{u_1^2 L}{A}$ (ft/in.²)	$\frac{u_2^2 L}{A}$ (ft/in.²)	$\frac{u_1 u_2 L}{A}$ (ft/in.²)	$S = S' + u_1 X_1 + u_2 X_2$ (kips)
ab	1	$+36$	$+1$	0	$+36$	0	$+1$	0	0	$36 - 25.6 + 0 = +10.4$
bc	1	$+36$	$+1$	0	$+36$	0	$+1$	0	0	$36 - 25.6 + 0 = +10.4$
cd	1	$+12$	$+1$	$-\frac{3}{5}$	$+12$	-7.2	$+1$	$+\frac{9}{25}$	$-\frac{3}{5}$	$12 - 25.6 + 6.4 = -7.0$
de	1	$+12$	$+1$	0	$+12$	0	$+1$	0	0	$12 - 25.6 + 0 = -13.6$
BC	1	-24	0	0	0	0	0	0	0	$-24 + 0 + 0 = -24$
CD	1	-24	0	$-\frac{3}{5}$	0	$+14.4$	0	$+\frac{9}{25}$	0	$-24 + 0 + 6.4 = -17.6$
aB	1	-60	0	0	0	0	0	0	0	$-60 + 0 + 0 = -60$
Bb	1	$+64$	0	0	0	0	0	0	0	$+64 + 0 + 0 = +64$
Bc	1	-20	0	0	0	0	0	0	0	$-20 + 0 + 0 = -20$
Cc	1	0	0	$-\frac{4}{5}$	0	0	0	$+\frac{16}{25}$	0	$0 + 0 + 8.5 = + 8.5$
Cd	1	0	0	$+1$	0	0	0	$+1$	0	$0 + 0 - 10.6 = -10.6$
cD	1	$+20$	0	$+1$	0	$+20$	0	$+1$	0	$20 + 0 - 10.6 = + 9.4$
Dd	1	0	0	$-\frac{4}{5}$	0	0	0	$+\frac{16}{25}$	0	$0 + 0 + 8.5 = + 8.5$
De	1	-20	0	0	0	0	0	0	0	$-20 + 0 + 0 = -20$
Σ					$+96$	$+27.2$	$+4$	$+4$	$-\frac{3}{5}$	

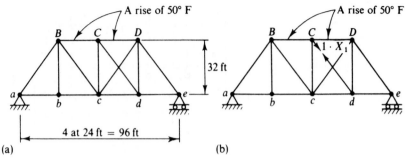

Figure 5-13

bar force X_1 as the redundant as shown in Fig. 5-13(b). The primary truss is then a simply supported truss subjected to the temperature rise in the top chords and the redundant axial force X_1. Since the relative axial displacement between the cut ends due to the combined effect of temperature rise and X_1 must be zero, we have

$$\Delta_1 = \Delta_1' + \delta_{11} X_1 = 0$$

or

$$\sum u_1(\alpha t° L) + X_1 \sum \frac{u_1^2 L}{AE} = 0$$

where Δ_1' = relative displacement between the cut ends of the primary truss due to the temperature rise = $\sum u_1(\alpha t° L)$ (see Eq. 4-26)

u_1 = internal force in any member of the primary truss due to a pair of unit axial forces acting at the ends of the cut section

The solution is shown in Table 5-4.

TABLE 5-4

Member	$\dfrac{L}{A}$ (ft/in.²)	u_1	$\alpha t° L$ (ft)	$u_1 \alpha t° L$ (ft)	$\dfrac{u_1^2 L}{A}$ (ft/in.²)	$S = u_1 X_1$ (kips)
ab	1	0	0	0	0	0
bc	1	0	0	0	0	0
cd	1	$-\frac{3}{5}$	0	0	$+\frac{9}{25}$	-21.1
de	1	0	0	0	0	0
BC	1	0	$+0.0078$	0	0	0
CD	1	$-\frac{3}{5}$	$+0.0078$	-0.00468	$+\frac{9}{25}$	-21.1
aB	1	0	0	0	0	0
Bb	1	0	0	0	0	0
Bc	1	0	0	0	0	0
Cc	1	$-\frac{4}{5}$	0	0	$+\frac{16}{25}$	-28.1
Cd	1	$+1$	0	0	$+1$	$+35.1$
cD	1	$+1$	0	0	$+1$	$+35.1$
Dd	1	$-\frac{4}{5}$	0	0	$+\frac{16}{25}$	-28.1
De	1	0	0	0	0	0
			Σ	-0.00468	$+4$	

$$\frac{4X_1}{30,000} - 0.00468 = 0$$

$$X_1 = 35.1 \text{ kips} \quad (\text{tension})$$

Although these illustrations are aimed at statically indeterminate trusses with one or two redundants, the procedure described can be extended to trusses with many degrees of redundancy.

5-5 CASTIGLIANO'S COMPATIBILITY EQUATION (METHOD OF LEAST WORK)

The method of consistent deformations hitherto discussed involves superposition equations for the elastic deformations of the primary structure at the points of application of the redundants $X_1, X_2, \ldots, X_n$, the primary structure being stable and determinate and subjected to external actions, together with n redundant forces. The expressions that the displacement at each of n redundants equals zero for a loaded structure with nonyielding supports may be set up by the use of Castigliano's theorem as

$$\begin{Bmatrix} \Delta_1 \\ \Delta_2 \\ \vdots \\ \Delta_n \end{Bmatrix} = \begin{Bmatrix} \dfrac{\partial W}{\partial X_1} \\ \dfrac{\partial W}{\partial X_2} \\ \vdots \\ \dfrac{\partial W}{\partial X_n} \end{Bmatrix} = \begin{Bmatrix} 0 \\ 0 \\ \vdots \\ 0 \end{Bmatrix} \tag{5-25}$$

where W is the *total strain energy* of the primary structure and is therefore a function of the external loads and the unknown redundant forces $X_1, X_2, \ldots, X_n$. There are as many simultaneous equations as the number of unknown redundants involved. Equation 5-25,

$$\frac{\partial W}{\partial X_1} = \frac{\partial W}{\partial X_2} = \cdots = \frac{\partial W}{\partial X_n} = 0$$

is known as Castigliano's compatibility equation and it may be stated as follows: *The redundants must have such value that the total strain energy of the structure is a minimum consistent with equilibrium*. For this reason it is sometimes referred to as the *theorem of least work*. Note that Castigliano's compatibility equation is limited to the computation of redundant forces produced only by external loads on a structure mounted on unyielding supports. It cannot be used to determine stresses caused by temperature change, support movements, fabrication errors, and the like.

In the analysis of statically indeterminate beams or rigid frames, we consider bending moment to be the only significant factor contributing to the internal energy.

Therefore, the total strain energy can be expressed by

$$W = \int \frac{M^2 \, dx}{2EI}$$

Setting the derivative of this expression with respect to any redundant X_i equal to zero gives

$$\int \frac{M(\partial M/\partial X_i) \, dx}{EI} = 0$$

Therefore, for a statically indeterminate beam (or rigid frame) with n redundants, we can write a set of n simultaneous compatibility equations:

$$\begin{Bmatrix} \dfrac{\partial W}{\partial X_1} \\ \dfrac{\partial W}{\partial X_2} \\ \vdots \\ \dfrac{\partial W}{\partial X_n} \end{Bmatrix} = \begin{Bmatrix} \int \dfrac{M(\partial M/\partial X_1) \, dx}{EI} \\ \int \dfrac{M(\partial M/\partial X_2) \, dx}{EI} \\ \vdots \\ \int \dfrac{M(\partial M/\partial X_n) \, dx}{EI} \end{Bmatrix} = \begin{Bmatrix} 0 \\ 0 \\ \vdots \\ 0 \end{Bmatrix} \tag{5-26}$$

to solve all the unknown redundants.

In the analysis of statically indeterminate trusses, the total strain energy can be expressed by

$$W = \sum \frac{S^2 L}{2AE}$$

Setting the derivative of this expression with respect to any redundant X_i equal to zero gives

$$\sum \frac{S(\partial S/\partial X_i)L}{AE} = 0$$

Thus, for a statically indeterminate truss with n redundant elements, we have a set of n simultaneous compatibility equations available for their solution:

$$\begin{Bmatrix} \sum \dfrac{S(\partial S/\partial X_1)L}{AE} \\ \sum \dfrac{S(\partial S/\partial X_2)L}{AE} \\ \vdots \\ \sum \dfrac{S(\partial S/\partial X_n)L}{AE} \end{Bmatrix} = \begin{Bmatrix} 0 \\ 0 \\ \vdots \\ 0 \end{Bmatrix} \tag{5-27}$$

Example 5-11

For the fixed-end beam under general loading shown in Fig. 5-14(a), derive a working formula for solving the end reactions at A.

We select the left-end reaction components M_A and V_A as redundants, as shown in Fig. 5-14(b). The primary structure is a cantilever subjected to the original loads on the span together with the redundant forces M_A and V_A at the left end. Applying the method of least work, we obtain

$$\frac{\partial W}{\partial M_A} = \int_0^l \frac{M(\partial M/\partial M_A)\,dx}{EI} = 0 \tag{5-28}$$

$$\frac{\partial W}{\partial V_A} = \int_0^l \frac{M(\partial M/\partial V_A)\,dx}{EI} = 0 \tag{5-29}$$

Since the bending moment at any section of the primary structure is given by

$$M = M' + M_A + V_A x$$

where M' indicates the bending moment at the same section of the primary structure resulting from the original loads on the span, we have

$$\frac{\partial M}{\partial M_A} = 1 \quad \text{and} \quad \frac{\partial M}{\partial V_A} = x$$

Substituting these in Eqs. 5-28 and 5-29 results in the following two equations:

$$\int_0^l \frac{M\,dx}{EI} = 0 \tag{5-30}$$

$$\int_0^l \frac{Mx\,dx}{EI} = 0 \tag{5-31}$$

to solve for redundants M_A and V_A.

For a beam of uniform section with constant EI, Eqs. 5-30 and 5-31 reduce to

$$\int_0^l M\,dx = 0 \tag{5-32}$$

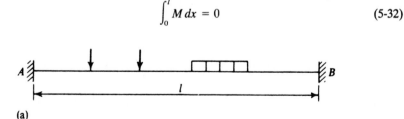

(a)

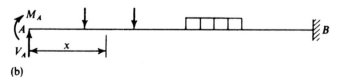

(b)

Figure 5-14

$$\int_0^l Mx\, dx = 0 \qquad\qquad (5\text{-}33)$$

As an illustration, let us find the fixed-end moments of the beam shown in Fig. 5-15. Taking the origin at A, we note that

$$M = M_A + V_A x, \qquad\qquad 0 \leqslant x \leqslant a$$

$$M = M_A + V_A x - P(x - a), \qquad a \leqslant x \leqslant l$$

Applying Eqs. 5-32 and 5-33 gives

$$\int_0^l M\, dx = \int_0^a (M_A + V_A x)\, dx + \int_a^l [M_A + V_A x - P(x - a)]\, dx$$

$$= \int_0^l (M_A + V_A x)\, dx + \int_a^l [-P(x - a)]\, dx = 0$$

or

$$M_A l + \frac{V_A l^2}{2} - \frac{Pb^2}{2} = 0 \qquad\qquad (5\text{-}34)$$

and

$$\int_0^l Mx\, dx = \int_0^a (M_A + V_A x)x\, dx + \int_a^l [M_A + V_A x - P(x - a)]x\, dx$$

$$= \int_0^l (M_A + V_A x)x\, dx + \int_a^l [-P(x - a)]x\, dx = 0$$

or

$$\frac{M_A l^2}{2} + \frac{V_A l^3}{3} - \frac{Pb^2(a + 2l)}{6} = 0 \qquad\qquad (5\text{-}35)$$

Solving Eqs. 5-34 and 5-35 simultaneously, we obtain

$$M_A = -\frac{Pab^2}{l^2}, \qquad V_A = \frac{Pb^2(l + 2a)}{l^3}$$

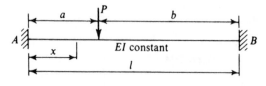

Figure 5-15

Similarly,

$$M_B = -\frac{Pa^2b}{l^2}, \qquad V_B = \frac{Pa^2(l + 2b)}{l^3}$$

Example 5-12

Analyze the frame shown in Fig. 5-16(a) by taking the internal shear, thrust, and moment in the midspan section of the beam as redundants.

Because of symmetry, the shear must be zero in the midspan section e of the beam, and only thrust and bending moment are left as redundants, as shown in Fig. 5-16(a). The solution can be simplified by considering only half of the frame, as shown in Fig. 5-16(b) and Table 5-5.

Applying

$$\frac{\partial W}{\partial M_e} = 0 \quad \text{or} \quad \int_F \frac{M(\partial M/\partial M_e)\, dx}{EI} = 0$$

we have

$$\frac{2}{EI}\left[\int_0^5 \left(M_e - \frac{(1.2)x^2}{2}\right)(1)\, dx + \int_0^{10} (M_e + H_e x - 15)(1)\, dx\right] = 0$$

or

$$3M_e + 10H_e - 35 = 0 \tag{5-36}$$

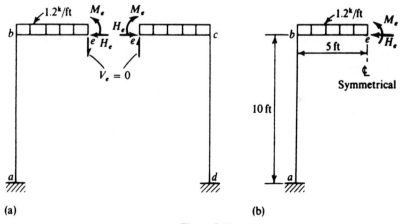

Figure 5-16

TABLE 5-5

Member	Origin	Limit (ft)	M (ft-kips)	$\dfrac{\partial M}{\partial M_e}$	$\dfrac{\partial M}{\partial H_e}$ (ft)
eb	e	0 to 5	$M_e - \dfrac{(1.2)x^2}{2}$	1	0
ba	b	0 to 10	$M_e + H_e x - 15$	1	x

Applying

$$\frac{\partial W}{\partial H_e} = 0 \quad \text{or} \quad \int_F \frac{M(\partial M/\partial H_e)\,dx}{EI} = 0$$

we have

$$\frac{2}{EI}\left[\int_0^{10} (M_e + H_e x - 15)x\,dx\right] = 0$$

or

$$3M_e + 20H_e - 45 = 0 \tag{5-37}$$

Solving Eqs. 5-36 and 5-37 simultaneously gives

$$H_e = 1.0 \text{ kip}, \qquad M_e = 8.33 \text{ ft-kips}$$

from which we obtain

$$H_a = 1.0 \text{ kip}, \qquad M_a = 3.33 \text{ ft-kips}$$

as previously found.

For a highly indeterminate rigid frame, such as the one shown in Fig. 5-17(a), the procedure of the analysis remains the same. The frame is statically indeterminate to the 24th degree. We may cut it back to three determinate structures and substitute the redundants $X_1, X_2, \ldots, X_{24}$ at the cut sections as shown in Fig. 5-17(b).

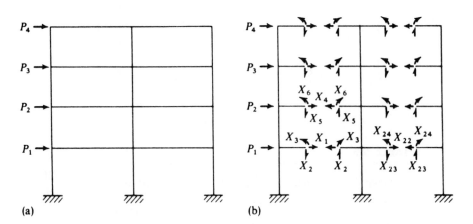

(a)   (b)

Figure 5-17

From least work, we have 24 equations to solve for all the redundants simultaneously:

$$\left\{\begin{array}{c} \dfrac{\partial W}{\partial X_1} \\ \dfrac{\partial W}{\partial X_2} \\ \vdots \\ \dfrac{\partial W}{\partial X_{24}} \end{array}\right\} = \left\{\begin{array}{c} 0 \\ 0 \\ \vdots \\ 0 \end{array}\right\}$$

where W is the total strain energy of the frame due to the external loads and redundant forces. The principle is neat and elegant, whereas the numerical calculations involved in the equations above are so cumbersome that it is almost impossible for a structural engineer to reach an exact solution for the system with only a slide rule or desk calculator. To handle a practical problem like this, a grossly simplified model of the actual structure was often used. However, with the advent of the digital computer, the solving of simultaneous equations can now be performed in a matter of seconds.

Example 5-13

Analyze the truss in Fig. 5-18(a). Assume that $E = 30{,}000$ kips/in.^{2} and L (ft)/A (in.^{2}) $= 1$ for all members.

The truss is statically indeterminate to the second degree. We may take bars bC and Cd as redundant members. As shown in Fig. 5-18(b), these bars are cut and replaced by redundant axial forces X_1 and X_2, respectively. The internal force for each bar is then computed in terms of the external load and redundant forces as indicated. The unknowns X_1 and X_2 are then solved by the simultaneous equations

$$\sum \frac{S(\partial S/\partial X_1)L}{AE} = 0 \quad \text{and} \quad \sum \frac{S(\partial S/\partial X_2)L}{AE} = 0$$

as prepared in Table 5-6. Setting

$$-78.4 + 4X_1 + 0.64X_2 = 0 \tag{5-38}$$

$$27.2 + 0.64X_1 + 4X_2 = 0 \tag{5-39}$$

and solving Eqs. 5-38 and 5-39 simultaneously, we obtain

$$X_1 = +21.2 \text{ kips}, \qquad X_2 = -10.2 \text{ kips}$$

The answer for each of the bar forces is given in the last column of Table 5-6. Note that this procedure can be extended to trusses with many redundants.

Structures made up of some members that are two-force members carrying only axial forces and others that are not are called *composite structures*. They are

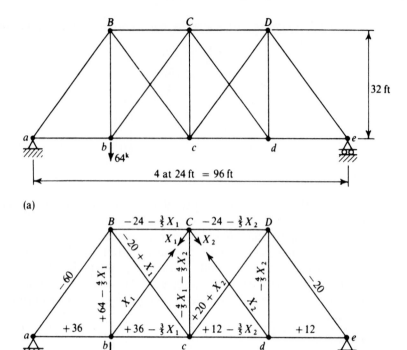

(a)

(b)

Figure 5-18

conveniently analyzed by the method of least work, as illustrated in the following example.

Example 5-14

Figure 5-19(a) shows a cantilever beam whose other end is supported by a rod. Find the force in the rod. $E = 30,000$ kips/in.^{2}.

The structure is statically indeterminate to the first degree. Select the force in the tie rod as the redundant X, as shown in Fig. 5-19(b). Then the internal work in the rod is

$$\frac{X^2 l_1}{2A_1 E}$$

and the internal work in the beam is equal to

$$\int_0^6 \frac{(0.6Xx)^2\, dx}{2EI} + \int_6^{12} \frac{[0.6Xx - 10(x-6)]^2\, dx}{2EI} + \frac{(-0.8X)^2 l_2}{2A_2 E}$$

Applying $\partial W/\partial X = 0$ gives

$$\frac{Xl_1}{A_1 E} + \int_0^6 \frac{(0.6Xx)(0.6x)\, dx}{EI} + \int_6^{12} \frac{[0.6Xx - 10(x-6)][0.6x]\, dx}{EI}$$

$$+ \frac{(-0.8X)(-0.8)l_2}{A_2 E} = 0$$

TABLE 5-6

Member	$\frac{L}{A}$ (ft/in.²)	S (kips)	$\frac{\partial S}{\partial X_1}$	$\frac{\partial S}{\partial X_2}$	$\frac{S(\partial S/\partial X_1)L}{A}$ (ft-kips/in.²)	$\frac{S(\partial S/\partial X_2)L}{A}$ (ft-kips/in.²)	Answer (kips)
ab	1	$36 + 0 + 0$	0	0	0	0	+36
bc	1	$36 - (\frac{3}{5})X_1 + 0$	$-\frac{3}{5}$	0	$-21.6 + (\frac{9}{25})X_1 + 0$	0	+23.3
cd	1	$12 + 0 - (\frac{3}{5})X_2$	0	$-\frac{3}{5}$	0	$-7.2 + 0 + (\frac{9}{25})X_2$	+18.2
de	1	$12 + 0 + 0$	0	0	0	0	+12
BC	1	$-24 - (\frac{3}{5})X_1 + 0$	$-\frac{3}{5}$	0	$14.4 + (\frac{9}{25})X_1 + 0$	0	-36.7
CD	1	$-24 + 0 - (\frac{3}{5})X_2$	0	$-\frac{3}{5}$	0	$14.4 + 0 + (\frac{9}{25})X_2$	-17.8
aB	1	$-60 + 0 + 0$	0	0	0	0	-60
Bb	1	$64 - (\frac{4}{5})X_1 + 0$	$-\frac{4}{5}$	0	$-51.2 + (\frac{16}{25})X_1 + 0$	0	+47
Bc	1	$-20 + X_1 + 0$	$+1$	0	$-20 + X_1 + 0$	0	+ 1.2
bC	1	$0 + X_1 + 0$	$+1$	0	$0 + X_1 + 0$	0	+21.2
Cc	1	$0 - (\frac{4}{5})X_1 - (\frac{4}{5})X_2$	$-\frac{4}{5}$	$-\frac{4}{5}$	$0 + (\frac{16}{25})X_1 + (\frac{16}{25})X_2$	$0 + (\frac{16}{25})X_1 + (\frac{16}{25})X_2$	- 8.8
Cd	1	$0 + 0 + X_2$	0	$+1$	0	$0 + 0 + X_2$	-10.2
cD	1	$20 + 0 + X_2$	0	$+1$	0	$20 + 0 + X_2$	+ 9.8
Dd	1	$0 + 0 - (\frac{4}{5})X_2$	0	$-\frac{4}{5}$	0	$0 + 0 + (\frac{16}{25})X_2$	+ 8.2
De	1	$-20 + 0 + 0$	0	0	0	0	-20
				Σ	$-78.4 + 4X_1 + 0.64X_2$	$27.2 + 0.64X_1 + 4X_2$	

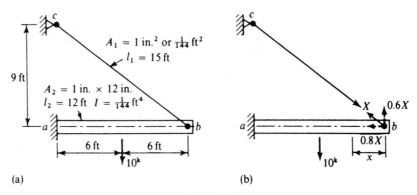

Figure 5-19

or

$$\frac{15X}{1/144} + \frac{207.4X - 3,024 + 1,944}{1/144} + \frac{(0.64X)(12)}{12/144} = 0$$

After simplifying, we find that

$$15X + 207.4X - 1,080 + 0.64X = 0$$

which yields

$$X = 4.84 \text{ kips} \quad \text{(tension)}$$

The effect of the axial force of beam on the strain energy is small and can be neglected.

5-6 MATRIX ANALYSIS OF STATICALLY INDETERMINATE TRUSSES

It is seen in the preceding sections that the key step in the method of consistent deformation is the generation of Eq. 5-11, the compatibility conditions. The process of finding the various elements in Eq. 5-11 is both tedious and error prone. Through a matrix formulation, however, the process can be made very straightforward. Consider a statically indeterminate truss. Let us denote the total *internal* member force vector by Q and the corresponding total elongation vector by q. Then the internal work W_I is simply

$$W_I = \frac{1}{2}Q^T q \tag{5-40}$$

After selecting the primary structure, an imaginary cut is placed at each of the redundant members. At each of these cuts, a pair of equal but opposite unknown forces is introduced. These unknown pairs of forces $X_1, X_2, \ldots$, form an unknown redundant force vector X, which is considered as *external*, just like the actually applied external force vector R. The external displacements corresponding to R constitute the nodal displacement vector r, and the external displacement corresponding to X is the null vector 0, because the compatibility condition dictates no relative axial movement across the cuts. The external work W_E is then

$$W_E = \frac{1}{2}\begin{Bmatrix} R \\ X \end{Bmatrix}^T \begin{Bmatrix} r \\ 0 \end{Bmatrix} \tag{5-41}$$

Equating the external work to the internal work and canceling the common factor $\frac{1}{2}$, we obtain

$$\begin{Bmatrix} R \\ X \end{Bmatrix}^T \begin{Bmatrix} r \\ 0 \end{Bmatrix} = Q^T q \tag{5-42}$$

Equation 5-42 links four vectors just as Eq. 4-36 of Sec. 4.8b links four vectors.

From equilibrium, we obtain the relationship between the member force Q and the applied external forces R and redundants X,

$$Q = b_R R + b_X X \tag{5-43}$$

where the matrices b_R and b_X are the force transformation matrices, which may be obtained by solving the primary structure for each of the applied forces $R_1, R_2, \ldots,$ and $X_1, X_2, \ldots,$ individually either by hand computation or by Gaussian elimination (Appendix A) using the computer. It should be noted that, just as in the method of consistent deformation, the member forces of the cut members must not be forgotten at this step. Equation 5-43 may be cast in the following *force transformation* form:

$$Q = [b_R \quad b_X]\begin{Bmatrix} R \\ X \end{Bmatrix} \tag{5-44}$$

Now, in view of the relationships expressed in Eqs. 5-42 and 5-44, the following *displacement transformation* equation is directly obtained by *contragredient transformation* (Sec. 4-8).

$$\begin{Bmatrix} r \\ 0 \end{Bmatrix} = \begin{bmatrix} b_R^T q \\ b_X^T \end{bmatrix} \tag{5-45}$$

The first part of Eq. 5-45 gives the nodal displacements r, and the second part is actually the compatibility condition that we are looking for.

Now the elongations are related to the member forces through the total member flexibility matrix f.

$$q = fQ \tag{5-46}$$

For trusses, the matrix f is diagonal and contains L/EA for all members and zero for regular support members or prescribed flexibility constants for elastic supports.

By substituting Eq. 5-46 and then Eq. 5-44 into Eq. 5-45, we obtain

$$\begin{Bmatrix} r \\ 0 \end{Bmatrix} = \begin{bmatrix} b_R^T \\ b_X^T \end{bmatrix} f \begin{bmatrix} b_R & b_X \end{bmatrix} \begin{Bmatrix} R \\ X \end{Bmatrix}$$

or

$$\begin{Bmatrix} r \\ 0 \end{Bmatrix} = \begin{bmatrix} F_{RR} & F_{RX} \\ F_{XR} & F_{XX} \end{bmatrix} \begin{Bmatrix} R \\ X \end{Bmatrix} \tag{5-47}$$

where

$$F_{RR} = b_R^T f b_R, \qquad F_{RX} = b_R^T f b_X$$
$$F_{XR} = b_X^T f b_R \qquad F_{XX} = b_X^T f b_X \tag{5-48}$$

The matrix F_{RR} relates the nodal displacement r and the nodal force R of the primary structure and is called the *flexibility matrix of the primary structure*.

Comparison of the second part of Eq. 5-47 to Eq. 5-9 and Eq. 5-11 reveals that the matrix F_{XX} is the F' matrix in Eq. 5-9 and Eq. 5-11, and $F_{XR} R$ corresponds to Δ' in Eq. 5-9 and Eq. 5-11. Obviously, if there are prescribed displacements Δ as indicated in Eq. 5-11, the 0 vector in the second part of Eq. 5-47 would be replaced by Δ. Thus, the second part of Eq. 5-47 is the compatibility condition, which results in the solution of the redundant force vector X:

$$X = -F_{XX}^{-1} F_{XR} R \tag{5-49}$$

The first part of Eq. 5-47 gives the nodal displacement solution:

$$r = F_{RR} R + F_{RX} X \tag{5-50}$$

This equation is also a compatibility statement that relates member deformation to nodal displacement.

Using the expression in Eq. 5-49, we finally reach the force displacement relationship of the indeterminate structure.

$$r = (F_{RR} - F_{RX} F_{XX}^{-1} F_{XR}) R$$

or

$$r = FR \tag{5-51}$$

where

$$F = F_{RR} - F_{RX} F_{XX}^{-1} F_{XR} \tag{5-52}$$

is the *flexibility matrix of the structure*.

This matrix procedure is now demonstrated through an example.

Example 5-15

Find the bar forces of the truss in Fig. 5-20(a) by the force method. Also find the nodal displacement corresponding to the applied load. Assume that $E = 30,000$ kips/in.^{2} and L (ft)/A (in.^{2}) = 1 for all members.

The truss shown in Fig. 5-20(a) is statically indeterminate to the first degree. Let us select bar e as the redundant and denote the external load of 12 kips by R_1, as shown in Fig. 5-20(b). The bar forces are denoted by $Q^a, Q^b, \ldots, Q^f$. From equilibrium based on the primary structure of Fig. 5-20(b),

$$
\begin{matrix} & R_1 = 1 \quad\quad X = 1 \end{matrix}
$$

$$
\begin{Bmatrix} Q^a \\ Q^b \\ Q^c \\ Q^d \\ Q^e \\ Q^f \end{Bmatrix} = \begin{bmatrix} 1 & -\frac{4}{5} \\ \frac{3}{4} & -\frac{3}{5} \\ 1 & -\frac{4}{5} \\ 0 & -\frac{3}{5} \\ 0 & 1 \\ -\frac{5}{4} & 1 \end{bmatrix} \begin{Bmatrix} R_1 \\ X \end{Bmatrix}
$$

$$
\begin{matrix} b_R \quad\quad b_x \end{matrix}
$$

Since $L/A = 1$ for all members,

$$
f = \frac{1}{E} \begin{bmatrix} 1 & & & & & \\ & 1 & & & & \\ & & 1 & & & \\ & & & 1 & & \\ & & & & 1 & \\ & & & & & 1 \end{bmatrix}
$$

Thus,

$$
F_{XR} = b_X^T f b_R
$$

$$
= [-\tfrac{4}{5} \quad -\tfrac{3}{5} \quad -\tfrac{4}{5} \quad -\tfrac{3}{5} \quad 1 \quad 1]\left(\frac{1}{E}\right) \begin{Bmatrix} 1 \\ \frac{3}{4} \\ 1 \\ 0 \\ 0 \\ -\frac{5}{4} \end{Bmatrix} = -\frac{3.3}{E}
$$

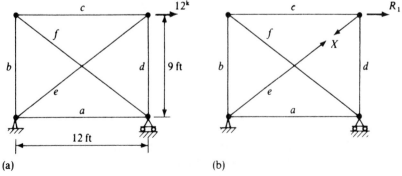

(a)   (b)

Figure 5-20

$$F_{XX} = b_X^T f b_X$$

$$= [-\tfrac{4}{5} \ -\tfrac{3}{5} \ -\tfrac{4}{5} \ -\tfrac{3}{5} \ 1 \ 1]\left(\frac{1}{E}\right)\begin{Bmatrix} -\tfrac{4}{5} \\ -\tfrac{3}{5} \\ -\tfrac{4}{5} \\ -\tfrac{3}{5} \\ 1 \\ 1 \end{Bmatrix} = \frac{4}{E}$$

$$F_{XX}^{-1} = \frac{E}{4}$$

The redundant force X is then solved by

$$X = -F_{XX}^{-1} F_{XR} R$$

$$= -\left(\frac{E}{4}\right)\left(-\frac{3.3}{E}\right)(12) = 9.9 \text{ kips}$$

Substituting in the equilibrium equation, we obtain

$$\begin{Bmatrix} Q^a \\ Q^b \\ Q^c \\ Q^d \\ Q^e \\ Q^f \end{Bmatrix} = \begin{bmatrix} 1 & -\tfrac{4}{5} \\ \tfrac{3}{4} & -\tfrac{3}{5} \\ 1 & -\tfrac{4}{5} \\ 0 & -\tfrac{3}{5} \\ 0 & 1 \\ -\tfrac{5}{4} & 1 \end{bmatrix} \begin{Bmatrix} 12 \\ 9.9 \end{Bmatrix} = \begin{Bmatrix} 4.08 \\ 3.06 \\ 4.08 \\ -5.94 \\ 9.90 \\ -5.10 \end{Bmatrix} \text{ kips}$$

To find r_1, we first calculate the flexibility matrix of structure F:

$$F = F_{RR} - F_{RX} F_{XX}^{-1} F_{XR}$$

$$= [1 \ \tfrac{3}{4} \ 1 \ 0 \ 0 \ -\tfrac{5}{4}]\left(\frac{1}{E}\right)\begin{Bmatrix} 1 \\ \tfrac{3}{4} \\ 1 \\ 0 \\ 0 \\ -\tfrac{5}{4} \end{Bmatrix} - \frac{3.3}{E} \frac{4}{E} \frac{3.3}{E}$$

$$= \frac{1.4}{E}$$

The displacement r_1 is then solved:

$$r_1 = FR_1$$

$$= \left(\frac{1.4}{E}\right)(12) = \frac{(1.4)(12)}{30,000} = 0.00056 \text{ ft}$$

in the direction of the applied load.

Note in this example that we did not include the support reactions explicitly as in Sec. 4-8. This is possible because we obtain the solution for Q with hand calculation, which may not involve the support reactions. Also, we include only the single applied nodal force R_1 in the formulation of the nodal force vector R, not the complete vector with zero applied forces included, as in Eq. 4-32 of Sec. 4-8. This is allowed because the zero applied forces contribute nothing in the computation. Consequently, however, we are able to solve for r_1 only. If all nodal displacements are desired, then we need to include even the zero applied nodal forces at the beginning.

PROBLEMS

5-1. Analyze the beam in Fig. 5-21 by the method of consistent deformations. (a) Use the reaction at center support b as redundant. (b) Use the internal moment at b as redundant. Assume constant EI.

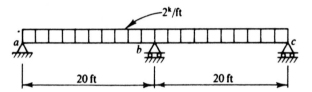

Figure 5-21

5-2. Determine the reaction at b in Fig. 5-22 by the method of consistent deformations. Assume constant EI.

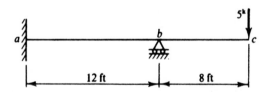

Figure 5-22

5-3. Find the reaction at b in Fig. 5-23 by the method of consistent deformations. Assume constant E.

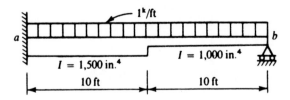

Figure 5-23

5-4. For the system shown in Fig. 5-24, determine, by the method of consistent deformations, the reaction at support e. The flexibility of the spring $f = 0.2$ cm/kN of force; the bending rigidity of the beam $EI = 30,000$ kN $\cdot$ m^2.

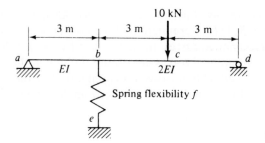

Figure 5-24

5-5. Find the fixed-end moments for the beams in Fig. 5-25 by the method of consistent deformations. Assume constant EI.

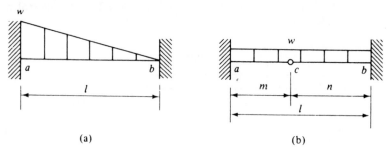

(a)   (b)

Figure 5-25

5-6. Use the method of consistent deformations to determine the horizontal reaction at support c of the rigid frame shown in Fig. 5-26. Assume that $E = 20,000$ kN/cm^2 and $I = 20,000$ cms.

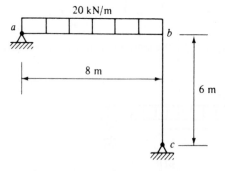

Figure 5-26

5-7. Analyze the rigid frame shown in Fig. 5-27 by the method of consistent deformations. Use the reaction components at support a as the redundants. All members have the same value of EI.

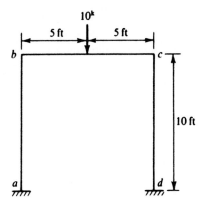

Figure 5-27

5-8. Repeat Problem 5-7 using the moment forces at joints b, c, and d as the redundants.

5-9. Analyze the truss in Fig. 5-28 by the method of consistent deformations. Assume that $E = 20,000$ kN/cm^2 and $A = 25$ cm^2 for all members.

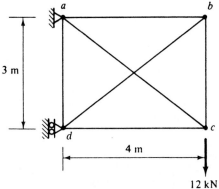

12 kN   **Figure 5-28**

5-10. Analyze each truss in Fig. 5-29 by the method of consistent deformations. Assume that $E = 30,000$ kips/in.^{2} and L (ft)/A (in.^{2}) = 2 for all members.

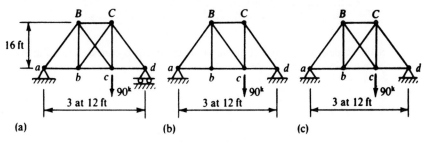

(a)   (b)   (c)

Figure 5-29

5-11. Analyze the truss in Fig. 5-29(a) (without the external load) subject to a rise in temperature of 50°F for member BC. Assume that $\alpha = 0.0000065$ in./in./1°F.

5-12. Repeat Problem 5-1 using Castigliano's compatibility equation.

5-13. Repeat Problem 5-5 using Castigliano's compatibility equation.

5-14. Repeat Problem 5-6 using Castigliano's compatibility equation.

5-15. Repeat Problem 5-9 using Castigliano's compatibility equation.

5-16. Find the internal force for the tie rod *ac* of the composite structure shown in Fig. 5-30, and sketch the moment diagram for member *ab*. E = 30,000 kips/in.^{2}.

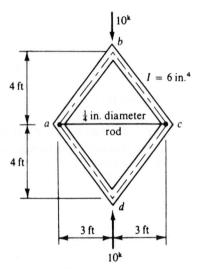

Figure 5-30

5-17. Find the internal forces for all rods of the composite structure shown in Fig. 5-31 and sketch the moment diagram for beam *ab*. E = 30,000 kips/in.^{2}.

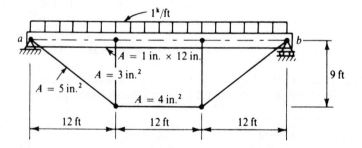

Figure 5-31

5-18. Repeat Problem 5-10 using the computer program described in Appendix B.

Chapter 6

Matrix Force Method

6-1 GENERAL

As illustrated in Sec. 2-8, there are two different methods of structural analysis, the force method and the displacement method. The material we covered in Chapters 3 through 5 is actually the force method. It is often considered a part of the *classical methods* of structural analysis as opposed to the more recently developed *matrix methods*. But, as we described in Sec. 3-5, Sec. 4-8, and Sec. 5-6, the classical method of analysis is easily cast in a matrix form for truss analysis. We will show in this chapter that the same matrix formulation also works for beams and frames, and we may call the matrix formulation the *matrix force method.* It would be misleading, however, to say that the difference between the classical methods and the matrix method is only a matter of form and notation. Certainly, the use of the contragredient transformation (Sec. 4-8) to form the compatibility condition in a matrix formulation is nowhere to be found in the classical procedure. More important, in a matrix method, the structure is discretized into members (or elements) and the members are connected through nodes (or joints), while in the classical procedure the structure is treated as a continuous body. This *discretization* process is a conceptual breakthrough that opens the door for a systematic formulation of a structural analysis procedure that is easily programmed for computer execution.

Before we unfold the general matrix force method, we point out that one of the differences between a truss problem and a beam or frame problem is that the former receives load only at discrete nodes, while the latter may have loads, concentrated or distributed, anywhere along the members. The treatment of loads between the nodes can be included in the general matrix force method, but it will disrupt the natural flow of the matrix formulation. Thus, we prefer an alternative but equivalent approach of replacing the loads between the nodes by loads at the nodes through the principle of superposition. Then we may deal with only nodal forces in the development of the matrix force method. To illustrate, let us consider the three-span continuous beam shown in Fig. 6-1(a), whose center span is subjected to a distributed

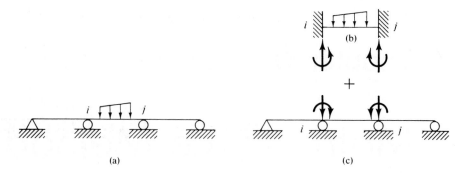

Figure 6-1

load. Let us first fix artificially the joints i and j of the center span [Fig. 6-1(b)] and then release them [Fig. 6-1(c)]. Since the application and removal of the artificial forces are neutralized, the original configuration of Fig. 6-1(a) is therefore statically equivalent to the combined effects of Fig. 6-1(b) and (c). The equivalent nodal loads at i and j in Fig. 6-1(c) are the reverse of fixed-end actions (moments and shears) in Fig. 6-1(b). Note that the final forces and displacements in the loaded member i–j must be obtained by superposing the effects of the fixed-end beam and those resulting from the nodal-force analysis of the original structure. The fixed-end moments induced by some commonly encountered loads are given in Appendix D. The fixed-end shears may be calculated from the fixed-end moments and loads by equilibrium.

In the remainder of the chapter, the matrix force method is first developed conceptually. Its solution procedure is then illustrated through examples that are designed for hand computation. At the end, the additional considerations needed for computer operation implementation are described.

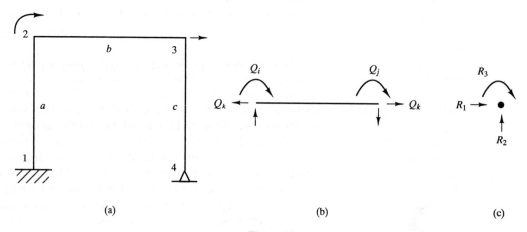

Figure 6-2

6-2 DISCRETIZATION

Consider the loaded frame in Fig. 6-2(a). The frame is composed of three frame members, a, b, and c, and reaction members (not shown in Fig. 6-2) at nodes 1 and 4. Each frame member has three representative member forces Q_i, Q_j, and Q_k, as shown in Fig. 6-2(b). The selection of these end moments, Q_i and Q_j, and the pair of axial tensile forces, Q_k, to represent the member force is arbitrary; that is, any three member forces will do. Other member forces such as end shears can be expressed in terms of these three member forces. The reaction forces (not shown in Fig. 6-2) are considered as member forces of reaction members.

We may use superscripts to identify the member to which the member forces belong and lump all the member forces, including those of the reaction members, into a single member force vector Q.

$$Q = \begin{Bmatrix} Q_i^a \\ Q_j^a \\ \vdots \\ Q_i^b \\ Q_j^b \\ \vdots \end{Bmatrix}$$

Corresponding to each of the member forces we may define a member deformation quantity, the detailed definition of which is given later in Sec. 6-5. Briefly, they represent the member end rotations and member elongation. These member deformation quantities, denoted by q_i, q_j, and q_k are arranged in the same order as that of the corresponding member forces and may be lumped into a single member deformation vector q.

$$q = \begin{Bmatrix} q_i^a \\ q_j^a \\ \vdots \\ q_i^b \\ q_j^b \\ \vdots \end{Bmatrix}$$

These two vectors, Q and q, constitute an *internal force and deformation pair* for the whole structure.

Now we turn our attention to the externally applied nodal forces. At each node, a maximum of three nodal forces, two forces and one moment, may be applied [Fig. 6-2(c)]. For example, there is only one applied force at each of nodes 2 and 3, respectively, in Fig. 6-2(a), and there are no applied forces at node 4, although an applied moment at 4 could be perfectly admissible. These applied nodal forces may be denoted by $R_1, R_2, \ldots$, and be represented by a single applied nodal force vector R.

$$R = \begin{Bmatrix} R_1 \\ R_2 \\ R_3 \\ \vdots \end{Bmatrix}$$

Corresponding to each of the applied force or moment, we may define a displacement quantity, which is either a translational displacement or a rotation. If they are arranged in the same order as that of the applied force, then we have a nodal displacement vector r.

$$r = \begin{Bmatrix} r_1 \\ r_2 \\ r_3 \\ \vdots \end{Bmatrix}$$

These two vectors, R and r, constitute an *external pair of force and displacement* for the whole structure.

6-3 EQUILIBRIUM, FORCE TRANSFORMATION MATRIX

For a statically determinate structure, each member force may be expressed in terms of the external nodal loads by using the equilibrium conditions of the system alone. Thus,

$$Q_1 = b_{11} R_1 + b_{12} R_2 + \cdots + b_{1n} R_n$$

$$Q_2 = b_{21} R_1 + b_{22} R_2 + \cdots + b_{2n} R_n$$

$$\vdots \tag{6-1}$$

$$Q_m = b_{m1} R_1 + b_{m2} R_2 + \cdots + b_{mn} R_n$$

in which $Q_1 = Q_i^a, Q_2 = Q_j^a, \ldots$. Observe that $R_1, R_2, \ldots, R_n$ represent the total set of applied loads and $Q_1, Q_2, \ldots, Q_m$ the total set of member forces. No connection between the subscripts on R and Q is implied.

The matrix form for Eq. 6-1 is

$$Q = bR \tag{6-2}$$

where

$$b = \begin{bmatrix} b_{11} & b_{12} & \cdots & b_{1n} \\ b_{21} & b_{22} & \cdots & b_{2n} \\ \vdots & \vdots & \ddots & \vdots \\ b_{m1} & b_{m2} & \cdots & b_{mn} \end{bmatrix} \tag{6-3}$$

is called the *force transformation matrix*, which relates the internal forces to the external forces. Matrix b is usually a rectangular matrix in which the typical element b_{ij} is the value of the internal force component Q_i caused by a unit value of external load R_j. Note that b is merely an expression of equilibrium for the system.

As for a statically indeterminate structure, the internal member forces cannot be expressed in terms of the external loads by equilibrium alone. However, as previously stated (see Sec. 5-1), a statically indeterminate structure can be made determinate by removing the redundant elements. The statically determinate and stable structure that remains after the removal of the extra restraints is called a *primary structure*. We then consider the original structure as equivalent to the primary structure subjected to the combined influences of the applied loads and the unknown redundant forces, thereby treating the redundants as a part of the external loads of unknown magnitude. In this way, we can express member forces in terms of the original applied loads R and the redundant forces X as

$$Q = b_R R + b_X X \qquad (6\text{-}4)$$

or

$$Q = [b_R \,|\, b_X]\left\{\frac{R}{X}\right\} \qquad (6\text{-}5)$$

where b_R and b_X are force transformation matrices representing the separate influences of the known applied loads R and the unknown redundants X on the member forces. They are generally rectangular matrices.

6-4 COMPATIBILITY, DISPLACEMENT TRANSFORMATION MATRIX

Compatibility is a continuity condition on the displacements of the structure after the external loads are applied to the structure. Compatibility must be brought into the analysis of statically indeterminate structures since the equilibrium equations alone do not suffice to solve the problem.

If we let r_X denote the prescribed displacement vector corresponding to the redundant force vector X, the compatibility conditions used in the force method for solving a static structure are that the displacements at all the cuts of redundant points caused by the original applied loads and the redundant forces must be made to be equal to r_X in order that the continuity of the structure can be maintained. For a loaded structure mounted on rigid supports, the gap in the displacements at redundant points resulting from applied loads is precisely removed by the redundant forces. Therefore, the compatibility condition is

$$r_X = 0 \qquad (6\text{-}6)$$

This null vector and the nodal displacement vector r constitute the total displacements corresponding to the redundant force X and the applied force R. Since these forces are external, the work done by the external forces is simply

$$W_E = \frac{1}{2}\left\{\frac{R}{X}\right\}^T \left\{\frac{r}{0}\right\} \qquad (6\text{-}7)$$

On the other hand, the internal work is

$$W_I = \frac{1}{2} Q^T q \tag{6-8}$$

Equating the external work to the internal work and canceling the common factor of $\frac{1}{2}$, we obtain

$$\begin{Bmatrix} R \\ X \end{Bmatrix}^T \begin{Bmatrix} r \\ 0 \end{Bmatrix} = Q^T q \tag{6-9}$$

In view of this work relationship and the force transformation relationship of Eq. 6-5, the following *displacement transformation* relationship is obtained by *contragredient transformation* (see Sec. 4-8b).

$$\begin{Bmatrix} r \\ 0 \end{Bmatrix} = \begin{bmatrix} b_R^T \\ b_X^T \end{bmatrix} q \tag{6-10}$$

The two matrices, b_R^T and b_X^T transform the member deformation vector q into nodal displacement r and the null relative displacement at the cuts, respectively, and may be called the displacement transformation matrices.

6-5 FORCE–DISPLACEMENT RELATIONSHIP, FLEXIBILITY COEFFICIENT, FLEXIBILITY MATRIX

A *flexibility coefficient* f_{ij} is the displacement at point i due to a unit action at point j, all other points being unloaded. Apparently, the flexibility coefficient constitutes a relationship between deformation and force. Applying the principle of superposition, we may express the deformation at any point of a system caused by a set of forces in terms of the flexibility coefficients.

Our intention is, first, to establish the relationship between the member displacements and the member forces of a structure. Consider a typical member a taken from a plane structure as shown in Fig. 6-3. As before, the member forces are represented by a vector Q^a:

$$Q^a = \begin{Bmatrix} Q_i^a \\ Q_j^a \\ Q_k^a \end{Bmatrix}$$

and the corresponding member deformations are represented by a vector q^a:

$$q^a = \begin{Bmatrix} q_i^a \\ q_j^a \\ q_k^a \end{Bmatrix}$$

The precise definition of the three member deformation quantities, q_i^a, q_j^a, and q_k^a, is now delineated. Referring to Fig. 6-3, we see that member a moves from its

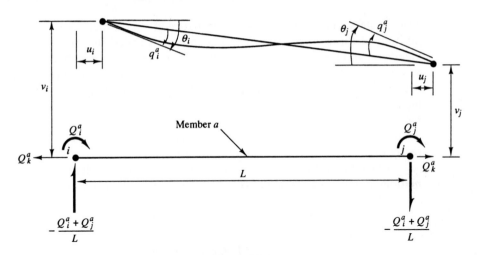

Figure 6-3

original position to a deformed and displaced position. This member deformation may be characterized by the two nodal translations u_i and v_i and a nodal rotation θ_i at node i and similar quantities u_j, v_j, and θ_j at node j. The nodal member forces, including the shear, are also shown in Fig. 6-3. Since we have already selected Q_i^a, Q_j^a, and Q_k^a as the representative member forces, the member end shear forces can be expressed in terms of these member forces as shown in Fig. 6-3 through the equilibrium of the member. The internal work of this member is then equal to the work done by all the member nodal forces.

$$
\begin{aligned}
W_I &= \frac{1}{2}\left[Q_i^a \theta_i + Q_j^a \theta_j - \frac{Q_i^a + Q_j^a}{L}(v_i - v_j) + Q_k^a(u_j - u_i) \right] \\
&= \frac{1}{2}\left[Q_i^a\left(\theta_i - \frac{v_i - v_j}{L} \right) + Q_j^a\left(\theta_j - \frac{v_i - v_j}{L} \right) + Q_k^a(u_j - u_i) \right]
\end{aligned}
\tag{6-11}
$$

On the other hand, the same internal work must also be expressed in terms of the representative member forces Q_i^a, Q_j^a, and Q_k^a and the corresponding representative member deformation q_i^a, q_j^a, and q_k^a.

$$
W_I = \frac{1}{2}[Q_i^a q_i^a + Q_j^a q_j^a + Q_k^a q_k^a]
\tag{6-12}
$$

Comparing Eqs. 6-11 and 6-12, we conclude that

$$
q_i^a = \theta_i - \frac{v_i - v_j}{L}
\tag{6-13a}
$$

$$
q_j^a = \theta_j - \frac{v_i - v_j}{L}
\tag{6-13b}
$$

$$
q_k^a = u_j - u_i
\tag{6-13c}
$$

The quantity $(v_i - v_j)/L$ is the angle between the dashed line and the original position of the member shown in Fig. 6-3. It is called the *rigid-body rotation of member a* and is positive if it rotates clockwise. Thus, the member rotations q_i^a and q_j^a are not the total rotations, but the relative rotations measured from the line connecting the displaced nodes i and j. This distinction disappears if the rigid-body member rotation is nil. Finally, the quantity q_k^a is simply the elongation of the member. Note that clockwise moments and rotations are considered positive. With the member force vector and the member deformation vector clearly defined, we are ready to explore the relationship between them.

Using the flexibility coefficient f_{ij}^a, we may express each of the member deformations in terms of the separate influences of the whole set of member forces:

$$q_i^a = f_{ii}^a Q_i^a + f_{ij}^a Q_j^a + f_{ik}^a Q_k^a$$

$$q_j^a = f_{ji}^a Q_i^a + f_{jj}^a Q_j^a + f_{jk}^a Q_k^a$$

$$q_k^a = f_{ki}^a Q_i^a + f_{kj}^a Q_j^a + f_{kk}^a Q_k^a$$

or, in matrix form,

$$q^a = f^a Q^a \tag{6-14}$$

in which

$$f^a = \begin{bmatrix} f_{ii}^a & f_{ij}^a & f_{ik}^a \\ f_{ji}^a & f_{jj}^a & f_{jk}^a \\ f_{ki}^a & f_{kj}^a & f_{kk}^a \end{bmatrix} \tag{6-15}$$

is defined as the *element flexibility matrix*. Clearly, the coefficient, for instance f_{ii}^a, is given by

$$f_{ii}^a = q_i^a \quad \text{as} \quad Q_i^a = 1, \quad Q_j^a = Q_k^a = 0$$

The rest can similarly be defined.

The descriptions above refer to an individual element. For a structure consisting of $a, b, \ldots$ elements, we have

$$q^a = f^a Q^a$$

$$q^b = f^b Q^b$$

$$\vdots$$

Let

$$q = \begin{Bmatrix} q^a \\ q^b \\ \vdots \end{Bmatrix} \quad \text{and} \quad Q = \begin{Bmatrix} Q^a \\ Q^b \\ \vdots \end{Bmatrix}$$

These equations can be put in the matrix form

$$q = fQ \tag{6-16}$$

where

$$f = \begin{bmatrix} f^a & & \\ & f^b & \\ & & \ddots \end{bmatrix} \tag{6-17}$$

which is a diagonal matrix with element flexibility matrices as its constituents.

Since the flexibility coefficients of Eq. 6-15 serve to relate the member deformations to the member forces, they are certainly governed by the geometric and material properties of the member. Suppose that the member is prismatic with length L, cross-sectional area A, moment of inertia I, and modulus of elasticity E and regarded as simply supported. The elements in the first column of f^a are, by definition, the member deformation resulting from $Q_i^a = 1$. These are found to be

$$f_{ii}^a = \text{rotation of the left end} = \frac{L}{3EI}$$

$$f_{ji}^a = \text{rotation at the right end} = -\frac{L}{6EI}$$

$$f_{ki}^a = \text{elongation of the member} = 0$$

Note that f_{ii}^a and f_{ji}^a can easily be determined by the conjugate beam method and that $f_{ki}^a = 0$ is apparent. All the other elements can be obtained similarly. Thus, the member flexibility matrix is given by

$$f^a = \begin{bmatrix} \dfrac{L}{3EI} & -\dfrac{L}{6EI} & 0 \\ -\dfrac{L}{6EI} & \dfrac{L}{3EI} & 0 \\ 0 & 0 & \dfrac{L}{AE} \end{bmatrix} \tag{6-18}$$

Note that the member flexibility matrix is symmetric because of reciprocity.

If the effect of axial forces in the member is neglected, as is usually done in rigid-frame analysis, then

$$f^a = \frac{L}{6EI} \begin{bmatrix} 2 & -1 \\ -1 & 2 \end{bmatrix} \tag{6-19}$$

For a truss member subjected to axial forces only,

$$f^a = \begin{bmatrix} \dfrac{L}{AE} \end{bmatrix} \tag{6-20}$$

6-6 SOLUTION FORMULAS

The equations developed in the preceding sections can now be synthesized to give the solution formulas for the unknown force and displacement vectors, Q, X, r, and q. We will consider the statically indeterminate structures; then the statically determinate structures are simply degenerated cases.

First, we need to solve for the redundant force vector X. This is achieved by combining Eqs. 6-10, 6-16, and 6-5 to yield

$$\begin{Bmatrix} r \\ 0 \end{Bmatrix} = \begin{bmatrix} b_R^T \\ b_X^T \end{bmatrix} q$$

$$= \begin{bmatrix} b_R^T \\ b_X^T \end{bmatrix} fQ$$

$$= \begin{bmatrix} b_R^T \\ b_X^T \end{bmatrix} f [b_R \quad b_X] \begin{Bmatrix} R \\ X \end{Bmatrix}$$

$$= \begin{bmatrix} b_R^T f b_R & b_R^T f b_X \\ b_X^T f b_R & b_X^T f b_X \end{bmatrix} \begin{Bmatrix} R \\ X \end{Bmatrix}$$

or

$$\begin{Bmatrix} r \\ 0 \end{Bmatrix} = \begin{bmatrix} F_{RR} & F_{RX} \\ F_{XR} & F_{XX} \end{bmatrix} \begin{Bmatrix} R \\ X \end{Bmatrix} \tag{6-21}$$

where

$$F_{RR} = b_R^T f b_R, \qquad F_{RX} = b_R^T f b_X$$
$$F_{XR} = b_X^T f b_R, \qquad F_{XX} = b_X^T f b_X \tag{6-22}$$

The second part of Eq. 6-21 is expanded into

$$F_{XR} R + F_{XX} X = 0$$

from which the formula for the redundant force is obtained:

$$X = -F_{XX}^{-1} F_{XR} R \tag{6-23}$$

The nodal displacement r may now be obtained by substituting the expression in Eq. 6-23 into the first part of Eq. 6-21:

$$r = FR \tag{6-24}$$

where

$$F = F_{RR} - F_{RX} F_{XX}^{-1} F_{XR} \tag{6-25}$$

The matrix F relates the applied loads to the corresponding displacements and is called the *flexibility matrix of the indeterminate structure*, whereas the matrix F_{RR} relates the applied load only to the nodal displacement of the primary structure (Eq. 6-21, if $X = 0$) and is called the *flexibility matrix of the primary structure*.

The solution of the member force vector Q is obtained from the combination of Eqs. 6-5 and 6-23.

$$Q = bR \qquad\qquad (6\text{-}26)$$

where

$$b = b_R - b_X F_{XX}^{-1} F_{XR} \qquad\qquad (6\text{-}27)$$

is the *force transformation matrix of the indeterminate structure*.

Finally, the member deformation vector q is obtained from Eq. 6-16.

The above derivation is easily extended to include the case in which the displacement r_X corresponding to the redundant force X is not zero. This happens, for example, when a support settles a prescribed amount and the support force is taken as a redundant force. The null vector 0 in Eq. 6-21 is replaced with r_X. Consequently, Eqs. 6-23, 6-24, and 6-26 become

$$X = F_{XX}^{-1} r_X - F_{XX}^{-1} F_{XR} R \qquad\qquad (6\text{-}23\text{a})$$

$$r = FR + F_{RX} F_{XX}^{-1} r_X \qquad\qquad (6\text{-}24\text{a})$$

$$Q = bR + b_X F_{XX}^{-1} r_X \qquad\qquad (6\text{-}26\text{a})$$

The other equations are not affected.

6-7 ANALYSIS OF STATICALLY DETERMINATE STRUCTURES BY THE MATRIX FORCE METHOD

As developed in Sec. 6-3, for a statically determinate structure, the internal forces Q can be solved by equilibrium alone:

$$Q = bR$$

See Eq. 6-2.

Also, the nodal displacements r can be solved by

$$r = b^T fbR$$

See Eqs. 6-22 and 6-24.

The procedure for analyzing a statically determinate structure by the force method is as follows:

1. Define the external nodal loads R.
2. Define the internal member forces Q.
3. Determine the force transformation matrix b.

Consider the elements of the first column of b. If we let

$$R_1 = 1, \qquad R_2 = R_3 = \cdots = R_n = 0$$

it is readily seen from Eq. 6-1 that $Q_1, Q_2, \ldots, Q_m$ are the elements of the first column. The rest can be obtained similarly.

4. The internal member forces Q are then solved by

$$Q = bR$$

5. Determine individual element flexibility matrices $f^a, f^b, \ldots$ according to Eq. 6-19 or 6-20, and assemble them as a diagonal matrix,

$$f = \begin{bmatrix} f^a & & \\ & f^b & \\ & & \ddots \end{bmatrix}$$

6. Compute the flexibility matrix of the structure.

$$F = b^T f b$$

7. Find the nodal displacements r.

$$r = FR$$

Example 6-1

Find the bar forces of the truss shown in Fig. 6-4. Find also the deflections corresponding to the applied loads R_1 and R_2. Assume that $L/A = 1$ for all members.

The load matrix is

$$R = \begin{Bmatrix} R_1 \\ R_2 \end{Bmatrix}$$

The truss has five bars designated by a, b, c, d, and e. The member force matrix is

$$Q = \begin{Bmatrix} Q^a \\ Q^b \\ Q^c \\ Q^d \\ Q^e \end{Bmatrix}$$

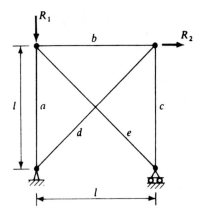

Figure 6-4

The force transformation matrix b is given by

$$b = \begin{bmatrix} -1 & 0 \\ 0 & 0 \\ 0 & -1 \\ 0 & \sqrt{2} \\ 0 & 0 \end{bmatrix}$$

in which the first column contains the bar forces of the truss in Fig. 6-4 in the order a, b, c, d, e, resulting from $R_1 = 1, R_2 = 0$. The second column contains the corresponding bar forces resulting from $R_2 = 1, R_1 = 0$. From equilibrium

$$\begin{Bmatrix} Q^a \\ Q^b \\ Q^c \\ Q^d \\ Q^e \end{Bmatrix} = \begin{bmatrix} -1 & 0 \\ 0 & 0 \\ 0 & -1 \\ 0 & \sqrt{2} \\ 0 & 0 \end{bmatrix} \begin{Bmatrix} R_1 \\ R_2 \end{Bmatrix}$$

For individual members the flexibility matrices are found to be

$$f^a = f^b = f^c = f^d = f^e = \frac{1}{E}$$

since $L/A = 1$ for all members. Thus, the diagonal matrix is

$$f = \begin{bmatrix} f^a & & & & \\ & f^b & & & \\ & & f^c & & \\ & & & f^d & \\ & & & & f^e \end{bmatrix} = \frac{1}{E} \begin{bmatrix} 1 & & & & \\ & 1 & & & \\ & & 1 & & \\ & & & 1 & \\ & & & & 1 \end{bmatrix}$$

The total flexibility matrix is then determined:

$$F = b^T f b$$

$$= \begin{bmatrix} -1 & 0 & 0 & 0 & 0 \\ 0 & 0 & -1 & \sqrt{2} & 0 \end{bmatrix} \frac{1}{E} \begin{bmatrix} 1 & & & & \\ & 1 & & & \\ & & 1 & & \\ & & & 1 & \\ & & & & 1 \end{bmatrix} \begin{bmatrix} -1 & 0 \\ 0 & 0 \\ 0 & -1 \\ 0 & \sqrt{2} \\ 0 & 0 \end{bmatrix}$$

$$= \frac{1}{E} \begin{bmatrix} 1 & 0 \\ 0 & 3 \end{bmatrix}$$

The nodal displacements r are solved by

$$r = FR$$

$$\begin{Bmatrix} r_1 \\ r_2 \end{Bmatrix} = \frac{1}{E} \begin{bmatrix} 1 & 0 \\ 0 & 3 \end{bmatrix} \begin{Bmatrix} R_1 \\ R_2 \end{Bmatrix}$$

or

$$r_1 = \frac{R_1}{E}, \qquad r_2 = \frac{3R_2}{E}$$

Example 6-2

Find the deflections corresponding to the applied loads for the cantilever beam shown in Fig. 6-5(a). Assume constant EI.

Since the loaded point of R_1 must be considered as a nodal point, it divides the beam into two segments, designated as member a and member b in Fig. 6-5(b). The internal member forces are shown by dashed lines. From equilibrium,

$$R_1 = 1 \quad R_2 = 1 \quad R_3 = 1$$

$$Q = bR, \qquad \begin{Bmatrix} Q_i^a \\ Q_j^a \\ Q_i^b \\ Q_j^b \end{Bmatrix} = \begin{bmatrix} -L_1 & -(L_1 + L_2) & -1 \\ 0 & L_2 & 1 \\ 0 & -L_2 & -1 \\ 0 & 0 & 1 \end{bmatrix} \begin{Bmatrix} R_1 \\ R_2 \\ R_3 \end{Bmatrix}$$

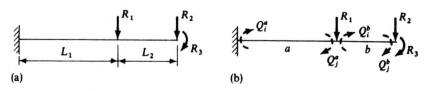

(a)   (b)

Figure 6-5

Note that the elements of the first column of matrix b are the member forces caused by $R_1 = 1, R_2 = R_3 = 0$ for the beam shown in Fig. 6-5(b). This gives

$$Q_i^a = -L_1, \qquad Q_j^a = Q_i^b = Q_j^b = 0$$

The second column of matrix b contains the member forces resulting from $R_2 = 1, R_1 = R_3 = 0$. Thus,

$$Q_i^a = -(L_1 + L_2), \qquad Q_j^a = L_2, \qquad Q_i^b = -L_2, \qquad Q_j^b = 0$$

And the third column of matrix b contains the member forces due to a unit couple applied only at the free end of the beam (i.e., $R_3 = 1, R_1 = R_2 = 0$). This gives

$$Q_i^a = -1, \qquad Q_j^a = 1, \qquad Q_i^b = -1, \qquad Q_j^b = 1$$

The individual member flexibility matrices are

$$f^a = \frac{1}{6EI}\begin{bmatrix} 2L_1 & -L_1 \\ -L_1 & 2L_1 \end{bmatrix}, \qquad f^b = \frac{1}{6EI}\begin{bmatrix} 2L_2 & -L_2 \\ -L_2 & 2L_2 \end{bmatrix}$$

from which

$$f = \frac{1}{6EI}\begin{bmatrix} 2L_1 & -L_1 & 0 & 0 \\ -L_1 & 2L_1 & 0 & 0 \\ 0 & 0 & 2L_2 & -L_2 \\ 0 & 0 & -L_2 & 2L_2 \end{bmatrix}$$

The total flexibility matrix F is obtained from

$$F = b^T f b = \begin{bmatrix} -L_1 & 0 & 0 & 0 \\ -(L_1 + L_2) & L_2 & -L_2 & 0 \\ -1 & 1 & -1 & 1 \end{bmatrix}\left(\frac{1}{6EI}\right)$$

$$\cdot \begin{bmatrix} 2L_1 & -L_1 & 0 & 0 \\ -L_1 & 2L_1 & 0 & 0 \\ 0 & 0 & 2L_2 & -L_2 \\ 0 & 0 & -L_2 & 2L_2 \end{bmatrix}\begin{bmatrix} -L_1 & -(L_1 + L_2) & -1 \\ 0 & L_2 & 1 \\ 0 & -L_2 & -1 \\ 0 & 0 & 1 \end{bmatrix}$$

$$= \begin{bmatrix} \dfrac{L_1^3}{3EI} & \dfrac{2L_1^3 + 3L_1^2 L_2}{6EI} & \dfrac{L_1^2}{2EI} \\[3mm] \dfrac{2L_1^3 + 3L_1^2 L_2}{6EI} & \dfrac{(L_1 + L_2)^3}{3EI} & \dfrac{(L_1 + L_2)^2}{2EI} \\[3mm] \dfrac{L_1^2}{2EI} & \dfrac{(L_1 + L_2)^2}{2EI} & \dfrac{L_1 + L_2}{EI} \end{bmatrix}$$

Thus,

$$\begin{Bmatrix} r_1 \\ r_2 \\ r_3 \end{Bmatrix} = \begin{bmatrix} \dfrac{L_1^3}{3EI} & \dfrac{2L_1^3 + 3L_1^2 L_2}{6EI} & \dfrac{L_1^2}{2EI} \\[3mm] \dfrac{2L_1^3 + 3L_1^2 L_2}{6EI} & \dfrac{(L_1 + L_2)^3}{3EI} & \dfrac{(L_1 + L_2)^2}{2EI} \\[3mm] \dfrac{L_1^2}{2EI} & \dfrac{(L_1 + L_2)^2}{2EI} & \dfrac{L_1 + L_2}{EI} \end{bmatrix}\begin{Bmatrix} R_1 \\ R_2 \\ R_3 \end{Bmatrix}$$

or

$$r_1 = \frac{R_1 L_1^3}{3EI} + \frac{R_2(2L_1^3 + 3L_1^2 L_2)}{6EI} + \frac{R_3 L_1^2}{2EI}$$

$$r_2 = \frac{R_1(2L_1^3 + 3L_1^2 L_2)}{6EI} + \frac{R_2(L_1 + L_2)^3}{3EI} + \frac{R_3(L_1 + L_2)^2}{2EI}$$

$$r_3 = \frac{R_1 L_1^2}{2EI} + \frac{R_2(L_1 + L_2)^2}{2EI} + \frac{R_3(L_1 + L_2)}{EI}$$

As a particular problem, find the vertical deflection and the rotation at the free end of the loaded cantilever beam shown in Fig. 6-6. To do this, we set $R_1 = P$, $R_2 = R_3 = 0$ in the preceding expression for r_2 to obtain

$$r_2 = \frac{P(2L_1^3 + 3L_1^2 L_2)}{6EI}$$

which is the resulting vertical deflection of the end of the beam. Similarly, we obtain

$$r_3 = \frac{PL_1^2}{2EI}$$

which is the resulting rotation of the end of the beam.

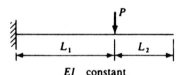

$$L_1 \qquad\qquad L_2$$

EI constant   **Figure 6-6**

6-8 ANALYSIS OF STATICALLY INDETERMINATE STRUCTURES BY THE MATRIX FORCE METHOD

As developed in Secs. 6-3 to 6-6, the procedures for analyzing a statically indeterminate structure by the force method are given as follows:

1. Define the external loads R.
2. Define the internal member forces Q, and specify the redundants X.
3. Calculate the force transformation matrices b_R and b_X from equilibrium:

$$Q = [b_R \,|\, b_X] \left\{ \frac{R}{X} \right\}$$

4. Determine the individual element flexibility matrices $f^a, f^b, \ldots$, and assemble them to obtain f:

$$f = \begin{bmatrix} f^a & & \\ & f^b & \\ & & \ddots \end{bmatrix}$$

5. Calculate F_{XR}:

$$F_{XR} = b_X^T f b_R$$

6. Calculate F_{XX}:

$$F_{XX} = b_X^T f b_X$$

7. Solve the redundants X by

$$X = -F_{XX}^{-1} F_{XR} R$$

and substitute X in the equilibrium equation to obtain the member forces Q.
8. Alternatively, we may find b by

$$b = b_R - b_X F_{XX}^{-1} F_{XR}$$

and obtain the member forces Q by

$$Q = bR$$

9. If the nodal displacements are desired, calculate F by

$$F = F_{RR} - F_{RX} F_{XX}^{-1} F_{XR}$$

and find r by

$$r = FR$$

As seen in the latter part of Example 6-2, if the points where the displacements are desired are not actually loaded, then we must apply fictitious loads of zero value at these points in order to carry out the procedures listed above.

Example 6-3

Find the member forces (end moments) of the rigid frame in Fig. 6-7(a) by the force method. E is constant.

The frame shown in Fig. 6-7(a) is statically indeterminate to the second degree. It may be made determinate by inserting two pins as in Fig. 6-7(b). Then the structure

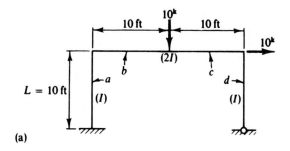

(a)

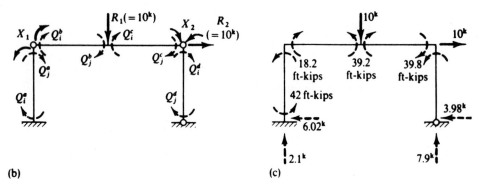

(b)

(c)

Figure 6-7

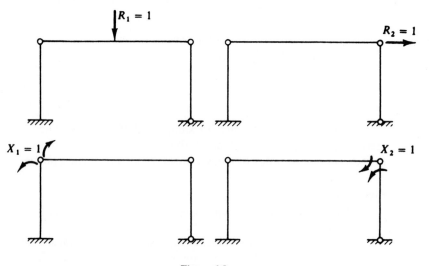

Figure 6-8

is subjected to the original applied loads denoted by R_1 and R_2 together with the redundant couples X_1 and X_2. The member forces (end moments) in Fig. 6-7(b), $Q_i^a, Q_j^a, \ldots$, are shown by dashed lines.

The force transformation matrix is obtained by considering the influences of $R_1 = 1, R_2 = 1, X_1 = 1$, and $X_2 = 1$ successively and separately, as shown in Fig. 6-8.

$$
\begin{bmatrix} Q_i^a \\ Q_j^a \\ Q_i^b \\ Q_j^b \\ Q_i^c \\ Q_j^c \\ Q_i^d \\ Q_j^d \end{bmatrix} = \left[\begin{array}{cc|cc} 0 & -L & 1 & 1 \\ 0 & 0 & -1 & 0 \\ 0 & 0 & 1 & 0 \\ -\frac{L}{2} & 0 & -\frac{1}{2} & \frac{1}{2} \\ \frac{L}{2} & 0 & \frac{1}{2} & -\frac{1}{2} \\ 0 & 0 & 0 & 1 \\ 0 & 0 & 0 & -1 \\ 0 & 0 & 0 & 0 \end{array}\right] \left\{ \begin{array}{c} R_1 \\ R_2 \\ \hline X_1 \\ X_2 \end{array} \right\}
$$

$$\underbrace{}_{b_R} \quad \underbrace{}_{b_x}$$

where $R_1 = 1 \quad R_2 = 1 \quad X_1 = 1 \quad X_2 = 1$ head the columns.

From individual member flexibility matrices, we form

$$
f = \frac{L}{6EI} \begin{bmatrix} 2 & -1 & & & & & & \\ -1 & 2 & & & & & & \\ & & 1 & -\frac{1}{2} & & & & \\ & & -\frac{1}{2} & 1 & & & & \\ & & & & 1 & -\frac{1}{2} & & \\ & & & & -\frac{1}{2} & 1 & & \\ & & & & & & 2 & -1 \\ & & & & & & -1 & 2 \end{bmatrix}
$$

Using b_R, b_x, and f found previously, we obtain

$$F_{XR} = b_x^T f b_R = \frac{L^2}{6EI} \begin{bmatrix} \frac{3}{4} & -3 \\ -\frac{3}{4} & -2 \end{bmatrix}$$

$$F_{XX} = b_x^T f b_x = \frac{L}{6EI} \begin{bmatrix} 8 & 2 \\ 2 & 6 \end{bmatrix}$$

and

$$F_{XX}^{-1} = \frac{6EI}{L} \frac{\begin{bmatrix} 6 & -2 \\ -2 & 8 \end{bmatrix}^T}{\begin{vmatrix} 8 & 2 \\ 2 & 6 \end{vmatrix}} = \left(\frac{6EI}{L}\right)\left(\frac{1}{44}\right)\begin{bmatrix} 6 & -2 \\ -2 & 8 \end{bmatrix}$$

The force transformation matrix of the indeterminate structure is

$$b = b_R - b_X F_{XX}^{-1} F_{XR}$$

$$
= \begin{bmatrix} 0 & -L \\ 0 & 0 \\ 0 & 0 \\ -\dfrac{L}{2} & 0 \\ \dfrac{L}{2} & 0 \\ 0 & 0 \\ 0 & 0 \\ 0 & 0 \end{bmatrix} - \begin{bmatrix} 1 & 1 \\ -1 & 0 \\ 1 & 0 \\ -\dfrac{1}{2} & \dfrac{1}{2} \\ \dfrac{1}{2} & -\dfrac{1}{2} \\ 0 & 1 \\ 0 & -1 \\ 0 & 0 \end{bmatrix}
$$

$$
\cdot \left(\frac{6EI}{L}\right)\left(\frac{1}{44}\right)\begin{bmatrix} 6 & -2 \\ -2 & 8 \end{bmatrix}\left(\frac{L^2}{6EI}\right)\begin{bmatrix} \frac{3}{4} & -3 \\ -\frac{3}{4} & -2 \end{bmatrix}
$$

$$
= \frac{L}{88}\begin{bmatrix} 0 & -88 \\ 0 & 0 \\ 0 & 0 \\ -44 & 0 \\ 44 & 0 \\ 0 & 0 \\ 0 & 0 \\ 0 & 0 \end{bmatrix} - \frac{L}{88}\begin{bmatrix} -3 & -48 \\ -12 & 28 \\ 12 & -28 \\ -13.5 & 4 \\ 13.5 & -4 \\ -15 & -20 \\ 15 & 20 \\ 0 & 0 \end{bmatrix} = \frac{L}{88}\begin{bmatrix} 3 & -40 \\ 12 & -28 \\ -12 & 28 \\ -30.5 & -4 \\ 30.5 & 4 \\ 15 & 20 \\ -15 & -20 \\ 0 & 0 \end{bmatrix}
$$

The end moments are then solved by $Q = bR$:

$$
\begin{Bmatrix} Q_i^a \\ Q_j^a \\ Q_i^b \\ Q_j^b \\ Q_i^c \\ Q_j^c \\ Q_i^d \\ Q_j^d \end{Bmatrix} = \frac{L}{88}\begin{bmatrix} 3 & -40 \\ 12 & -28 \\ -12 & 28 \\ -30.5 & -4 \\ 30.5 & 4 \\ 15 & 20 \\ -15 & -20 \\ 0 & 0 \end{bmatrix}\begin{Bmatrix} R_1 \\ R_2 \end{Bmatrix}
$$

Using $L = 10$ ft and $R_1 = R_2 = 10$ kips, we obtain

$$Q_i^a = -42 \text{ ft-kips}$$

$$Q_j^a = -Q_i^b = -18.2 \text{ ft-kips}$$

$$Q_j^b = -Q_i^c = -39.2 \text{ ft-kips}$$

$$Q_j^c = -Q_i^d = 39.8 \text{ ft-kips}$$

$$Q_j^d = 0$$

The answer diagram for the end moments together with the reactions at the supports found by statics is shown by the dashed line in Fig. 6-7(c).

Example 6-4

Find the end moments for the rigid frame shown in Fig. 6-9(a) by the force method. Assume constant EI.

The equivalent form of the given loaded frame is shown in Fig. 6-9(b). Because of symmetry, the vertical reaction at each support of the frame is known to be 6 kips acting upward, as indicated. If only flexural deformation is considered, then the nodal axial forces, shown in the frame in Fig. 6-9(b), only increase the compression in the two columns but cause no effect on the end moments of the frame and can therefore be neglected in the nodal force analysis for obtaining end moments. The primary structure may be chosen as the one shown in Fig. 6-10, subjected to nodal moments R_1 and R_2 and redundant reaction components of the left support, denoted by X_1 and X_2. Those

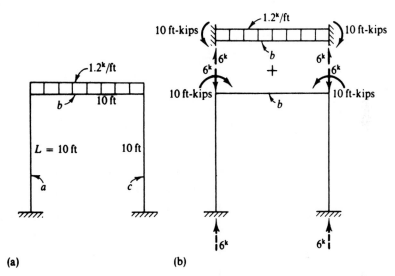

Figure 6-9

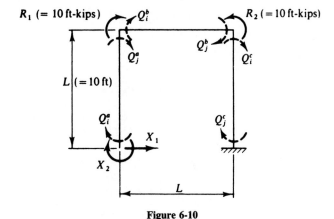

Figure 6-10

shown by dashed lines are member end moments $Q_i^a, Q_j^a, \ldots$. They can be expressed in terms of R and X as

$$R_1 = 1 \quad R_2 = 1 \qquad X_1 = 1 \quad X_2 = 1$$

$$\begin{Bmatrix} Q_i^a \\ Q_j^a \\ Q_i^b \\ Q_j^b \\ Q_i^c \\ Q_j^c \end{Bmatrix} \quad \begin{bmatrix} 0 & 0 & 0 & 1 \\ 0 & 0 & L & -1 \\ 1 & 0 & -L & 1 \\ -1 & 0 & L & -1 \\ 1 & -1 & -L & 1 \\ -1 & 1 & 0 & -1 \end{bmatrix} \begin{Bmatrix} R_1 \\ R_2 \\ \overline{} \\ X_1 \\ X_2 \end{Bmatrix}$$

$$ b_R b_X$$

From the member flexibility matrices, we form

$$f = \frac{L}{6EI} \begin{bmatrix} 2 & -1 & & & & \\ -1 & 2 & & & & \\ & & 2 & -1 & & \\ & & -1 & 2 & & \\ & & & & 2 & -1 \\ & & & & -1 & 2 \end{bmatrix}$$

Thus,

$$F_{XR} = b_X^T f b_R$$

$$= \begin{bmatrix} 0 & L & -L & L & -L & 0 \\ 1 & -1 & 1 & -1 & 1 & -1 \end{bmatrix} \left(\frac{L}{6EI}\right)$$

$$\cdot \begin{bmatrix} 2 & -1 & & & & \\ -1 & 2 & & & & \\ & & 2 & -1 & & \\ & & -1 & 2 & & \\ & & & & 2 & -1 \\ & & & & -1 & 2 \end{bmatrix} \begin{bmatrix} 0 & 0 \\ 0 & 0 \\ 1 & 0 \\ -1 & 0 \\ 1 & -1 \\ -1 & 1 \end{bmatrix}$$

$$= \frac{L}{6EI} \begin{bmatrix} -9L & 3L \\ 12 & -6 \end{bmatrix}$$

Similarly,

$$F_{XX} = b_X^T f b_X$$

$$= \frac{L}{6EI} \begin{bmatrix} 10L^2 & -12L \\ -12L & 18 \end{bmatrix}$$

from which

$$F_{XX}^{-1} = \frac{6EI}{L} \frac{\begin{bmatrix} 18 & 12L \\ 12L & 10L^2 \end{bmatrix}^T}{(180L^2 - 144L^2)} = \frac{6EI}{L} \frac{\begin{bmatrix} 18 & 12L \\ 12L & 10L^2 \end{bmatrix}}{36L^2}$$

The force transformation matrix of the indeterminate structure is

$$b = b_R - b_X F_{XX}^{-1} F_{XR}$$

$$
= \begin{bmatrix} 0 & 0 \\ 0 & 0 \\ 1 & 0 \\ -1 & 0 \\ 1 & -1 \\ -1 & 1 \end{bmatrix} - \begin{bmatrix} 0 & 1 \\ L & -1 \\ -L & 1 \\ L & -1 \\ -L & 1 \\ 0 & -1 \end{bmatrix} \left(\frac{1}{36L^2} \right) \begin{bmatrix} 18 & 12L \\ 12L & 10L^2 \end{bmatrix} \begin{bmatrix} -9L & 3L \\ 12 & -6 \end{bmatrix}
$$

$$
= \begin{bmatrix} 0 & 0 \\ 0 & 0 \\ 1 & 0 \\ -1 & 0 \\ 1 & -1 \\ -1 & 1 \end{bmatrix} - \begin{bmatrix} \frac{1}{3} & -\frac{2}{3} \\ -\frac{5}{6} & \frac{1}{6} \\ \frac{5}{6} & -\frac{1}{6} \\ -\frac{5}{6} & \frac{1}{6} \\ \frac{5}{6} & -\frac{1}{6} \\ -\frac{1}{3} & \frac{2}{3} \end{bmatrix} = \begin{bmatrix} -\frac{1}{3} & \frac{2}{3} \\ \frac{5}{6} & -\frac{1}{6} \\ \frac{1}{6} & \frac{1}{6} \\ -\frac{1}{6} & -\frac{1}{6} \\ \frac{1}{6} & -\frac{5}{6} \\ -\frac{2}{3} & \frac{1}{3} \end{bmatrix}
$$

The end moments based on the nodal force analysis are then solved by $Q = bR$:

$$
\begin{Bmatrix} Q_i^a \\ Q_j^a \\ Q_i^b \\ Q_j^b \\ Q_i^c \\ Q_j^c \end{Bmatrix} = \begin{bmatrix} -\frac{1}{3} & \frac{2}{3} \\ \frac{5}{6} & -\frac{1}{6} \\ \frac{1}{6} & \frac{1}{6} \\ -\frac{1}{6} & -\frac{1}{6} \\ \frac{1}{6} & -\frac{5}{6} \\ -\frac{2}{3} & \frac{1}{3} \end{bmatrix} \begin{Bmatrix} 10 \\ 10 \end{Bmatrix} = \begin{Bmatrix} \frac{10}{3} \\ \frac{20}{3} \\ \frac{10}{3} \\ -\frac{10}{3} \\ -\frac{20}{3} \\ -\frac{10}{3} \end{Bmatrix} \text{ ft-kips}
$$

The final result is obtained by adding the fixed-end moments [see upper part of Fig. 6-9(b)] to the end moments of member b. Thus,

$$
\begin{Bmatrix} Q_i^a \\ Q_j^a \\ Q_i^b \\ Q_j^b \\ Q_i^c \\ Q_j^c \end{Bmatrix} = \begin{Bmatrix} \frac{10}{3} \\ \frac{20}{3} \\ \frac{10}{3} \\ -\frac{10}{3} \\ -\frac{20}{3} \\ -\frac{10}{3} \end{Bmatrix} \begin{Bmatrix} \\ \\ -10 \\ +10 \\ \\ \end{Bmatrix} = \begin{Bmatrix} \frac{10}{3} \\ \frac{20}{3} \\ -\frac{20}{3} \\ \frac{20}{3} \\ -\frac{20}{3} \\ -\frac{10}{3} \end{Bmatrix} \text{ ft-kips}
$$

Example 6-5

Use the matrix force method to find the reaction at support C and the deflection and slope at B for the beam shown in Fig. 6-11(a). Assume that the spring flexibility is f_s.

We consider the spring as a member and therefore the system is composed of the beam portion, denoted as member a, and the spring, denoted as member b. The whole can be separated into two parts: the fixed-end beam under a uniform load and the system subjected to nodal forces R_1, R_2 at B and redundant reaction X at C, as shown in Fig. 6-11(b). To obtain the nodal displacements at B and reaction at C, it is necessary only to analyze the nodal load system of Fig. 6-11(b).

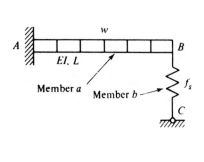

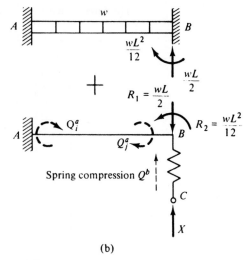

(a)   (b)

Figure 6-11

We first relate the end moments Q_i^a, Q_j^a of member a, and the spring force Q^b to the external loads R_1, R_2, and X as

$$\begin{Bmatrix} Q_i^a \\ Q_j^a \\ Q^b \end{Bmatrix} = \begin{bmatrix} -L & 1 & \vdots & L \\ 0 & -1 & \vdots & 0 \\ 0 & 0 & \vdots & 1 \end{bmatrix} \begin{Bmatrix} R_1 \\ R_2 \\ X \end{Bmatrix}$$

$$\underbrace{\phantom{\begin{matrix} -L & 1 \\ 0 & -1 \\ 0 & 0 \end{matrix}}}_{b_R} \quad \underbrace{\phantom{\begin{matrix} L \\ 0 \\ 1 \end{matrix}}}_{b_X}$$

The flexibility matrix of member a is

$$f^a = \begin{bmatrix} \dfrac{L}{3EI} & -\dfrac{L}{6EI} \\ -\dfrac{L}{6EI} & \dfrac{L}{3EI} \end{bmatrix}$$

The flexibility of member b (spring) is f_s. Therefore, the assembled flexibility is

$$f = \begin{bmatrix} \dfrac{L}{3EI} & -\dfrac{L}{6EI} & \\ -\dfrac{L}{6EI} & \dfrac{L}{3EI} & \\ & & f_s \end{bmatrix}$$

With b_R, b_X, and f obtained, we have

$$F_{XR} = b_X^T f b_R = \begin{bmatrix} -\dfrac{L^3}{3EI} & \dfrac{L^2}{2EI} \end{bmatrix}$$

$$F_{XX} = b_X^T f b_X = \dfrac{L^3}{3EI} + f_s$$

$$F_{XX}^{-1} = \dfrac{1}{L^3/3EI} + f_s$$

The redundant force X, which is equal to the spring force Q^b, is determined by

$$X = -F_{XX}^{-1} F_{XR} R$$

$$= -\left(\frac{1}{L^3/3EI + f_s}\right)\left[-\frac{L^3}{3EI} \quad \frac{L^2}{2EI}\right]\left\{\begin{array}{c} \dfrac{wL}{2} \\ \dfrac{wL^2}{12} \end{array}\right\}$$

$$= \frac{3}{8} wL \left(\frac{1}{1 + 3EIf_s/L^3}\right)$$

Apparently, if $f_s = 0$,

$$X = \tfrac{3}{8} wL$$

To find the deflection and slope at B, we use

$$r_R = F_{RR} R + F_{RX} X$$

Now, since

$$F_{RR} = b_R^T f b_R = \left[\begin{array}{cc} \dfrac{L^3}{3EI} & -\dfrac{L^2}{2EI} \\ -\dfrac{L^2}{2EI} & \dfrac{L}{EI} \end{array}\right]$$

$$F_{RX} = b_R^T f b_X = \left[\begin{array}{c} -\dfrac{L^3}{3EI} \\ \dfrac{L^2}{2EI} \end{array}\right]$$

we reach

$$\left\{\begin{array}{c} r_1 \\ r_2 \end{array}\right\} = \left[\begin{array}{cc} \dfrac{L^3}{3EI} & -\dfrac{L^2}{2EI} \\ -\dfrac{L^2}{2EI} & \dfrac{L}{EI} \end{array}\right]\left\{\begin{array}{c} R_1 \\ R_2 \end{array}\right\} + \left[\begin{array}{c} -\dfrac{L^3}{3EI} \\ \dfrac{L^2}{2EI} \end{array}\right](X)$$

Using

$$R_1 = \frac{wL}{2}, \qquad R_2 = \frac{wL^2}{12}, \qquad X = \frac{3}{8} wL \left(\frac{1}{1 + 3EIf_s/L^3}\right)$$

we obtain

$$r_1 \text{ (deflection)} = \frac{wL^4}{8EI} - \frac{L^3}{3EI}\left(\frac{\frac{3}{8}wL}{1 + 3EIf_s/L^3}\right)$$

$$= \frac{3}{8} wL \left(\frac{1}{3EI/L^3 + 1/f_s}\right)$$

$$r_2 \text{ (slope)} = -\frac{wL^3}{6EI} + \frac{L^2}{2EI}\left(\frac{\frac{3}{8}wL}{1 + 3EIf_s/L^3}\right)$$

$$= \left(-\frac{w}{2} + \frac{wL^3}{48EIf_s}\right)\left(\frac{1}{3EI/L^3 + 1/f_s}\right)$$

As a check, if $f_s = 0$ (rigid support), we have

$$r_1 = 0, \qquad r_2 = \frac{wL^3}{48EI} \quad \text{\large\texthookuparrow}$$

If $f_s = \infty$ (free end),

$$r_1 = \frac{wL^4}{8EI} \quad \downarrow, \qquad r_2 = -\frac{wL^3}{6EI} \quad \text{\large\texthookdownarrow}$$

The foregoing procedure for fixing a loaded beam is not limited to the case of distributed loads. The procedure can also be applied to members subjected to a set of concentrated loads if reducing the number of nodes is desirable.

6-9 ON THE NOTION OF PRIMARY STRUCTURE

The procedures for the analysis of statically indeterminate structures by the force method already discussed are based on the concept of *primary structure* previously developed in the method of consistent deformations. The notion of primary structure serves a convenient means of setting up an equilibrium equation. However, if we, without considering the notion of primary structure, examine the basic equation

$$Q = b_R R + b_X X$$

we observe that it merely states that Q is linearly related to a set of applied forces R and a set of unknown forces X. The equation itself does not necessarily suggest a primary structure. As a result, we may separate these two sets of influences from the two independent force systems imposed on the original structure. Doing so does not violate the truth of the preceding equation, but certainly broadens our view of handling the problem.

Now b_R represents an array of member forces in equilibrium with unit applied loads based on the original structure. More specifically, each column of b_R represents member forces in equilibrium with a certain unit load applied to the original structure. Since the original structure is statically indeterminate, many equilibrating systems may be chosen from to establish each column of b_R.

Likewise, each column of b_X can be thought of as an independent self-equilibrating internal force system for the original structure. For a structure indeterminate to the nth degree, b_X will represent any group of n independent self-equilibrating member force systems, one for each redundant.

If it is convenient, these member forces may be determined by introducing a primary structure. However, in a larger sense, the traditional notion of primary structure is not essential to the analysis of a statically indeterminate structure; rather, it introduces unnecessary restrictions to the analysis.

Example 6-6

Solve the bar forces of the truss in Fig. 5-20(a) (Example 5-15) by the preceding generalized procedures.

Solution 1   Disregarding the notion of a primary structure, we may choose a set of member forces in equilibrium with external load $R_1 = 1$, as shown in Fig. 6-12(a), and a set of self-equilibrating internal forces, as shown in Fig. 6-12(b). Thus,

$$b_R = \begin{Bmatrix} 5 \\ \frac{15}{4} \\ 5 \\ 3 \\ -5 \\ -\frac{25}{4} \end{Bmatrix}, \qquad b_X = \begin{Bmatrix} -4 \\ -3 \\ -4 \\ -3 \\ 5 \\ 5 \end{Bmatrix}$$

There are, of course, many other choices that might be made.

$$F_{XR} = b_X^T f b_R$$

$$= [-4 \quad -3 \quad -4 \quad -3 \quad 5 \quad 5]\left(\frac{1}{E}\right)\begin{Bmatrix} 5 \\ \frac{15}{4} \\ 5 \\ 3 \\ -5 \\ -\frac{25}{4} \end{Bmatrix} = -\frac{116.5}{E}$$

$$F_{XX} = b_X^T f b_X$$

$$= [-4 \quad -3 \quad -4 \quad -3 \quad 5 \quad 5]\left(\frac{1}{E}\right)\begin{Bmatrix} -4 \\ -3 \\ -4 \\ -3 \\ 5 \\ 5 \end{Bmatrix} = \frac{100}{E}$$

$$F_{XX}^{-1} = \frac{E}{100}$$

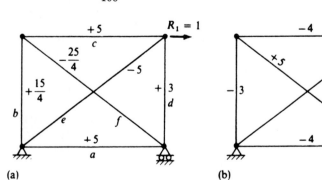

(a)   (b)

Figure 6-12

The force transformation matrix is then determined:

$$b = b_R - b_X F_{XX}^{-1} F_{XR}$$

$$= \left\{ \begin{array}{c} 5 \\ \frac{15}{4} \\ 5 \\ 3 \\ -5 \\ -\frac{25}{4} \end{array} \right\} - \left\{ \begin{array}{c} -4 \\ -3 \\ -4 \\ -3 \\ 5 \\ 5 \end{array} \right\} \left(\frac{E}{100} \right) \left(\frac{-116.5}{E} \right) = \left\{ \begin{array}{c} 5 \\ 3.75 \\ 5 \\ 3 \\ -5 \\ -6.25 \end{array} \right\} - \left\{ \begin{array}{c} 4.660 \\ 3.495 \\ 4.660 \\ 3.495 \\ -5.825 \\ -5.825 \end{array} \right\} = \left\{ \begin{array}{c} 0.340 \\ 0.255 \\ 0.340 \\ -0.495 \\ 0.825 \\ -0.425 \end{array} \right\}$$

We obtain Q by $Q = bR$:

$$\left\{ \begin{array}{c} Q^a \\ Q^b \\ Q^c \\ Q^d \\ Q^e \\ Q^f \end{array} \right\} = \left\{ \begin{array}{c} 0.340 \\ 0.255 \\ 0.340 \\ -0.495 \\ 0.825 \\ -0.425 \end{array} \right\} (12) = \left\{ \begin{array}{c} 4.08 \\ 3.06 \\ 4.08 \\ -5.94 \\ 9.90 \\ -5.10 \end{array} \right\} \text{kips}$$

Solution 2 It may be interesting to point out that, when primary structure is used in analyzing an indeterminate structure, the same final results will be obtained if different primary structures are chosen in developing b_R and b_X.

To illustrate, let us first take member e as the redundant. The bar forces associated with the given primary structure due to external load $R_1 = 1$ are elements of b_R, as indicated in Fig. 6-13(a). Next, let member a be chosen as the redundant. Setting the redundant force equal to unity, we obtain a set of internal forces in equilibrium [Fig. 6-13(b)], which forms b_X.

$$b_R = \left\{ \begin{array}{c} 1 \\ \frac{3}{4} \\ 1 \\ 0 \\ 0 \\ -\frac{5}{4} \end{array} \right\}, \qquad b_X = \left\{ \begin{array}{c} 1 \\ \frac{3}{4} \\ 1 \\ \frac{3}{4} \\ -\frac{5}{4} \\ -\frac{5}{4} \end{array} \right\}$$

$$F_{XR} = b_X^T f b_R$$

$$= [1 \quad \tfrac{3}{4} \quad 1 \quad \tfrac{3}{4} \quad -\tfrac{5}{4} \quad -\tfrac{5}{4}] \left(\frac{1}{E} \right) \left\{ \begin{array}{c} 1 \\ \frac{3}{4} \\ 1 \\ 0 \\ 0 \\ -\frac{5}{4} \end{array} \right\} = \frac{66}{16E}$$

$$F_{XX} = b_X^T f b_X$$

$$= [1 \quad \tfrac{3}{4} \quad 1 \quad \tfrac{3}{4} \quad -\tfrac{5}{4} \quad -\tfrac{5}{4}] \left(\frac{1}{E} \right) \left\{ \begin{array}{c} 1 \\ \frac{3}{4} \\ 1 \\ \frac{3}{4} \\ -\frac{5}{4} \\ -\frac{5}{4} \end{array} \right\} = \frac{100}{16E}$$

$$F_{XX}^{-1} = \frac{16E}{100}$$

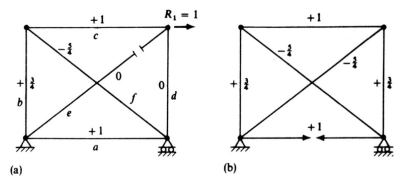

Figure 6-13

The force transformation matrix b is found to be

$$b = b_R - b_X F_{XX}^{-1} F_{XR} = \left\{ \begin{matrix} 1 \\ \frac{3}{4} \\ 1 \\ 0 \\ 0 \\ -\frac{5}{4} \end{matrix} \right\} - \left\{ \begin{matrix} 1 \\ \frac{3}{4} \\ 1 \\ \frac{3}{4} \\ -\frac{5}{4} \\ -\frac{5}{4} \end{matrix} \right\} \left(\frac{16E}{100} \right) \left(\frac{66}{16E} \right) = \left\{ \begin{matrix} 0.340 \\ 0.255 \\ 0.340 \\ -0.495 \\ 0.825 \\ -0.425 \end{matrix} \right\}$$

the same as previously obtained.

6-10 COMPUTER IMPLEMENTATION OF THE MATRIX FORCE METHOD

As shown in the example problems in the previous two sections, the computational procedure of the matrix forced method is straightforward. If it is executed by hand computation, however, the amount of computation is no different from that of the more conventional methods. The advantage of the matrix method lies in the ease of computer implementation. Two issues need to be considered before automated computation can be implemented.

6-10a Automatic Generation of Equilibrium Equations

In computer implementation, the matrices b_R and b_X will be solved from a set of equilibrium equations instead of being given from hand computation. The equilibrium equations are the collection of nodal equilibrium conditions of all the nodes.

Consider the loaded frame as shown in Fig. 6-14(a). There are $3 \times 5 = 15$ equilibrium equations, three from each of the five nodes. There are 17 unknown member forces (12 from the four members, 3 from support 1, and 2 from support 4). The structure is statically indeterminate to the second degree. By assigning an x–y coordinate system as shown in Fig. 4-16(a), we may express all the external load accordingly.

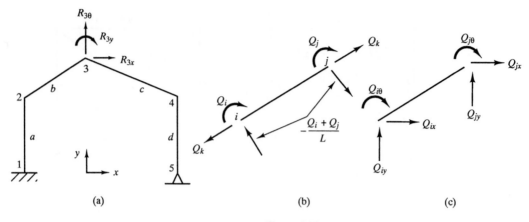

Figure 6-14

Let us consider a typical node, say node 3. The three equilibrium equations at node 3 will include the member forces of member b and member c. These member forces are defined according to their *local coordinate system* as shown in Fig. 6-14(b) for any typical member. They must be transformed into the *global coordinate system* $(x-y)$ as shown in Fig. 6-14(c) before being summed up to balance the external loads. Note that in Fig. 6-14(b) and (c) we have dropped the superscript for member designation in the interest of clarity. By equating the nodal force and moment in Figs. 6-14(b) and 6-14(c), we arrive at the following two transformation equations. For node i,

$$\begin{Bmatrix} Q_{ix} \\ Q_{iy} \\ Q_{i\theta} \end{Bmatrix} = \begin{bmatrix} \dfrac{S}{L} & \dfrac{S}{L} & -C \\ -\dfrac{C}{L} & -\dfrac{C}{L} & -S \\ 1 & 0 & 0 \end{bmatrix} \begin{Bmatrix} Q_i \\ Q_j \\ Q_k \end{Bmatrix} \tag{6-28}$$

For node j,

$$\begin{Bmatrix} Q_{jx} \\ Q_{jy} \\ Q_{j\theta} \end{Bmatrix} = \begin{bmatrix} -\dfrac{S}{L} & -\dfrac{S}{L} & C \\ \dfrac{C}{L} & \dfrac{C}{L} & S \\ 0 & 1 & 0 \end{bmatrix} \begin{Bmatrix} Q_i \\ Q_j \\ Q_k \end{Bmatrix} \tag{6-29}$$

where

$$C = \frac{x_j - x_i}{L}, \qquad S = \frac{y_j - y_i}{L} \tag{6-30}$$

are the cosine and sine of the angle of orientation of the member. Note that the orientation of the member is defined by the direction from the starting node (i) to the terminating node (j), and the angle is measured counterclockwise from the x axis to the member direction.

The three equilibrium equations at node 3 are

$$Q_{jx}^b + Q_{ix}^c = R_{3X}$$

$$Q_{jy}^b + Q_{iy}^c = R_{3Y}$$

$$Q_{j\theta}^b + Q_{i\theta}^c = R_{3\theta}$$

Now the superscripts are necessary to indicate the member to which the forces belong. Upon substituting Eqs. 6-28 and 6-29 for the two members, the three equations become

$$
\begin{bmatrix}
-\left(\dfrac{S}{L}\right)_b & -\left(\dfrac{S}{L}\right)_b & C_b & \left(\dfrac{S}{L}\right)_c & \left(\dfrac{S}{L}\right)_c & -C_c \\[2mm]
\left(\dfrac{C}{L}\right)_b & \left(\dfrac{C}{L}\right)_b & S_b & -\left(\dfrac{C}{L}\right)_c & -\left(\dfrac{C}{L}\right)_c & -S_c \\[2mm]
0 & 1 & 0 & 1 & 0 & 0
\end{bmatrix}
\begin{Bmatrix}
Q_i^b \\ Q_j^b \\ Q_k^b \\ Q_i^c \\ Q_j^c \\ Q_k^c
\end{Bmatrix}
=
\begin{Bmatrix}
R_{3X} \\ R_{3Y} \\ R_{3\theta}
\end{Bmatrix}
$$

where the member designation is either in the superscripts or in the subscripts. We may repeat the same procedure at nodes 2 and 4.

At the support nodes 1 and 5, however, additional convention is needed. The supports are replaced with reaction members as shown in Fig. 6-15 for general support conditions. The constraint against translation is represented by a link and that against rotation is represented by a torsional spring. The force in each link and the moment in each torsional spring are the reactional forces and moments, respectively. If the flexibility coefficient in these links and springs is put to zero, then the movements at the supports are suppressed. Otherwise, nonzero constants may be assigned to allow movements.

With these conventions introduced, the support at node 5, for example, is replaced with two links as shown in Fig. 6-16(a), and the forces involved at node 5

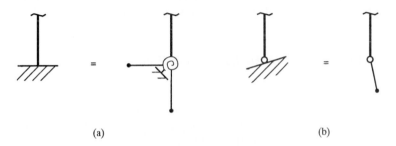

(a)   (b)

Figure 6-15

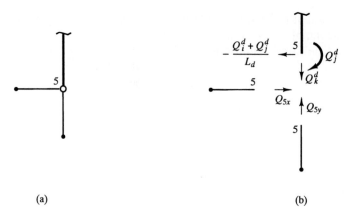

(a)   (b)

Figure 6-16

are shown in Fig. 6-16(b). The three equilibrium equations at node 5 are then established.

$$\begin{bmatrix} \left(\frac{1}{L}\right)_d & \left(\frac{1}{L}\right)_d & 0 & 1 & 0 \\ 0 & 0 & -1 & 0 & 1 \\ 0 & 1 & 0 & 0 & 0 \end{bmatrix} \begin{Bmatrix} Q_i^d \\ Q_j^d \\ Q_k^d \\ Q_{5x} \\ Q_{5y} \end{Bmatrix} = \begin{Bmatrix} 0 \\ 0 \\ 0 \end{Bmatrix}$$

When all the equations are generated and arranged according to the node number and the unknown member forces properly numbered in sequence, the equilibrium equations may be represented by the matrix equation

$$AQ = R \qquad\qquad (6\text{-}31)$$

where A is a rectangular matrix containing all the coefficients on the left-hand side of the equilibrium equation, Q contains all the unknown member forces, including reaction forces, and R is the applied force vector. In the computer memory, only the matrix A and the vector R need to be stored. For the frame under consideration, the size of matrix A is 15×17, and R is a vector of length 15.

6-10b Solution of the Equilibrium Equation

Note that Eq. (6-31) is established without the notion of primary structure. Now we need to introduce the imaginary cuts and pairs of external loads denoted by a vector X. We may also write the following equation, which simply states that the internal member forces corresponding to the cuts are equal to the external loads X.

$$A_X Q = X \qquad\qquad (6\text{-}32)$$

The matrix A_X contains zero and a single 1 in each row to identify the member forces. For example, if we decide to select the support forces Q_{5x} and Q_{5y} as redundant forces, then the links in Fig. 6-16(a) will be cut, and two pairs of external forces X_1 and X_2 are inserted at the cuts. The A_x matrix is 2×17. The 16th element in row 1 and the 17th element in row 2 are of the value 1, and all other elements are zero.

By combining Eqs. 6-31 and 6-32, we obtain

$$A'Q = \begin{Bmatrix} R \\ X \end{Bmatrix} \tag{6-33}$$

where

$$A' = \begin{bmatrix} A \\ A_X \end{bmatrix} \tag{6-34}$$

is now a square matrix (17×17).

Using the Gaussian elimination method (Appendix A), we may obtain the inverse of A' and denote it by b'. In other words,

$$Q = b' \begin{Bmatrix} R \\ X \end{Bmatrix} \tag{6-35}$$

Comparing Eq. 6-35 to Eq. 6-5, we conclude that the matrix b' actually contains the two submatrices b_R and b_X.

$$b' = \begin{bmatrix} b_R & b_X \end{bmatrix} \tag{6-36}$$

Once the matrices b_R and b_X are obtained, the rest of the solution may be obtained using the formulas given in Sec. 6-6 through simple matrix multiplications.

It is seen that the matrix force method can be programmed easily for computer execution. The selection of redundant forces can be made in one of two ways: (1) random selection by computer and (2) user input. In random selection by computer, there is a risk of selecting a primary structure that is unstable, rendering the matrix A' singular. Thus, a trial-and-error scheme must be implemented. For simplicity, therefore, the programs described in Appendix B for the matrix force method require user input in redundant force selection. Users are encouraged to use the programs given in Appendix B either to check or to replace hand computation in the following problems.

PROBLEMS

6-1. Use the force method to find the vertical deflection at each of the loaded points of the beam shown in Fig. 6-17. Assume constant EI.

6-2. Use the force method to find the slope and deflection at the loaded point of the beam shown in Fig. 6-18.

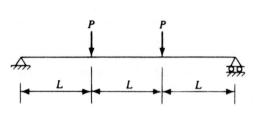

Figure 6-17   Figure 6-18

6-3. Find, by the force method, all the bar forces and the vertical deflection at each of the loaded joints of the truss shown in Fig. 6-19. Assume that $A = 10$ in.^{2} and $E = 30,000$ kips/in.^{2} for all members.

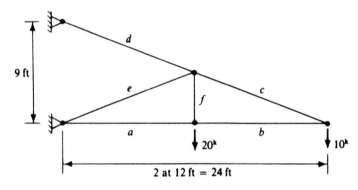

Figure 6-19

6-4. Find, by the force method, all the member forces (end moments) and the nodal displacements corresponding to the applied loads for the frame in Fig. 6-20. Assume constant EI.

6-5. Find, by the force method, the slope and deflection at the loaded end of the beam shown in Fig. 6-21. Assume constant EI.

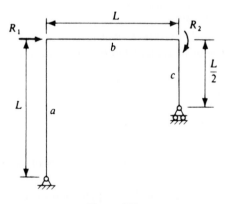

Figure 6-20

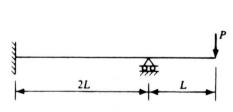

Figure 6-21

6-6. Find, by the force method, the bar forces and the deflection components at the loaded point of the truss in Fig. 6-22. Assume that $A = 10$ in.^{2} and $E = 30,000$ kips/in.^{2} for all members.

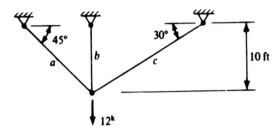

12^k **Figure 6-22**

6-7. The truss shown in Fig. 6-23 is statically indeterminate to the first degree. Choose the axial force in bar c as redundant. Use the force method to find the bar forces and the deflection components corresponding to the applied loads. Assume that $A = 50$ cm^2 and $E = 20,000$ kN/cm^2 for all bars.

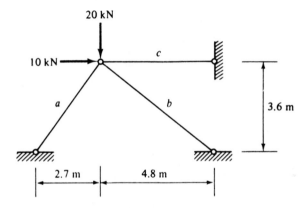

Figure 6-23

6-8. Use the force method to obtain the member end moments for the frame shown in Fig. 6-24. Assume constant EI.

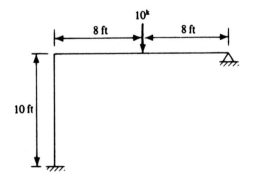

Figure 6-24

6-9. Use the force method to find the member end moments for the frame shown in Fig. 6-25. Assume constant EI.

6-10. Refer to Fig. 6-26. Find, by the force method, the slope and deflection of the beam at the point B.

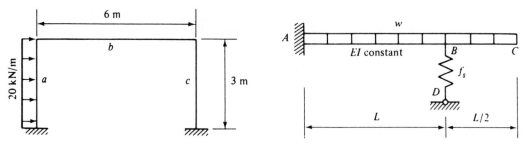

Figure 6-25   Figure 6-26

6-11. Use the force method to find the member end moments for the gable bent in Fig. 6-27. Assume constant EI.

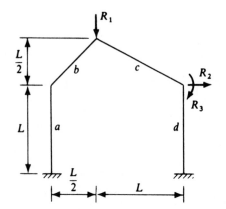

Figure 6-27

6-12. Solve Problem 6-6 disregarding the notion of primary structure.

6-13. Solve Problem 6-7 disregarding the notion of primary structure.

6-14. Solve Problem 6-8 by using different primary structures for developing the force transformation matrices b_R and b_X.

Chapter 7

Moment Distribution Method

7-1 GENERAL

Throughout the preceding chapters we have used forces as the basic unknowns in the analysis of structures. Accordingly, these methods of analysis are referred to as *force methods*. We have learned that in the force methods the *static determinacy* of a structure plays a major role in the process of analysis. In this and the next two chapters, we will use displacements as the basic unknowns. The methods we introduce will be referred to as *displacement methods*. In displacement methods, static determinacy does not affect the solution process at all. Rather, the number of displacement unknowns, often called *degrees of freedom* (dof) dictates the cost of computing.

The method of moment distribution was originated by Hardy Cross in 1930 in a paper entitled "Analysis of Continuous Frames by Distributing Fixed-end Moments." It is a highly efficient method for beams and frames with only a few nodal rotational dof's but high degrees of static indeterminacy. As we shall see, the use of displacements in the moment distribution method is actually implicit. In other words, the displacement unknowns do not appear explicitly in the solution process, but the effect of displacement, that moments get distributed, does. In the following sections, we will use the word *joint* to replace *node*, just to conform to tradition.

7-2 LOCKING AND FIXED-END MOMENT

Let us consider the frame shown in Fig. 7-1(a) loaded by a single moment at joint j. Because of the clamped support conditions, the only joint displacement unknown is the rotation of joint j, which may be denoted by θ_j.

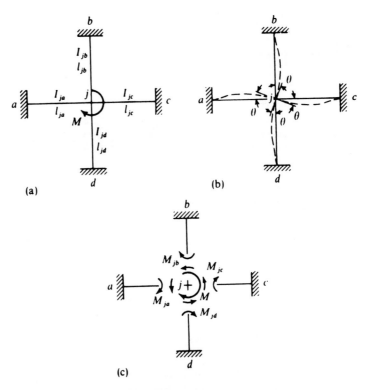

Figure 7-1

Note that joint j does not have translational displacements because the axial deformation of each member is neglected. Before the moment is applied, clearly θ_j is zero. The effect of the applied joint moment is to turn the rigid joint clockwise [Fig. 7-1(b)]. In that process, the applied joint moment is distributed to each of the four members [Fig. 7-1(c)]. Intuitively, we may conclude that the moment is equally distributed to the four members, if they are identical. Thus, without even knowing how much is the joint rotation θ_j, we may still be able to obtain the member-end moments, $M_{ja} = M_{jb} = M_{jc} = M_{jd} = M/4$. Note that clockwise moments and rotations are considered positive. The subscripts associated with moments identify the member and the joint at which the moments are acting. Thus, M_{ja} is the member-end moment of member a–j acting at j, the first subscript.

Now consider the same frame loaded by a uniformly distributed load on the member j–c, as shown in Fig. 7-2(a). The effect of the uniformly distributed load may be recognized by first *locking* the joint j to allow no rotation [Fig. 7-2(b)]. This will introduce no moment at the unloaded members, but the loaded member j–c is now in a state of being fixed at both ends. As far as the member j–c is concerned, the moments at the fixed ends, called fixed-end moments, may be found by the method of consistent deformations as described in Chapter 5. For typical loadings, including the uniformly distributed load, the fixed-end moments, denoted by M^F or F.E.M. in tables and illustrations, are given in Appendix D.

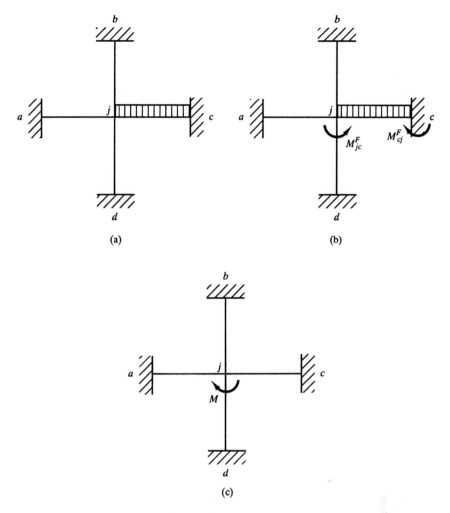

Figure 7-2

The locking process introduces an artificial device that supplies the joint moment at j needed to maintain the fixed-end moment MF_{jc}^F. Thus, $M = M_{jc}^F$. To obtain the solution of the original frame without the artificial device, we need to cancel the effect of locking by applying an equal and opposite joint moment M, as shown in Fig. 7-2(c). Now the situation in Fig. 7-2(c) is identical to that of Fig. 7-1(a). If the members are identical, the member-end moments $M_{ja} = M_{jb} = M_{jc} = M_{jd} = M/4$. The final solution is obtained by superposing the solutions of Figs. 7-2(b) and (c). The process of canceling the locking effect is called *unlocking*, and its effect is to distribute the unbalanced joint moment. If the four members are not identical, then we must know the *stiffness* of each member before we may distribute the joint moment.

7-3 UNLOCKING, STIFFNESS, AND CARRY-OVER FACTOR

During unlocking, the rigid joint j in Fig. 7-1(b) rotates by a certain amount, θ_j, and so is the end of all members connected at j. This process introduces member-end moments at each of the members [Fig. 7-1(c)]. Equilibrium of the joint requires that

$$M_{ja} + M_{jb} + M_{jc} + M_{jd} = M \tag{7-1}$$

Each of the member-end moments in Eq. 7-1 is obviously proportional to the joint rotation, but the proportional constant depends on the properties of each member. To find the relationship between the member-end moment and the joint rotation, basically we need to solve the problem shown in Fig. 7-3. This is the problem that allows no translation and rotation at the far end, b, and allows only rotation at the near end, a.

Many methods may be used to solve this problem. We choose to solve the differential equation

$$EI\frac{d^4 y}{dx^4} = 0 \tag{7-2}$$

which is obtained by differentiating twice Eq. 4-4a,

$$\frac{d^2 y}{dx^2} = -\frac{M}{EI} \tag{4-4a}$$

and noting that

$$\frac{dM}{dx} = V$$

and

$$\frac{dV}{dx} = -w = 0$$

See Sec. 4-3. In these equations, the x axis originates at a in Fig. 7-3 and points to the right, and the deflection y is downward.

The solution of Eq. 7-2 is obviously a cubic function in x, because the equation is a homogeneous equation in the fourth order. Let us assume that $y(x) = a_0 + a_1 x + a_2 x^2 + a_3 x^3$. Using the four conditions $y(0) = 0$, $y(l) = 0$, $y'(0) = \theta_a$,

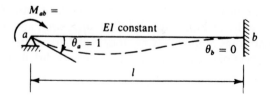

$M_{ab} =$

EI constant

$\theta_a = 1$

$\theta_b = 0$

l

Figure 7-3

and $y'(l) = 0$, where the prime denotes differentiation with respect to x, we obtain $a_0 = 0$, $a_1 = \theta_a$, $a_2 = -2\theta_a/l$, and $a_3 = \theta_a/l^2$. Thus,

$$y = x\left(1 - \frac{x}{l}\right)^2 \theta_a \tag{7-3}$$

From Eq. 4-4a, the moment is calculated as

$$M = E\frac{I}{l}\left(4 - 6\frac{x}{l}\right)\theta_a \tag{7-4}$$

By putting $x = 0$ in Eq. 7-4, we get

$$M_{ab} = 4E\frac{I}{l}\theta_a \tag{7-5}$$

It is customary to denote the ratio of I to l by K and call it the *stiffness factor of the member*.

$$K = \frac{I}{l} \tag{7-6}$$

Equation 7-5 can then be rewritten as

$$M_{ab} = 4EK\theta_a \tag{7-7}$$

This equation indicates that to produce a unit rotation at a, as shown in Fig. 7-3, the amount of moment at a is $4EK$. This proportional constant is called the *member stiffness* and is denoted by S.

$$S = 4EK \tag{7-8}$$

Now that we have the member stiffness, we may return to Fig. 7-1 and write the member-end moments for the four members at joint j, which rotates by an angle θ.

$$M_{ja} = 4E\frac{I_{ja}}{l_{ja}}\theta = 4EK_{ja}\theta = S_{ja}\theta$$

$$M_{jb} = 4E\frac{I_{jb}}{l_{jb}}\theta = 4EK_{jb}\theta = S_{jb}\theta$$

$$M_{jc} = 4E\frac{I_{jc}}{l_{jc}}\theta = 4EK_{jc}\theta = S_{jc}\theta \tag{7-9}$$

$$M_{jd} = 4E\frac{I_{jd}}{l_{jd}}\theta = 4EK_{ja}\theta = S_{jd}\theta$$

Substituting Eq. 7-8 in Eq. 7-1, we obtain

$$(S_{ja} + S_{jb} + S_{jc} + S_{jd})\theta = M$$

or

$$4E(K_{ja} + K_{jb} + K_{jc} + K_{jd})\theta = M$$

Thus,

$$\theta = \frac{M}{4E \Sigma K} \tag{7-10}$$

where $\Sigma K = K_{ja} + K_{jb} + K_{jc} + K_{jd}$.

From Eqs. 7-9 and 7-10, we see that

$$M_{ja} = \frac{K_{ja}}{\Sigma K} M = D_{ja} M$$

$$M_{jb} = \frac{K_{jb}}{\Sigma K} M = D_{jb} M$$

$$M_{jc} = \frac{K_{jc}}{\Sigma K} M = D_{jc} M \tag{7-11}$$

$$M_{jd} = \frac{K_{jd}}{\Sigma K} M = D_{jd} M$$

in which the ratio $K_{ji}/\Sigma K$ or D_{ji} $(i = a, b, c, d)$ is defined as the *distribution factor*. Thus, a moment resisted by a joint will be distributed among the connecting members in proportion to their distribution factors. In determining the distribution factors, only the relative K values for connected members are needed. Thus, in most cases we are concerned with the *relative stiffness* rather than the absolute stiffness (Eq. 7-8).

As the moment at joint j is distributed to each member according to their stiffness through a rotation, there are moments induced at the far end of these members. For a typical member, the far end moment may be obtained also from the solution in Eq. 7-4.

Referring to Fig. 7-4, we put $x = l$ in Eq. 7-4 to obtain

$$M_{ba} = 2EK\theta_a \tag{7-12}$$

where a minus sign in the moment is removed because M_{ba} is already plotted as clockwise in Fig. 7-4. It should be cautioned that a distinction must be made about the sign conventions for moment diagrams and the member-end moment used herein. The latter is positive if acting in the clockwise direction irrespective of which end it acts on.

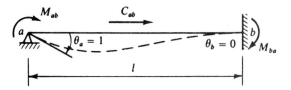

Figure 7-4

In the context of the moment distribution method, if joint a rotates, the moment at a is a *distributed moment*, which is carried over to the other end (Fig. 7-4) to induce M_{ba}. The ratio between the *carry-over moment* M_{ba} and the distributed moment M_{ab} is called the *carry-over factor* and is denoted by C_{ab}.

$$M_{ba} = C_{ab} M_{ab} \tag{7-13}$$

The stiffness factor and the carry-over factor remain the same if we consider b as the rotating joint and a as the far end because the beam is assumed to be prismatic. From Eqs. 7-7, 7-12, and 7-13, we note that

$$C_{ab} = C_{ba} = \frac{1}{2} \tag{7-14}$$

Referring to Fig. 7-1 again, we obtain the moments at the far ends (fixed ends) of the four members as

$$M_{aj} = 2E\frac{I_{ja}}{l_{ja}}\theta = \left(\frac{1}{2}\right)M_{ja}$$

$$M_{bj} = 2E\frac{I_{jb}}{l_{jb}}\theta = \left(\frac{1}{2}\right)M_{jb}$$

$$M_{cj} = 2E\frac{I_{jc}}{l_{jc}}\theta = \left(\frac{1}{2}\right)M_{jc} \tag{7-15}$$

$$M_{dj} = 2E\frac{I_{jd}}{l_{jd}}\theta = \left(\frac{1}{2}\right)M_{jd}$$

We recapitulate some of the main points of Secs. 7-2 and 7-3 as follows. When an external moment is applied to a joint whose translation is prevented, the joint rotates; but the rotation is checked by members meeting at the joint. The resisting moment is then distributed to the near ends of the connected members according to their distribution factors, provided that all the far ends of these members are fixed. The distributed moment to the near end for each member based on the free body of the member (not the joint) equals the applied moment times the distribution factor bearing the same sign as that of the applied moment. Meanwhile, moment is carried over to the far end of each member, which equals one-half the distributed moment to the near end and bears the same sign.

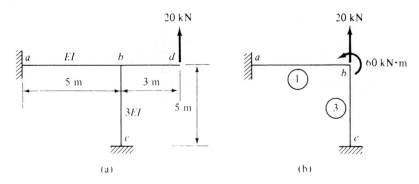

Figure 7-5

In subsequent illustrations and tables we often use the symbols D.M. to denote the distributed moment; D.F., the distribution factor; C.O.M., the carry-over moment; and C.O.F., the carry-over factor.

Example 7-1

For the loaded frame shown in Fig. 7-5(a), find the end moments at a and c.

We begin by putting the portion abc of Fig. 7-5(a) into its equivalent [Fig. 7-5(b)] and obtaining the relative K values for members ab and bc (circled). It is then readily seen that the end moments at a and c are the carry-over moments due to the external moment 60 kN · m applied to joint b. Thus,

$$M_{ab} = \frac{1}{2}M_{ba} = \left(\frac{1}{2}\right)(-60)\left(\frac{1}{3+1}\right) = -7.5 \text{ kN} \cdot \text{m}$$

$$M_{cb} = \frac{1}{2}M_{bc} = \left(\frac{1}{2}\right)(-60)\left(\frac{3}{3+1}\right) = -22.5 \text{ kN} \cdot \text{m}$$

The negative signs indicate counterclockwise moments.

7-4 PROCESS OF LOCKING AND UNLOCKING: ONE JOINT

The essence of moment distribution lies in locking and unlocking the joints based on the principle of superposition; that is, the effect of an artificial moment applied to a rigid joint of the frame and then eliminated is the same as no effect on the actual structure, since the two actions are neutralized. In this section our attention is confined to those frames that have all joints (including supported ends) fixed except one, which is allowed to rotate. Figure 7-6(a) shows the case, which may then be considered as the superposition of effects of Fig. 7-6(b) and (c).

In connection with the setup in Fig. 7-6, we note the following:

1. Suppose that the artificial moment M imposed on joint e [see Fig. 7-6(b)] is so chosen as to just lock the joint against rotation (keeping $\theta_e = 0$) under the original loading (in the present case, the uniform load over span ae). Each member

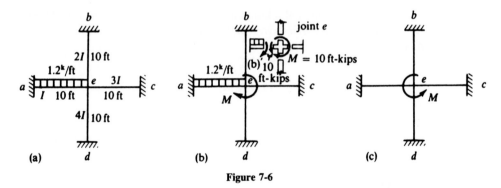

Figure 7-6

of the frame is then in the state of a fixed-end beam; consequently, fixed-end moments will be developed at the ends of member ae:

$$M_{ea}^F = -M_{ae}^F = \frac{(1.2)(10)^2}{12} = 10 \text{ ft-kips}$$

all other member ends being subjected to no moment. The results are shown in row 1 of Table 7-1.

Referring to Fig. 7-6(b), we find that the equilibrium condition

$$\sum M_{\text{joint } e} = 0$$

requires that the locking moment

$$M = 10 \text{ ft-kips}$$

act clockwise on joint e.

2. Next, let us release the joint e from the artificial restraint, that is, apply to it an unlocking moment equal and opposite to the locking moment. Referring to Fig. 7-6(c), we see a counterclockwise M equal to the value of 10 ft-kips:

$$M = -10 \text{ ft-kips}$$

is thus applied to joint e.

TABLE 7-1

		ae		be		ce		de	
		ae		be		ce		de	
Row	Step	M_{ae}	M_{ea}	M_{be}	M_{eb}	M_{ce}	M_{ec}	M_{de}	M_{ed}
1	F.E.M.	−10	+10	0	0	0	0	0	0
2	D.M.	0	−1	0	−2	0	−3	0	−4
3	C.O.M.	−0.5	0	−1	0	−1.5	0	−2	0
4	Σ	−10.5	+9	−1	−2	−1.5	−3	−2	−4

As a result of this unlocking moment, the resisting moment will be distributed at the near ends and carried over to the far ends, as described in preceding sections. Thus,

$$M_{ea} = (-10)\left(\frac{1}{10}\right) = -1.0 \text{ ft-kip}, \qquad M_{ae} = (-1)\left(\frac{1}{2}\right) = -0.5 \text{ ft-kip}$$

$$M_{eb} = (-10)\left(\frac{2}{10}\right) = -2.0 \text{ ft-kips}, \qquad M_{be} = (-2)\left(\frac{1}{2}\right) = -1.0 \text{ ft-kip}$$

$$M_{ec} = (-10)\left(\frac{3}{10}\right) = -3.0 \text{ ft-kips}, \qquad M_{ce} = (-3)\left(\frac{1}{2}\right) = -1.5 \text{ ft-kips}$$

$$M_{ed} = (-10)\left(\frac{4}{10}\right) = -4.0 \text{ ft-kips}, \qquad M_{de} = (-4)\left(\frac{1}{2}\right) = -2.0 \text{ ft-kips}$$

They are shown in rows 2 and 3 of Table 7-1, respectively.

3. The sum of the results from steps 1 to 3 gives the solution, as shown in row 4 of Table 7-1.

In analyzing problems like this, with all ends fixed except one rigid joint allowed to rotate, the method of moment distribution provides a very rapid tool, since it involves only one round of locking and unlocking. More examples to illustrate this process follow.

Example 7-2

The end moments at a, b, and c for the beam and loading shown in Fig. 7-7(a) may be obtained by locking joint b and then unlocking it, as indicated in Fig. 7-7(b) and (c). The complete analysis is shown in Fig. 7-7(d), which contains the following steps:

1. The values of stiffness for members ab and bc are found to be

$$K_{ab} = \frac{4EI}{60}, \qquad K_{bc} = \frac{4EI}{40}$$

Multiplying each by $30/EI$ gives the relative K values (circled).

2. The distribution factors are computed according to $K/\Sigma K$. Thus,

$$D_{ba} = \frac{2}{2+3} = 0.4, \qquad D_{bc} = \frac{3}{2+3} = 0.6$$

We consider the immovable supports at a and c with infinite stiffness so that

$$D_{ab} = D_{cb} = 0$$

The distribution factors are indicated in the attached box at each joint.

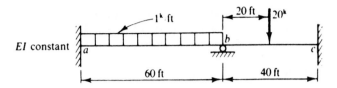

(a)

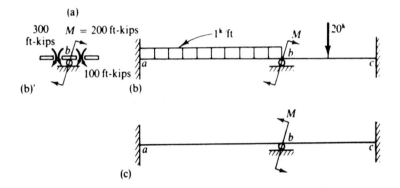

(b)'   (b)

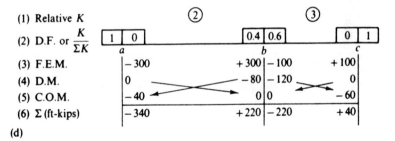

(c)

(1) Relative K		②		③	
(2) D.F. or $\dfrac{K}{\Sigma K}$	1	0	0.4	0.6	0	1
	a		b			c
(3) F.E.M.	-300		$+300$	-100	$+100$	
(4) D.M.	0		-80	-120	0	
(5) C.O.M.	-40		0	0	-60	
(6) Σ (ft-kips)	-340		$+220$	-220	$+40$	

(d)

Figure 7-7

3. The locking joint b artificially puts members ab and bc in the state of fixed-end beams. We write the fixed-end moments as

$$M_{ab}^F = -M_{ba}^F = -\frac{(1)(60)^2}{12} = -300 \text{ ft-kips}$$

$$M_{bc}^F = -M_{cb}^F = -\frac{(20)(40)}{8} = -100 \text{ ft-kips}$$

Note that locking joint b means applying an external clockwise moment equal to 200 ft-kips, required by the equilibrium of moments for that joint [see Fig. 7-7(b)'].

4. Unlocking joint b (i.e., eliminating the artificial restraint acting on joint b) means applying an external counterclockwise moment equal to 200 ft-kips. We write the distributed moment for each of the near ends according to the distribution factor.

5. Write down the carry-over moment for each of the far ends equal to one-half the distributed moment of the near end.

6. The sum of the results from steps 3, 4, and 5 gives the solution.

Example 7-3

Find the end moments for the frame shown in Fig. 7-8(a) resulting from the rotational yield of support a 0.0016 rad clockwise. EI = 10,000 kips-ft^2.

The moment required to produce a rotation of 0.0016 rad at a is given by

$$M = \frac{4EI_{ab}\,\theta_a}{l_{ab}} = \frac{(4)(10.000)(0.0016)}{10} = 6.4 \text{ ft-kips}$$

if joint b is temporarily fixed. Half the amount of this moment will be carried over to end b of member ab. By releasing joint b, a process of distribution and carry-over takes place, as recorded in Fig. 7-8(b). This gives

$$M_{ab} = 5.6 \text{ ft-kips}, \qquad M_{ba} = -M_{bc} = 1.6 \text{ ft-kips}, \qquad M_{cb} = -0.8 \text{ ft-kip}$$

7-5 PROCESS OF LOCKING AND UNLOCKING: TWO OR MORE JOINTS

For a rigid frame or continuous beam having no joint translation but involving more than one joint permitted to rotate, the process of moment distribution consists of the repeated application of the principle of superposition, as stated briefly in the following steps:

1. The joints are first locked; all members, accordingly, are fixed end. Write the fixed-end moments for all members.

2. The joints are then unlocked. Only one joint at a time is selected to be unlocked. While one joint is unlocked, the rest of joints are assumed to be held against rotation. Calculate the unlocking moment at this joint, and write distributed moments for the near ends of the members meeting at this joint.

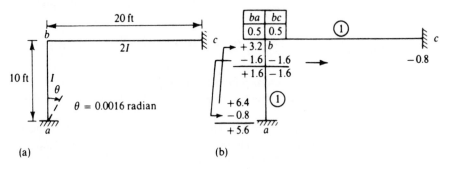

(a)   (b)

Figure 7-8

3. Also write down the carry-over moments at the far ends of these members. Note that the carry-over moments constitute a new set of fixed-end moments for the far ends.

4. Relock the joint, and select the next joint to be unlocked. Repeat steps 2 and 3. Note that after a joint is unlocked and the moments at a joint distributed, the joint is in balance, or in equilibrium, since the artificial restraint is removed. However, there are other joints still locked by external means; hence, the next step is to relock the joint and then proceed to unlock the next joint. The process of locking and unlocking each joint only once constitutes *one cycle* of moment distribution.

5. Joints are unlocked and relocked one by one; therefore, steps 2 and 3 are repeated several times. The process can be halted as soon as the carry-over moments are so small that we are willing to neglect them.

6. Sum up the moments to obtain the final result.

We see that the analysis starts from an alteration of the original structure by locking all joints against rotation. This means that artificial restraints are actually applied to the original structure. The altered structure, consisting of a number of fixed-end members, is then modified by unlocking and relocking joints one by one until all artificial restraints are removed or diminished to a sufficiently small amount. Thus, moment distribution is a method of successive approximations by which the exact results can be approached with the desired degree of precision.

The complete analysis of a loaded three-span continuous beam by moment distribution, shown in Fig. 7-9, will illustrate the foregoing procedure.

The presentation of moment distribution in Fig. 7-9, may be rearranged as shown in Fig. 7-10. At first glance it seems as if joints *b* and *c* were locked and then unlocked simultaneously. However, the performance can still be considered under the restriction of unlocking one joint at a time. For the loads given, the fixed-end moments are recorded in step 1 (see Fig. 7-10). Next, we may consider joint *c* as being held against rotation and joint *b* as being unlocked first. The unlocking moment $+10$ at *b* is then equally distributed to the near ends of members *ba* and *bc* as indicated in step 2, and one-half of the amount is carried over the far ends of these members as indicated in step 3. Next, we consider joint *b* as locked and joint *c* as released, but only partially, by applying an unlocking moment of $-(40 - 30)$ or -10 to it, since the complete releasing of joint *c* would require an unlocking moment of $-(40 - 30 + 2.5)$ or -12.5 for the time being. This unlocking moment -10 is equally distributed to the near ends of members *cb* and *cd*, and one-half of the amount is carried over to the far ends of these members as indicated in steps 2 and 3, leaving the just-received carry-over moment $+2.5$ to be handled later.

Referring to step 3 of Fig. 7-10, we find the carry-over moments form a new set of fixed-end moments for the beam, and a process of unlocking joints can be carried out in a similar manner. The process will thus be repeated in a cyclic fashion until the carry-over moments are neglected.

In fact, if the carry-over moments are neglected, the joints, after being unlocked, are in balance (i.e., no external constraint exists). This gives the approximate solution for the analysis. For instance, the first approximation may be obtained from

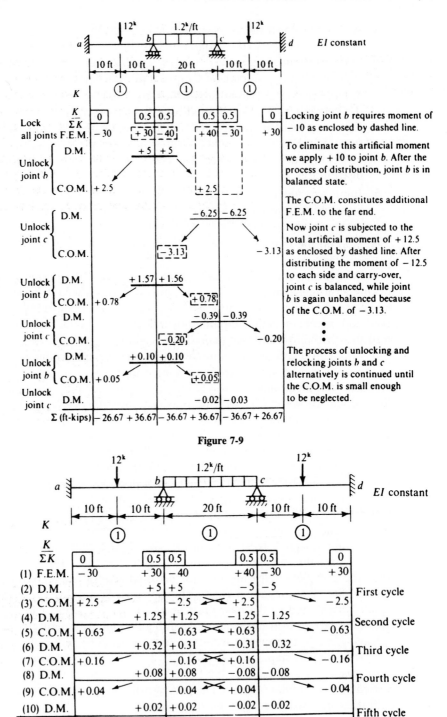

Figure 7-9

Figure 7-10

the sum of steps 1 and 2, the result of the first cycle; the second approximation may be obtained from the sum of steps 1 to 4, the result up to the second cycle; and so on. It is interesting to note that, in this particular problem, even the first cycle yields a good approximation of the exact solution. After two or three cycles, the carry-over values become negligible.

Note that the beam and the loading shown in Fig. 7-10 are symmetrical; the data presented on each side of the line of symmetry are equal in magnitude but opposite in sign. This special display suggests that some modification could be made in order to facilitate the process of moment distribution by working with only half the structure. See Sec. 7-6 for *modified stiffness*. This problem will be re-solved in Example 7-5 by using modified stiffness.

More examples are given to illustrate the cyclic process.

Example 7-4

Analyze the frame in Fig. 7-11 by moment distribution. The relative stiffnesses for the frame members are computed first as

$$K_{ab \atop (cd)} = \frac{2I}{30}, \quad \text{say } 4$$

$$K_{bc} = \frac{2I}{40}, \quad \text{say } 3$$

$$K_{be \atop (cf)} = \frac{I}{20}, \quad \text{say } 3$$

Next, the fixed-end moments for the loaded member bc are found to be

$$M_{bc}^F = -\frac{(60)(10)(30)^2}{(40)^2} + \frac{(60)(30)(10)^2}{(40)^2} = -225 \text{ ft-kips}$$

$$M_{cb}^F = +\frac{(60)(30)(10)^2}{(40)^2} - \frac{(60)(10)(30)^2}{(40)^2} = -225 \text{ ft-kips}$$

The complete analysis is shown in Fig. 7-12. Note that the intermediate values of the moments at fixed ends e and f are not shown. Since members be and cf are not loaded, it is evident that

$$M_{eb} = \tfrac{1}{2}M_{be} = 32.2 \text{ ft-kips}, \qquad M_{fc} = \tfrac{1}{2}M_{cf} = 32.2 \text{ ft-kips}$$

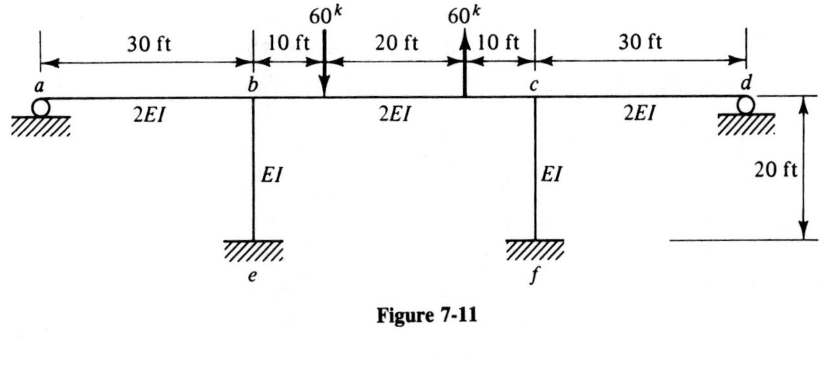

Figure 7-11

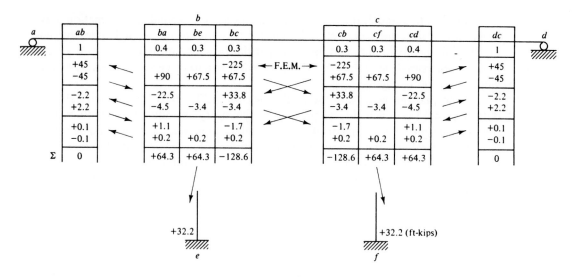

Figure 7-12

From Fig. 7-12 the values of the moments obtained on the left side of the center line of the structure are exactly the same as those on the right. Such a special display is referred to as *antisymmetry*, which yields

$$\theta_b = \theta_c$$

An adjustment can be made to the stiffness of the center beam *bc* that will permit the analyst to work with only half the structure. We also find that the final result $M_{ab} = M_{dc} = 0$ is known beforehand. The convergence of moment distribution may be improved by using modified stiffness in beams *ab* and *dc*. See Sec. 7-6 for modified stiffness. This problem is re-solved in Example 7-7.

7-6 MODIFIED STIFFNESSES

The examples given in Sec. 7-5 have illustrated three special cases that suggest that some modifications for simplifying the moment distribution process might be found by recognizing certain known conditions.

Consider the frame subjected to a clockwise external moment M applied to the connecting joint shown in Fig. 7-13(a), for which we note the following:

1. $\theta_a = 0$; that is, the member is fixed at end a.
2. $M_b = 0$; that is, the member is simply supported at end b.
3. $\theta_c = -\theta$; that is, the member rotates through an equal but opposite angle at the other end c as in the case of symmetry.
4. $\theta_d = \theta$; that is, the member rotates through the same angle at the other end d as in the case of antisymmetry.

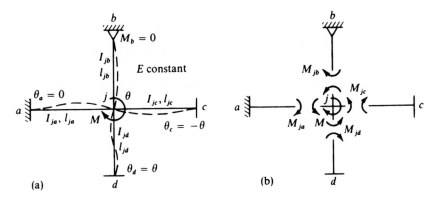

Figure 7-13

Among the four members, only member a–j is in the regular condition with the far end fixed.

$$M_{ja} = 4EK_{ja}\,\theta \qquad (7\text{-}16)$$

The stiffness of the other three members may be found by the principle of superposition utilizing the fundamental solution, as shown in Fig. 7-14.

Take member j–b for example. The far end b is to have zero moment because of the hinge at b. The standard beam shown in the middle of Fig. 7-14(a) would produce a moment of $2EK\theta$, which should be neutralized by adding an opposite $2EK\theta$, as shown in the rightmost figure of Fig. 7-14(a). Thus,

$$M_{jb} = 3EK_{jb}\,\theta = 4E(\tfrac{3}{4}K_{jb})\theta = 4EK_{jb}'\,\theta \qquad (7\text{-}17)$$

where we let

$$K_{jb}' = \tfrac{3}{4}K_{jb} \qquad (7\text{-}18)$$

K_{jb}' is called the *modified stiffness factor* for member jb. Similarly,

$$M_{jc} = 2EK_{jc}\,\theta = 4E(\tfrac{1}{2}K_{jc})\theta = 4EK_{jc}'\,\theta \qquad (7\text{-}19)$$

where

$$K_{jc}' = \tfrac{1}{2}K_{jc} \qquad (7\text{-}20)$$

and

$$M_{jd} = 6EK_{jd}\,\theta = 4E(\tfrac{3}{2}K_{jd})\theta = 4EK_{jd}'\,\theta \qquad (7\text{-}21)$$

where

$$K_{jd}' = \tfrac{3}{2}K_{jd} \qquad (7\text{-}22)$$

Referring to Fig. 7-13(b), we find the equilibrium of joint j requires that

$$M_{ja} + M_{jb} + M_{jc} + M_{jd} = M \tag{7-23}$$

Substituting Eqs. 7-16, 7-17, 7-19, and 7-21 in Eq. 7-23 yields

$$4E(K_{ja} + K_{jb}' + K_{jc}' + K_{jd}')\theta = M$$

or

$$\theta = \frac{M}{4E \sum K'} \tag{7-24}$$

where

$$\sum K' = K_{ja} + K_{jb}' + K_{jc}' + K_{jd}'$$

Substituting Eq. 7-24 in Eqs. 7-16, 7-17, 7-19, and 7-21 yields

$$M_{ja} = \frac{K_{ja}}{\sum K'} M$$

$$M_{jb} = \frac{K_{jb}'}{\sum K'} M$$

$$\tag{7-25}$$

$$M_{jc} = \frac{K_{jc}'}{\sum K'} M$$

$$M_{jd} = \frac{K_{jd}'}{\sum K'} M$$

Thus, it is seen that when an external moment is applied to joint j the distributed moments to the near ends of the members meeting at the joint are in direct proportion to their modified stiffness factors if the conditions of the far ends are known. By using the modified stiffness factor for one end, we actually eliminate the carry-over to the other end except for writing down the final result for that part.

Let us recapitulate the modified stiffness factors for various end conditions:

1. If the one end is simply supported, the modified stiffness factor for the other end is given by

$$K' = \tfrac{3}{4} K \tag{7-26}$$

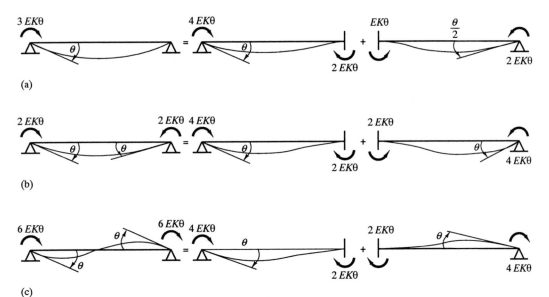

Figure 7-14

2. If the one end is symmetrical to the other end, then

$$K' = \tfrac{1}{2}K \qquad\qquad (7\text{-}27)$$

3. If the one end is antisymmetrical to the other end, then

$$K' = \tfrac{3}{2}K \qquad\qquad (7\text{-}28)$$

K' denotes the modified stiffness factor. In parallel with Eq. 7-8, we may have

$$S' = 4EK' \qquad\qquad (7\text{-}29)$$

S' being called the *modified stiffness*. A general definition for *modified stiffness* is the end moment required to produce a unit rotation at this end (simple end), while the other end remains in the actual conditions.

The following examples illustrate the process of moment distribution by using the modified K values.

Example 7-5

Analyze the symmetrical beam in Fig. 7-15 by using the modified K value in the center span.

Example 7-6

Analyze the symmetrical frame in Fig. 7-16, which was solved by the methods of consistent deformations and least work. Once again the method of moment distribution demonstrates its superiority over any other method previously discussed.

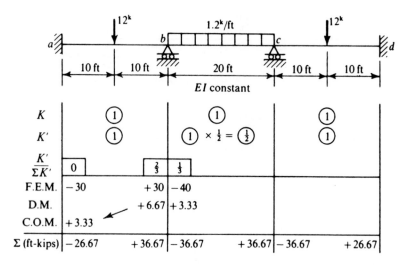

Figure 7-15

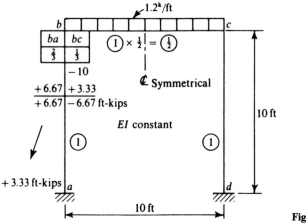

Figure 7-16

Example 7-7

Analyze the frame in Fig. 7-11 by using the modified stiffness in beams ab, bc, and cd. The solution is given in Fig. 7-17, which agrees with the result of Example 7-4.

7-7 TREATMENT OF JOINT TRANSLATIONS

The procedure of moment distribution discussed thus far is based on the restriction that the joints of the structure do not move. However, many frames encountered in practice undergo joint translations. There are, in general, two types of loaded frames in which joint translations are involved. The first is a frame under the action of a lateral force applied at a joint, such as the one shown in Fig. 7-18(a); the second is

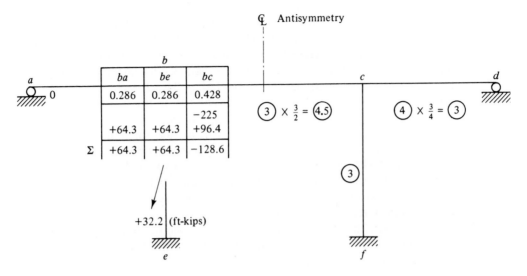

Figure 7-17

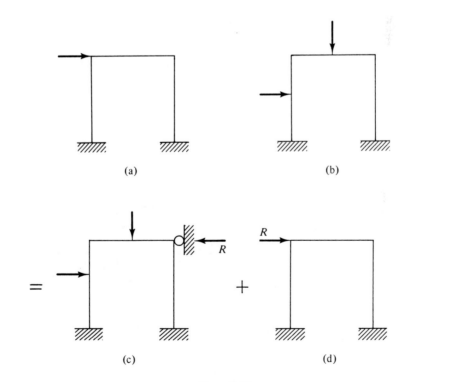

Figure 7-18

a frame that, together with loads acting on its members, forms an unsymmetrical system, such as the one shown in Fig. 7-18(b). To handle the latter type of frame, we may resort to the principle of superposition. An artificial holding force to prevent joint translation is imposed on the structure and is subsequently eliminated. Thus, the frame in Fig. 7-18(b) can be considered as the superposed effect of the two separate systems indicated in Fig. 7-18(c) and (d). In the first place [Fig. 7-18(c)], the translation of joints is prevented by providing an artificial support at the top of the column so that moment distribution can be carried out in the usual manner. The required holding force R is then obtained by statics. The next step [Fig. 7-18(d)] is to eliminate the artificial restraint by applying to the top of the column a lateral force equal to R but opposite in direction. The resulting configuration is the same as that shown in Fig. 7-18(a). Therefore, the problem now reduces to dealing with a frame under lateral forces applied at the joints.

To handle this type of frame, we consider the frame in Fig. 7-19(a) in which joints a and d are fixed, whereas joints b and c undergo both translation and rotation because of the lateral force P applied at the top of column. It is obvious that if the joint translation of b is specified as Δ then the joint translation of c is determined

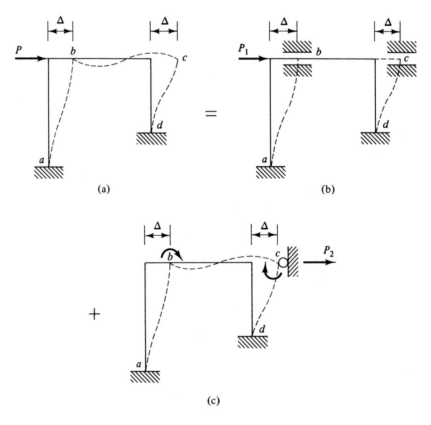

Figure 7-19

and, in this case, is also Δ. Now the distortion imposed on joints b and c may be regarded as the superposed effect of the two following separate steps:

1. Translation without rotation [see Fig. 7-19(b)]
2. Rotation without translation [see Fig. 7-19(c)]

In step 1, joints b and c are locked against rotation ($\theta_b = \theta_c = 0$), and the joint translation Δ is produced by applying a lateral force P_1. It is clear that some external restraints (i.e., locking moments) are required at joints b and c in order to hold both joints against rotation. Also, end moments will be induced in the members having relative joint translation. The amount of end moments can be found by the principle of superposition as shown in Fig. 7-20, utilizing results shown in Fig. 7-14 and Eq. 7-21. The *rigid-body rotation of the member* is defined by

$$R = \frac{\Delta}{l} \qquad (7\text{-}30)$$

which is positive if it rotates clockwise. The end moments induced by joint translation are then

$$M_{ab} = M_{ba} = -6EKR \qquad (7\text{-}31)$$

This means an end moment of $-6EI\Delta/l^2$ is induced for each column end in the present case. We call them the F.E.M. due to joint translation, from which the lateral force P_1 can be figured.

In step 2, further joint translations are checked by providing an artificial support at the top of the column. Joints b and c are then unlocked so that they finally rotate to their actual positions. Recall that to unlock a joint means to apply a moment equal but opposite to the locking moment at the joint. From the resulting end moments, the holding force P_2 at the artificial support can be figured.

The preceding two steps complete the procedure of moment distribution for frames having joint translations under joint loads. The procedure differs from that for frames without joint translation under member loads only in the source of fixed-end moments. In the former case, the fixed-end moments arise from pure joint translations, whereas in the latter case the fixed-end moments are due to loads acting on the fixed beams as described in Sec. 7-2.

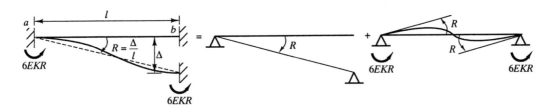

Figure 7-20

Referring to Fig. 7-19, we notice that the lateral force applied at the joints, that is, the sum of P_1 and P_2, is found to be a function of Δ, a value that we usually do not know at the outset. However, Δ can be solved by the force condition

$$P_1 + P_2 = P$$

After the value of Δ is found, the resulting end moments, which are also expressed in terms of Δ, can readily be determined.

As a simple illustration, let us analyze the frame shown in Fig. 7-21(a) by the method of moment distribution. Because of the lateral force acting on the column top, joint b and also joint c will move to the right a distance Δ, causing a relative deflection between joints a and b. We thus write the fixed-end moments due to joint translation equal to $-6EI\Delta/l^2$ at column ends a and b. Since $M_c = 0$ is known beforehand, we use modified stiffness for member bc to simplify the calculation. Next, we perform the process of distribution and carry-over. The complete analysis is given in Fig. 7-21(b). The resulting end moments are found to be consistent with

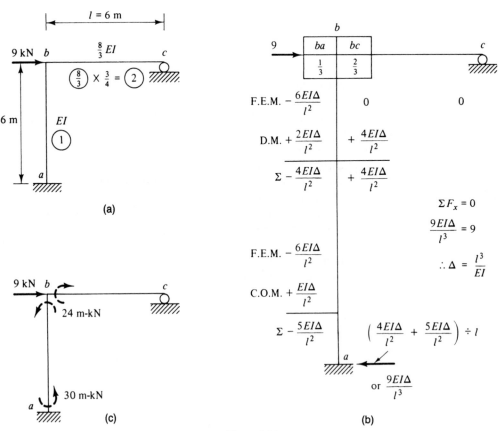

Figure 7-21

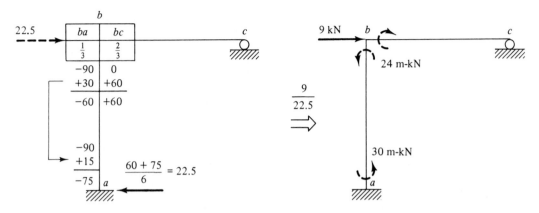

Figure 7-22

a horizontal reaction $9EI\Delta/l^3$ at support a, which should be equal to the applied lateral force of 9 kN from $\Sigma F_X = 0$. Thus, we have

$$\frac{9EI\Delta}{l^3} = 9$$

or

$$\Delta = \frac{l^3}{EI}$$

Substituting this value in the result shown in Fig. 7-21(b), we obtain the answer diagram given in Fig. 7-21(c).

Practically, we often start with a convenient value for Δ, or F.E.M., to carry out the moment distribution process and then correct the result thus obtained by a constant of proportionality. The problem is re-solved in Fig. 7-22.

Note that we choose F.E.M. $= -90$ as a start. The final result of end moments is associated with a lateral force equal to 22.5 kN. Multiplying the obtained result by a correction ratio of 9/22.5 will give the answer.

Example 7-8

Determine all the end moments of the loaded frame in Fig. 7-23(a).
The complete analysis is as follows:

1. Hold the loaded frame at the top of the column, say at joint c, against sidesway, and obtain the end moments by the usual moment distribution procedures [Fig. 7-23(b)].

2. From $\Sigma F_x = 0$ for the entire frame, calculate the holding force needed to prevent sidesway. In this case, it is

$$4 - 1.5 = 2.5 \text{ kN}$$

acting to the left, as indicated in Fig. 7-23(b).

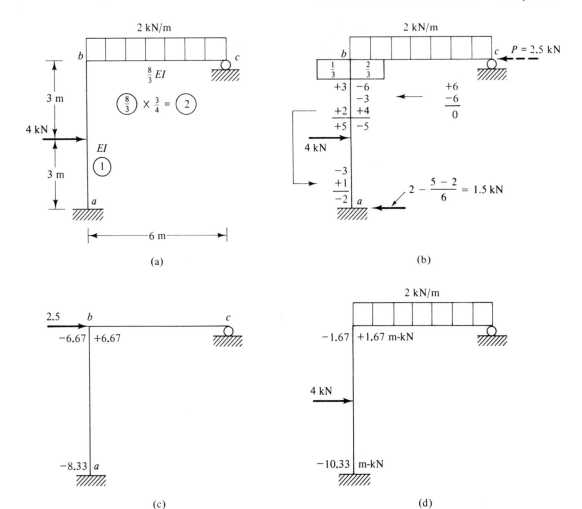

Figure 7-23

3. Remove the artificial holding force by the application of an equal and opposite force at the top of the column, and find the resulting end moments [see Fig. 7-23(c)].

4. Add the end moments from steps 1 and 3 to obtain the final solution [see Fig. 7-23(d)].

The foregoing procedure may be extended to two or more joint translational degrees-of-freedom problems, but the bookkeeping part of it becomes cumbersome. In fact, for problems with more than 3 degrees of freedom, rotational or translational, the moment distribution method is not practical.

In retrospect, we see the moment distribution method as an iterative solution method for solving the joint equilibrium equations. Even though the joint displacements do not appear explicitly, they are implicitly changed whenever an unlocking process is executed. The basic unknowns are still the displacements. When the number of displacement unknowns becomes large, it is more efficient to solve for these unknowns directly from the equilibrium equations without iteration. That is the essence of the slope-deflection method described in Chapter 8.

PROBLEMS

7-1. Find all the end moments of the beam shown in Fig. 7-24 by moment distribution.

7-2. Figure 7-25 shows a frame of uniform cross section. Find all the end moments by moment distribution.

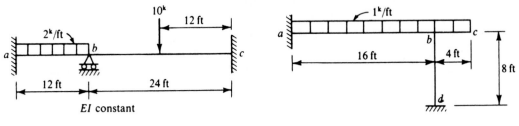

Figure 7-24   **Figure 7-25**

7-3. Find all the end moments of the beam shown in Fig. 7-26 by moment distribution.

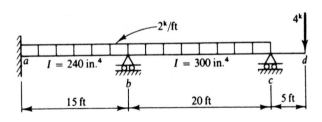

Figure 7-26

7-4. Find the end moments of the frame shown in Fig. 7-27 by moment distribution (a) not using modified stiffness, and (b) using a modified K value in the center span.

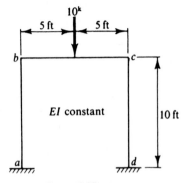

Figure 7-27

7-5. Analyze the box shown in Fig. 7-28 by moment distribution. Assume constant *EI*.

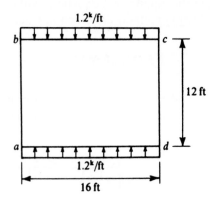

Figure 7-28

7-6. Analyze the continuous beam in Fig. 7-29 by moment distribution. Assume constant *EI*.

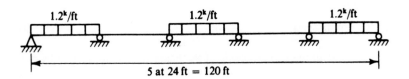

Figure 7-29

7-7. Analyze the continuous beam in Fig. 7-30 by moment distribution. Take advantage of modified stiffnesses, replacing the unsymmetrical loading system with a symmetrical and an antisymmetrical system. Assume constant *EI*.

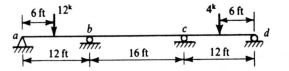

Figure 7-30

7-8. Analyze the frame in Fig. 7-31 by moment distribution and find the reaction at support *c*.

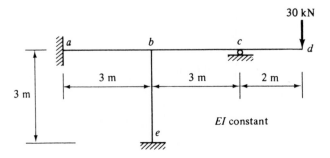

Figure 7-31

7-9. With reference to Fig. 7-32, find the stiffness for end *a* of member *ab* if a hinge connection is inserted in the member at *c* as shown.

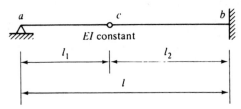

Figure 7-32

7-10. Use the method of moment distribution to find the fixed-end moment and the spring force for the beam shown in Fig. 7-33.

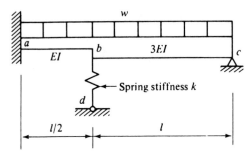

Figure 7-33

7-11. Analyze each frame in Fig. 7-34 by moment distribution.

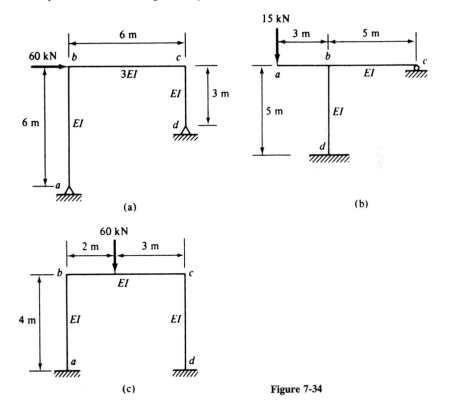

(a)

(b)

(c)

Figure 7-34

7-12. Find the fixed-end moments for the beams shown in Fig. 7-35 by moment distribution. Assume that $w = 3$ kN/m and $l = 4$ m.

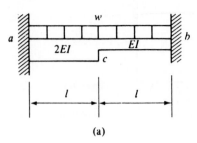
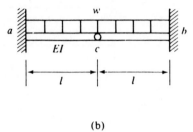

(a)   (b)

Figure 7-35

Chapter 8

Slope-Deflection Method

8-1 GENERAL

The slope-deflection method is a displacement method for beam and rigid frame analysis. The axial deformation of members is neglected. Thus, the deformed configuration is defined by joint rotations and joint translations resulting from bending of members. The basic unknowns are joint rotations (slopes) and joint translations (deflections) subjected to the kinematic constraint that axial deformation of any member is zero. These unknowns are solved from equilibrium equations that are equal in number to the unknowns, whether the structure is statically indeterminate or not. The number of displacement unknowns is usually referred to as displacement *degrees of freedom* or *kinematic indeterminacy*, as opposed to static indeterminacy in the forced method.

The slope-deflection method may be used in analyzing beams and rigid frames composed of prismatic or nonprismatic members. In this chapter, we discuss exclusively beams and rigid frames of prismatic members.

8-2 BASIC SLOPE-DEFLECTION EQUATIONS

The basis of the slope deflection method lies in the *slope-deflection equations*, which express the end moments of each member in terms of the end distortions of that member.

Consider member *ab* shown in Fig. 8-1, which is isolated from a loaded statically indeterminate beam or rigid frame (not shown). The member is deformed

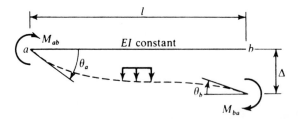

Figure 8-1

(see the dashed line) with end rotations θ_a and θ_b and relative deflection Δ between the ends. Obviously, the induced end moments at a and b, called M_{ab} and M_{ba}, are related to the elastic distortions at both ends as well as to the load on span ab, if any. Thus,

$$M_{ab} = f(\theta_a, \theta_b, \Delta, \text{load on span}) \tag{8-1}$$

$$M_{ba} = g(\theta_a, \theta_b, \Delta, \text{load on span}) \tag{8-2}$$

where f and g are symbols for functions.

To find the expressions of Eqs. 8-1 and 8-2, let us first establish the following sign convention for slope deflection:

1. The moment acting on the end of a member (not a joint) is positive when clockwise.
2. The rotation at the end of a member is positive when the tangent to the deformed curve at the end rotates clockwise from its original position.
3. The relative deflection between ends of a member is positive when it corresponds to a clockwise rotation of the member (the straight line joining the ends of the elastic curve).

All signs of end distortions and moments shown in Fig. 8-1 are positive. The sign conventions established here are purely arbitrary and could be replaced by any other convenient system; but once these conventions have been adopted, we will restrict ourselves to this system.

Next, let us refer to Fig. 8-1 and observe that the end moments M_{ab} and M_{ba} may be considered as the algebraic sum of four separate effects:

1. The moment due to end rotation θ_a while the other end b is fixed [Fig. 8-2(a)].
2. The moment due to end rotation θ_b while end a is fixed [Fig. 8-2(b)].
3. The moment due to a relative deflection Δ between the ends of the member without altering the existing slopes of tangents at the ends [Fig. 8-2(c)].
4. The moment caused by placing the actual loads on the span without altering the existing end distortions [Fig. 8-2(d)].

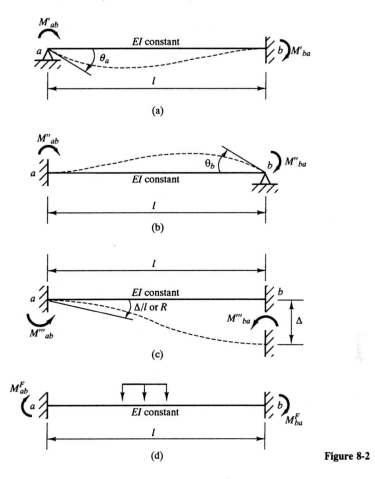

Figure 8-2

The solution of each of these four cases may be obtained by the method of consistent deformations or by a direct solution of the beam equation as described in Chapter 7. We will simply list the solutions here:

$$M'_{ab} = \frac{4EI\theta_a}, \qquad M'_{ba} = \frac{2EI\theta_a}{l} \tag{8-3}$$

$$M''_{ab} = \frac{2EI\theta_b}{l}, \qquad M''_{ba} = \frac{4EI\theta_b}{l} \tag{8-4}$$

$$M'''_{ab} = -\frac{6EI\Delta}{l^2}, \qquad M'''_{ba} = -\frac{6EI\Delta}{l^2} \tag{8-5}$$

and the fixed end moments M^F_{ab} and M^F_{ba} are given for various loadings in a table in Appendix D.

Summing up the four elements listed above, we have

$$M_{ab} = M'_{ab} + M''_{ab} + M'''_{ab} + M^F_{ab}$$

$$M_{ba} = M'_{ba} + M''_{ba} + M'''_{ba} + M^F_{ba}$$

Using Eqs. 8-3, 8-4, and 8-5, we find that

$$M_{ab} = \frac{4EI\theta_a}{l} + \frac{2EI\theta_b}{l} - \frac{6EI\Delta}{l^2} + M^F_{ab}$$

$$M_{ba} = \frac{2EI\theta_a}{l} + \frac{4EI\theta_b}{l} - \frac{6EI\Delta}{l^2} + M^F_{ba}$$

Rearranging gives

$$M_{ab} = 2E\frac{I}{l}\left(2\theta_a + \theta_b - 3\frac{\Delta}{l}\right) + M^F_{ab} \qquad\qquad (8\text{-}6)$$

$$M_{ba} = 2E\frac{I}{l}\left(2\theta_b + \theta_a - 3\frac{\Delta}{l}\right) + M^F_{ba} \qquad\qquad (8\text{-}7)$$

which are the basic equations of slope-deflection for a general deformed member of uniform cross section. The equations express end moments M_{ab} and M_{ba} in terms of the end slopes (θ_a, θ_b), the relative deflection between the two ends (Δ), and the loading on the span ab.

If we let

$$\frac{I}{l} = K, \qquad \frac{\Delta}{l} = R$$

K being the *stiffness factor of the member* and R the rigid-body *rotation of the member* [see Fig. 8-2(c)], the equations become

$$M_{ab} = 2EK(2\theta_a + \theta_b - 3R) + M^F_{ab} \qquad\qquad (8\text{-}8)$$

$$M_{ba} = 2EK(2\theta_b + \theta_a - 3R) + M^F_{ba} \qquad\qquad (8\text{-}9)$$

The signs and values of M^F_{ab} and M^F_{ba} depend on the loading condition on span ab. If the member ab carries no load itself, then $M^F_{ab} = M^F_{ba} = 0$.

8-3 PROCEDURE OF ANALYSIS BY THE SLOPE-DEFLECTION METHOD

The slope-deflection method consists of writing a series of slope-deflection equations expressing the end moments for all members in terms of the slope (rotation) and the deflection (relative translation) of various joints, or of quantities proportional to them, and of solving these unknown displacements by a number of equilibrium equations that these end moments must satisfy. Once the displacements have been determined, the end moments for each member may be figured. The solution thus obtained is unique, since it satisfies the equilibrium equations and end conditions (compatibility conditions) embedded in the slope-deflection equations.

To illustrate, let us consider the frame in Fig. 8-3(a). First we draw the free-body diagrams for all members, as shown in Fig. 8-3(b), where the unknown end moments for each member are assumed positive (i.e., acting clockwise according to our sign convention).

Next, we observe that ends a and d of the frame are fixed and will undergo no rotation ($\theta_a = \theta_d = 0$) or linear displacement. Joint b, owing to the restriction of length ab (we neglect the small change in length in ab due to the axial forces) and the support a, cannot move otherwise, but rotates about a. However, since the deformations of the frame are extremely small as compared to the length, we may replace arc length with tangent length without appreciable error. With joint b, and therefore c, moving a horizontal distance Δ to the right [see Fig. 8-3(a)], there is a relative deflection Δ between joints a and b and also joints c and d. There is no relative deflection between joints b and c if the small lengthening or shortening in ab or cd, caused primarily by axial forces, is neglected. There are some joint rotations at b and c. Attention should be paid to the fact that, when a rigid frame is deformed, each rigid joint is considered to rotate as a whole. For instance, members ba and bc rotate the same angle θ_b at joint b. Similarly, members cb and cd rotate the same angle θ_c at joint c.

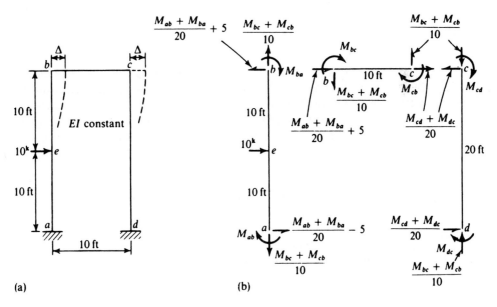

(a)   (b)

Figure 8-3

To determine the end moments for each member shown in Fig. 8-3(b), we write a series of slope-deflection equations as follows:

$$M_{ab} = 2EK_{ab}(\theta_b - 3R) - M_{ab}^F = 2E\left(\frac{I}{20}\right)(\theta_b - 3R) - 25$$

$$M_{ba} = 2EK_{ab}(2\theta_b - 3R) + M_{ba}^F = 2E\left(\frac{I}{20}\right)(2\theta_b - 3R) + 25$$

$$M_{bc} = 2EK_{bc}(2\theta_b + \theta_c) = 2E\left(\frac{I}{10}\right)(2\theta_b + \theta_c)$$

$$M_{cb} = 2EK_{bc}(2\theta_c + \theta_b) = 2E\left(\frac{I}{10}\right)(2\theta_c + \theta_b)$$ (8-10)

$$M_{cd} = 2EK_{cd}(2\theta_c - 3R) = 2E\left(\frac{I}{20}\right)(2\theta_c - 3R)$$

$$M_{dc} = 2EK_{cd}(\theta_c - 3R) = 2E\left(\frac{I}{20}\right)(\theta_c - 3R)$$

Involved in these expressions are three unknowns: θ_b, θ_c, and R (or $\Delta/20$). These can be solved by the three equations of statics the end moments must satisfy.

By taking joints b and c as free bodies, we immediately obtain two equilibrium equations:

$$\sum M_{\text{joint } b} = 0 \quad \text{or} \quad M_{ba} + M_{bc} = 0 \tag{8-11}$$

$$\sum M_{\text{joint } c} = 0 \quad \text{or} \quad M_{cb} + M_{cd} = 0 \tag{8-12}$$

Usually, we have as many joint equilibrium equations as the number of joint displacement unknowns involved. However, with the member rotation R unknown, a third equation may be more conveniently secured from the equilibrium of the structure. Referring to Fig. 8-3, by taking the whole frame as free body, we see that the horizontal shear in ends a and d must balance the horizontal external force acting on the frame. Thus,

$$10 + \left(\frac{M_{ab} + M_{ba}}{20} - 5\right) + \left(\frac{M_{cd} + M_{dc}}{20}\right) = 0$$

or

$$M_{ab} + M_{ba} + M_{cd} + M_{dc} + 100 = 0 \tag{8-13}$$

Before we try to substitute the expressions of Eq. 8-10 in Eqs. 8-11, 8-12, and 8-13, we should note that, if our purpose is to determine the end moments but not to obtain the exact values of the slope and deflection of each joint, then we may substitute the relative values for the coefficients $2EI/l$, usually some simple integers, in the slope-deflection equations to facilitate the calculation. This can be done because such a substitution will only magnify the values of θ and Δ, but will not affect the final result of the end moments. Thus, if we set

$$2E\frac{I}{20} = 1$$

accordingly,

$$2E\left(\frac{I}{10}\right) = 2$$

and the moment expressions of Eq. 8-10 become

$$M_{ab} = \theta_b - 3R - 25$$

$$M_{ba} = 2\theta_b - 3R + 25$$

$$M_{bc} = 2(2\theta_b + \theta_c)$$

$$M_{cb} = 2(2\theta_c + \theta_b) \tag{8-14}$$

$$M_{cd} = 2\theta_c - 3R$$

$$M_{dc} = \theta_c - 3R$$

Substituting these in Eqs. 8-11, 8-12, and 8-13 yields

$$6\theta_b + 2\theta_c - 3R + 25 = 0 \tag{8-15}$$

$$2\theta_b + 6\theta_c - 3R = 0 \tag{8-16}$$

$$3\theta_b + 3\theta_c - 12R + 100 = 0 \tag{8-17}$$

Solving Eqs. 8-15, 8-16, and 8-17 simultaneously, we obtain

$$\theta_b = -1.20, \qquad \theta_c = 5.05, \qquad R = 9.30$$

Note that the values thus obtained are only the relative values of the slope and the deflection for the various joints. They must be divided by the factor $2EI/20$ to give the absolute values of the slope and deflection.

To determine the end moments for each member of the frame, we substitute $\theta_b = -1.20$, $\theta_c = 5.05$, and $R = 9.30$ in Eq. 8-14 and obtain

$$M_{ab} = -54.10 \text{ ft-kips} \qquad \text{(counterclockwise)}$$

$$M_{ba} = -5.30 \text{ ft-kips} \qquad \text{(counterclockwise)}$$

$$M_{bc} = +5.30 \text{ ft-kips} \qquad \text{(clockwise)}$$

$$M_{cb} = +17.80 \text{ ft-kips} \qquad \text{(clockwise)}$$

$$M_{cd} = -17.80 \text{ ft-kips} \qquad \text{(counterclockwise)}$$

$$M_{dc} = -22.80 \text{ ft-kips} \qquad \text{(counterclockwise)}$$

The answer diagram for the end actions for each member of the frame is shown in Fig. 8-4(a), which is based on Fig. 8-3(b).

The moment diagram for the frame is drawn as in Fig. 8-4(b). The moment is plotted on the compressive side of each member. In this particular case each member has one point of inflection corresponding to the point of zero moment.

Finally, we can sketch the elastic curve of the deformed structure, as shown in Fig. 8-4(c) by using the values (or relative values) of the joint rotations

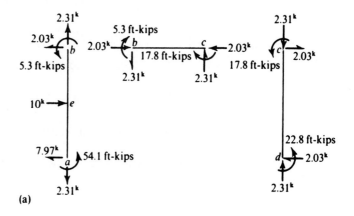

(a)

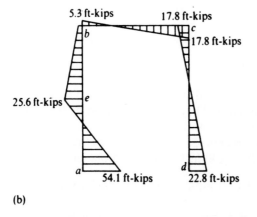

(b)

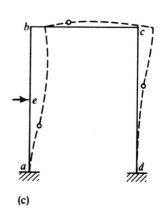

(c)

Figure 8-4

and deflections together with the bending moment diagram. Note particularly the following:

1. The elastic curve of the deformed frame bends according to the bending moment diagram.
2. Both joints b and c deflect to the right the same horizontal distance.
3. Joint b rotates counterclockwise while joint c rotates clockwise.
4. Since joints b and c are rigid, the tangents to the elastic curves ba and bc at b and the tangents to the elastic curves cb and cd at c should be perpendicular to each other so as to maintain the original formation at the joints of the unloaded frame.

8-4 ANALYSIS OF BEAMS BY THE SLOPE-DEFLECTION METHOD

The application of the slope-deflection method in solving beam problems will be illustrated in the following examples.

Example 8-1

Figure 8-5(a) shows a continuous, two-section beam, all the supports of which are immovable. We wish to draw the shear and bending moment diagrams for the beam. We solve for the end moments and shears as follows:

1. Since $2EK_{ab} = 2E(2I)/16 = EI/4$ and $2EK_{bc} = 2EI/12 = EI/6$, if we let $2EK_{ab} = 3$, then $2EK_{bc} = 2$ relatively. The relative values of $2EK$ are shown circled in Fig. 8-5(a).
2. By inspection, $\theta_a = 0$ (fixed end at a) and $R_{ab} = R_{bc} = 0$ (immovable supports at a, b, c).
3. We calculate the fixed-end moments as follows:

$$M_{ab}^F = -\frac{(7.5)(16)}{8} = -15 \text{ ft-kips}$$

$$M_{ba}^F = +\frac{(7.5)(16)}{8} = +15 \text{ ft-kips}$$

$$M_{bc}^F = -\frac{(1)(12)^2}{12} = -12 \text{ ft-kips}$$

$$M_{cb}^F = +\frac{(1)(12)^2}{12} = +12 \text{ ft-kips}$$

4. We write the slope-deflection equations using the relative $2EK$ values.

$$M_{ab} = (3)(\theta_b) - 15 \tag{8-18}$$

$$M_{ba} = (3)(2\theta_b) + 15 = 6\theta_b + 15 \tag{8-19}$$

$$M_{bc} = (2)(2\theta_b + \theta_c) - 12 = 4\theta_b + 2\theta_c - 12 \tag{8-20}$$

$$M_{cb} = (2)(2\theta_c + \theta_b) + 12 = 2\theta_b + 4\theta_c + 12 \tag{8-21}$$

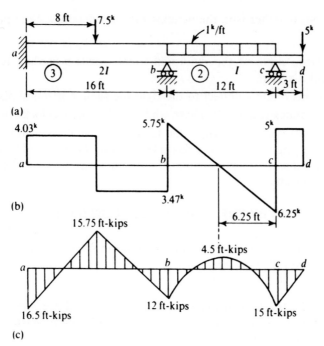

(a)

(b)

(c)

Figure 8-5

5. Involved in the equations above are two unknowns, θ_b and θ_c, that can be solved by two joint conditions:

$$\sum M_{\text{joint } b} = M_{ba} + M_{bc} = 0 \tag{8-22}$$

$$M_{cb} = (5)(3) = 15 \tag{8-23}$$

Substituting Eqs. 8-19 and 8-20 in Eq. 8-22 and Eq. 8-21 in Eq. 8-23 yields

$$10\theta_b + 2\theta_c + 3 = 0 \tag{8-24}$$

and

$$2\theta_b + 4\theta_c - 3 = 0 \tag{8-25}$$

Solving yields

$$\theta_b = -\tfrac{1}{2}, \qquad \theta_c = 1$$

6. Substituting the above values in step 4, we obtain

$$M_{ab} = -16.5 \text{ ft-kips}$$

$$M_{ba} = +12.0 \text{ ft-kips}$$

$$M_{bc} = -12.0 \text{ ft-kips}$$

$$M_{cb} = +15.0 \text{ ft-kips}$$

7. Having determined the end moments for each member, we can find the end shears and, therefore, the reactions,

$$R_a = V_{ab} = \frac{7.5}{2} + \frac{16.5 - 12}{16} = 4.03 \text{ kips} \qquad \text{(up)}$$

$$V_{ba} = \frac{-7.5}{2} + \frac{16.5 - 12}{16} = -3.47 \text{ kips} \quad \text{(up)}$$

$$V_{bc} = \frac{12}{2} - \frac{15 - 12}{12} = 5.75 \text{ kips} \qquad \text{(up)}$$

$$R_b = 3.47 + 5.75 = 9.22 \text{ kips} \qquad \text{(up)}$$

$$V_{cb} = -\frac{12}{2} - \frac{15 - 12}{12} = -6.25 \text{ kips} \qquad \text{(up)}$$

$$V_{cd} = 5 \text{ kips} \qquad \text{(up)}$$

$$R_c = 6.25 + 5 = 11.25 \text{ kips} \qquad \text{(up)}$$

8. We now draw the shear and moment diagrams, as shown in Fig. 8-5(b) and (c), respectively.

Example 8-2

For the system and load shown in Fig. 8-6, find a general expression for the spring force. Given $E = 20,000 \text{ kN/cm}^2$, $I = 5,000 \text{ cm}^4$, $k = 5 \text{ kN/cm}$, $w = 4 \text{ kN/m}$, and $l = 3 \text{ m}$, determine the value of the spring force.

Assuming that the contraction of spring at b is Δ, we write the moment equations as

$$M_{ab} = 2E\frac{I}{l}\left(\theta_b - 3\frac{\Delta}{l}\right) - \frac{wl^2}{12} \qquad (8\text{-}26)$$

$$M_{ba} = 2E\frac{I}{l}\left(2\theta_b - 3\frac{\Delta}{l}\right) + \frac{wl^2}{12} \qquad (8\text{-}27)$$

Using $M_{ba} = 0$, we have

$$\theta_b = \frac{3\Delta}{2l} - \frac{wl^3}{48EI} \qquad (8\text{-}28)$$

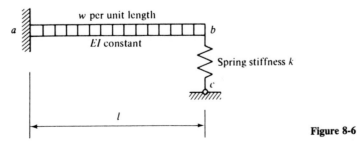

w per unit length
a
EI constant
b
Spring stiffness k
c
l

Figure 8-6

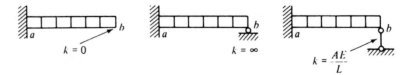

Figure 8-7

Substituting Eq. 8-28 in Eq. 8-26 gives

$$M_{ab} = -\left(\frac{3EI\Delta}{l^2} + \frac{wl^2}{8}\right) \tag{8-29}$$

Let the spring force be X; hence, $X = k\Delta$ or $\Delta = X/k$. Thus,

$$M_{ab} = -\left(\frac{3EIX}{kl^2} + \frac{wl^2}{8}\right) \tag{8-30}$$

Since the compressive force in the spring is equal to the end shear at b,

$$X = \frac{wl}{2} + \frac{M_{ab}}{l}$$

Using Eq. 8-30, we obtain

$$X = \frac{3}{8}wl\left(\frac{1}{1 + \frac{3EI}{kl^3}}\right) \tag{8-31}$$

A substitution of $E = 20,000$ kN/cm^2, $I = 5,000$ cm^4, $k = 5$ kN/cm, $l = 3$ m $= 300$ cm, and $wl = (4)(3) = 12$ kN in Eq. 8-31 yields

$$X = \left(\frac{3}{8}\right)(12)\left(\frac{1}{1 + \frac{(3)(10)^8}{(5)(3)^3(10)^6}}\right) = 1.2 \text{ kN}$$

Some special cases can be derived by specifying the value of spring stiffness. They are given in Fig. 8-7. For instance, $k = 0$ means no axial resistance (free end) (i.e., $X = 0$); $k = \infty$ means an unyielding support, $X = \frac{3}{8}wl$. If the spring is replaced by an elastic link with length L, cross-sectional area A, and modulus of elasticity E, then we use $k = AE/L$ in Eq. 8-31.

8-5 ANALYSIS OF RIGID FRAMES WITHOUT JOINT TRANSLATION BY THE SLOPE-DEFLECTION METHOD

Some rigid frames, such as those shown in Fig. 8-8(a) to (d), are so constructed that translations of joints are prevented. Others, although capable of joint translation in construction, will undergo no joint translation because of the symmetry of the

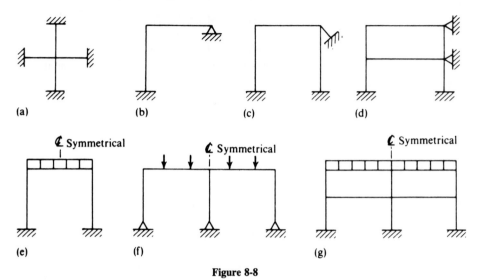

(a)   (b)   (c)   (d)

(e)   (f)   (g)

Figure 8-8

structure and the loading about a certain axis, such as those shown in Fig. 8-8(e) to (g).

In both cases

$$R = 0$$

in the equations of slope-deflection, so the analysis is considerably simplified, as we shall see in the following examples.

Example 8-3

The end moments for the frame shown in Fig. 8-9 were solved by the force method (Examples 5-7 and 5-12) and will be re-solved by slope-deflection.

The analysis is as follows:

1. The relative $2EK$ values for all members are shown encircled.
2. $\theta_a = \theta_d = R = 0$, and because of symmetry, $\theta_c = -\theta_b$.
3. $M^F_{bc} = -M^F_{cb} = -(1.2)(10)^2/12 = -10$ ft-kips.
4. Equations of slope-deflection are then given by

$$M_{ab} = -M_{dc} = (1)(\theta_b) \qquad (8\text{-}32)$$

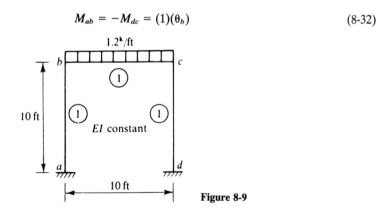

Figure 8-9

$$M_{ba} = -M_{cd} = (1)(2\theta_b) \qquad\qquad (8\text{-}33)$$

$$M_{bc} = -M_{cb} = (1)(2\theta_b - \theta_b) - 10 \qquad\qquad (8\text{-}34)$$

5. There is only one unknown, θ_b, involved in this analysis, and it can be solved by

$$\sum M_{\text{joint } b} = M_{ba} + M_{bc} = 0 \qquad\qquad (8\text{-}35)$$

Substituting Eqs. 8-33 and 8-34 in Eq. 8-35 gives

$$3\theta_b - 10 = 0$$

from which

$$\theta_b = 3.33$$

6. Going back to step 4, we obtain

$$M_{ab} = -M_{dc} = 3.33 \text{ ft-kips}$$

$$M_{ba} = -M_{cd} = 6.67 \text{ ft-kips}$$

$$M_{bc} = -M_{cb} = -6.67 \text{ ft-kips}$$

Example 8-4

Analyze the frame in Fig. 8-10 if the support at a yields 0.0016 rad clockwise. Assume that $EI = 10{,}000$ kips-ft^2.

$$M_{ab} = \frac{2EI}{10}(2\theta_a + \theta_b) = \frac{EI}{5}[(2)(0.0016) + \theta_b]$$

$$M_{ba} = \frac{2EI}{10}(2\theta_b + \theta_a) = \frac{EI}{5}(2\theta_b + 0.0016)$$

$$M_{bc} = \frac{2E(2I)}{20}(2\theta_b + \theta_c) = \frac{EI}{5}(2\theta_b), \qquad \theta_c = 0$$

$$M_{cb} = \frac{2E(2I)}{20}(2\theta_c + \theta_b) = \frac{EI}{5}(\theta_b)$$

The unknown θ_b is solved by

$$\sum M_{\text{joint } b} = M_{ba} + M_{bc} = 0$$

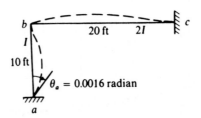

Figure 8-10

or

$$4\theta_b + 0.0016 = 0$$

from which

$$\theta_b = -0.0004$$

With θ_b determined, all end moments can be figured as

$$M_{ab} = \frac{10{,}000}{5}(0.0032 - 0.0004) = 5.6 \text{ ft-kips}$$

$$M_{ba} = \frac{10{,}000}{5}(-0.0008 + 0.0016) = 1.6 \text{ ft-kips}$$

$$M_{bc} = \frac{10{,}000}{5}(-0.0008) = -1.6 \text{ ft-kips}$$

$$M_{cb} = \frac{10{,}000}{5}(-0.0004) = -0.8 \text{ ft-kip}$$

The deformed structure is indicated by the dashed lines in Fig. 8-10.

8-6 ANALYSIS OF RIGID FRAMES WITH ONE DEGREE OF FREEDOM OF JOINT TRANSLATION BY THE SLOPE-DEFLECTION METHOD

Figure 8-11 shows several examples of rigid frames with 1 degree of freedom of joint translation. In each of these examples, if the translation of one joint is given or assumed, the translation of all other joints can be deduced from it.

For instance, suppose that, in the frame in Fig. 8-11(a), joint a moves to a' a distance Δ. Since we neglect any slight change in the length of a member due to axial forces, and since the rotations of members are small, joint a moves essentially perpendicular to member Aa and, in this case, horizontally. Similarly, joint b at the top of column Bb must move horizontally. Furthermore, as b is the end of member ab and the change of axial length of ab is neglected, the horizontal movement of b [see bb' in Fig. 8-11(a)] must also be Δ (i.e., $aa' = bb' = \Delta$).

In the same manner, we reason that if joint a in Fig. 8-11(b) moves a horizontal distance Δ to a', the tops of all the other columns must have the same horizontal displacement.

Let us now consider the case of Fig. 8-11(c) in which the frame is acted on by a lateral force at the top of column Aa. Joint a cannot move other than horizontally, say a distance Δ_1 to a'. To find the final location of joint b, we imagine that the frame is temporarily disconnected at b. Point b, being the end of member ab, will move to b' the displacement Δ_1, if free of other effects except that due to the movement of a. However, b is also the end of member Bb; the final position of b, called b'',

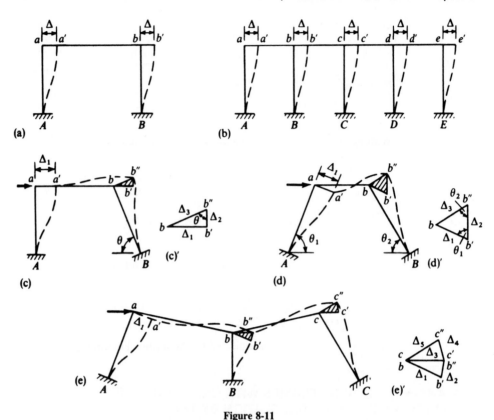

Figure 8-11

must be determined by two arcs that restrict the motion of b', one from a' with a radius equal to ab (or $a'b'$) and the other from B with a radius equal to Bb. Since the deformations of the frame are very small in proportion to the length, it is permissible to substitute the tangents for the arcs, as shown in Fig. 8-11(c). The displacement diagram is shown separately in Fig. 8-11(c)', for which we note that Δ_1 is the relative displacement between the ends of member Aa, Δ_2 that between the ends of ab, and Δ_3 that between the ends of Bb. The relationship between Δ_1, Δ_2, and Δ_3 can be expressed by the sine law:

$$\frac{\Delta_1}{\sin \theta} = \frac{\Delta_2}{\sin (90° - \theta)} = \frac{\Delta_3}{\sin 90°}$$

from which

$$\Delta_1 = \Delta_2 \tan \theta = \Delta_3 \sin \theta$$

The joint displacements of Fig. 8-11(d) are similar to that described for Fig. 8-11(c), noting that joint a should move perpendicularly to member Aa. From the displacement diagram shown in Fig. 8-11(d)', we see that

$$\frac{\Delta_1}{\sin \theta_2} = \frac{\Delta_2}{\sin (\theta_1 + \theta_2)} = \frac{\Delta_3}{\sin \theta_1}$$

The procedure described above is now extended to a two-span frame such as the one shown in Fig. 8-11(e) together with the joint displacement diagram in Fig. 8-11(e)′. It may be extended to any number of spans. With the relative deflection between the ends for each member clarified, it becomes a simple matter to apply the slope-deflection equations.

Example 8-5

Find the end moments for each member of the portal frame shown in Fig. 8-12(a) resulting from a lateral force P acting on the top of the column. Assume constant EI throughout the entire frame.

Because of the lateral force P acting at b, the frame deflects to the right. Both joints b and c move the same horizontal distance Δ, as indicated. There are also rotations θ_b at joint b and θ_c at joint c. Now, since an equal and opposite force P acting at c would completely balance the original force at b and would thus return the structure to the original position (except for some small change of length in bc), θ_b must be equal to θ_c. Thus,

$$M_{ab} = M_{dc} = (1)(\theta_b - 3R), \qquad \theta_a = \theta_d = 0$$

$$M_{ba} = M_{cd} = (1)(2\theta_b - 3R)$$

$$M_{bc} = M_{cb} = (2)(2\theta_b + \theta_b) = 6\theta_b$$

This special case in which the end moments and joint rotations of one side of the center-line axis of the structure are the same as those of the other side is termed *antisymmetry*, in contrast to the case of *symmetry*, in which the values of the end moments and joint rotations of one side of the center-line axis of the structure are equal but opposite to those of the other side, according to the sign convention of slope-deflection.

The unknowns, θ_b and R, are then solved by two equilibrium equations, one for joint b and the other for the entire frame:

$$\sum M_{\text{joint } b} = M_{ba} + M_{bc} = 0$$

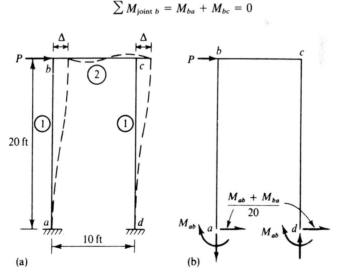

(a)   (b)

Figure 8-12

or

$$8\theta_b - 3R = 0 \qquad (8\text{-}36)$$

By isolating the frame from the supports [Fig. 8-12(b)],

$$\Sigma F_x = (2)\frac{M_{ab} + M_{ba}}{20} + P = 0$$

or

$$3\theta_b - 6R + 10P = 0 \qquad (8\text{-}37)$$

Solving Eqs. 8-36 and 8-37 simultaneously, we obtain

$$\theta_b = \frac{10}{13}P, \qquad 3R = \frac{80}{13}P$$

Substituting these in equations for end moments, we obtain

$$M_{ab} = M_{dc} = -\frac{70}{13}P$$

$$M_{ba} = M_{cd} = -\frac{60}{13}P$$

$$M_{bc} = M_{cb} = +\frac{60}{13}P$$

Example 8-6

Draw the bending moment diagram for the frame shown in Fig. 8-13(a). The relative values of $2EK$ are circled.

   To find the end moments, we begin by sketching the relative displacement diagram, as shown in Fig. 8-13(b). Thus,

$$R_{ab} = \frac{\Delta}{l_{ab}} = \frac{\Delta}{15}$$

$$R_{bc} = -\frac{\frac{3}{4}\Delta}{l_{bc}} = -\frac{\frac{3}{4}\Delta}{15} = -\frac{\Delta}{20}$$

$$R_{cd} = \frac{\frac{5}{4}\Delta}{l_{cd}} = \frac{\frac{5}{4}\Delta}{25} = \frac{\Delta}{20}$$

   If we let $R_{ab} = R$, then $R_{bc} = -3R/4$ and $R_{cd} = 3R/4$. The expressions for the various end moments are now written as

$$M_{ab} = (1)(\theta_b - 3R), \qquad \theta_a = 0$$

$$M_{ba} = (1)(2\theta_b - 3R)$$

$$M_{bc} = (2)[2\theta_b + \theta_c + (3)(\tfrac{3}{4}R)]$$

$$M_{cb} = (2)[2\theta_c + \theta_b + (3)(\tfrac{3}{4}R)]$$

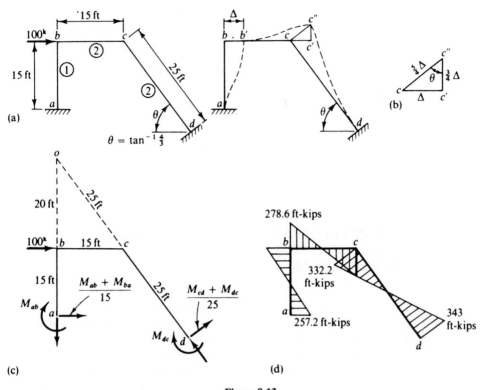

Figure 8-13

$$M_{cd} = (2)[2\theta_c - (3)(\tfrac{3}{4}R)], \qquad \theta_d = 0$$

$$M_{dc} = (2)[\theta_c - (3)(\tfrac{3}{4}R)]$$

Two of the three condition equations required to evaluate the three independent unknowns θ_b, θ_c, and R are from $\Sigma M = 0$ for joints b and c. Thus,

$$M_{ba} + M_{bc} = 0$$

$$6\theta_b + 2\theta_c + 1.5R = 0 \qquad\qquad (8\text{-}38)$$

$$M_{cb} + M_{cd} = 0$$

$$\theta_b + 4\theta_c = 0 \qquad\qquad (8\text{-}39)$$

The third condition equation can best be found by expressing $\Sigma M_o = 0$ for the entire frame, o being the center of moment chosen at the intersection of the two legs [see Fig. 8-13(c)], since this eliminates the axial forces from the equation. Thus,

$$M_{ab} + M_{dc} - (100)(20) - \left(\frac{M_{ab} + M_{ba}}{15}\right)35 - \left(\frac{M_{cd} + M_{dc}}{25}\right)50 = 0$$

$$-6\theta_b - 10\theta_c + 24.5R - 2{,}000 = 0 \qquad (8\text{-}40)$$

Solving Eqs. 8-38, 8-39, and 8-40 simultaneously, we obtain

$$\theta_b = -21.4, \qquad \theta_c = 5.36, \qquad R = 78.6$$

Substitution of these values in the moment expressions yields

$$M_{ab} = -257.2 \text{ ft-kips} \qquad M_{ba} = -278.6 \text{ ft-kips}$$

$$M_{bc} = 278.6 \text{ ft-kips} \qquad M_{cb} = 332.2 \text{ ft-kips}$$

$$M_{cd} = -332.2 \text{ ft-kips}, \qquad M_{dc} = -343.0 \text{ ft-kips}$$

as shown in Fig. 8-13(d).

8-7 ANALYSIS OF RIGID FRAMES WITH TWO DEGREES OF FREEDOM OF JOINT TRANSLATION BY THE SLOPE-DEFLECTION METHOD

The number of degrees of freedom for joint translation in a rigid frame equals the number of independent joint translations that can be given to the frame. Figure 8-14 shows several examples of rigid frames with 2 degrees of freedom of joint translation.

Figure 8-14(a) shows an unsymmetrical gable bent subjected to a vertical load at the top. Under this pressure, joint b will move a distance Δ_1 to b' and joint d a distance Δ_2 to d', as indicated. To locate the position of c, let us imagine that joint c is temporarily disconnected. Joint c, being the end of member bc, will move to c' ($cc' = bb' = \Delta_1$). Joint c, being the end of member cd, will move to c'' ($cc'' = dd' = \Delta_2$). The final position of c is c''', which is the intersection of the line perpendicular to bc drawn at c' and the line perpendicular to cd drawn at c'', as indicated in Fig. 8-14(a). From the displacement diagram Δ_3 (the relative displacement between ends b and c) and Δ_4 (that between c and d) is related to Δ_1 (that between a and b) and Δ_2 (that between d and e) by the sine law,

$$\frac{\Delta_1 + \Delta_2}{\sin(\phi_1 + \phi_2)} = \frac{\Delta_3}{\sin(90° - \phi_2)} = \frac{\Delta_4}{\sin(90° - \phi_1)}$$

or

$$\frac{\Delta_1 + \Delta_2}{\sin(\phi_1 + \phi_2)} = \frac{\Delta_3}{\cos \phi_2} = \frac{\Delta_4}{\cos \phi_1}$$

so Δ_3 and Δ_4 can be deduced from Δ_1 and Δ_2.

The case shown in Fig. 8-14(b) is similar to that of Fig. 8-14(a) except that we assume the tops of the two legs move in the same direction as the result of a lateral force applied at b. The relationships of joint displacements are expressed by

$$\frac{\Delta_1 - \Delta_2}{\sin(\phi_1 + \phi_2)} = \frac{\Delta_3}{\sin(90° - \phi_2)} = \frac{\Delta_4}{\sin(90° - \phi_1)}$$

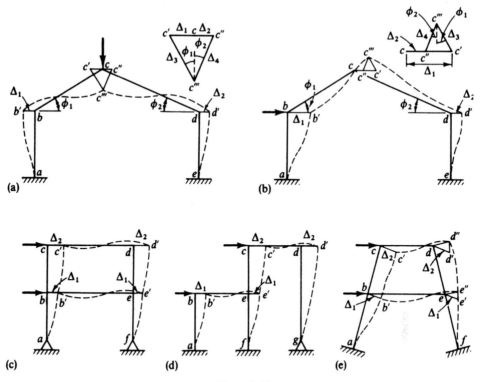

Figure 8-14

or

$$\frac{\Delta_1 - \Delta_2}{\sin(\phi_1 + \phi_2)} = \frac{\Delta_3}{\cos\phi_2} = \frac{\Delta_4}{\cos\phi_1}$$

Figure 8-14(c) and (e) show the joint displacements in two-story frames, and Fig. 8-14(d) shows the joint displacements in a two-stage frame. In each of these cases, the arrangement of the structure is such that the joint translations of the first floor are not required to be in any fixed relationship to those of the second floor (i.e., the translations of joints *b* and *e* are not in a fixed ratio to the translations of joints *c* and *d*). The procedure for finding joint displacements on each floor is the same as that discussed in Sec. 8-6 for one-story frames. With the relative end displacement for each member consistently determined, it becomes rather easy to analyze the frame by the method of slope-deflection.

Example 8-7

Find all the end moments for the gable bent shown in Fig. 8-15(a). Assume constant *EI* throughout the entire frame so that the relative 2*EK* values are the circled numbers.

We start by sketching the joint displacements of the frame as shown in Fig. 8-15(b), for which we note that

$$\Delta_3 = \frac{(\Delta_1 + \Delta_2)\sin(90° - \phi_2)}{\sin(\phi_1 + \phi_2)} = \frac{(\Delta_1 + \Delta_2)\cos\phi_2}{\sin[180° - (\phi_1 + \phi_2)]} = \frac{4}{5}(\Delta_1 + \Delta_2)$$

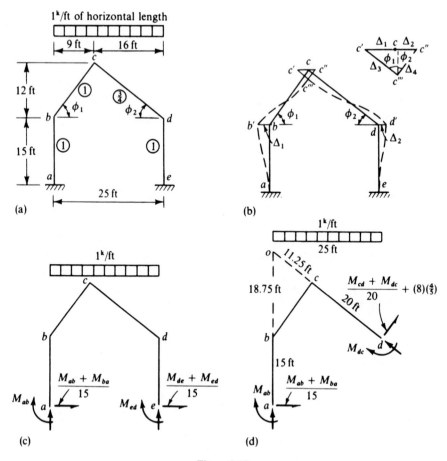

Figure 8-15

since, if we refer to Fig. 8-15(a), $\cos \phi_2 = \frac{4}{5}$ and $180° - (\phi_1 + \phi_2) = \measuredangle c = 90°$ in this case. Similarly,

$$\Delta_4 = \frac{(\Delta_1 + \Delta_2) \cos \phi_1}{\sin[180° - (\phi_1 + \phi_2)]} = \frac{3}{5}(\Delta_1 + \Delta_2)$$

Thus, the rotation of each member can be expressed in terms of Δ_1 and Δ_2.

$$R_{ab} = -\frac{\Delta_1}{15}, \qquad\qquad R_{bc} = \left(\frac{1}{15}\right)\left(\frac{4}{5}\right)(\Delta_1 + \Delta_2)$$

$$R_{cd} = -\left(\frac{1}{20}\right)\left(\frac{3}{5}\right)(\Delta_1 + \Delta_2), \qquad R_{de} = \frac{\Delta_2}{15}$$

If we let $\Delta_1/15 = R_1$ and $\Delta_2/15 = R_2$, we have

$$R_{ab} = -R_1, \qquad\qquad R_{bc} = 0.8(R_1 + R_2)$$

$$R_{cd} = -0.45(R_1 + R_2), \qquad R_{de} = R_2$$

The fixed-end moments are found to be

$$M_{bc}^F = -M_{cb}^F = -\frac{(1)(9)^2}{12} = -6.750 \text{ ft-kips}$$

$$M_{cd}^F = -M_{dc}^F = -\frac{(1)(16)^2}{12} = -21.333 \text{ ft-kips}$$

The expressions for various end moments are then written as

$$M_{ab} = (1)(\theta_b + 3R_1), \qquad \theta_a = 0$$

$$M_{ba} = (1)(2\theta_b + 3R_1)$$

$$M_{bc} = (1)[2\theta_b + \theta_c - 2.4(R_1 + R_2)] - 6.750$$

$$M_{cb} = (1)[2\theta_c + \theta_b - 2.4(R_1 + R_2)] + 6.750$$

$$M_{cd} = (\tfrac{3}{4})[2\theta_c + \theta_d + 1.35(R_1 + R_2)] - 21.333$$

$$M_{dc} = (\tfrac{3}{4})[2\theta_d + \theta_c + 1.35(R_1 + R_2)] + 21.333$$

$$M_{de} = (1)(2\theta_d - 3R_2), \qquad \theta_e = 0$$

$$M_{ed} = (1)(\theta_d - 3R_2)$$

Five statical equations are needed to solve the independent unknowns θ_b, θ_c, θ_d, R_1, and R_2, three from $\Sigma M = 0$ for joints b, c, and d, one from shear balance ($\Sigma F_x = 0$) for the entire frame [see Fig. 8-15(c)], and one from $\Sigma M_o = 0$ for the portion of the frame shown in Fig. 8-15(d). Thus,

$$\Sigma M_{\text{joint } b} = M_{ba} + M_{bc} = 0$$

$$4\theta_b + \theta_c + 0.6R_1 - 2.4R_2 - 6.750 = 0 \tag{8-41}$$

$$\Sigma M_{\text{joint } c} = M_{cb} + M_{cd} = 0$$

$$\theta_b + 3.5\theta_c + 0.75\theta_d - 1.387(R_1 + R_2) - 14.583 = 0 \tag{8-42}$$

$$\Sigma M_{\text{joint } d} = M_{dc} + M_{de} = 0$$

$$0.75\theta_c + 3.5\theta_d + 1.013R_1 - 1.987R_2 + 21.333 = 0 \tag{8-43}$$

$\Sigma F_x = 0$ for the frame of Fig. 8-15(c):

$$\frac{M_{ab} + M_{ba}}{15} + \frac{M_{de} + M_{ed}}{15} = 0$$

$$\theta_b + \theta_d + 2R_1 - 2R_2 = 0 \tag{8-44}$$

$\Sigma M_o = 0$ for the portion of the frame [Fig. 8-15(d)]:

$$M_{ab} - \left(\frac{M_{ab} + M_{ba}}{15}\right)33.75 - \left(\frac{M_{cd} + M_{dc}}{20}\right)31.25 - (8)\left(\frac{4}{5}\right)31.25$$

$$+ M_{dc} + \frac{(1)(25)^2}{2} = 0$$

$$(\theta_b + 3R_1) - 2.25(3\theta_b + 6R_1) - 1.5625[2.25\theta_c + 2.25\theta_d + 2.025(R_1 + R_2)]$$

$$- 200 + [0.75\theta_c + 1.5\theta_d + 1.013(R_1 + R_2) + 21.333] + 312.5 = 0$$

or

$$5.75\theta_b + 2.766\theta_c + 2.016\theta_d + 12.651R_1 + 2.151R_2 - 133.833 = 0 \quad (8\text{-}45)$$

Solving Eqs. 8-41 through 8-45 simultaneously, we obtain

$$\theta_b = 0.385, \qquad \theta_c = 11.039, \qquad \theta_d = -8.340$$

$$R_1 = 8.542, \qquad R_2 = 4.565$$

Substituting these in the expressions for the various end moments, we obtain

$$M_{ab} = 26 \text{ ft-kips}$$

$$M_{ba} = -M_{bc} = 26.3 \text{ ft-kips}$$

$$M_{cb} = -M_{cd} = -2.3 \text{ ft-kips}$$

$$M_{dc} = -M_{de} = 30.3 \text{ ft-kips}$$

$$M_{ed} = -22 \text{ ft-kips}$$

Example 8-8

Analyze the frame in Fig. 8-16(a). Assume that all members are of uniform cross section, so the relative values of $2EK$ are the circled numbers. Because of the action of the lateral forces, the frame will deflect to the right. Assume that joints b and e, on the first-floor level, move a horizontal distance Δ_1; joints c and d, on the second-floor level, move a horizontal distance Δ_2, as shown in Fig. 8-16(b). Antisymmetry exists in this case. Thus,

$$\theta_b = \theta_e, \qquad \theta_c = \theta_d, \qquad R_{ab} = R_{ef} = \frac{\Delta_1}{20}, \qquad R_{bc} = R_{de} = \frac{\Delta_2 - \Delta_1}{20}$$

Now since

$$\theta_a = \theta_f = R_{be} = R_{cd} = 0$$

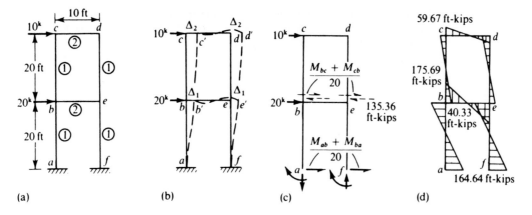

Figure 8-16

the problem involves a total of four unknowns, θ_b, θ_c, R_{ab}, and R_{bc}, which are to be solved by four equations of statics, two from $\Sigma M = 0$ for joints b and c and the other two from shear balance for the frame.

The equations expressing end moments are then written as

$$M_{ab} = M_{fe} = (1)(\theta_b - 3R_{ab}), \qquad \theta_a = 0$$

$$M_{ba} = M_{ef} = (1)(2\theta_b - 3R_{ab})$$

$$M_{bc} = M_{ed} = (1)(2\theta_b + \theta_c - 3R_{bc})$$

$$M_{be} = M_{eb} = (2)(2\theta_b + \theta_e) = 6\theta_b, \qquad \theta_b = \theta_e$$

$$M_{cb} = M_{de} = (1)(2\theta_c + \theta_b - 3R_{bc})$$

$$M_{cd} = M_{dc} = (2)(2\theta_c + \theta_d) = 6\theta_c, \qquad \theta_c = \theta_d$$

The equations from joint equilibrium in moment are then established:

$$M_{ba} + M_{bc} + M_{be} = 0$$

$$10\theta_b + \theta_c - 3R_{ab} - 3R_{bc} = 0 \tag{8-46}$$

$$M_{cb} + M_{cd} = 0$$

$$\theta_b + 8\theta_c - 3R_{bc} = 0 \tag{8-47}$$

The third equation is from shear balance for the entire frame isolated from the supports [see Fig. 8-16(c)]:

$$2\left(\frac{M_{ab} + M_{ba}}{20}\right) + 20 + 10 = 0$$

$$\theta_b - 2R_{ab} + 100 = 0 \tag{8-48}$$

The fourth equation results from considering the free body cut out by a horizontal section just above *be*; the shear in the two legs [see the dashed lines in Fig. 8-16(c)] must balance the lateral force of 10 kips. Thus,

$$2\left(\frac{M_{bc} + M_{cb}}{20}\right) + 10 = 0$$

$$3\theta_b + 3\theta_c - 6R_{bc} + 100 = 0 \qquad (8\text{-}49)$$

Solving Eqs. 8-46 through 8-49 simultaneously, we obtain

$$\theta_b = 29.282, \qquad \theta_c = 9.945$$

$$R_{ab} = 64.641, \qquad R_{cd} = 36.282$$

Substituting these in the moment equations, we arrive at

$$M_{ab} = M_{fe} = -164.64 \text{ ft-kips}$$

$$M_{ba} = M_{ef} = -135.36 \text{ ft-kips}$$

$$M_{bc} = M_{ed} = -40.33 \text{ ft-kips}$$

$$M_{be} = M_{eb} = +175.69 \text{ ft-kips}$$

$$M_{cb} = M_{de} = -59.67 \text{ ft-kips}$$

$$M_{cd} = M_{dc} = +59.67 \text{ ft-kips}$$

as plotted in Fig. 8-16(d).

8-8 MATRIX FORMULATION OF THE SLOPE-DEFLECTION PROCEDURE

In the slope-deflection method, the joint displacements appear as the basic unknown in the simultaneous equations that express the joint equilibrium of forces in terms of joint rotations and translations. The matrix formulation of these equilibrium equations will readily throw light on the analysis, revealing the essence of the matrix stiffness procedure. This can best be illustrated by going over the problem in Fig. 8-3.

We start by Eq. 8-10 and, with some modifications, rewrite the slope-deflection equations as

$$M_{ab} = 2E\frac{I_{ab}}{l_{ab}}\left(\theta_b - \frac{3\Delta}{l_{ab}}\right) - 25$$

$$M_{ba} = 2E\frac{I_{ab}}{l_{ab}}\left(2\theta_b - \frac{3\Delta}{l_{ab}}\right) + 25$$

$$M_{bc} = 2E\frac{I_{bc}}{l_{bc}}(2\theta_b + \theta_c)$$

$$M_{cb} = 2E\frac{I_{bc}}{l_{bc}}(2\theta_c + \theta_b)$$

(8-50)

$$M_{cd} = 2E\frac{I_{cd}}{l_{cd}}\left(2\theta_c - \frac{3\Delta}{l_{cd}}\right)$$

$$M_{dc} = 2E\frac{I_{cd}}{l_{cd}}\left(\theta_c - \frac{3\Delta}{l_{cd}}\right)$$

We also rewrite the joint equilibrium equations as

$$M_{ba} + M_{bc} = 0$$

$$M_{cb} + M_{cd} = 0$$

(8-51)

$$\frac{M_{ab} + M_{ba}}{l_{ab}} + \frac{M_{cd} + M_{dc}}{l_{cd}} + 5 = 0$$

Substituting the various expressions of eq. 8-50 in Eq. 8-51, we have

$$\left(\frac{4EI_{ab}}{l_{ab}} + \frac{4EI_{bc}}{l_{bc}}\right)\theta_b + \frac{2EI_{bc}}{l_{bc}}\theta_c - \frac{6EI_{ab}}{l_{ab}^2}\Delta + 25 = 0$$

$$\frac{2EI_{bc}}{l_{bc}}\theta_b + \left(\frac{4EI_{bc}}{l_{bc}} + \frac{4EI_{cd}}{l_{cd}}\right)\theta_c - \frac{6EI_{cd}}{l_{cd}^2}\Delta = 0$$

(8-52)

$$\frac{6EI_{ab}}{l_{ab}^2}\theta_b + \frac{6EI_{cd}}{l_{cd}^2}\theta_c - \left(\frac{12EI_{ab}}{l_{ab}^3} + \frac{12EI_{cd}}{l_{cd}^3}\right)\Delta + 5 = 0$$

Equation 8-52 in matrix form is

FJA $\theta_b = 1$ $\theta_c = 1$ $\Delta = 1$

$$\begin{Bmatrix} 25 \\ 0 \\ -5 \end{Bmatrix} + \begin{bmatrix} \dfrac{4EI_{ab}}{l_{ab}} + \dfrac{4EI_{bc}}{l_{bc}} & \dfrac{2EI_{bc}}{l_{bc}} & -\dfrac{6EI_{ab}}{l_{ab}^2} \\[3mm] \dfrac{2EI_{bc}}{l_{bc}} & \dfrac{4EI_{bc}}{l_{bc}} + \dfrac{4EI_{cd}}{l_{cd}} & -\dfrac{6EI_{cd}}{l_{cd}^2} \\[3mm] -\dfrac{6EI_{ab}}{l_{ab}^2} & -\dfrac{6EI_{cd}}{l_{cd}^2} & \dfrac{12EI_{ab}}{l_{ab}^3} + \dfrac{12EI_{cd}}{l_{cd}^3} \end{bmatrix} \begin{Bmatrix} \theta_b \\ \theta_c \\ \Delta \end{Bmatrix} = \begin{Bmatrix} 0 \\ 0 \\ 0 \end{Bmatrix}$$

(8-53)

Equation 8-53 can be put into generalized form

$$F' + SD = F$$

(8-54)

We notice that the column matrix F' on the left-hand side of Eq. 8-53 or 8-54 represents the fixed-joint action (FJA) under applied member loads, while the square matrix S is a stiffness matrix, each column of which gives the various joint actions required to produce a certain unit joint displacement. Note that the stiffness matrix is symmetrical. The column matrix D represents joint displacements. The column matrix F on the right-hand side of the same equation contains the actual joint loads (JL) corresponding to the joint displacements. In our case there are no loads actually acting on joints b and c, so the elements in the JL matrix are zeros.

It may be interesting to compare Eq. 8-54 with Eq. 5-11 and find out the duality between the displacement method (stiffness method) and the force method (flexibility method).

The analysis therefore can be performed as follows:

1. Analyze a restrained structure with all joints fixed (kinematically determinate) and subjected to member loads only [Fig. 8-17(a)]. With reference to Fig. 8-17(b), we see that locking the joint b against rotation requires an artificial moment

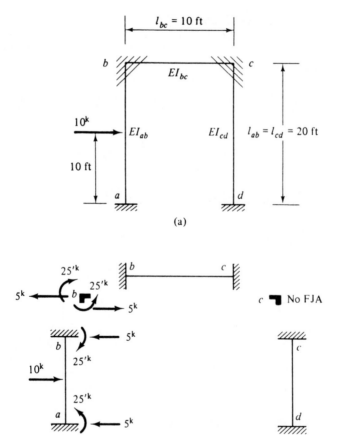

(a)

(b)   **Figure 8-17**

force of 25 ft-kips acting clockwise in order to balance the internal moment exerted by member ab at that joint. Likewise, preventing the lateral translation of joint b requires a lateral force of 5 kips acting to the left to balance the internal shear exerted by member ab at joint b. Simply, the fixed-joint action is obtained from the algebraic sum of fixed-end actions of the related members.

2. Apply joint displacements individually and successively to joints b and c (free joints) so that the altered structure is restored to the actual displaced configuration. Figure 8-18 shows the separate cases of unit joint displacement from which we obtained the joint forces corresponding to these displacements. For instance, turning a unit rotation of joint b would require a moment force of $(4EI_{ab}/l_{ab} + 4EI_{bc}/l_{bc})$ at joint b, a moment force of $2EI_{bc}/l_{bc}$ at joint c, and a lateral force of $-6EI_{ab}/l_{ab}^2$ (acting to the left) at b. The rest can similarly be explained. These are stiffness coefficients that construct the stiffness matrix of Eq. 8-53.

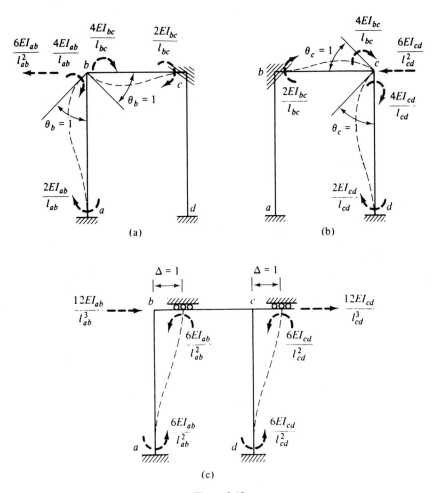

(a)

(b)

(c)

Figure 8-18

3. Steps 1 and 2 accomplish the geometric configuration (compatibility). It remains for us to say that the sum of joint forces thus obtained must be equal to the actual joint loads (equilibrium). This completes our formulation.

Using $2EI_{ab}/l_{ab} = 2EI_{cd}/l_{cd} = 1$, $2EI_{bc}/l_{bc} = 2$, and $l_{ab} = l_{cd} = 2l_{bc} = 20$, we reduce Eq. 8-53 to

$$\begin{Bmatrix} 25 \\ 0 \\ -5 \end{Bmatrix} + \begin{bmatrix} 6 & 2 & -\frac{3}{20} \\ 2 & 6 & -\frac{3}{20} \\ -\frac{3}{20} & -\frac{3}{20} & \frac{12}{400} \end{bmatrix} \begin{Bmatrix} \theta_b \\ \theta_c \\ \Delta \end{Bmatrix} = \begin{Bmatrix} 0 \\ 0 \\ 0 \end{Bmatrix} \tag{8-55}$$

Replacing Δ with R ($R = \Delta/20$) in Eq. 8-55 and multiplying the last equation by 20 gives

$$\begin{Bmatrix} 25 \\ 0 \\ -100 \end{Bmatrix} + \begin{bmatrix} 6 & 2 & -3 \\ 2 & 6 & -3 \\ -3 & -3 & 12 \end{bmatrix} \begin{Bmatrix} \theta_b \\ \theta_c \\ R \end{Bmatrix} = \begin{Bmatrix} 0 \\ 0 \\ 0 \end{Bmatrix} \tag{8-56}$$

which is identical to the set of simultaneous equations given in Eqs. 8-15 to 8-17.

PROBLEMS

8-1. Analyze the beam shown in Fig. 8-19 by slope-deflection. Draw the shear and moment diagrams.

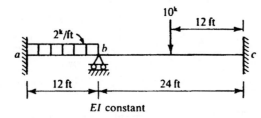

EI constant   **Figure 8-19**

8-2. Figure 8-20 shows a frame of uniform cross section. Find all the end moments by slope-deflection, and sketch the deformed structure.

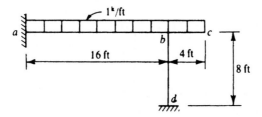

Figure 8-20

8-3. Analyze the beam shown in Fig. 8-21 by slope-deflection. Draw the shear and moment diagrams.

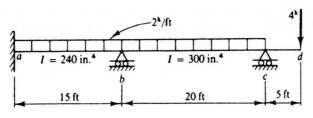

Figure 8-21

8-4. Find all the end moments by slope-deflection for the rigid frame shown in Fig. 8-22. Draw the moment diagram, and sketch the deformed structure.

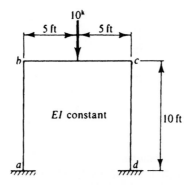

Figure 8-22

8-5. In Fig. 8-21, remove all the loads, and assume that the support b settles vertically 0.5 in. Find all the end moments by slope-deflection. $E = 30,000$ kips/in.^{2}.

8-6. In Fig. 8-22, remove the load, and assume that a rotational yield of 0.002 rad clockwise and a linear yield downward of 0.1 in. occur at support a. Find the moment diagram. $EI = 10,000$ kips-ft^2.

8-7. For the system and load shown in Fig. 8-23, use the method of slope-deflection to find the spring force if $EI = 2 \times 10^8$ kN-cm^2 and the axial stiffness of the spring $k = 8$ kN/cm.

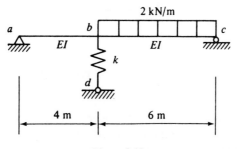

Figure 8-23

8-8. For the load and frame shown in Fig. 8-24, use the method of slope-deflection to find the reaction at supports a and c, and sketch the deformed structure.

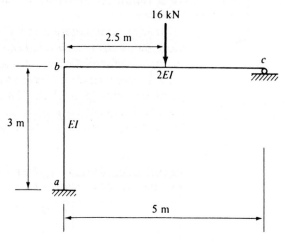

Figure 8-24

8-9. Find all the end moments by slope-deflection for the rigid frame shown in Fig. 8-25. Draw the moment diagram, and sketch the deformed structure. [*Hint:* There are two slopes at c (i.e., θ_{cb} and θ_{cd}). Use the condition $M_{cb} = M_{cd} = 0$ to evaluate the two unknowns.]

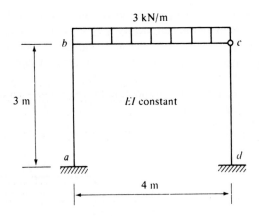

Figure 8-25

8-10. For the system shown in Fig. 8-26, use the method of slope-deflection to find the reaction at support d if $E = 20{,}000$ kN/cm^2, $I = 40{,}000$ cm^4, and the axial stiffness of the spring $k = 5$ kN/cm.

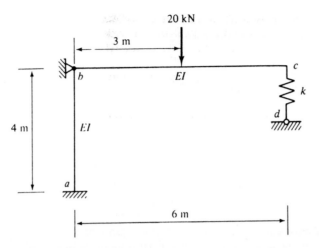

Figure 8-26

8-11. Analyze each frame shown in Fig. 8-27 by slope-deflection, and draw the moment diagram. Assume constant EI.

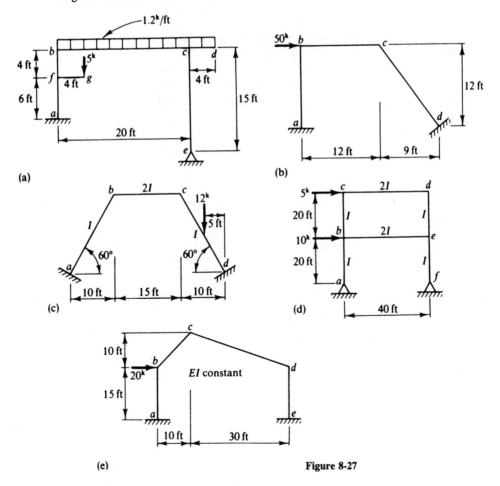

Figure 8-27

8-12. Find the fixed-end moments for the beams shown in Fig. 8-28 by slope deflection. Assume that $w = 3$ kN/m and $l = 4$ m.

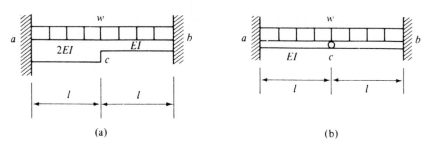

Figure 8-28

8-13. Repeat Problem 8-3 by the matrix stiffness procedure.

8-14. Repeat Problem 8-11 shown in Fig. 8-27(b) by the matrix stiffness procedure.

8-15. Use the matrix stiffness method to analyze the frame shown in Fig. 8-29.

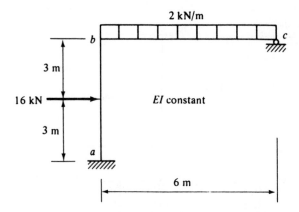

Figure 8-29

Chapter 9

Matrix Displacement Method

9-1 GENERAL

We have seen that the slope-deflection method is a displacement method. We may easily develop a matrix displacement method that, when applied to rigid frame problems, is equivalent to the slope-deflection method. We have also seen that the slope deflection method becomes cumbersome when a frame has inclined members. In that case the kinematic relationship between joint translation and member rotation needs to be carefully derived. Thus, a matrix displacement method that is equivalent to the slope deflection method will have the same difficulty and is not easily programmable for computer applications. This kinematic problem results from the assumption of zero axial deformation for all members. If this assumption is relaxed, a more general matrix displacement method can be formulated. We will follow this general approach to formulate a matrix displacement method for rigid frames and trusses. At the heart of this method is a simple way of assembling the equilibrium equations of the whole structure by the *direct stiffness method*.

   We start the formulation by discretizing the structure into elements (or members) connected by nodes (or joints). The treatment of load between the nodes is similar to that of the matrix force method; that is, statically equivalent nodal forces are derived from the applied load and the final solution is obtained by the principle of superposition (see Sec. 6-1 and Fig. 6-1). Thus, we will consider forces applied only at nodes in the formulation of the method. We begin by deriving the force–displacement relationship of a typical element.

9-2 ELEMENT STIFFNESS EQUATION IN LOCAL COORDINATES

Let us isolate a typical prismatic element with constant EI from a rigid frame and place it in a *global coordinate system* $X–Y$ as shown in Fig. 9-1(a). The location of the element is defined by a starting node, i, at (x_i, y_i) and a terminating node, j, at (x_j, y_j). The orientation of the element is defined by the direction from node i to node j. A local coordinate $\overline{X}–\overline{Y}$ system is then defined by placing the origin at node i and the $\overline{X}$ axis in the direction of the element [Fig. 9-1(a)]. The two coordinate systems are related by an angle ϕ measured from the local $\overline{X}$ axis to the global X axis. A clockwise angle is defined as positive.

After deformation, the new position of the element is shown in Fig. 9-1(b). The nodal displacement is characterized by two translational displacements, $\overline{u}$ and $\overline{v}$, and a rotational displacement, $\overline{\theta}$, for each node, all defined in the local coordinate system. These nodal displacements are vector quantities that can be represented as shown in Fig. 9-1(c), where clockwise rotation is considered positive. The corresponding two nodal forces and a moment, $\overline{F}_X$, $\overline{F}_Y$, and $\overline{M}$ for each node are shown in Fig. 9-1(d). We will now find the relationship between the nodal displacements and the nodal forces.

There are several ways to derive this relationship. In fact, we could have simply used the results from the matrix force method or the formulas derived in the moment distribution method. We will use the following three equivalent methods, however, because they are general methods (see Appendix C) used in deriving similar relationship in finite element methods for two- and three-dimensional elasticity problems.

9-2a Method of Virtual Displacement

This method is often called the principle of virtual work. To distinguish it from the method of virtual force (see Sec. 4-5), which is also a virtual work method, we call it the method of virtual displacement. It states that *a necessary and sufficient condition for the equilibrium of a deformable body is the equivalence of the work done by internal forces on an imaginary virtual displacement from the equilibrium position and the work done by the external forces on the same virtual displacement*. The external virtual work is often denoted by δW and the internal virtual work, also called virtual strain energy, is denoted by δU. Thus, the method of virtual displacement is expressed as

$$\delta W = \delta U \qquad (9-1)$$

In its application, the real displacement (still unknown) is assumed in the form of some known functions with unknown parameters. The internal forces are then derived from the assumed displacement. A virtual displacement function is then assumed upon which δW and δU are calculated. Equation 9-1 is then used to give the equilibrium condition.

In the present case, we will treat the axial deformation separately from the

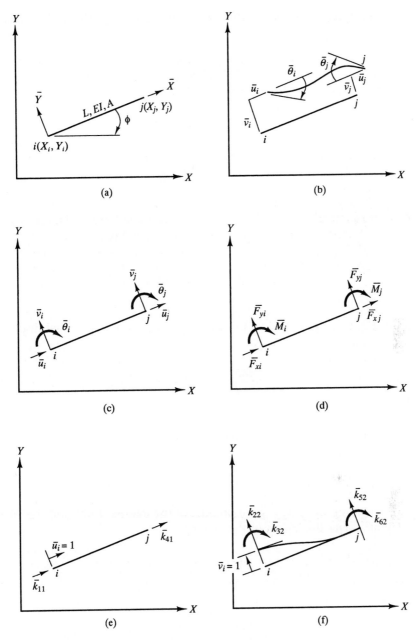

Figure 9-1

bending deformation because they are independent from each other. We assume a linear function for the real axial displacement $\bar{u}(\bar{x})$,

$$\bar{u}(\bar{x}) = \left(1 - \frac{\bar{x}}{L}\right)\bar{u}_i + \frac{\bar{x}}{L}\bar{u}_j \tag{9-2}$$

in terms of the unknown nodal displacements $\bar{u}_i$ and $\bar{u}_j$. The internal axial force $\bar{F}_X$ is then

$$\bar{F}_X = EA\frac{d\bar{u}}{d\bar{x}}$$

$$= EA(-\bar{u}_i + \bar{u}_j)\frac{1}{L} \tag{9-3}$$

$$= EA\left[-\frac{1}{L}\ \ \frac{1}{L}\right]\left\{\begin{matrix}\bar{u}_i\\\bar{u}_j\end{matrix}\right\}$$

Now, we assume a virtual displacement in the same form as the real displacement, but in terms of virtual nodal displacements $\delta\bar{u}_i$ and $\delta\bar{u}_j$.

$$\delta\bar{u}(\bar{x}) = \left(1 - \frac{\bar{x}}{L}\right)\delta\bar{u}_i + \frac{\bar{x}}{L}\delta\bar{u}_j \tag{9-4}$$

From Eq. 9-4, the virtual strain (i.e., strain based on the virtual displacement) is obtained as

$$\frac{d\delta\bar{u}(\bar{x})}{d\bar{x}} = -\frac{1}{L}\delta\bar{u}_i + \frac{1}{L}\delta\bar{u}_j$$

$$= \left\{\begin{matrix}\delta\bar{u}_i\\\delta\bar{u}_j\end{matrix}\right\}^T\left\{\begin{matrix}-\frac{1}{L}\\\frac{1}{L}\end{matrix}\right\} \tag{9-5}$$

The virtual strain energy is the product of the internal force and the virtual strain integrated over the length of the element.

$$\delta U_a = \int_0^L \frac{d\delta\bar{u}(\bar{x})}{d\bar{x}}\bar{F}_X\,d\bar{x}$$

$$= \int_0^L \left\{\begin{matrix}\delta\bar{u}_i\\\delta\bar{u}_j\end{matrix}\right\}^T\left\{\begin{matrix}-\frac{1}{L}\\\frac{1}{L}\end{matrix}\right\}EA\left[-\frac{1}{L}\ \ \frac{1}{L}\right]\left\{\begin{matrix}\bar{u}_i\\\bar{u}_j\end{matrix}\right\}d\bar{x} \tag{9-6}$$

$$= \left\{\begin{matrix}\delta\bar{u}_i\\\delta\bar{u}_j\end{matrix}\right\}^T\left[\begin{matrix}\frac{EA}{L} & -\frac{EA}{L}\\-\frac{EA}{L} & \frac{EA}{L}\end{matrix}\right]\left\{\begin{matrix}\bar{u}_i\\\bar{u}_j\end{matrix}\right\}$$

The virtual work of the external forces, in this case the nodal forces, is simply

$$\delta W = \left\{ \begin{array}{c} \delta\bar{u}_i \\ \delta\bar{u}_j \end{array} \right\}^T \left\{ \begin{array}{c} \bar{F}_{xi} \\ \bar{F}_{xj} \end{array} \right\} \tag{9-7}$$

Equating δW from Eq. 9-7 to δU from Eq. 9-6, we obtain

$$\left\{ \begin{array}{c} \delta\bar{u}_i \\ \delta\bar{u}_j \end{array} \right\}^T \left[\begin{array}{cc} \dfrac{EA}{L} & -\dfrac{EA}{L} \\ -\dfrac{EA}{L} & \dfrac{EA}{L} \end{array} \right] \left\{ \begin{array}{c} \bar{u}_i \\ \bar{u}_j \end{array} \right\} = \left\{ \begin{array}{c} \delta\bar{u}_i \\ \delta\bar{u}_j \end{array} \right\}^T \left\{ \begin{array}{c} \bar{F}_{xi} \\ \bar{F}_{xj} \end{array} \right\} \tag{9-8}$$

This is a single scalar equation. But, the virtual nodal displacements, $\delta\bar{u}_i$ and $\delta\bar{u}_j$, are arbitrary. For Eq. 9-8 to hold for any $\delta\bar{u}_i$ and $\delta\bar{u}_j$, we must have

$$\underbrace{\left[\begin{array}{cc} \dfrac{EA}{L} & -\dfrac{EA}{L} \\ -\dfrac{EA}{L} & \dfrac{EA}{L} \end{array} \right]}_{\bar{k}_a} \underbrace{\left\{ \begin{array}{c} \bar{u}_i \\ \bar{u}_j \end{array} \right\}}_{\bar{q}_a} = \underbrace{\left\{ \begin{array}{c} \bar{F}_{xi} \\ \bar{F}_{xj} \end{array} \right\}}_{\bar{Q}_a} \tag{9-9}$$

or

$$\bar{k}_a \bar{q}_a = \bar{Q}_a \tag{9-10}$$

Equation 9-9 relates the axial nodal displacements to the axial nodal forces through a stiffness matrix, $\bar{k}_a$. Each column of the stiffness matrix gives the force induced at each node by a unit displacement at one of the two nodes. Equation 9-9 is the axial element stiffness equation, and the matrix $\bar{k}_a$ is the element stiffness matrix for axial deformation.

9-2b Principle of Minimum Total Potential Energy

The principle of minimum total potential energy states that *at a stable equilibrium position the total potential energy of a deformable body is at a minimum with respect to any change in displacements*. The total potential energy, denoted by Π_p, is defined as the strain energy, U, plus a force potential, V, which is defined as the negative of the product of external forces and the corresponding displacements.

$$\Pi_p = U + V \tag{9-11}$$

We now use this principle to derive the element bending stiffness equation.

For beam in bending, the strain energy is, from Eq. 4-15,

$$U_b = \int_0^L \frac{M^2}{2EI} d\bar{x} \tag{9-12}$$

For this principle to work, the strain energy must be expressed in terms of displacement variables. We recall, from Eq. 4-4,

$$\frac{d^2 \bar{v}}{d\bar{x}^2} = \frac{M}{EI} \tag{4-4}$$

Thus, the strain energy in terms of transverse displacement becomes

$$U_b = \int_0^L \frac{EI}{2} \left(\frac{d^2 \bar{v}}{d\bar{x}^2} \right)^2 d\bar{x} \tag{9-13}$$

We now need an expression for the transverse displacement. We know, from Fig. 9-1(c), that

$$\bar{v} = \bar{v}_i, \qquad \frac{d\bar{v}}{d\bar{x}} = -\bar{\theta}_i, \qquad \text{at node } i$$

$$\bar{v} = \bar{v}_j, \qquad \frac{d\bar{v}}{d\bar{x}} = -\bar{\theta}_j, \qquad \text{at node } j \tag{9-14}$$

These four conditions may be used to determine the four constants of a cubic function. The transverse displacement is then expressed in terms of these four nodal displacements, each with an associated cubic function (see Problem 9-1).

$$\bar{v}(x) = f_1 \bar{v}_i + f_2 \bar{\theta}_i + f_3 \bar{v}_j + f_4 \bar{\theta}_j \tag{9-15}$$

where

$$f_1 = 1 - 3\left(\frac{\bar{x}}{L}\right)^2 + 2\left(\frac{\bar{x}}{L}\right)^3$$

$$f_2 = L\left[-\frac{\bar{x}}{L} + 2\left(\frac{\bar{x}}{L}\right)^2 - \left(\frac{\bar{x}}{L}\right)^3 \right]$$

$$f_3 = 3\left(\frac{\bar{x}}{L}\right)^2 - 2\left(\frac{\bar{x}}{L}\right)^3 \tag{9-16}$$

$$f_4 = L\left[\left(\frac{\bar{x}}{L}\right)^2 - \left(\frac{\bar{x}}{L}\right)^3 \right]$$

From Eqs. 9-15 and 9-16,

$$\frac{d^2 \bar{v}}{d\bar{x}^2} = f_1'' \bar{v}_i + f_2'' \bar{\theta}_i + f_3'' \bar{v}_j + f_4'' \bar{\theta}_j \tag{9-17}$$

where the double prime denotes double differentiation with respect to x, and

$$f_1'' = \frac{1}{L^2}\left[-6 + 12\left(\frac{\bar{x}}{L}\right)\right]$$

$$f_2'' = \frac{1}{L}\left[4 - 6\left(\frac{\bar{x}}{L}\right)\right]$$

$$f_3'' = \frac{1}{L^2}\left[6 - 12\left(\frac{\bar{x}}{L}\right)\right]$$

(9-18)

$$f_4'' = \frac{1}{L}\left[2 - 6\left(\frac{\bar{x}}{L}\right)\right]$$

We may execute the integration in Eq. 9-13 to obtain

$$U_b = \int_0^L \frac{EI}{2}\left(\frac{d^2\bar{v}}{d\bar{x}^2}\right)\left(\frac{d^2\bar{v}}{d\bar{x}^2}\right) dx$$

$$= \int_0^L \frac{EI}{2}\begin{Bmatrix}\bar{v}_i\\\theta_i\\\bar{v}_j\\\theta_j\end{Bmatrix}^T \begin{Bmatrix}f_1''\\f_2''\\f_3''\\f_4''\end{Bmatrix}[f_1''\ \ f_2''\ \ f_3''\ \ f_4'']\begin{Bmatrix}\bar{v}_i\\\theta_i\\\bar{v}_j\\\theta_j\end{Bmatrix} d\bar{x}$$

$$= \int_0^L \frac{EI}{2}\begin{Bmatrix}\bar{v}_i\\\theta_i\\\bar{v}_j\\\theta_j\end{Bmatrix}^T \begin{bmatrix}f_1''f_1'' & f_1''f_2'' & f_1''f_3'' & f_1''f_4''\\ f_2''f_1'' & f_2''f_2'' & f_2''f_3'' & f_2''f_4''\\ f_3''f_1'' & f_3''f_2'' & f_3''f_3'' & f_3''f_4''\\ f_4''f_1'' & f_4''f_2'' & f_4''f_3'' & f_4''f_4''\end{bmatrix}\begin{Bmatrix}\bar{v}_i\\\theta_i\\\bar{v}_j\\\theta_j\end{Bmatrix} d\bar{x}$$

(9-19)

$$= \frac{1}{2}\underbrace{\begin{Bmatrix}\bar{v}_i\\\theta_i\\\bar{v}_j\\\theta_j\end{Bmatrix}^T}_{\bar{q}_b^T} \underbrace{\begin{bmatrix}\dfrac{12EI}{L^3} & -\dfrac{6EI}{L^2} & -\dfrac{12EI}{L^3} & -\dfrac{6EI}{L^2}\\[2mm] -\dfrac{6EI}{L^2} & \dfrac{4EI}{L} & \dfrac{6EI}{L^2} & \dfrac{2EI}{L}\\[2mm] -\dfrac{12EI}{L^3} & \dfrac{6EI}{L^2} & \dfrac{12EI}{L^3} & \dfrac{6EI}{L^2}\\[2mm] -\dfrac{6EI}{L^2} & \dfrac{2EI}{L} & \dfrac{6EI}{L^2} & \dfrac{4EI}{L}\end{bmatrix}}_{\bar{k}_b}\underbrace{\begin{Bmatrix}\bar{v}_i\\\theta_i\\\bar{v}_j\\\theta_j\end{Bmatrix}}_{\bar{q}_b}$$

or

$$U_b = \tfrac{1}{2}\bar{q}_b^T \bar{k}_b \bar{q}_b$$

(9-20)

The force potential in this case is simply

$$V = -\begin{Bmatrix} \overline{v}_i \\ \theta_i \\ \overline{v}_j \\ \theta_j \end{Bmatrix}^T \begin{Bmatrix} \overline{F}_{yi} \\ \overline{M}_i \\ \overline{F}_{yj} \\ \overline{M}_j \end{Bmatrix} \qquad (9\text{-}21)$$

$$\overline{q}_b^T \qquad \overline{Q}_b$$

or

$$V = -\overline{q}_b^T \overline{Q}_b \qquad (9\text{-}22)$$

Substituting Eqs. 9-20 and 9-21 into Eq. 9-11, we obtain

$$\Pi_p = \tfrac{1}{2}\overline{q}_b^T \overline{k}_b \overline{q}_b - \overline{q}_b^T \overline{Q}_b \qquad (9\text{-}23)$$

To find the minimum, we take differentiation of Π_p with respect to each of the nodal displacements and put the result to zero.

$$\frac{\partial \Pi_p}{\partial \overline{q}_{b_n}} = 0, \qquad n = 1, 2, 3, \text{ and } 4 \qquad (9\text{-}24)$$

The result (see Problem 9-2) is

$$\overline{k}_b \overline{q}_b = \overline{Q}_b \qquad (9\text{-}25)$$

This is the element stiffness equation for bending, and the matrix $\overline{k}_b$ is called the element stiffness matrix for bending.

9-2c Castigliano's First Theorem

We learned Castigliano's second theorem in Sec. 4-6 in the context of the force method. In displacement method, there is a counterpart called Castigliano's first theorem. It states that *a structure subjected to N external forces (moments), Q_n, $n = 1, 2, \ldots, N$, is in equilibrium if the partial derivative of the strain energy with respect to the individual deflection under the load equals the load itself.* In other words,

$$\frac{\partial U}{\partial q_n} = Q_n, \qquad n = 1, 2, \ldots, N \qquad (9\text{-}26)$$

We will now use Castigliano's first theorem to derive the complete element stiffness including both axial and bending deformations. The total strain energy is the sum of the strain energy due to axial deformation and that of bending deformation.

$$U = U_a + U_b \tag{9-27}$$

We already have the expression for U_b in terms of the nodal displacements q_b (Eqs. 9-19 and 9-20). Similarly, U_a can be expressed in terms of $\bar{q}_a$ (see Problem 9-3).

$$U_a = \tfrac{1}{2}\bar{q}_a^T \bar{k}_a \bar{q}_a \tag{9-28}$$

Thus, the total strain energy is

$$U = \tfrac{1}{2}\bar{q}_a^T \bar{k}_a \bar{q}_a + \tfrac{1}{2}\bar{q}_b^T \bar{k}_b \bar{q}_b \tag{9-29}$$

Referring to Eqs. 9-9 and 9-19 for the expression of the stiffness matrices and defining a nodal displacement vector $\bar{q}$ to include both $\bar{q}_a$ and $\bar{q}_b$, we obtain

$$U = \frac{1}{2}
\begin{Bmatrix} \bar{u}_i \\ \bar{u}_j \\ \bar{v}_i \\ \bar{\theta}_i \\ \bar{v}_j \\ \bar{\theta}_j \end{Bmatrix}^T
\begin{bmatrix}
\dfrac{EA}{L} & -\dfrac{EA}{L} & 0 & 0 & 0 & 0 \\[2mm]
-\dfrac{EA}{L} & \dfrac{EA}{L} & 0 & 0 & 0 & 0 \\[2mm]
0 & 0 & \dfrac{12EI}{L^3} & -\dfrac{6EI}{L^2} & -\dfrac{12EI}{L^3} & -\dfrac{6EI}{L^2} \\[2mm]
0 & 0 & -\dfrac{6EI}{L^2} & \dfrac{4EI}{L} & \dfrac{6EI}{L^2} & \dfrac{2EI}{L} \\[2mm]
0 & 0 & -\dfrac{12EI}{L^3} & \dfrac{6EI}{L^2} & \dfrac{12EI}{L^3} & \dfrac{6EI}{L^2} \\[2mm]
0 & 0 & -\dfrac{6EI}{L^2} & \dfrac{2EI}{L} & \dfrac{6EI}{L^2} & \dfrac{4EI}{L}
\end{bmatrix}
\begin{Bmatrix} \bar{u}_i \\ \bar{u}_j \\ \bar{v}_i \\ \bar{\theta}_i \\ \bar{v}_j \\ \bar{\theta}_j \end{Bmatrix}$$

A more convenient form, with displacements of the same node grouped together, is

$$U = \frac{1}{2}
\underbrace{\begin{Bmatrix} \bar{u}_i \\ \bar{v}_i \\ \bar{\theta}_i \\ \bar{u}_j \\ \bar{v}_j \\ \bar{\theta}_j \end{Bmatrix}^T}_{\bar{q}^T}
\underbrace{\begin{bmatrix}
\dfrac{EA}{L} & 0 & 0 & -\dfrac{EA}{L} & 0 & 0 \\[2mm]
0 & \dfrac{12EI}{L^3} & -\dfrac{6EI}{L^2} & 0 & -\dfrac{12EI}{L^3} & -\dfrac{6EI}{L^2} \\[2mm]
0 & -\dfrac{6EI}{L^2} & \dfrac{4EI}{L} & 0 & \dfrac{6EI}{L^2} & \dfrac{2EI}{L} \\[2mm]
-\dfrac{EA}{L} & 0 & 0 & \dfrac{EA}{L} & 0 & 0 \\[2mm]
0 & -\dfrac{12EI}{L^3} & \dfrac{6EI}{L^2} & 0 & \dfrac{12EI}{L^3} & \dfrac{6EI}{L^2} \\[2mm]
0 & -\dfrac{6EI}{L^2} & \dfrac{2EI}{L} & 0 & \dfrac{6EI}{L^2} & \dfrac{4EI}{L}
\end{bmatrix}}_{\bar{k}}
\underbrace{\begin{Bmatrix} \bar{u}_i \\ \bar{v}_i \\ \bar{\theta}_i \\ \bar{u}_j \\ \bar{v}_j \\ \bar{\theta}_j \end{Bmatrix}}_{\bar{q}}
\tag{9-30}$$

or

$$U = \tfrac{1}{2}\bar{q}^T \bar{k}\bar{q} \tag{9-31}$$

Now, we may apply Eq. 9-26, which has a similar operation of differentiation as that in Eq. 9-24, to obtain the matrix equation

$$
\begin{bmatrix}
\dfrac{EA}{L} & 0 & 0 & -\dfrac{EA}{L} & 0 & 0 \\[2mm]
0 & \dfrac{12EI}{L^3} & -\dfrac{6EI}{L^2} & 0 & -\dfrac{12EI}{L^3} & -\dfrac{6EI}{L^2} \\[2mm]
0 & -\dfrac{6EI}{L^2} & \dfrac{4EI}{L} & 0 & \dfrac{6EI}{L^2} & \dfrac{2EI}{L} \\[2mm]
-\dfrac{EA}{L} & 0 & 0 & \dfrac{EA}{L} & 0 & 0 \\[2mm]
0 & -\dfrac{12EI}{L^3} & \dfrac{6EI}{L^2} & 0 & \dfrac{12EI}{L^3} & \dfrac{6EI}{L^2} \\[2mm]
0 & -\dfrac{6EI}{L^2} & \dfrac{2EI}{L} & 0 & \dfrac{6EI}{L^2} & \dfrac{4EI}{L}
\end{bmatrix}
\begin{Bmatrix}
\bar{u}_i \\ \bar{v}_i \\ \bar{\theta}_i \\ \bar{u}_j \\ \bar{v}_j \\ \bar{\theta}_j
\end{Bmatrix}
=
\begin{Bmatrix}
\bar{F}_{xi} \\ \bar{F}_{yi} \\ \bar{M}_i \\ \bar{F}_{xj} \\ \bar{F}_{yj} \\ \bar{M}_j
\end{Bmatrix}
\tag{9-32}
$$

$$\underbrace{\qquad\qquad\qquad\qquad}_{\bar{k}} \qquad \underbrace{\quad}_{\bar{q}} \qquad \underbrace{\quad}_{\bar{Q}}$$

or

$$\bar{k}\bar{q} = \bar{Q} \tag{9-33}$$

This is the complete force–displacement relationship, where the 6×6 matrix $\bar{k}$ is the element stiffness matrix of a frame element. For truss problems, the bending deformation is absent and we may use Eq. 9-10 and the $\bar{k}_a$ matrix.

It is important to note the following:

1. The three different approaches are equivalent in the present context (see Problem 9-4). They all start with an assumption on the real displacement function in terms of some unknown parameters (nodal displacements) and end up with the stiffness equation, which is basically a force–displacement relationship containing the geometric and material property of an element. We could have used any one of them for the derivation of the complete stiffness equation, Eq. 9-33. The foregoing presentation is designed to introduce all three methods.

2. Castigliano's First Theorem is restricted to discrete (concentrated) external loads, while both the minimum total potential energy method and the virtual displacement method are applicable to distributed external loadings as well. The force potential of distributed loads is simply the integration of force times displacement over the distributed length.

3. The resulting element stiffness matrix for frame elements is exact. This is because the displacements that we assumed, linear in axial and cubic in transverse directions, are the correct functions for the actual deflection. If we

assume a polynomial function that is only an approximation to the correct function, the resulting stiffness matrix is also approximate.

4. In the method of virtual displacement, the correct stiffness matrix will be obtained even if the assumed virtual displacement is different in form from the real displacement (see Problem 9-5).

5. The element stiffness matrix is symmetric. This is not a coincidence but a property. It is due to the quadratic form of the strain energy expression, Eq. 9-13.

6. The element stiffness matrices, as defined in Eqs. 9-9, 9-19, and 9-30, are *unconstrained stiffness matrices* because no constraints are placed on the nodal displacements. Such unconstrained stiffness matrices must be singular (see Problem 9-6).

7. From Eq. 9-32, it is clear that column 1 of matrix $\bar{k}$ contains the forces required to produce a unit translation of $\bar{u}_i$ [Fig. 9-1(e)], column 2 contains the forces to produce a unit translation of $\bar{v}_i$, [Fig. 9-1(f)], and so on. Thus, the stiffness matrix may be obtained directly by solving the problems posed in Fig. 9-1(e), (f), ..., using the results from Chapter 7 or 8.

9-3 ELEMENT STIFFNESS EQUATION IN GLOBAL COORDINATES

The nodal displacements and forces in the last section are defined in the local coordinate system of each element. In the next section, the nodal forces of all elements will be summed up at each node to balance the applied forces. Before they can be summed up, they must be expressed in a common coordinate system, the global coordinate system.

We now define the element nodal displacements and nodal forces as shown in Figs. 9-2(a) and (b), respectively. The two pairs of nodal displacements and nodal forces in Figs. 9-1(c) and 9-2(a) and Figs. 9-1(d) and 9-2(b) are equivalent. In both the local and the global coordinates, the rotations and moments are about an axis perpendicular to the plane of $\bar{X}-\bar{Y}$ (or $X-Y$). Thus,

$$\bar{\theta}_i = \theta_i, \qquad \bar{M}_i = M_i$$

$$\bar{\theta}_j = \theta_j, \qquad \bar{M}_j = M_j \tag{9-34}$$

The relationship between the translational displacements and forces in two coordinates can be easily obtained by vector decomposition.

$$\bar{u}_i = C \cdot u_i + S \cdot v_i, \qquad \bar{F}_{Xi} = C \cdot F_{Xi} + S \cdot F_{Yi}$$

$$\bar{v}_i = -S \cdot u_i + C \cdot v_i \qquad \bar{F}_{Yi} = -S \cdot F_{Xi} + C \cdot F_{Yi}$$

$$\bar{u}_j = C \cdot u_j + S \cdot v_j, \qquad \bar{F}_{Xj} = C \cdot F_{Xj} + S \cdot F_{Yj}$$

$$\bar{v}_j = -S \cdot u_j + C \cdot v_j, \qquad \bar{F}_{Yj} = S \cdot F_{Xj} + C \cdot F_{Yj} \tag{9-35}$$

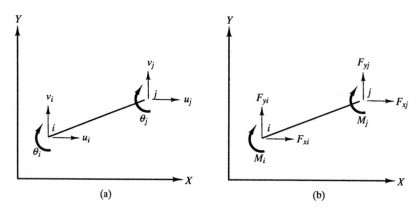

Figure 9-2

where

$$C = \text{Cos}\,\phi \qquad S = \text{Sin}\,\phi$$

$$= \frac{x_j - x_i}{L}, \qquad = \frac{y_j - y_i}{L}$$

(9-36)

Equations 9-34 and 9-35 may be combined into a pair of transformation equations:

$$\begin{Bmatrix} \bar{u}_i \\ \bar{v}_i \\ \bar{\theta}_i \\ \bar{u}_j \\ \bar{v}_j \\ \bar{\theta}_j \end{Bmatrix} = \begin{bmatrix} C & S & 0 & 0 & 0 & 0 \\ -S & C & 0 & 0 & 0 & 0 \\ 0 & 0 & 1 & 0 & 0 & 0 \\ 0 & 0 & 0 & C & S & 0 \\ 0 & 0 & 0 & -S & C & 0 \\ 0 & 0 & 0 & 0 & 0 & 1 \end{bmatrix} \begin{Bmatrix} u_i \\ v_i \\ \theta_i \\ u_j \\ v_j \\ \theta_j \end{Bmatrix},$$

$$\qquad \bar{q} \qquad\qquad\qquad T \qquad\qquad\qquad q$$

(9-37)

$$\begin{Bmatrix} \bar{F}_{xi} \\ \bar{F}_{yi} \\ \bar{M}_i \\ \bar{F}_{xj} \\ \bar{F}_{yj} \\ \bar{M}_j \end{Bmatrix} = \begin{bmatrix} C & S & 0 & 0 & 0 & 0 \\ -S & C & 0 & 0 & 0 & 0 \\ 0 & 0 & 1 & 0 & 0 & 0 \\ 0 & 0 & 0 & C & S & 0 \\ 0 & 0 & 0 & -S & C & 0 \\ 0 & 0 & 0 & 0 & 0 & 1 \end{bmatrix} \begin{Bmatrix} F_{xi} \\ F_{yi} \\ M_i \\ F_{xj} \\ F_{yj} \\ M_j \end{Bmatrix}$$

$$\qquad \bar{Q} \qquad\qquad\qquad T \qquad\qquad\qquad Q$$

or

$$\bar{q} = Tq, \qquad \bar{Q} = TQ$$

(9-38)

We now use Castigliano's first theorem to derive the element stiffness equation in the global coordinate system. The strain energy in terms of the local coordinate nodal displacements is expressed in Eq. 9-31. Upon substituting Eqs. 9-38 into Eq. 9-31, the new expression becomes

$$U = \tfrac{1}{2} q^T T^T \bar{k} T q \tag{9-39}$$

Defining

$$k = T^T \bar{k} T \tag{9-40}$$

we may write Eq. 9-39 in the following form:

$$U = \tfrac{1}{2} q^T k q \tag{9-41}$$

Comparing Eq. 9-41 to Eq. 9-31, we conclude that k in Eq. 9-41 is the element stiffness matrix in global coordinate system and it is related to the element stiffness matrix in local coordinate system by Eq. 9-40. An application of Castigliano's first theorem on Eq. 9-41 immediately yields

$$kq = Q \tag{9-42}$$

This is the element stiffness equation in a global coordinate system. We may use Eq. 9-40 to obtain k from the $\bar{k}$ in Eq. 9-30. Then Eq. 9-42 appears as

$$
\begin{bmatrix}
C^2\dfrac{EA}{L}+S^2\dfrac{12EI}{L^3} & & & & & \\[2ex]
CS\left(\dfrac{EA}{L}-\dfrac{12EI}{L^3}\right) & C^2\dfrac{12EI}{L^3}+S^2\dfrac{EA}{L} & & \text{Sym.} & & \\[2ex]
S\dfrac{6EI}{L^2} & -C\dfrac{6EI}{L^2} & \dfrac{4EI}{L} & & & \\[2ex]
-C^2\dfrac{EA}{L}-S^2\dfrac{12EI}{L^3} & CS\left(\dfrac{12EI}{L^3}-\dfrac{EA}{L}\right) & -S\dfrac{6EI}{L^2} & C^2\dfrac{EA}{L}+S^2\dfrac{12EI}{L^3} & & \\[2ex]
CS\left(\dfrac{12EI}{L^3}-\dfrac{EA}{L}\right) & -C^2\dfrac{12EI}{L^3}-S^2\dfrac{EA}{L} & C\dfrac{6EI}{L^2} & CS\left(\dfrac{EA}{L}-\dfrac{12EI}{L^3}\right) & C^2\dfrac{12EI}{L^3}+S^2\dfrac{EA}{L} & \\[2ex]
S\dfrac{6EI}{L^2} & -C\dfrac{6EI}{L^2} & \dfrac{2EI}{L} & -S\dfrac{6EI}{L^2} & C\dfrac{6EI}{L^2} & \dfrac{4EI}{L}
\end{bmatrix}
\begin{Bmatrix} u_i \\ v_i \\ \theta_i \\ u_j \\ v_j \\ \theta_j \end{Bmatrix}
= \begin{Bmatrix} F_{xi} \\ F_{yi} \\ M_i \\ F_{xj} \\ F_{yj} \\ M_j \end{Bmatrix}
\tag{9-43}
$$

$$\underbrace{\qquad\qquad\qquad}_{k} \qquad \underbrace{\qquad}_{q} \qquad \underbrace{\qquad}_{Q}$$

We note that, because

$$\bar{q}^T \overline{Q} = q^T Q \qquad (9\text{-}44)$$

and (from Eq. 9-38)

$$\bar{q} = Tq$$

we must have

$$Q = T^T \overline{Q} \qquad (9\text{-}45)$$

according to contragredient transformation (see Sec. 4-8b). Comparing this relationship with that of the second part of Eq. 9-38, we conclude that

$$T^T T = I$$

or

$$T^T = T^{-1} \qquad (9\text{-}46)$$

Such a matrix is called an *orthonormal matrix*.

9-4 COMPATIBILITY

So far we have worked on individual element relationships. These elements are part of the structure. They are linked to each other or to supports at nodes. How they are linked is expressed in nodal displacement relationships.

A convenient way of expressing nodal displacement relationships is to define structural, or global, nodal displacements for the entire structure and then relate each element nodal displacement to the global nodal displacement. Consider the loaded frame in Fig. 9-3(a). We see there are three nodes and each has three nodal displacements, as shown in Fig. 9-3(b). Thus, there are nine global nodal displacements. We denote the vector containing these global nodal displacements by r.

For elements a and b, the element nodal displacements, q^a and q^b, are related to the global nodal displacement vector r by the following equations [see Figs. 9-3(c) and (d)].

$$\begin{Bmatrix} u_i^a \\ v_i^a \\ \theta_i^a \\ u_j^a \\ v_j^a \\ \theta_j^a \end{Bmatrix} = \begin{bmatrix} 1 & 0 & 0 & 0 & 0 & 0 & 0 & 0 & 0 \\ 0 & 1 & 0 & 0 & 0 & 0 & 0 & 0 & 0 \\ 0 & 0 & 1 & 0 & 0 & 0 & 0 & 0 & 0 \\ 0 & 0 & 0 & 1 & 0 & 0 & 0 & 0 & 0 \\ 0 & 0 & 0 & 0 & 1 & 0 & 0 & 0 & 0 \\ 0 & 0 & 0 & 0 & 0 & 1 & 0 & 0 & 0 \end{bmatrix} \begin{Bmatrix} r_1 \\ r_2 \\ r_3 \\ r_4 \\ r_5 \\ r_6 \\ r_7 \\ r_8 \\ r_9 \end{Bmatrix} \qquad (9\text{-}47)$$

$$\qquad\quad q^a \qquad\qquad\qquad\qquad \Gamma^a \qquad\qquad\qquad\qquad\quad r$$

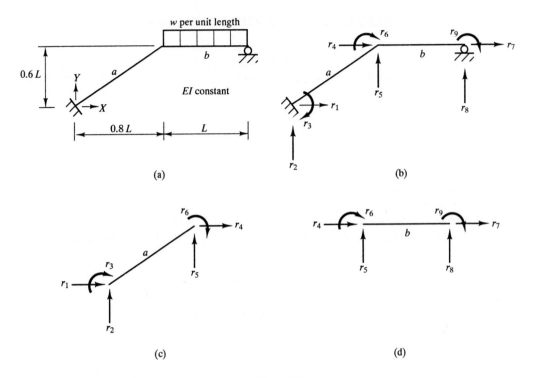

Figure 9-3

or

$$q^a = \Gamma^a r \tag{9-48}$$

and

$$
\begin{Bmatrix} u_i^b \\ v_i^b \\ \theta_i^b \\ u_j^b \\ v_j^b \\ \theta_j^b \end{Bmatrix} =
\begin{bmatrix}
0 & 0 & 0 & 1 & 0 & 0 & 0 & 0 & 0 \\
0 & 0 & 0 & 0 & 1 & 0 & 0 & 0 & 0 \\
0 & 0 & 0 & 0 & 0 & 1 & 0 & 0 & 0 \\
0 & 0 & 0 & 0 & 0 & 0 & 1 & 0 & 0 \\
0 & 0 & 0 & 0 & 0 & 0 & 0 & 1 & 0 \\
0 & 0 & 0 & 0 & 0 & 0 & 0 & 0 & 1
\end{bmatrix}
\begin{Bmatrix} r_1 \\ r_2 \\ r_3 \\ r_4 \\ r_5 \\ r_6 \\ r_7 \\ r_8 \\ r_9 \end{Bmatrix} \tag{9-49}
$$

$$\qquad\qquad q^b \qquad\qquad\qquad\qquad \Gamma^b \qquad\qquad\qquad\qquad r$$

or

$$q^b = \Gamma^b r \tag{9-50}$$

The matrices Γ^a and Γ^b are element-to-structure transformation matrices and they consist of only 0 and 1. Equations 9-48 and 9-50 are compatibility equations.

9-5 GLOBAL STIFFNESS EQUATION: DIRECT STIFFNESS METHOD

The equilibrium of the structure as a whole is now to be addressed. This can be done either by directly writing equilibrium equations for each node or by indirectly deriving the equilibrium equations using one of the three methods introduced in Sec. 9-2. We choose to use Castigliano's first theorem.

For each global nodal displacement, there is a corresponding global nodal force (moment). The global nodal displacements are represented by a vector, r, and the corresponding vector for the global nodal forces is denoted by R. Since the nodal forces are discrete forces, Castigliano's first theorem is readily applicable. We need an expression for the strain energy of the whole structure first. The strain energy of a single element has been derived in Sec. 9-2c and Sec. 9-3 and is given by Eq. 9-41, with the element stiffness matrix defined in Eq. 9-40 and its expression given in Eq. 9-43. With the transformation indicated in Eq. 9-48 or 9-50, the strain energy of a single element becomes

$$U^e = \tfrac{1}{2}(q^e)^T(k^e)(q^e)$$

$$= \tfrac{1}{2}(r)^T(\Gamma^e)^T(k^e)(\Gamma^e)(r) \tag{9-51}$$

$$= \tfrac{1}{2}(r)^T(K^e)(r)$$

where

$$K^e = (\Gamma^e)^T(k^e)(\Gamma^e) \tag{9-52}$$

is the expanded element stiffness matrix. The superscript e designates the element and is either a or b in the example problem under consideration. The total strain energy is the summation of the strain energy of all the elements.

$$U = \Sigma\, U^e$$

$$= \Sigma \tfrac{1}{2}(r)^T(K^e)(r) \tag{9-53}$$

$$= \tfrac{1}{2}(r)^T(K)(r)$$

where

$$K = \Sigma\, K^e \tag{9-54}$$

Now we apply Castigliano's first theorem by differentiating the right-hand side of Eq. 9-53 with respect to the components of r, the nodal displacement, and equating the result to the corresponding components of R, the nodal force. This yields

$$Kr = R \tag{9-55}$$

This equation is called the *unconstrained global stiffness equation*, because no constraints are put on the nodal displacements. It basically represents the nodal equilibrium conditions. The matrix K is called the *unconstrained global stiffness matrix*.

Let us examine the composition of K. Consider the problem shown in Fig. 9-3 again. According to Eq. 9-54,

$$K = K^a + K^b \tag{9-56}$$

The expanded element stiffness matrix K^a is the product of the original element stiffness matrix k^a and the element-to-structure transformation matrix Γ^a, according to Eq. 9-52.

$$K^a = (\Gamma^a)^T (k^a)(\Gamma^a) \tag{9-57}$$

The original element stiffness matrix is a 6×6 matrix.

$$k^a = \begin{bmatrix} k_{11}^a & k_{12}^a & k_{13}^a & k_{14}^a & k_{15}^a & k_{16}^a \\ k_{21}^a & k_{22}^a & k_{23}^a & k_{24}^a & k_{25}^a & k_{26}^a \\ k_{31}^a & k_{32}^a & k_{33}^a & k_{34}^a & k_{35}^a & k_{36}^a \\ k_{41}^a & k_{42}^a & k_{43}^a & k_{44}^a & k_{45}^a & k_{46}^a \\ k_{51}^a & k_{52}^a & k_{53}^a & k_{54}^a & k_{55}^a & k_{56}^a \\ k_{61}^a & k_{62}^a & k_{63}^a & k_{64}^a & k_{65}^a & k_{66}^a \end{bmatrix} \tag{9-58}$$

Using the transformation matrix Γ^a given in Eq. 9-47, we obtain the following expanded matrix.

$$K^a = \begin{bmatrix} k_{11}^a & k_{12}^a & k_{13}^a & k_{14}^a & k_{15}^a & k_{16}^a & 0 & 0 & 0 \\ k_{21}^a & k_{22}^a & k_{23}^a & k_{24}^a & k_{25}^a & k_{26}^a & 0 & 0 & 0 \\ k_{31}^a & k_{32}^a & k_{33}^a & k_{34}^a & k_{35}^a & k_{36}^a & 0 & 0 & 0 \\ k_{41}^a & k_{42}^a & k_{43}^a & k_{44}^a & k_{45}^a & k_{46}^a & 0 & 0 & 0 \\ k_{51}^a & k_{52}^a & k_{53}^a & k_{54}^a & k_{55}^a & k_{56}^a & 0 & 0 & 0 \\ k_{61}^a & k_{62}^a & k_{63}^a & k_{64}^a & k_{65}^a & k_{66}^a & 0 & 0 & 0 \\ 0 & 0 & 0 & 0 & 0 & 0 & 0 & 0 & 0 \\ 0 & 0 & 0 & 0 & 0 & 0 & 0 & 0 & 0 \\ 0 & 0 & 0 & 0 & 0 & 0 & 0 & 0 & 0 \end{bmatrix} \tag{9-59}$$

Similarly, if the element stiffness matrix for element b is designated by

$$k^b = \begin{bmatrix} k_{11}^b & k_{12}^b & k_{13}^b & k_{14}^b & k_{15}^b & k_{16}^b \\ k_{21}^b & k_{22}^b & k_{23}^b & k_{24}^b & k_{25}^b & k_{26}^b \\ k_{31}^b & k_{32}^b & k_{33}^b & k_{34}^b & k_{35}^b & k_{36}^b \\ k_{41}^b & k_{42}^b & k_{43}^b & k_{44}^b & k_{45}^b & k_{46}^b \\ k_{51}^b & k_{52}^b & k_{53}^b & k_{54}^b & k_{55}^b & k_{56}^b \\ k_{61}^b & k_{62}^b & k_{63}^b & k_{64}^b & k_{65}^b & k_{66}^b \end{bmatrix} \tag{9-60}$$

then the expanded matrix is

$$
K^b = \begin{bmatrix}
0 & 0 & 0 & 0 & 0 & 0 & 0 & 0 & 0 \\
0 & 0 & 0 & 0 & 0 & 0 & 0 & 0 & 0 \\
0 & 0 & 0 & 0 & 0 & 0 & 0 & 0 & 0 \\
0 & 0 & 0 & k_{11}^b & k_{12}^b & k_{13}^b & k_{14}^b & k_{15}^b & k_{16}^b \\
0 & 0 & 0 & k_{21}^b & k_{22}^b & k_{23}^b & k_{24}^b & k_{25}^b & k_{26}^b \\
0 & 0 & 0 & k_{31}^b & k_{32}^b & k_{33}^b & k_{34}^b & k_{35}^b & k_{36}^b \\
0 & 0 & 0 & k_{41}^b & k_{42}^b & k_{43}^b & k_{44}^b & k_{45}^b & k_{46}^b \\
0 & 0 & 0 & k_{51}^b & k_{52}^b & k_{53}^b & k_{54}^b & k_{55}^b & k_{56}^b \\
0 & 0 & 0 & k_{61}^b & k_{62}^b & k_{63}^b & k_{64}^b & k_{65}^b & k_{66}^b
\end{bmatrix}
\tag{9-61}
$$

The total global stiffness matrix K is simply the superposition of the two expanded stiffness matrices K^a and K^b according to Eq. 9-56. We observe that the effect of the triple product that changes the element stiffness matrix into an expanded matrix (Eq. 9-52) is simply assigning the coefficients in the element stiffness matrix to the proper location in the expanded matrix according to the one-to-one correspondence between the element nodal displacements and the global displacements. For element a, the six nodal displacements correspond to the first six global displacements; thus, Eq. 9-59 results. For element b, the six element displacements correspond to the last six global displacements and Eq. 9-61 results. In general, this correspondence may be in any order, and the element stiffness matrix may be dispersed into the expanded form according to the order of the global nodal displacements. The fact remains that it is not necessary even to create the matrix Γ^e in order to carry out the triple product. We need only to keep track of the one-to-one correspondence of the displacements and superpose the coefficients of the element stiffness matrix onto the global stiffness matrix directly. This procedure is called the *direct stiffness method*.

Let us apply the direct stiffness method to the problem shown in Fig. 9-3. Before we calculate the element stiffness matrices, we introduce a normalization method that is often convenient for hand computation and for computer programming as well. We first select a characteristic length, usually the length of a particular element, and denote it by L_G, where the subscript stands for "global." All the translational nodal displacements, u and v, are normalized by L_G to become dimensionless. Correspondingly, we multiply the nodal forces, F_X and F_Y, by L_G so that the nodal "force" vectors will all have the same dimension as that of a moment. With this change, the content of an element stiffness matrix must have the dimension of a moment (force times length). If we take out a factor of EI/L, which has the dimension of a moment, then the inside content of the stiffness matrix will be dimensionless. We can easily show that by further defining the following dimensionless quantities

$$
\alpha^2 = \frac{L^2 A}{I}
\tag{9-62}
$$

and

$$
\beta = \frac{L_G}{L}
\tag{9-63}
$$

the element stiffness equation, Eq. 9-43, becomes

$$
\frac{EI}{L}
\begin{bmatrix}
(\alpha^2 C^2 + 12S^2)\beta^2 & & & & & \\
(\alpha^2 - 12)CS\beta^2 & (12C^2 + \alpha^2 S^2)\beta^2 & & \text{Sym.} & & \\
6S\beta & -6C\beta & 4 & & & \\
-(\alpha^2 C^2 + 12S^2)\beta^2 & (12 - \alpha^2)CS\beta^2 & -6S\beta & (\alpha^2 C^2 + 12S^2)\beta^2 & & \\
(12 - \alpha^2)CS\beta^2 & (-12C^2 - \alpha^2 S^2)\beta^2 & 6C\beta & (\alpha^2 - 12)CS\beta^2 & (12C^2 + \alpha^2 S^2)\beta^2 & \\
6S\beta & -6C\beta & 2 & -6S\beta & 6C\beta & 4
\end{bmatrix}
\begin{Bmatrix}
u_i/L_G \\
v_i/L_G \\
\theta_i \\
u_j/L_G \\
v_j/L_G \\
\theta_j
\end{Bmatrix}
$$

$$
= \begin{Bmatrix}
F_{xi} L_G \\
F_{yi} L_G \\
M_i \\
F_{xj} L_G \\
F_{yj} L_G \\
M_j
\end{Bmatrix}
\qquad (9\text{-}64)
$$

We recall that the dimensionless quantity α is actually the slenderness ratio of the element. For the frame shown in Fig. 9-3, the two elements are identical. Thus, $L_G = L$ and $\beta = 1$. The slenderness ratio is to be 44.7, which gives $\alpha^2 = 2,000$. We list the element stiffness equations next.

Element a: $C = \text{Cos } \phi = 0.8, S = \text{Sin } \phi = 0.6$

$$
\frac{EI}{L}
\begin{bmatrix}
1{,}284.32 & & & & & \\
954.24 & 727.68 & & \text{Sym.} & & \\
3.60 & -4.80 & 4.00 & & & \\
-1{,}284.32 & -954.24 & -3.60 & 1{,}284.32 & & \\
-954.24 & -727.68 & 4.80 & 954.24 & 727.68 & \\
3.60 & -4.80 & 2.00 & -3.60 & 4.80 & 4.00
\end{bmatrix}
\begin{Bmatrix}
u_i^a/L \\
v_i^a/L \\
\theta_i^a \\
u_j^a/L \\
v_j^a/L \\
\theta_j^a
\end{Bmatrix}
$$

$$
= \begin{Bmatrix}
F_{xi}^a L \\
F_{yi}^a L \\
M_i^a \\
F_{xj}^a L \\
F_{yj}^a L \\
M_j^a
\end{Bmatrix}
\qquad (9\text{-}65)
$$

Element b: $C = \text{Cos } \phi = 1, S = \text{Sin } \phi = 0$

$$
\frac{EI}{L}
\begin{bmatrix}
2{,}000.00 & & & & & \\
0 & 12.00 & & \text{Sym.} & & \\
0 & -6.00 & 4.00 & & & \\
-2{,}000.00 & 0 & 0 & 2{,}000.00 & & \\
0 & -12.00 & 6.00 & 0 & 12.00 & \\
0 & -6.00 & 2.00 & 0 & 6.00 & 4.00
\end{bmatrix}
\begin{Bmatrix}
u_i^b/L \\
v_i^b/L \\
\theta_i^b \\
u_j^b/L \\
v_j^b/L \\
\theta_j^b
\end{Bmatrix}
=
\begin{Bmatrix}
F_{xi}^b L \\
F_{yi}^b L \\
M_i^b \\
F_{xj}^b L \\
F_{yj}^b L \\
M_j^b
\end{Bmatrix}
\qquad (9\text{-}66)
$$

Referring to Fig. 9-3 for the ordering of the global displacements and to Fig. 9-4 for the nodal forces caused by the uniform loading, we arrive at the following unconstrained global stiffness equation via Eq. 9-55.

$$\frac{EI}{L}\begin{bmatrix}
1{,}284.32 & & & & & & & & \\
954.24 & 727.68 & & & & \text{Sym.} & & & \\
3.60 & -4.80 & 4.00 & & & & & & \\
1{,}284.32 & -954.24 & -3.60 & 3{,}284.32 & & & & & \\
-954.24 & -727.68 & 4.80 & 954.24 & 739.68 & & & & \\
3.60 & -4.80 & 2.00 & -3.60 & -1.20 & 8.00 & & & \\
0 & 0 & 0 & -2{,}000.00 & 0 & 0 & 2{,}000.00 & & \\
0 & 0 & 0 & 0 & -12.00 & 6.00 & 0 & 12.00 & \\
0 & 0 & 0 & 0 & -6.00 & 2.00 & 0 & 6.00 & 4.00
\end{bmatrix}$$

$$\begin{Bmatrix} r_1 \\ r_2 \\ r_3 \\ r_4 \\ r_5 \\ r_6 \\ r_7 \\ r_8 \\ r_9 \end{Bmatrix} = \begin{Bmatrix} R_1 \\ R_2 \\ R_3 \\ R_4 = 0 \\ R_5 = -\dfrac{wL^2}{2} \\ R_6 = \dfrac{wL^3}{12} \\ R_7 = 0 \\ R_8 \\ R_9 = -\dfrac{wL^3}{12} \end{Bmatrix} \qquad (9\text{-}67)$$

The nodal displacements are defined in a similar way as those of the element nodal displacement; that is, $r_1 = u_1/L_G$, $r_2 = v_2/L_G$, and so on. The nodal forces are also defined similarly and all have the dimension of a moment.

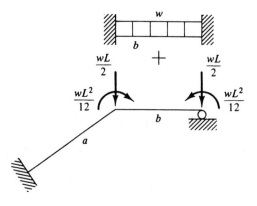

Figure 9-4

9-6 CONSTRAINING AND SOLUTION OF THE GLOBAL STIFFNESS EQUATION

The nine equations in Eq. 9-67 contains exactly nine unknowns. Out of the nine nodal displacements, the following four are known: $r_1 = r_2 = r_3 = r_8 = 0$. These known displacements may be grouped together symbolically as a constrained displacement vector r_c. Corresponding to the constrained displacements are the reactions R_1, R_2, R_3, and R_8, which are unknown and may be grouped together as a force vector R_c. The remaining unknown displacements, r_4, r_5, r_6, r_7, and r_9, are grouped together as a free displacement vector r_f, with the corresponding nodal forces designated as R_f, which are known.

$$
\frac{EI}{L}
\begin{bmatrix}
3{,}284.32 & & & & & & & & \\
954.24 & 739.68 & & & & \text{Sym.} & & & \\
-3.60 & -1.20 & 8.00 & & & & & & \\
-2{,}000.00 & 0 & 0 & 2{,}000.00 & & & & & \\
0 & -6.00 & 2.00 & 0 & 4.00 & & & & \\
\hline
1{,}284.32 & -954.24 & 3.60 & 0 & 0 & 1{,}284.32 & & & \\
-954.24 & -727.68 & 4.80 & 0 & 0 & 954.24 & 727.68 & & \\
-3.60 & 4.80 & 2.00 & 0 & 0 & 3.60 & -4.80 & 4.00 & \\
0 & -12.00 & 6.00 & 0 & 6.00 & 0 & 0 & 0 & 12.00
\end{bmatrix}
$$

$$
\cdot
\begin{Bmatrix}
r_4 \\
r_5 \\
r_6 \\
r_7 \\
r_9 \\
\hline
r_1 = 0 \\
r_2 = 0 \\
r_3 = 0 \\
r_8 = 0
\end{Bmatrix}
=
\begin{Bmatrix}
R_4 = 0 \\
R_5 = -\dfrac{wL^2}{2} \\
R_6 = \dfrac{wL^3}{12} \\
R_7 = 0 \\
R_9 = -\dfrac{wL^3}{12} \\
\hline
R_1 \\
R_2 \\
R_3 \\
R_8
\end{Bmatrix}
\tag{9-68}
$$

or

$$
\begin{bmatrix}
K_{ff} & \vdots & K_{fc} \\
\cdots & & \cdots \\
K_{cf} & \vdots & K_{cc}
\end{bmatrix}
\begin{Bmatrix}
r_f \\
\cdots \\
r_c
\end{Bmatrix}
=
\begin{Bmatrix}
R_f \\
\cdots \\
R_c
\end{Bmatrix}
\tag{9-69}
$$

The first part of Eq. 9-69 contains the unknown displacement vector r_f,

$$
K_{ff}r_f + K_{fc}r_c = R_f
$$

the solution of which may be expressed symbolically as

$$
r_f = K_{ff}^{-1}(R_f - K_{fc}r_c)
\tag{9-70}
$$

Note that in general the constrained displacement r_c need not be zero. Equation 9-70 gives the solution for the unknown nodal displacements. To find the unknown support forces (reactions), R_c, we use the second part of Eq. 9-69.

$$R_c = K_{cf}r_f + K_{cc}r_c \qquad (9\text{-}71)$$

or, upon substituting r_f with the expression in Eq. 9-70,

$$R_c = K_{cf}K_{ff}^{-1}(R_f - K_{fc}r_c) + K_{cc}r_c$$

$$= K_{cf}K_{ff}^{-1}R_f + (K_{cc} - K_{cf}K_{ff}^{-1}K_{fc})r_c \qquad (9\text{-}72)$$

In actual computation, the solution for the unknown displacements r_f need not involve the inversion of K_{ff}, but may be obtained through Gaussian elimination (see Appendix A). In the present case, the normalized nodal displacements are found to be

$$\begin{Bmatrix} r_4 \\ r_5 \\ r_6 \\ r_7 \\ r_9 \end{Bmatrix} = \begin{Bmatrix} 0.0279 \\ -0.0375 \\ 0.0419 \\ 0.0279 \\ -0.0979 \end{Bmatrix} \frac{wL^3}{EI} \qquad (9\text{-}73)$$

and the normalized reactions are

$$\begin{Bmatrix} R_1 \\ R_2 \\ R_3 \\ R_8 \end{Bmatrix} = \begin{Bmatrix} 0 \\ 0.387 \\ -0.197 \\ 0.113 \end{Bmatrix} wL^2 \qquad (9\text{-}74)$$

Referring to Fig. 9-4, we see the total reaction $R_8 (= F_y L)$ should also include the $(wL/2)L$ from the uniform loading. Thus, the total $R_8 = (0.113 + 0.5)wL^2 = 0.613wL^2$.

This completes the solution of the global stiffness equation.

9-7 SOLUTION FOR ELEMENT FORCES

The element nodal forces may now be computed using Eqs. 9-65 and 9-66 for elements a and b, respectively.

Element a:

$$\frac{EI}{L}\begin{bmatrix} 1,284.32 & & & & & \\ 954.24 & 727.68 & & & \text{Sym.} & \\ 3.60 & -4.80 & 4.00 & & & \\ -1,284.32 & -954.24 & -3.60 & 1,284.32 & & \\ -954.24 & -727.68 & 4.80 & 954.24 & 727.68 & \\ 3.60 & -4.80 & 2.00 & -3.60 & 4.80 & 4.00 \end{bmatrix} \begin{Bmatrix} 0 \\ 0 \\ 0 \\ 0.0279 \\ -0.0375 \\ 0.0419 \end{Bmatrix} \frac{wL^3}{EI}$$

$$= \begin{Bmatrix} 0 \\ 0.387 \\ -0.190 \\ 0 \\ -0.387 \\ -0.113 \end{Bmatrix} wL^2 \qquad (9\text{-}75)$$

Element b:

$$\frac{EI}{L}\begin{bmatrix} 2,000.00 & & & & & \\ 0 & 12.00 & & & \text{Sym.} & \\ 0 & -6.00 & 4.00 & & & \\ -2,000.00 & 0 & 0 & 2,000.00 & & \\ 0 & -12.00 & 6.00 & 0 & 12.00 & \\ 0 & -6.00 & 2.00 & 0 & 6.00 & 4.00 \end{bmatrix} \begin{Bmatrix} 0.0279 \\ -0.0375 \\ 0.0419 \\ 0.0279 \\ 0 \\ -0.0979 \end{Bmatrix} \frac{wL^3}{EI}$$

$$= \begin{Bmatrix} 0 \\ -0.113 \\ 0.196 \\ 0 \\ 0.113 \\ -0.0833 \end{Bmatrix} wL^2 \qquad (9\text{-}76)$$

These nodal forces at the right-hand side are in the global coordinate system. It is
more convenient, for plotting shear and moment diagrams, for example, to have
them in the element local coordinate system. This is easily achieved by multiplying
the element nodal forces by the transformation matrix T using Eq. 9-38.

Element a: $C = \text{Cos }\phi = 0.8, S = \text{Sin }\phi = 0.6$

$$\begin{bmatrix} 0.8 & 0.6 & 0 & 0 & 0 & 0 \\ -0.6 & 0.8 & 0 & 0 & 0 & 0 \\ 0 & 0 & 1 & 0 & 0 & 0 \\ 0 & 0 & 0 & 0.8 & 0.6 & 0 \\ 0 & 0 & 0 & -0.6 & 0.8 & 0 \\ 0 & 0 & 0 & 0 & 0 & 1 \end{bmatrix} \begin{Bmatrix} 0 \\ 0.387 \\ -0.197 \\ 0 \\ -0.387 \\ -0.113 \end{Bmatrix} wL^2 = \begin{Bmatrix} 0.232 \\ 0.310 \\ -0.197 \\ -0.232 \\ -0.310 \\ -0.113 \end{Bmatrix} wL^2$$

Element b: $C = \text{Cos}\,\phi = 1, S = \text{Sin}\,\phi = 0$

The transformation matrix is an identity matrix, and there is no change after the transformation in the value of nodal forces. The total element forces, however, should include the fixed-end forces (moments) due to the uniform load.

$$\begin{Bmatrix} 0 \\ -0.113 \\ 0.196 \\ 0 \\ 0.113 \\ -0.0833 \end{Bmatrix} wL^2 + \begin{Bmatrix} 0 \\ \frac{1}{2} \\ -\frac{1}{12} \\ 0 \\ \frac{1}{2} \\ \frac{1}{12} \end{Bmatrix} wL^2 = \begin{Bmatrix} 0 \\ 0.387 \\ 0.113 \\ 0 \\ 0.613 \\ 0 \end{Bmatrix} wL^2$$

From these member-end forces and moments, also referring to Fig. 9-3(a) for the effect of uniform load, the shear, moment, and deflection diagrams are obtained as shown in Fig. 9-5(a), (b) and (c). The axial force in element a is $0.232wL$ (compression), and there is no axial force in element b.

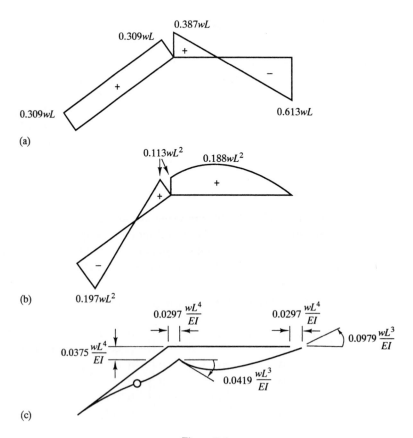

Figure 9-5

9-8 A SPECIAL CASE: TRUSS ANALYSIS

The above procedure of analysis is equally applicable to truss analysis since it may be considered as a special case of frame analysis by deleting the bending stiffness terms and rotational degrees of freedom. The element stiffness equation in the global coordinate system as given by Eq. 9-43 degenerates into the following form:

$$\frac{EA}{L}\begin{bmatrix} C^2 & & \text{Sym.} & \\ CS & S^2 & & \\ -C^2 & -CS & C^2 & \\ -CS & -S^2 & CS & S^2 \end{bmatrix}\begin{Bmatrix} u_i \\ v_i \\ u_j \\ v_j \end{Bmatrix} = \begin{Bmatrix} F_{xi} \\ F_{yi} \\ F_{xj} \\ F_{yj} \end{Bmatrix} \tag{9-77}$$

where $C = \text{Cos}\,\phi$ and $S = \text{Sin}\,\phi$, and ϕ is the angle of element orientation as shown in Fig. 9-6. Each node will have only two translational degrees of freedom and will receive only nodal forces (without moments).

Example 9-1

Analyze the truss shown in Fig. 9-7(a) by the direct stiffness method. Assume that $EA/L = 1$ for all elements.

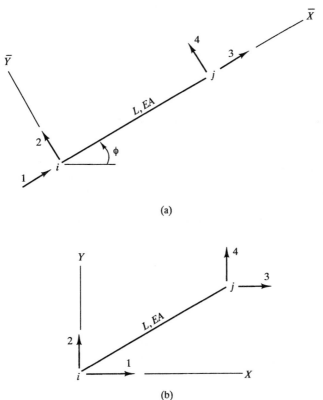

(a)

(b)   **Figure 9-6**

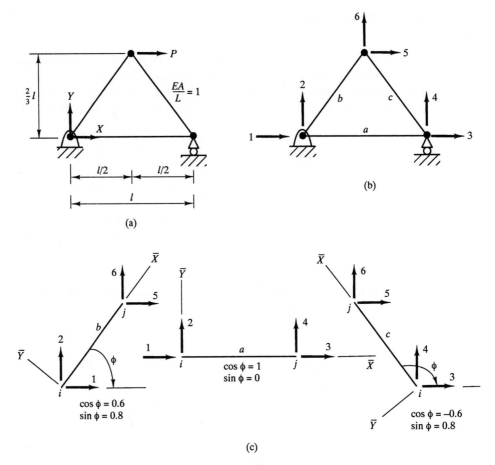

Figure 9-7

There are three elements and three nodes. We number the nodal degrees of freedom as shown in Fig. 9-7(b). The orientations and the local coordinate systems of the three elements are shown in Fig. 9-7(c).

The element stiffness matrices and the associated global nodal displacement numbers are listed below.

Element a: $\quad \dfrac{EA}{L} = 1, C = \text{Cos}\,\phi = 1, S = \text{Sin}\,\phi = 0$

$$
k^a =
\begin{array}{c}
\begin{array}{cccc} 1 & 2 & 3 & 4 \end{array} \\
\left[
\begin{array}{cccc}
1 & & \text{Sym.} & \\
0 & 0 & & \\
-1 & 0 & 1 & \\
0 & 0 & 0 & 0
\end{array}
\right]
\begin{array}{c} 1 \\ 2 \\ 3 \\ 4 \end{array}
\end{array}
\qquad (9\text{-}78)
$$

Element b: $\dfrac{EA}{L} = 1, C = \text{Cos}\,\phi = 0.6, S = \text{Sin}\,\phi = 0.8$

$$k^b = \begin{array}{c} \begin{array}{cccc} 1 \quad\; & 2 \quad\; & 5 \quad\; & 6 \quad \end{array} \\ \left[\begin{array}{cccc} 0.36 & & \text{Sym.} & \\ 0.48 & 0.64 & & \\ -0.36 & -0.48 & 0.36 & \\ -0.48 & -0.64 & 0.48 & 0.64 \end{array}\right] \begin{array}{c} 1 \\ 2 \\ 5 \\ 6 \end{array} \end{array} \qquad (9\text{-}79)$$

Element c: $\dfrac{EA}{L} = 1, C = \text{Cos}\,\phi = -0.6, S = \text{Sin}\,\phi = 0.8$

$$k^c = \begin{array}{c} \begin{array}{cccc} 3 \quad\; & 4 \quad\; & 5 \quad\; & 6 \quad \end{array} \\ \left[\begin{array}{cccc} 0.36 & & \text{Sym.} & \\ -0.48 & 0.64 & & \\ -0.36 & 0.48 & 0.36 & \\ 0.48 & -0.64 & -0.48 & 0.64 \end{array}\right] \begin{array}{c} 3 \\ 4 \\ 5 \\ 6 \end{array} \end{array} \qquad (9\text{-}80)$$

The global stiffness equation is established by the direct stiffness method.

$$\begin{array}{c} \begin{array}{cccccc} 1 \quad\;\; & 2 \quad\;\; & 3 \quad\;\; & 4 \quad\;\; & 5 \quad\;\; & 6 \quad \end{array} \\ \left[\begin{array}{cccccc} 1.36 & & & & \text{Sym.} & \\ 0.48 & 0.64 & & & & \\ -1.00 & 0.00 & 1.36 & & & \\ 0.00 & 0.00 & -0.48 & 0.64 & & \\ -0.36 & -0.48 & -0.36 & 0.48 & 0.72 & \\ -0.48 & -0.64 & 0.48 & -0.64 & 0.00 & 1.28 \end{array}\right] \left\{\begin{array}{c} r_1 \\ r_2 \\ r_3 \\ r_4 \\ r_5 \\ r_6 \end{array}\right\} = \left\{\begin{array}{c} R_1 \\ R_2 \\ R_3 \\ R_4 \\ R_5 \\ R_6 \end{array}\right\} \end{array} \qquad (9\text{-}81)$$

The following nodal displacements are constrained to zero: $r_1 = r_2 = r_4 = 0$. After rearranging the global nodal displacements and applying the known nodal forces, Eq. 9-81 becomes

$$\begin{array}{c} \begin{array}{cccccc} 3 \quad\;\; & 5 \quad\;\; & 6 \quad\;\; & 1 \quad\;\; & 2 \quad\;\; & 4 \quad \end{array} \\ \left[\begin{array}{ccc|ccc} 1.36 & & \text{Sym.} & & & \\ -0.36 & 0.72 & & & & \\ 0.48 & 0.00 & 1.28 & & & \\ \hline -1.00 & -0.36 & -0.48 & 1.36 & & \\ 0.00 & -0.48 & -0.64 & 0.48 & 0.64 & \\ -0.48 & 0.48 & -0.64 & 0.00 & 0.00 & 0.64 \end{array}\right] \left\{\begin{array}{c} r_3 \\ r_5 \\ r_6 \\ \hline 0 \\ 0 \\ 0 \end{array}\right\} = \left\{\begin{array}{c} 0 \\ P \\ 0 \\ \hline R_1 \\ R_2 \\ R_4 \end{array}\right\} \end{array} \qquad (9\text{-}82)$$

The solution of the first three equations by Gaussian elimination gives

$$\left\{\begin{array}{c} r_3 \\ r_5 \\ r_6 \end{array}\right\} = \left\{\begin{array}{c} 0.500 \\ 1.639 \\ 0.188 \end{array}\right\} P \qquad (9\text{-}83)$$

Substituting Eq. 9-83 into the last three equations of Eq. 9-82 gives the reaction forces:

$$\begin{Bmatrix} R_1 \\ R_2 \\ R_4 \end{Bmatrix} = \begin{Bmatrix} -1.000 \\ -0.667 \\ 0.667 \end{Bmatrix} P \tag{9-84}$$

The element nodal forces in the global coordinate system are found by using Eqs. 9-78, 9-79, and 9-80, respectively.

Element a:
$$\begin{bmatrix} 1 & & \text{Sym.} & \\ 0 & 0 & & \\ -1 & 0 & 1 & \\ 0 & 0 & 0 & 0 \end{bmatrix} \begin{Bmatrix} 0 \\ 0 \\ 0.500 \\ 0 \end{Bmatrix} P = \begin{Bmatrix} -0.500 \\ 0 \\ 0.500 \\ 0 \end{Bmatrix} P$$

Element b:
$$\begin{bmatrix} 0.36 & & \text{Sym.} & \\ 0.48 & 0.64 & & \\ -0.36 & -0.48 & 0.36 & \\ -0.48 & -0.64 & 0.48 & 0.64 \end{bmatrix} \begin{Bmatrix} 0 \\ 0 \\ 1.639 \\ -0.188 \end{Bmatrix} P = \begin{Bmatrix} -0.500 \\ -0.667 \\ 0.500 \\ 0.667 \end{Bmatrix} P$$

Element c:
$$\begin{bmatrix} 0.36 & & \text{Sym.} & \\ -0.48 & 0.64 & & \\ -0.36 & 0.48 & 0.36 & \\ 0.48 & -0.64 & -0.48 & 0.64 \end{bmatrix} \begin{Bmatrix} 0.500 \\ 0 \\ 1.639 \\ -0.188 \end{Bmatrix} P = \begin{Bmatrix} -0.500 \\ 0.667 \\ 0.500 \\ -0.667 \end{Bmatrix} P$$

To find the element forces in the local coordinate, we need to use the degenerated form of the second part of Eq. 9-37.

$$\begin{Bmatrix} \overline{F}_{Xi} \\ \overline{F}_{Yi} \\ \overline{F}_{Xj} \\ \overline{F}_{Yj} \end{Bmatrix} = \begin{bmatrix} C & S & 0 & 0 \\ -S & C & 0 & 0 \\ 0 & 0 & C & S \\ 0 & 0 & -S & C \end{bmatrix} \begin{Bmatrix} F_{Xi} \\ F_{Yi} \\ F_{Xj} \\ F_{Yj} \end{Bmatrix} \tag{9-85}$$

Using Eq. 9-85, the following nodal forces in local coordinates are obtained.

Element a: $C = \text{Cos}\,\phi = 1, S = \text{Sin}\,\phi = 0$

$$\begin{Bmatrix} \overline{F}_{Xi} \\ \overline{F}_{Yi} \\ \overline{F}_{Xj} \\ \overline{F}_{Yj} \end{Bmatrix} = \begin{bmatrix} 1 & 0 & 0 & 0 \\ 0 & 1 & 0 & 0 \\ 0 & 0 & 1 & 0 \\ 0 & 0 & 0 & 1 \end{bmatrix} \begin{Bmatrix} -0.500 \\ 0 \\ 0.500 \\ 0 \end{Bmatrix} P = \begin{Bmatrix} -0.500 \\ 0 \\ 0.500 \\ 0 \end{Bmatrix} P$$

Element b: $C = \text{Cos}\,\phi = 0.6, S = \text{Sin}\,\phi = 0.8$

$$\begin{Bmatrix} \overline{F}_{Xi} \\ \overline{F}_{Yi} \\ \overline{F}_{Xj} \\ \overline{F}_{Yj} \end{Bmatrix} = \begin{bmatrix} 0.6 & 0.8 & 0 & 0 \\ -0.8 & 0.6 & 0 & 0 \\ 0 & 0 & 0.6 & 0.8 \\ 0 & 0 & -0.8 & 0.6 \end{bmatrix} \begin{Bmatrix} -0.500 \\ -0.667 \\ 0.500 \\ 0.667 \end{Bmatrix} P = \begin{Bmatrix} -0.833 \\ 0 \\ 0.833 \\ 0 \end{Bmatrix} P$$

Element c: $C = \text{Cos}\,\phi = -0.6, S = \text{Sin}\,\phi = 0.8$

$$\begin{Bmatrix} \bar{F}_{Xi} \\ \bar{F}_{Yi} \\ \bar{F}_{Xj} \\ \bar{F}_{Yj} \end{Bmatrix} = \begin{bmatrix} -0.6 & 0.8 & 0 & 0 \\ -0.8 & -0.6 & 0 & 0 \\ 0 & 0 & -0.6 & 0.8 \\ 0 & 0 & -0.8 & -0.6 \end{bmatrix} \begin{Bmatrix} -0.500 \\ 0.667 \\ 0.500 \\ -0.667 \end{Bmatrix} P = \begin{Bmatrix} 0.833 \\ 0 \\ -0.833 \\ 0 \end{Bmatrix} P$$

Thus, the axial forces in elements a, b, and c are $0.500P$ (tension), $0.833P$ (tension), and $0.833P$ (compression), respectively.

9-9 MODIFIED ELEMENT STIFFNESS MATRIX

As described in Sec. 7-6, some circumstances call for the use of modified stiffnesses. One such is a member with a hinged end as shown in Fig. 9-8. The case in Fig. 9-8(a) has two beam members with one hinged end each, while the columns are continuous. The case in Fig. 9-8(b) has six members with one hinged end each, with discontinuous column bending stiffness (which is highly unlikely in practice). A simple approach is to assign an additional nodal rotational degree of freedom for each member-end hinge. Thus, the hinged node in Fig. 9-8(a) would have two rotational nodal degrees of freedom, while that in Fig. 9-8(b) would have three rotational degrees of freedom. This means that the total number of nodal displacement unknowns would be increased, which is undesirable in the matrix displacement method of analysis.

An alternative approach is to use a modified stiffness matrix in the same way as in the modified stiffness approach in the moment distribution method. We start with the element stiffness equation in local coordinate, Eq. 9-33.

$$\begin{bmatrix} \dfrac{EA}{L} & 0 & 0 & -\dfrac{EA}{L} & 0 & 0 \\ 0 & \dfrac{12EI}{L^3} & -\dfrac{6EI}{L^2} & 0 & -\dfrac{12EI}{L^3} & -\dfrac{6EI}{L^2} \\ 0 & -\dfrac{6EI}{L^2} & \dfrac{4EI}{L} & 0 & \dfrac{6EI}{L^2} & \dfrac{2EI}{L} \\ -\dfrac{EA}{L} & 0 & 0 & \dfrac{EA}{L} & 0 & 0 \\ 0 & -\dfrac{12EI}{L^3} & \dfrac{6EI}{L^2} & 0 & \dfrac{12EI}{L^3} & \dfrac{6EI}{L^2} \\ 0 & -\dfrac{6EI}{L^2} & \dfrac{2EI}{L} & 0 & \dfrac{6EI}{L^2} & \dfrac{4EI}{L} \end{bmatrix} \begin{Bmatrix} \bar{u}_i \\ \bar{v}_i \\ \bar{\theta}_i \\ \bar{u}_j \\ \bar{v}_j \\ \bar{\theta}_j \end{Bmatrix} = \begin{Bmatrix} \bar{F}_{xi} \\ \bar{F}_{yi} \\ \bar{M}_i \\ \bar{F}_{xj} \\ \bar{F}_{yj} \\ \bar{M}_j \end{Bmatrix} \qquad (9\text{-}86)$$

Assuming that node j is a hinged node, and thus $\bar{M}_j = 0$, we may solve for $\bar{\theta}_j$ using the last equation in Eq. 9-86.

$$\bar{\theta}_j = \frac{3}{2L}\bar{v}_i - \frac{1}{2}\bar{\theta}_i - \frac{3}{2L}\bar{v}_j \qquad (9\text{-}87)$$

Eliminating $\bar{\theta}_j$ by substituting Eq. 9-87 into the first five equations in Eq. 9-86, we obtain the following modified stiffness equation with a 5×5 modified stiffness matrix in the local coordinate system.

$$
\begin{bmatrix}
\dfrac{EA}{L} & 0 & 0 & -\dfrac{EA}{L} & 0 \\
0 & \dfrac{3EI}{L^3} & -\dfrac{3EI}{L^2} & 0 & -\dfrac{3EI}{L^3} \\
0 & -\dfrac{3EI}{L^2} & \dfrac{3EI}{L} & 0 & \dfrac{3EI}{L^2} \\
-\dfrac{EA}{L} & 0 & 0 & \dfrac{EA}{L} & 0 \\
0 & -\dfrac{3EI}{L^3} & \dfrac{3EI}{L^2} & 0 & \dfrac{3EI}{L^3}
\end{bmatrix}
\begin{Bmatrix} \bar{u}_i \\ \bar{v}_i \\ \bar{\theta}_i \\ \bar{u}_j \\ \bar{v}_j \end{Bmatrix}
=
\begin{Bmatrix} \bar{F}_{xi} \\ \bar{F}_{yi} \\ \bar{M}_i \\ \bar{F}_{xj} \\ \bar{F}_{yj} \end{Bmatrix}
\tag{9-88}
$$

Thus, $\bar{\theta}_j$ will not appear as an additional degree of freedom, but rather as a dependent variable obtainable through Eq. 9-87. Because the element has $\bar{M}_j = 0$, it does not contribute to the global moment equilibrium of that particular node.

The local-to-global transformation matrix is also reduced to a 5×5 matrix from Eq. 9-37.

$$
\begin{Bmatrix} \bar{u}_i \\ \bar{v}_i \\ \bar{\theta}_i \\ \bar{u}_j \\ \bar{v}_j \end{Bmatrix}
=
\begin{bmatrix}
C & S & 0 & 0 & 0 \\
-S & C & 0 & 0 & 0 \\
0 & 0 & 1 & 0 & 0 \\
0 & 0 & 0 & C & S \\
0 & 0 & 0 & -S & C
\end{bmatrix}
\begin{Bmatrix} u_i \\ v_i \\ \theta_i \\ u_j \\ v_j \end{Bmatrix}
\tag{9-89}
$$

Using Eq. 9-40, we obtain the modified stiffness equation in the global coordinate system with a 5×5 modified stiffness matrix.

$$
\begin{bmatrix}
C^2\dfrac{EA}{L} + S^2\dfrac{3EI}{L^3} & & & \text{Sym.} & \\
CS\left(\dfrac{EA}{L} - \dfrac{3EI}{L^3}\right) & C^2\dfrac{3EI}{L^3} + S^2\dfrac{EA}{L} & & & \\
S\dfrac{3EI}{L^2} & -C\dfrac{3EI}{L^2} & \dfrac{3EI}{L} & & \\
-C^2\dfrac{EA}{L} - S^2\dfrac{3EI}{L^3} & CS\left(\dfrac{3EI}{L^3} - \dfrac{EA}{L}\right) & -S\dfrac{3EI}{L^2} & C^2\dfrac{EA}{L} + S^2\dfrac{3EI}{L^3} & \\
CS\left(\dfrac{3EI}{L^3} - \dfrac{EA}{L}\right) & -C^2\dfrac{3EI}{L^3} - S^2\dfrac{EA}{L} & C\dfrac{3EI}{L^2} & CS\left(\dfrac{EA}{L} - \dfrac{3EI}{L^3}\right) & C^2\dfrac{3EI}{L^3} + S^2\dfrac{EA}{L}
\end{bmatrix}
\begin{Bmatrix} u_i \\ v_i \\ \theta_i \\ u_j \\ v_j \end{Bmatrix}
$$

$$
= \begin{Bmatrix} F_{xi} \\ F_{yi} \\ M_i \\ F_{xj} \\ F_{yj} \end{Bmatrix}
\tag{9-90}
$$

The application of this modified stiffness matrix is now illustrated with an example.

Example 9-2

Analyze the rigid frame shown in Fig. 9-9(a) using modified stiffness matrix for element b. Assume that $AL^2/I = 2{,}000$.

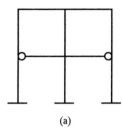 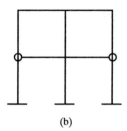

(a)   (b)   **Figure 9-8**

This is the same problem used in Secs. 9-4 through 9-7 to illustrate the direct stiffness method. Because the modified stiffness matrix is to be used for element b, the global number of nodal displacements is 8 as shown in Fig. 9-9(b).

From Figs. 9-9(c) and 9-9(d), the element stiffness equations in the global coordinate system are obtained as follows:

Element a: $C = \text{Cos } \phi = 0.8, S = \text{Sin } \phi = 0.6$

$$
\frac{EI}{L}
\begin{array}{cccccc}
1 & 2 & 3 & 4 & 5 & 6
\end{array}
$$

$$
\frac{EI}{L}
\begin{bmatrix}
1{,}284.32 & & & \text{Sym.} & & \\
954.24 & 727.68 & & & & \\
3.60 & -4.80 & 4.00 & & & \\
-1{,}284.32 & -954.24 & -3.60 & 1{,}284.32 & & \\
-954.24 & -727.68 & 4.80 & 954.24 & 727.68 & \\
3.60 & -4.80 & 2.00 & -3.60 & 4.80 & 4.00
\end{bmatrix}
\begin{Bmatrix}
u_i^a/L \\
v_i^a/L \\
\theta_i^a \\
u_j^a/L \\
v_j^a/L \\
\theta_j^a
\end{Bmatrix}
=
\begin{Bmatrix}
F_{xi}^a L \\
F_{yi}^a L \\
M_i^a \\
F_{xj}^a L \\
F_{yj}^a L \\
M_j^a
\end{Bmatrix}
$$

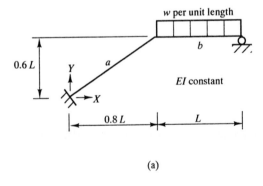 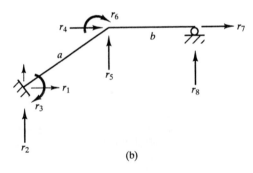

(a)   (b)

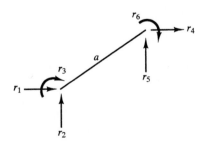 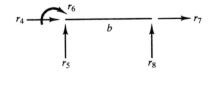

(c)   (d)

Figure 9-9

Element b: $C = \text{Cos}\,\phi = 1, S = \text{Sin}\,\phi = 0$

$$
\frac{EI}{L}
\begin{bmatrix}
2{,}000.00 & & & & \text{Sym.} \\
0 & 3.00 & & & \\
0 & -3.00 & 3.00 & & \\
-2{,}000.00 & 0 & 0 & 2{,}000.00 & \\
0 & -3.00 & 3.00 & 0 & 3.00
\end{bmatrix}
\begin{Bmatrix}
u_i^b/L \\ v_i^b/L \\ \theta_i^b \\ u_j^b/L \\ v_j^b/L
\end{Bmatrix}
=
\begin{Bmatrix}
F_{xi}^b L \\ F_{yi}^b L \\ M_i^b \\ F_{xj}^b L \\ F_{yj}^b L
\end{Bmatrix}
$$

The global stiffness equation, with nodal displacements rearranged, appears as

$$
\frac{EI}{L}
\left[
\begin{array}{cccc:cccc}
3{,}284.32 & & & & & \text{Sym.} & & \\
954.24 & 730.68 & & & & & & \\
-3.60 & 1.80 & 7.00 & & & & & \\
-2{,}000.00 & 0 & 0 & 2{,}000.00 & & & & \\ \hdashline
-1{,}284.32 & -954.24 & 3.60 & 0 & 1{,}284.32 & & & \\
-954.24 & -727.68 & -4.80 & 0 & 954.24 & 727.68 & & \\
-3.60 & 4.80 & 2.00 & 0 & 3.60 & -4.80 & 4.00 & \\
0 & -3.00 & 3.00 & 0 & 0 & 0 & 0 & 3.00
\end{array}
\right]
\begin{Bmatrix}
r_4 \\ r_5 \\ r_6 \\ r_7 \\ 0 \\ 0 \\ 0 \\ 0
\end{Bmatrix}
$$

$$
=
\begin{Bmatrix}
0 \\ -\frac{5}{8} \\ \frac{1}{8} \\ 0 \\ R_1 \\ R_2 \\ R_3 \\ R_8
\end{Bmatrix} wL^2
$$

where the nodal forces are obtained from Fig. 9-10. The unknown nodal displacements are found to be

$$
\begin{Bmatrix}
r_4 \\ r_5 \\ r_6 \\ r_7
\end{Bmatrix}
=
\begin{Bmatrix}
0.0279 \\ -0.0375 \\ 0.0419 \\ 0.0279
\end{Bmatrix}
\frac{wL^3}{EI}
$$

the same as obtained before (see Eq. 9-73). The rest of the computation would give the same results as before also.

The modified stiffness approach can also be used in symmetrical and anti-symmetrical cases in a way similar to that for the moment distribution method. If a member is in a symmetrical situation, then $\bar{u}_i = -\bar{u}_j$, $\bar{v}_i = \bar{v}_j$, and $\bar{\theta}_i = -\bar{\theta}_j$ [Fig. 9-11(a)].

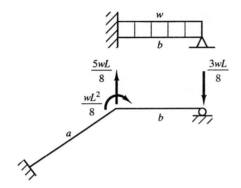

Figure 9-10

Following the same procedure as in the hinged-end case, we eliminate the nodal displacement unknowns at node j from Eq. 9-86 and obtain the following element stiffness equation with a 2×2 stiffness matrix in the local coordinate system.

$$\begin{bmatrix} \dfrac{2EA}{L} & 0 \\ 0 & \dfrac{2EI}{L} \end{bmatrix} \left\{ \begin{matrix} \bar{u}_i \\ \bar{\theta}_i \end{matrix} \right\} = \left\{ \begin{matrix} \bar{F}_{xi} \\ \bar{M}_i \end{matrix} \right\} \tag{9-91}$$

Note the absence of $\bar{v}_i$ and $\bar{F}_{yi}$ in Eq. 9-91. This is because, under $\bar{v}_i = \bar{v}_j$ and $\bar{\theta}_i = -\bar{\theta}_j$, the nodal shear forces are zero, and $\bar{v}_i = \bar{v}_j$ will not require any nodal moments and axial forces.

Similarly, for antisymmetrical cases [Fig. 9-11(b)], using $\bar{u}_i = \bar{u}_j$, $\bar{v}_i = -\bar{v}_j$, and $\bar{\theta}_i = \bar{\theta}_j$, we obtain the following stiffness equation with a 2×2 stiffness matrix.

$$\begin{bmatrix} \dfrac{24EI}{L^3} & -\dfrac{12EI}{L^2} \\ -\dfrac{12EI}{L^2} & \dfrac{6EI}{L} \end{bmatrix} \left\{ \begin{matrix} \bar{v}_i \\ \bar{\theta}_i \end{matrix} \right\} = \left\{ \begin{matrix} \bar{F}_{yi} \\ \bar{M}_i \end{matrix} \right\} \tag{9-92}$$

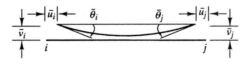

(a)

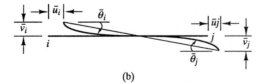

(b)   Figure 9-11

The application of these modified stiffness equations is now illustrated with the following examples.

Example 9-3

The end moments of the rigid frame shown in Fig. 9-12(a) were solved by the force method in Example 6-4 and will now be resolved by the displacement method. Assume that $AL^2/I = 2,000$.

The original problem is equivalent to the superposition of two separate problems as shown in Fig. 9-12(b). The problem in Fig. 9-12(b) with nodal forces only is clearly a symmetrical one. The global nodal degrees of freedom are arranged in the order shown in Fig. 9-12(c). The global degrees of freedom associated with elements a and b are shown in Figs. 9-12(d) and (e), respectively. Note that for element b only two displacements are needed because of symmetry. The element stiffness equations in global coordinate system are listed next.

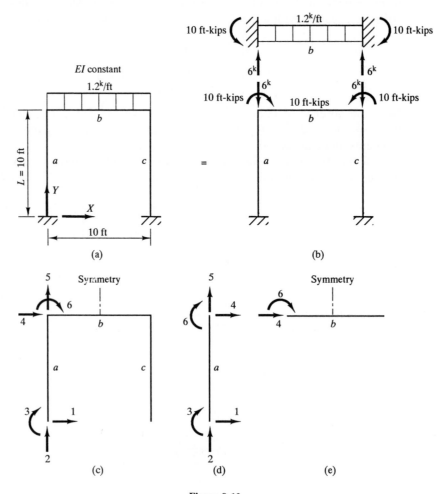

Figure 9-12

Element a: $C = \text{Cos } \phi = 0, S = \text{Sin } \phi = 1$, regular element

$$
\frac{EI}{L}
\begin{bmatrix}
12 & & & & & \text{Sym.} \\
0 & 2{,}000 & & & & \\
6 & 0 & 4 & & & \\
-12 & 0 & -6 & 12 & & \\
0 & -2{,}000 & 0 & 0 & 2{,}000 & \\
6 & 0 & 2 & -6 & 0 & 4
\end{bmatrix}
\begin{Bmatrix}
u_i^a/L \\
v_i^a/L \\
\theta_i^a \\
u_j^a/L \\
v_j^a/L \\
\theta_j^a
\end{Bmatrix}
=
\begin{Bmatrix}
F_{xi}^a L \\
F_{yi}^a L \\
M_i^a \\
F_{xj}^a L \\
F_{yj}^a L \\
M_j^a
\end{Bmatrix}
\tag{9-93}
$$

with column indices 1 2 3 4 5 6.

Element b: $C = \text{Cos } \phi = 1, S = \text{Sin } \phi = 0$, symmetrical element

$$
\frac{EI}{L}
\begin{bmatrix}
4{,}000 & 0 \\
0 & 2
\end{bmatrix}
\begin{Bmatrix}
u_i^b/L \\
\theta_i^b
\end{Bmatrix}
=
\begin{Bmatrix}
F_{xi}^b \\
M_i^b
\end{Bmatrix}
\tag{9-94}
$$

with column indices 4 6.

The global stiffness equation with rearranged displacements appears as

$$
\frac{EI}{L}
\begin{bmatrix}
4{,}012 & & & \text{Sym.} & & \\
0 & 2{,}000 & & & & \\
-6 & 0 & 6 & & & \\
-12 & 0 & 6 & 12 & & \\
0 & -2{,}000 & 0 & 0 & 2{,}000 & \\
-6 & 0 & 2 & 6 & 0 & 4
\end{bmatrix}
\begin{Bmatrix}
r_4 \\
r_5 \\
r_6 \\
0 \\
0 \\
0
\end{Bmatrix}
=
\begin{Bmatrix}
0 \\
-60 \\
10 \\
R_1 \\
R_2 \\
R_3
\end{Bmatrix}
\tag{9-95}
$$

with column indices 4 5 6 1 2 3.

The normalized unknown displacements are solved from the first three equations of Eq. 9-95.

$$
\begin{Bmatrix}
r_4 \\
r_5 \\
r_6
\end{Bmatrix}
=
\begin{Bmatrix}
\dfrac{100}{4006EI} \\[2mm]
-\dfrac{3}{10EI} \\[2mm]
\dfrac{50}{3EI} + \dfrac{100}{4006EI}
\end{Bmatrix}
$$

From the nodal displacements, we may calculate the element nodal forces using Eqs. 9-93 and 9-94 to obtain the member-end moments (after adding the fixed-end moment of -10 ft-kips to M_i^b).

$$
\begin{Bmatrix}
M_i^a \\
M_j^a \\
M_i^b
\end{Bmatrix}
=
\begin{Bmatrix}
\dfrac{10}{3} - \dfrac{40}{4006} \\[2mm]
\dfrac{20}{3} - \dfrac{20}{4006} \\[2mm]
-\dfrac{20}{3} + \dfrac{20}{4006}
\end{Bmatrix}
\text{ft-kips}
$$

We deliberately express these moment solutions in two terms, the second term being the effect of axial deformation of element b. We note the effect is indeed negligible (less than 1%), and the first term solutions are identical to those obtained in Example 6-4 using the matrix force method.

Example 9-4

Find the end moments of the rigid frame shown in Fig. 9-13(a). Assume that EI = constant and $AL^2/I = 2,000$.

Since the axial deformation effect is negligible, we may treat the original problem as equivalent to that in Fig. 9-13(b), which is antisymmetric. The global degrees of freedom numbering is shown in Fig. 9-13(c), and the element degrees of freedom are shown in Fig. 9-13(d) and (e) for elements a and b, respectively.

The element stiffness equation for element a is identical to that in Eq. 9-93. The element stiffness equation for element b, taking into account of the antisymmetric nature, is

$$\frac{EI}{L}\begin{bmatrix} 24 & -12 \\ -12 & 6 \end{bmatrix}\begin{Bmatrix} v_i^b/L \\ \theta_i \end{Bmatrix} = \begin{Bmatrix} F_{yi}^b L \\ M_i^b \end{Bmatrix}$$

with columns labeled 5 and 6.

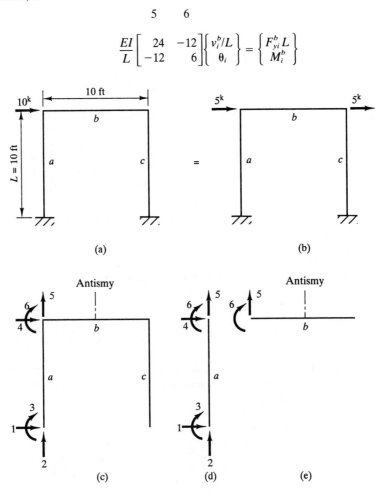

(a)

(b)

(c)

(d)

(e)

Figure 9-13

The global stiffness equation after rearranging the nodal displacements appears as

$$
\frac{EI}{L}
\begin{bmatrix}
12 & & & & \text{Sym.} & \\
0 & 2{,}024 & & & & \\
-6 & -12 & 10 & & & \\
-12 & 0 & 6 & 12 & & \\
0 & -2{,}000 & 0 & 0 & 2{,}000 & \\
-6 & 0 & 2 & 6 & 0 & 4
\end{bmatrix}
\begin{bmatrix} r_4 \\ r_5 \\ r_6 \\ 0 \\ 0 \\ 0 \end{bmatrix}
=
\begin{bmatrix} 50 \\ 0 \\ 0 \\ R_1 \\ R_2 \\ R_3 \end{bmatrix}
$$

with column headers 4 5 6 1 2 3.

The normalized unknown displacements are solved from the first three equations.

$$
\begin{Bmatrix} r_4 \\ r_5 \\ r_6 \end{Bmatrix}
=
\begin{Bmatrix}
5.97\dfrac{L}{EI} \\[2mm]
0.0214\dfrac{L}{EI} \\[2mm]
3.61\dfrac{L}{EI}
\end{Bmatrix}
$$

The member-end moments are obtained from the element stiffness equations.

$$
\begin{Bmatrix} M_i^a \\ M_j^a \\ M_i^b \end{Bmatrix}
=
\begin{Bmatrix} -28.6 \\ -21.4 \\ 21.4 \end{Bmatrix} \text{ ft-kips}
$$

9-10 COMPOSITE STRUCTURES

A composite structure consists of both frame members and truss members. In fact, a frame member having both ends hinged becomes a truss member. The element stiffness equations are established using Eq. 9-43 for frame members and Eq. 9-77 for truss members. The use of normalized quantities in the way of Eq. 9-64 is not appropriate because truss members have no bending stiffness. The handling of both truss and frame members in the development of the global stiffness equation through the direct stiffness method is illustrated with an example.

Example 9-5

The axial force in the rod of the composite structure shown in Fig. 9-14(a) has been solved by the method of consistent deformations in Example 5-14. It will now be solved by the matrix displacement method. $E = 30{,}000$ kips/in.^{2}.

The problem is separated into two parts as shown in Fig. 9-14(b). The numbering of the global degrees of freedom is shown in Fig. 9-14(c), and the element nodal degrees of freedom for elements 1 and 2 are given in Figs. 9-14(d) and (e), respectively. Note that no global rotational degree of freedom is defined at node c.

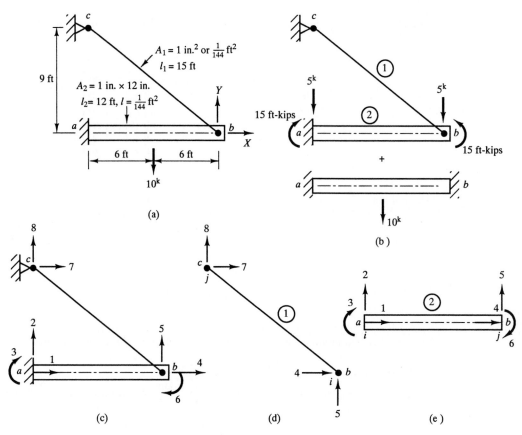

(a)

(b)

(c)

(d)

(e)

Figure 9-14

The element stiffness equations are given below.

Element 1: $C = \text{Cos}\,\phi = -0.8, S = \text{Sin}\,\phi = 0.6$, truss element

$$
\frac{E}{144}
\begin{bmatrix}
0.04267 & & \text{Sym.} & \\
-0.03200 & 0.02400 & & \\
-0.04267 & 0.03200 & 0.04267 & \\
0.03200 & -0.02400 & -0.03200 & 0.02400
\end{bmatrix}
\begin{Bmatrix}
u_i^1 \\ v_i^1 \\ u_j^1 \\ v_j^1
\end{Bmatrix}
=
\begin{Bmatrix}
F_{xi}^1 \\ F_{yi}^1 \\ F_{xj}^1 \\ F_{yj}^1
\end{Bmatrix}
$$

$$\quad\quad 4 \quad\quad\quad 5 \quad\quad\quad 7 \quad\quad\quad 8$$

Element 2: $C = \text{Cos}\,\phi = 1, S = \text{Sin}\,\phi = 0$, frame element

$$\quad 1 \quad\quad 2 \quad\quad 3 \quad\quad 4 \quad\quad 5 \quad\quad 6$$

$$
\frac{E}{144}
\begin{bmatrix}
1 & & & \text{Sym.} & & \\
0 & 0.00694 & & & & \\
0 & -0.04167 & 0.33333 & & & \\
-1 & 0 & 0 & 1 & & \\
0 & -0.00694 & 0.04167 & 0 & 0.00694 & \\
0 & -0.04167 & 0.16667 & 0 & 0.04167 & 0.33333
\end{bmatrix}
\begin{Bmatrix}
u_i^2 \\ v_i^2 \\ \theta_i^2 \\ u_j^2 \\ v_j^2 \\ \theta_j^2
\end{Bmatrix}
=
\begin{Bmatrix}
F_{xi}^2 \\ F_{yi}^2 \\ M_i^2 \\ F_{xj}^2 \\ F_{yj}^2 \\ M_j^2
\end{Bmatrix}
$$

The global stiffness equation has eight equations in it. The three related to the unknown displacements, r_4, r_5, and r_6, appear as

$$\frac{E}{144}\begin{bmatrix} 1.04267 & & \text{Sym.} \\ -0.03200 & 0.03094 & \\ 0 & 0.04167 & 0.33333 \end{bmatrix}\begin{Bmatrix} r_4 \\ r_5 \\ r_6 \end{Bmatrix} = \begin{Bmatrix} 0 \\ -5 \\ -15 \end{Bmatrix}$$

The solutions for the three nodal displacements are

$$\begin{Bmatrix} r_4 \\ r_5 \\ r_6 \end{Bmatrix} = \begin{Bmatrix} -3.87 \\ -126.52 \\ -29.18 \end{Bmatrix}\frac{144}{E}$$

The horizontal and vertical nodal forces at node b of the truss element are found to be 3.87 and -2.90 kips, respectively, from which the axial force in the rod is calculated to be 4.84 kips in tension, the same as found before.

9-11 TREATMENT OF INCLINED SUPPORTS

Consider the truss shown in Fig. 9-15. The inclined roller support at the right end provides a constraining equation containing both the horizontal and the vertical displacements at that node. When the global stiffness equation is formed, this constraining equation cannot be easily incorporated into it. We could define an inclined global coordinate system to accommodate this support condition, but other roller supports would require a regular horizontal–vertical system. Thus, the standard approach with one global coordinate system is not workable without some modification.

There are more than one way of treating the inclined support problem. We will discuss one that defines a separate coordinate system for that particular node. We choose this approach because it is the simplest in concept and easily programmable for computer applications. We will illustrate the method with a truss problem, but the approach is equally applicable to frame problems.

The central idea is simply to define a separate coordinate system only for the supporting node. We recall that the global coordinate system is necessary only because we need a common coordinate system so that nodal forces calculated from different elements at a node can be summed up in the same coordinate system. There is no reason why we cannot use different systems for different nodes. The effect of

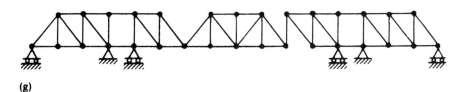

(g)

Figure 9-15

using a separate nodal coordinate system at the supporting node is that all joining members at that node will have two different systems at their end nodes, as shown in Fig. 9-16.

A different system, $X'-Y'$, is defined for node j as shown in Fig. 9-16(b). This means that we need to have two angles of rotation for coordinate transformation: one between the $\overline{X}$ axis and X axis and the other between the $\overline{X}$ axis and X' axis. They are denoted by ϕ_i and ϕ_j in Fig. 9-16(a). As a result, the transformation between the local and "global" degrees of freedom becomes, from Eq. 9-38,

$$\begin{Bmatrix} \bar{u}_i \\ \bar{v}_i \\ \bar{u}_j \\ \bar{v}_j \end{Bmatrix} = \begin{bmatrix} C_i & S_i & 0 & 0 \\ -S_i & C_i & 0 & 0 \\ 0 & 0 & C_j & S_j \\ 0 & 0 & -S_j & C_j \end{bmatrix} \begin{Bmatrix} u_i \\ v_i \\ u'_j \\ v'_j \end{Bmatrix} \tag{9-96}$$

where $C_i = \mathrm{Cos}\,\phi_i$, $S_i = \mathrm{Sin}\,\phi_i$, $C_j = \mathrm{Cos}\,\phi_j$, and $S_j = \mathrm{Sin}\,\phi_j$. The element stiffness equation (Eq. 9-77) in the "global" coordinate system changes into

$$\frac{EA}{L} \begin{bmatrix} C_i^2 & & & \\ C_i S_i & S_i^2 & & \\ -C_i C_j & -C_j S_i & C_j^2 & \\ -C_i S_j & -S_i S_j & C_j S_j & S_j^2 \end{bmatrix} \begin{Bmatrix} u_i \\ v_i \\ u'_j \\ v'_j \end{Bmatrix} = \begin{Bmatrix} F_{xi} \\ F_{yi} \\ F'_{xj} \\ F'_{yj} \end{Bmatrix} \tag{9-97}$$

The global stiffness equation can then be assembled according to the direct stiffness method.

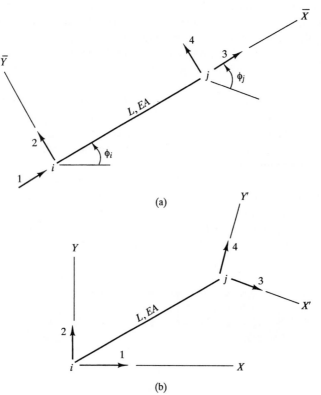

(a)

(b)   **Figure 9-16**

Example 9-6

Analyze the truss shown in Fig. 9-17(a). Assume $EA/L = 1$ for all elements. Note that the truss is the same as that in Example 9-1, except the roller support is inclined.

The separate coordinate system, $X'-Y'$, defined at the roller support node is shown in Fig. 9-17(a) and the global degrees of freedom are defined in Fig. 9-17(b). Element b is not affected by the new $X'-Y'$ system, but the other two elements are and have different angles of transformation at the two ends, as shown in Fig. 9-17(c).

The element stiffness matrices and the associated global nodal displacement numbers are listed next.

Element a: $C_i = \text{Cos } \phi_i = 1, S_i = \text{Sin } \phi_i = 0, C_j = \text{Cos } \phi_j = 0.8, S_j = \text{Sin } \phi_j = -0.6$

$$k^a = \begin{matrix} & \begin{matrix} 1 & \quad 2 & \quad 3 & \quad 4 \end{matrix} & \\ & \left[\begin{matrix} 1.00 & & \text{Sym.} & \\ 0 & 0 & & \\ -0.80 & 0 & 0.64 & \\ 0.60 & 0 & -0.48 & 0.36 \end{matrix} \right] & \begin{matrix} 1 \\ 2 \\ 3 \\ 4 \end{matrix} \end{matrix}$$

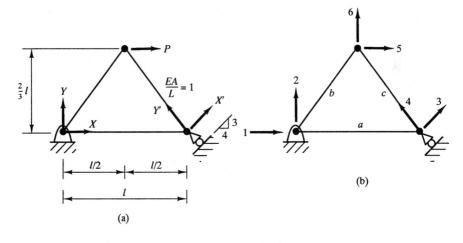

(a)

(b)

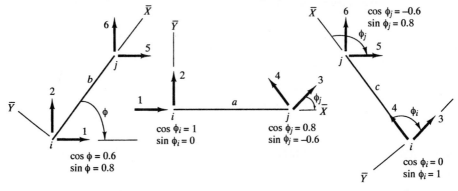

$\cos \phi = 0.6$
$\sin \phi = 0.8$

$\cos \phi_i = 1$
$\sin \phi_i = 0$

$\cos \phi_j = 0.8$
$\sin \phi_j = -0.6$

$\cos \phi_j = -0.6$
$\sin \phi_j = 0.8$

$\cos \phi_i = 0$
$\sin \phi_i = 1$

(c)

Figure 9-17

Element b: $C = \text{Cos } \phi = 0.6, S = \text{Sin } \phi = 0.8$

$$k^b = \begin{array}{c} \\ \\ \\ \end{array} \begin{matrix} 1 & 2 & 5 & 6 \\ \begin{bmatrix} 0.36 & & \text{Sym.} & \\ 0.48 & 0.64 & & \\ -0.36 & -0.48 & 0.36 & \\ -0.48 & -0.64 & 0.48 & 0.64 \end{bmatrix} & \begin{matrix} 1 \\ 2 \\ 5 \\ 6 \end{matrix} \end{matrix}$$

Element c: $C_i = \text{Cos } \phi_i = 0, S_i = \text{Sin } \phi_i = 1, C_j = \text{Cos } \phi_j = -0.6, S_j = \text{Sin } \phi_i = 0.8$

$$k^c = \begin{matrix} 3 & 4 & 5 & 6 \\ \begin{bmatrix} 0 & & \text{Sym.} & \\ 0 & 1.00 & & \\ 0 & 0.60 & 0.36 & \\ 0 & -0.80 & -0.48 & 0.64 \end{bmatrix} & \begin{matrix} 3 \\ 4 \\ 5 \\ 6 \end{matrix} \end{matrix}$$

The global stiffness equation, after being rearranged to put unknown displacements first, appears as

$$\begin{matrix} 3 & 5 & 6 & 1 & 2 & 4 \\ \begin{bmatrix} 0.64 & & & & \text{Sym.} & \\ 0.00 & 0.72 & & & & \\ 0.00 & 0.00 & 1.28 & & & \\ -0.80 & -0.36 & -0.48 & 1.36 & & \\ 0.00 & -0.48 & -0.64 & 0.48 & 0.64 & \\ -0.48 & 0.60 & -0.80 & 0.60 & 0.00 & 1.36 \end{bmatrix} \end{matrix} \begin{Bmatrix} r_3 \\ r_5 \\ r_6 \\ 0 \\ 0 \\ 0 \end{Bmatrix} = \begin{Bmatrix} 0 \\ P \\ 0 \\ R_1 \\ R_2 \\ R_4 \end{Bmatrix}$$

The solution of the first three equations is

$$\begin{Bmatrix} r_3 \\ r_5 \\ r_6 \end{Bmatrix} = \begin{Bmatrix} 0.000 \\ 1.389 \\ 0.000 \end{Bmatrix} P$$

The reaction forces are

$$\begin{Bmatrix} R_1 \\ R_2 \\ R_4 \end{Bmatrix} = \begin{Bmatrix} -0.500 \\ -0.667 \\ 0.833 \end{Bmatrix} P$$

The member forces are 0 for element a, $0.833P$ (tension) for element b, and $0.833P$ (compression) for element c.

9-12 COMPUTER IMPLEMENTATION

With the direct stiffness method, the computer implementation of the displacement method is very simple. A computer program will involve the following ingredients.

1. Input of data:
   a. *Geometric data:* nodal coordinates of all nodes with respect to a single global coordinate system. The nodes are numbered.
   b. *Element connectivity and properties:* the global node number of the starting node, i, and the terminating node, j, and EI and EA of all elements. Elements are also numbered.
   c. *Displacement constraints:* inclination of the constrained nodes (supports) and the value of constrained displacements, which may not be zero.
   d. *Applied forces at each degree of freedom:* usually only nonzero forces need to be input. The zero forces are internally established by the program.

2. *Establishment of the unconstrained global stiffness equation:* The element stiffness matrices are established and directly added to the global stiffness matrix via the element connectivity information.

3. *Establishment of the constrained global stiffness equation:* The applied forces and given displacement constraints are properly incorporated into the force and displacement vectors. There are a variety of ways of treating the displacement constraints. It is seldom necessary to actually rearrange the global stiffness equation as shown in all of our examples, which are designed for hand computation.

4. *Solution of nodal displacements, reaction forces, and element forces:* Either Gaussian elimination or one of its equivalent methods may be used.

5. Output of results.

Two computer programs written according to the matrix displacement method are given in Appendix B. One is for truss analysis only and the other is for frame and/or composite structures. Readers are encouraged to use it not only for assigned problems but for self-designed problems as well.

PROBLEMS

9-1. Derive the functions f_1, f_2, f_3, and f_4 in Eq. 9-16 by assuming a cubic function of the form

$$v(\bar{x}) = a_0 + a_1\bar{x} + a_2\bar{x}^2 + a_3\bar{x}^3$$

and applying the four conditions in Eq. 9-14.

9-2. Derive Eq. 9-25 by taking the derivative of the total potential energy with respect to the displacements q_{bn} one by one.

9-3. Use the principle of minimum total potential energy to derive the stiffness equation of an axial element by assuming a displacement function in the form of Eq. 9-2.

9-4. Use the axial element as an example to derive (a) the principle of minimum total potential energy formula and (b) Castigliano's first theorem formula using the method of virtual displacement. *Hint:* Since virtual displacement may be any assumed function, select virtual displacement as the differential quantity of the real displacement.

9-5. Derive the stiffness equation of an axial element by assuming a real displacement the same as in Eq. 9-2, but a virtual displacement $\delta\bar{u}(\bar{x}) = [1 - (\bar{x}/L)^2]\delta\bar{u}_i + (\bar{x}/L)^2\,\delta\bar{u}_j$.

9-6. A singular matrix A is defined as one with a zero determinant or, equivalently, as one that satisfies $AX = 0$, where X is a vector with at least one nonzero coefficient and 0 is a vector of all zero coefficients. Use the latter definition to prove that the element stiffness matrix of an axial element is singular by finding a vector X such that $AX = 0$. Explain the meaning of the vector X in terms of the displacement pattern it represents.

9-7. Find the support reactions of the beam shown in Fig. 9-18 by the matrix displacement method.

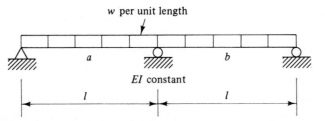

Figure 9-18

9-8. Determine, by the matrix displacement method, the member end forces and support reactions for the beam shown in Fig. 9-19.

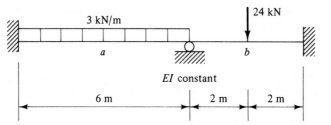

Figure 9-19

9-9. Determine, by the matrix displacement method, the bar forces, support reactions, and nodal displacements for the truss shown in Fig. 9-20. Assume the same constant axial rigidity EA for all members.

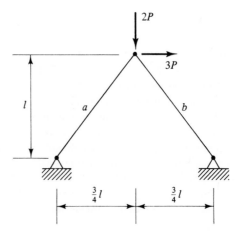

Figure 9-20

9-10. Determine, by the matrix displacement method, the bar forces and support reactions for the truss shown in Fig. 9-21. Assume that $A/L = 1$ for all members.

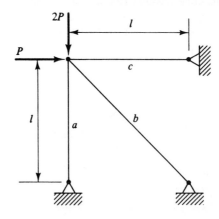

Figure 9-21

9-11. Find, by the matrix displacement method, the member-end forces and support reactions for the frame shown in Fig. 9-22. Assume that $L^2 A/I = 2,000$.

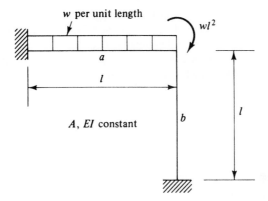

Figure 9-22

9-12. Find, by the matrix displacement method, the member-end forces and support reactions for the rigid frame shown in Fig. 9-23 using the modified stiffness matrix for elements with a hinged end. Assume that $L^2 A/I = 2,000$.

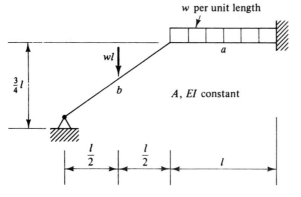

Figure 9-23

9-13. Use the matrix displacement method to solve for nodal displacements for the rigid frame shown in Fig. 9-24 by separating the problem into a symmetrical one and an anti-symmetrical one. Assume that $L^2 A/I = 2,000$.

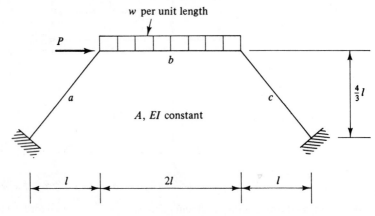

Figure 9-24

9-14. Resolve Problems 9-7 through 9-13 using the computer programs for the matrix displacement method described in Appendix B. In each problem, assign a convenient numerical value for quantities such as EI, w, and P.

9-15. Resolve Problems 5-16 and 5-17 using the computer programs for the matrix displacement method described in Appendix B.

Chapter 10

Influence Lines

10-1 CONCEPT OF THE INFLUENCE LINE

In the design of a structure, as discussed in Sec. 1-2, the loading conditions for the structure must be established before the stress analysis can be made. For a static structure, we are mainly concerned with two kinds of load, dead load and live load (the impact load being a fraction of the live load). The dead load remains stationary with the structure, whereas the live load, either the moving or the movable load, may vary in position on the structure. When designing any specific part of a structure, we should know where to place the live load so that it will cause the maximum live stresses for the part considered. The part of the structure and the type of stress may be the reaction of a support, the shear or moment of a beam section, or the bar force in a truss. The position of the load that causes the maximum bending moment at a section will not necessarily cause the maximum shear at the same section, and the condition of loading that causes the maximum axial force at one member may not cause the maximum axial force at some other member. To handle these, it is advisable to plot curves that show the individual effect on a desired force element at a certain location of the structure caused by a unit load moving across the structure span. This can be done by taking the x axis to indicate the path of the unit moving load, and the y axis, the corresponding force variation at the given location. The graphic representation of the relationship $y = f(x)$ is called the *influence line*.

As an illustration, let us draw a bending moment influence line for the midspan section of a simple beam 10 ft long [Fig. 10-1(a)]. We may first divide the span into equal segments, say 10 segments $AB, BC, \ldots, JK$, to indicate the position of load. As the unit load moves continuously from the left to the right, we focus our attention on the midspan section F and compute the bending moment at F for each 1-ft interval. The results are plotted in Fig. 10-1(b), which gives the bending moment influence line for section F. The abscissa coincides with the beam axis, indicating the position of the load, and the ordinate gives the corresponding moment at F due to the single unit load placed at the ordinate. For instance, the ordinate at D is 1.5, which is the value of the moment at F caused by a unit load at D.

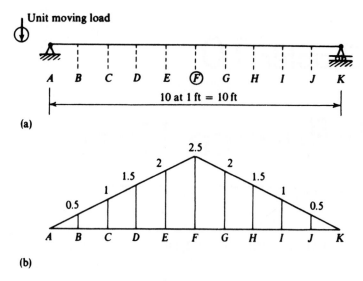

Figure 10-1

We need not always plot the influence line in this fashion, since it is time consuming. In most cases we can find an equation $y = f(x)$ expressing the desired force y at the given section in terms of the load position x. The plane curve represented by the equation gives the desired influence line. To illustrate this technique, let us use the same problem but picture it in a different way, as shown in Fig. 10-2(a). The unit load is placed at a distance x from the left end A. The reactions at ends A and K are expressed as functions of x,

$$R_A = \frac{(10-x)(1)}{10} = 1 - \frac{x}{10}, \qquad R_K = \left(\frac{x}{10}\right)(1) = \frac{x}{10}$$

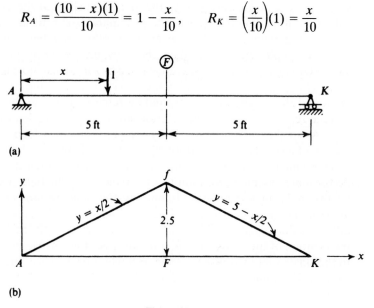

Figure 10-2

respectively. When the moving load is confined to the left of section F (as shown), the bending moment at F may be found from R_K:

$$M_F = 5R_K = \frac{x}{2}$$

or

$$y = \frac{x}{2}$$

where y denotes M_F. As the moving load is confined to the right of section F (not shown), the bending moment at F may be found from R_A:

$$M_F = 5R_A = (5)\left(1 - \frac{x}{10}\right) = 5 - \frac{x}{2}$$

or

$$y = 5 - \frac{x}{2}$$

Selecting the coordinate axes as shown in Fig. 10-2(b), we plot $y = x/2$ and $y = 5 - (x/2)$. The curve AfK given in Fig. 10-2(b) is the desired *bending moment influence line* for section F, and the corresponding diagram $AFKf$ is called the *bending moment influence diagram* for section F.

A generalized definition of the influence line may be given as follows: *An influence line is a curve whose ordinate (y value) gives the value of the function* (shear, moment, reaction, bar force, etc.) *in a fixed element* (member section, support, bar in truss, etc.) *when a unit load is at the ordinate*.

Although in this particular case the influence diagram of Fig. 10-2(b) is identical with the moment diagram for the same beam under a unit load at midspan, we must not confuse the influence diagram with a bending moment diagram for the beam. Whereas the ordinate in the latter shows the bending moment at the corresponding section due to a fixed load, the ordinate in the influence diagram shows the bending moment at a fixed section due to a unit load placed at that point.

10-2 USE OF THE INFLUENCE LINE

An influence line is a useful tool in stress analysis in two ways:

1. It serves as a criterion in determining the maximum stress; that is, it is a guide for determining what portion of the structure should be loaded in order to cause the maximum effect on the part under consideration.
2. It simplifies the computation.

To illustrate, consider a simple beam 10 ft long subjected to the passage of a moving uniform load of 1 kip/ft without limit in length and a movable concentrated load of 10 kips that may be placed at any point of the span [see Fig. 10-3(a)]. Determine the maximum bending moment at the midspan section C.

We start by drawing the bending moment influence line for section C, as in Fig. 10-3(b). It is apparent from the influence line that to obtain the maximum M_C the single concentrated load of 10 kips should be placed at the midpoint of the span, where the maximum ordinate of the influence line occurs, and the uniform load should be spread over the entire span.

Next, to compute the bending moment at C due to the live loads so placed, we simply multiply each load by the corresponding influence ordinate and add. Referring to Fig. 10-3(b) and (c), we obtain

$$M_C = P(2.5) + \sum (w\,dx)y$$

Note that the uniform load is treated as a series of infinitesimal concentrated loads each of magnitude $w\,dx$, and the total effect of the uniform load is the summation

$$\sum (w\,dx)y$$

Now,

$$\sum (w\,dx)y = \int_0^l wy\,dx = w\int_0^l y\,dx$$

$$= \text{(load intensity)} \times \text{(area of influence diagram)}$$

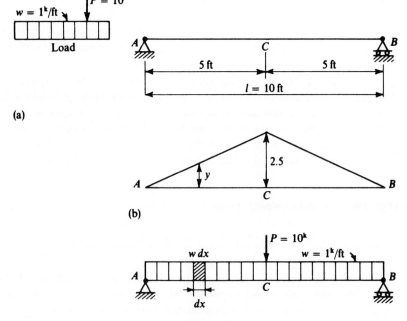

(a)

(b)

Figure 10-3

Therefore, the total bending moment at C is

$$M_C = (10)(2.5) + (1)\frac{(2.5)(10)}{2} = 25 + 12.5 = 37.5 \text{ ft-kips}$$

This value may be checked by the conventional method of computing M_C:

$$M_C = \left(\frac{10}{2}\right)(5) + \frac{(1)(10)^2}{8} = 25 + 12.5 = 37.5 \text{ ft-kips}$$

In this simple case, such a conclusion may be drawn without the aid of the influence diagram; but for more complicated moving load systems, we find that the influence diagram can be of substantial help, as discussed in Sec. 10-5.

10-3 INFLUENCE LINES FOR STATICALLY DETERMINATE BEAMS

The basic approach to drawing influence lines for a statically determinate beam is to apply the equilibrium based on the procedure of taking the appropriate free body as the unit load travels along the beam span. It is often convenient to construct the reaction influence lines first and then deduce the shear and moment influences.

Example 10-1

Consider the simple beam with an overhang shown in Fig. 10-4(a). To construct the influence line for R_B, we place a unit load distance x from end A and apply $\Sigma M_C = 0$ to obtain

$$R_B = \frac{20 - x}{16}$$

The expression represents a straight line with a maximum ordinate of $\frac{5}{4}$ at A and a minimum ordinate of 0 at C, as shown in Fig. 10-4(b). Note that when the unit load is placed at B the influence ordinate for R_B should be equal to unity.

The influence line for R_C may be found by applying $\Sigma F_y = 0$:

$$R_C = 1 - R_B = 1 - \frac{20 - x}{16} = \frac{x - 4}{16}$$

which is also a linear function of x, as shown in Fig. 10-4(c). As a check, the ordinate at C should be equal to unity and that at B to zero.

The influence line for the shear at the section just to the left of B, called $(V_B)_L$, is given in Fig. 10-4(d). As long as the unit load is on the overhanging portion of beam, $(V_B)_L = -1$; as the load passes B to the right, $(V_B)_L = 0$.

The influence line for the shear at the section just to the right of B, called $(V_B)_R$, is shown in Fig. 10-4(e). As long as the unit load is on the overhanging portion of beam, $(V_B)_R$ equals R_C but with opposite sign. When the load is on the simple beam portion, $(V_B)_R$ equals R_B.

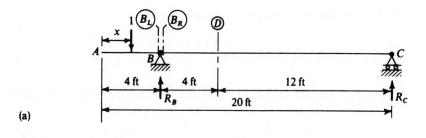

(a)

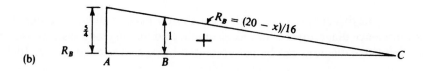

(b)

$R_B = (20 - x)/16$

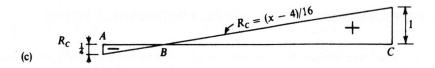

(c)

$R_C = (x - 4)/16$

(d)

$(V_B)_L$

$(V_B)_L = 0$

$(V_B)_L = -1$

(e)

$(V_B)_R$

$(V_B)_R = -R_C$

$(V_B)_R = R_B$

(f)

V_D

$V_D = -R_C$

$V_D = R_B$

(g)

M_D

$M_D = 12R_C$

$M_D = 4R_B$

(h)

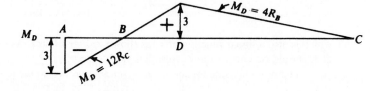

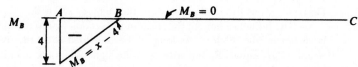

M_B

$M_B = 0$

$M_B = x - 4$

Figure 10-4

By a similar approach, we construct the influence line for shear at section D, as shown in Fig. 10-4(f). As a check, when the unit load passes D from the left to the right, the shear at D increases suddenly from $-\frac{1}{4}$ to $+\frac{3}{4}$ (i.e., there is an abrupt change of shear equal to unity at D).

The influence line for the moment at D is shown in Fig. 10-4(g). We note that as long as the unit load is confined to the portion AD, the moment at D may be found from R_C:

$$M_D = 12R_C = (12)\left(\frac{x-4}{16}\right) = \frac{3x-12}{4}, \qquad 0 \leqslant x \leqslant 8$$

which represents a straight line from A to D with ordinates of -3 at A and $+3$ at D. When the load passes D to the right, the moment at D may be found from R_B:

$$M_D = 4R_B = (4)\left(\frac{20-x}{16}\right) = \frac{20-x}{4}, \qquad 8 \leqslant x \leqslant 20$$

which represents a straight line from D to C with ordinates of $+3$ at D and 0 at C.

Finally, we construct the influence line for the moment at B, as in Fig. 10-4(h). When the load is placed at A, M_B has its greatest negative value of 4. As the load travels from A to B, the moment varies linearly from -4 to 0. As the load enters the portion BC, there is no moment at B.

A more simple and elegant way to construct beam influence lines is to apply Müller–Breslau's principle, which can be stated as follows:

1. To obtain an influence line for the reaction of any statically determinate beam, remove the support and make a positive unit displacement of its point of application. The deflected beam is the influence line for the reaction.

2. To obtain an influence line for the shear at a section of any statically determinate beam, cut the section and induce a unit relative transverse sliding displacement between the portion to the left of the section and the portion to the right of the section, keeping all other constraints (both external and internal) intact. The deflected beam is the influence line for the shear at the section.

3. To obtain the influence line for the moment at a section of any statically determinate beam, cut the section and induce a unit rotation between the portion to the left of the section and the portion to the right of the section, keeping all other constraints (both external and internal) intact. The deflected beam is the influence line for the moment at the section.

Müller–Breslau's principle is based on the theorem of virtual work, which states that, if a compatible virtual displacement is induced in an ideal system in equilibrium under balanced forces, the total virtual work δW done by all active forces is equal to zero.

To prove the theory, we take the case of a simple beam. The proof is generally applicable to more complicated beams. Figure 10-5(a) shows a simple beam subjected to a single unit moving load. To find the reaction at A by the method of virtual work, we remove the constraint at A, substitute R_A for it, and let A travel a small virtual displacement δs_A along R_A. We then have a deflected beam $A'B$, as shown

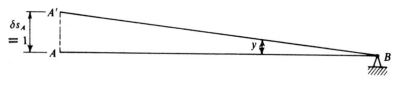

(a)

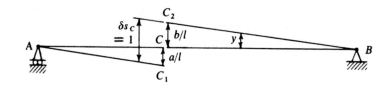

(b)

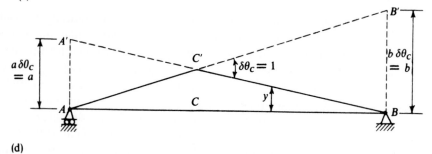

(c)

(d)

Figure 10-5

in Fig. 10-5(b), where y indicates the transverse displacement at the point of unit load. Applying $\delta W = 0$, we obtain

$$(R_A)(\delta s_A) - (1)(y) = 0$$

from which

$$R_A = \frac{y}{\delta s_A}$$

If we let

$$\delta s_A = 1$$

then

$$R_A = y$$

Since y is, on the one hand, the ordinate of the deflected beam at the point where the unit load stands and is, on the other hand, the value of function R_A due to the unit moving load (i.e., the influence ordinate at the point), we conclude that the deflected beam $A'B$ of Fig. 10-5(b) is the influence line for R_A if δs_A is set to be unity.

To determine the shearing force at any beam cross section C, we cut the beam at C and let the two portions AC and CB have a relative virtual transverse displacement δs_C at C without causing relative rotation between the two portions. This is equivalent to rotating AC and BC the same small angle about A and B, respectively. Applying $\delta W = 0$, we obtain

$$(V_C)(\delta s_C) - (1)(y) = 0$$

from which

$$V_C = \frac{y}{\delta s_C}$$

If we let

$$\delta s_C = 1$$

then

$$V_C = y$$

This proves that the deflected beam $AC_1 C_2 B$ of Fig. 10-5(c) is the influence line for V_C. It should be pointed out that the virtual displacement is supposed to be vanishingly small, and that when we say $\delta s_C = 1$ we do not mean that $\delta s_C = 1$ ft or 1 in., but one unit of very small distance for which the expressions

$$CC_1 = \frac{a}{l}$$

$$CC_2 = \frac{b}{l}$$

shown in Fig. 10-5(c) are justified.

To determine the moment at any beam cross section C by the method of virtual work, we cut the beam at C and induce a relative virtual rotation between the two portions AC and CB at C without producing relative transverse sliding between the two. Thus, by $\delta W = 0$.

$$(M_C)(\delta\theta_C) - (1)(y) = 0$$

from which

$$M_C = \frac{y}{\delta\theta_C}$$

If we let

$$\delta\theta_C = 1$$

then

$$M_C = y$$

This proves that the deflected beam $AC'B$ of Fig. 10-5(d) is the influence line for M_C. Note that when we say $\delta\theta_C = 1$ we do not mean that $\delta\theta_C = 1$ radian. One unit of $\delta\theta_C$ may be as small as $\frac{1}{100}$ radian, for which it is justified to write

$$AA' = a \cdot \delta\theta_C = a \text{ units}, \qquad BB' = b \cdot \delta\theta_C = b \text{ units}$$

as indicated in Fig. 10-5(d).

Example 10-2

Figure 10-6(a) shows a compound beam. Draw influence lines for R_A, V_D, M_D, V_E, and M_E by Müller–Breslau's principle.

To construct the influence line for R_A, we remove support A and move end A up a unit distance. The deflected beam $A'CB$ shown in Fig. 10-6(b) is the influence line for R_A. Note that portion CB is a cantilever and will remain unmoved.

To construct the influence line for V_D, we cut the beam through D and let the left portion of beam have a relative transverse displacement equal to unity with respect to the right portion of beam at D without causing relative rotation between the two. The deflected beam AD_1D_2CB shown in Fig. 10-6(c) is the influence line for V_D.

To construct the influence line for M_D, we cut the beam through D and let the left portion of beam rotate a unit angle with respect to the right portion at D. The deflected beam $AD'CB$ of Fig. 10-6(d) is the influence line for M_D.

The influence line for V_E is shown in Fig. 10-6(e) by $AC'E'EB$, which results from cutting the beam through E and moving the left portion of beam down a unit distance with respect to the right portion of beam at E while keeping the deflected portion $C'E'$ parallel to BE.

The influence line for M_E is shown in Fig. 10-6(f) by $AC'EB$, which results from cutting the beam through E and rotating the left portion of beam a unit angle with respect to the right portion of beam at E. Point E is kept fixed in the original position.

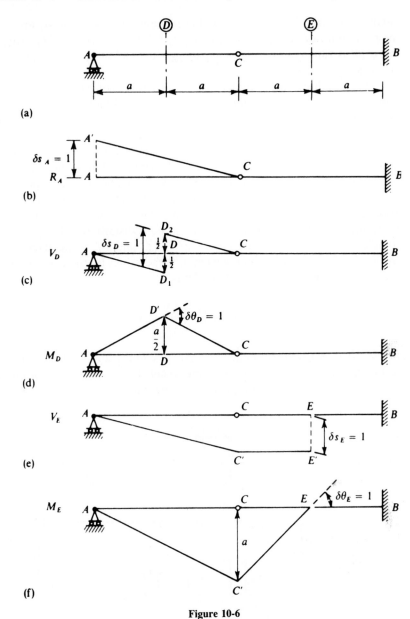

Figure 10-6

10-4 INFLUENCE LINES FOR STATICALLY DETERMINATE BRIDGE TRUSSES

As stated in Sec. 3-6, the live loads on the deck of a bridge are transmitted to the loaded chords of main trusses through the system of stringers and floor beams. The stringers running parallel to the main trusses are usually assumed to act as simple beams supported by the adjacent floor beams, which, in turn, are connected to the panel points (truss joints) of the loaded chords (see Fig. 3-21). Any live load on the deck is thus considered as a panel-point load at the loaded chord in a truss analysis.

We can draw influence lines for the bar forces of a bridge truss by placing the unit load at each successive panel point of the loaded chord, computing the bar forces as the influence ordinates, and connecting adjacent influence ordinates by straight lines. The reason that the influence line between consecutive panel points will be a straight line can be explained as follows. Refer to Fig. 10-7(a) for a diagram of a truss chord loaded with cross beams and stringers. Let a unit load travel along a panel $m–n$. When the unit load is at m, we let y_m be the corresponding influence ordinate for it; when the unit load is at n, we let y_n be the corresponding influence ordinate for it [see Fig. 10-7(b)]. Now, when the unit load is in any intermediate position, say at distance x from m, it will be transmitted to the girder through the floor beams at m and n with values. $(l - x)/l$ and x/l, respectively. The effect of the load is found by multiplying each of these values by the corresponding value of the influence ordinate and adding. Thus,

$$(1)(y) = \left(\frac{l - x}{l}\right)(y_m) + \left(\frac{x}{l}\right)(y_n)$$

in which y denotes the influence ordinate where the unit load is located as indicated in Fig. 10-7(b). This expression, being linear in x, specifies the influence ordinate for the general intermediate position in the panel.

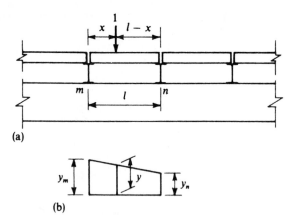

(a)

(b)

Figure 10-7

Example 10-3

For the truss shown in Fig. 10-8(a), draw the influence lines for forces in members aB, Bb, Bc, and bc.

We start with a unit load at joint a and then move it to b, c, and d successively. Each time we place the unit load at a joint, we compute the bar forces (or components) in the desired members and we erect the ordinates to the respective influence lines, as shown in Fig. 10-8(b) to (e). Finally, we connect the consecutive ordinates by straight lines to complete the influence lines.

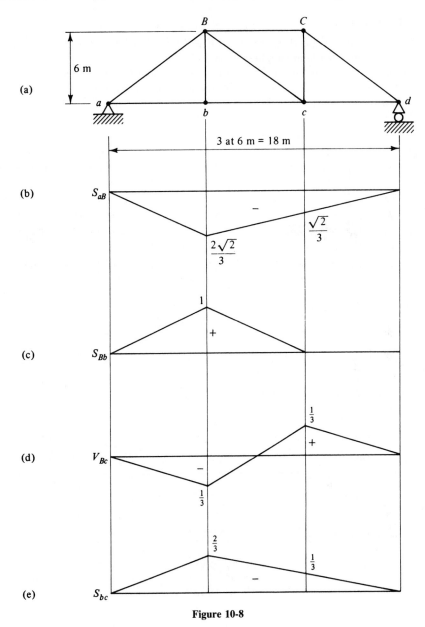

Figure 10-8

Although it is always possible to obtain the ordinates to an influence line for any element for a unit load at each point of a truss, the method may become time consuming when dealing with a truss involving many panels without the aid of a computer. Alternatively, we may first seek the influence lines for support reactions since they are related in a simple manner to the unit load of variable position. After that we can deduce the influence lines for bar forces very quickly, as can be seen in the following example.

Example 10-4

Figure 10-9(a) shows a Warren truss. Let us draw the influence lines for bar forces (or components) in members cd and Cc.

The influence lines for reactions R_a and R_g are readily drawn as shown in Fig. 10-9(b) and (c). They are constructed in the same way as the influence lines for the

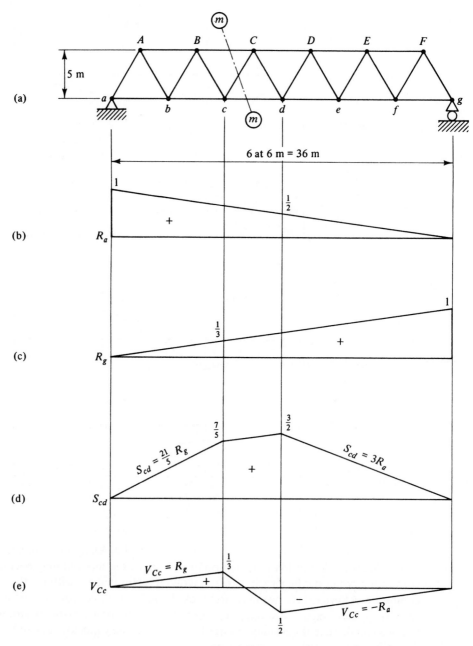

Figure 10-9

reactions of a simple beam 36 m long, because end reactions of a truss are not affected by the presence of the floor system.

To construct the influence line for the force in bar cd, denoted by S_{cd}, we pass a section m–m through bars cd, Cc, and BC, as shown in Fig. 10-9(a). With the unit load at or to the left of panel point c, we find that

$$S_{cd} = \frac{21R_g}{5}$$

by using the right portion of truss as a free body and applying $\Sigma M_C = 0$. With a unit load at or to the right of panel point d, we find that

$$S_{cd} = \frac{(R_a)(15)}{5} = 3R_a$$

by using the left portion and the same moment equation. This procedure results in two straight lines similar to the respective segments of influence lines for R_a and R_g, but with multipliers. Connecting the influence ordinates at c and d by a straight line gives the influence line for S_{cd}, as shown in Fig. 10-9(d).

We employ the same procedure to obtain the influence line for the vertical component force in bar Cc, denoted by V_{Cc}, except that we apply $\Sigma F_y = 0$ instead of the moment equation to compute the bar force. As the unit load travels from a to c, we use the right portion of the truss and observe that

$$V_{Cc} = R_g$$

which represents a straight line identical to the segment of influence line for R_g. As the unit load travels from d to g, we use the left portion of truss and find that

$$V_{Cc} = -R_a$$

which represents a straight line opposite to the segment of the influence line for R_a. Connecting the influence ordinates at c and d by a straight line completes the influence line for V_{Cc}, as shown in Fig. 10-9(e).

10-5 INFLUENCE LINES AND CONCENTRATED LOAD SYSTEMS

As mentioned in Sec. 10-2, the influence line serves a guide for determining the maximum live stresses. Under a single concentrated load or a uniform load, the critical position causing a certain maximum live stress can be spotted at once by inspection of the influence line. For more complicated conditions of loading of various magnitudes and spacings, such as a series of moving wheels on a locomotive, we cannot tell the critical position by just looking at the influence line. The method that should be followed in such cases is essentially one of trial and error with reference to the influence line in order to minimize computations.

Example 10-5

Figure 10-10(a) shows a simple beam subjected to the passage of wheel loads. We wish to find the maximum reaction at the left end A, the influence line of which is also shown in the same figure.

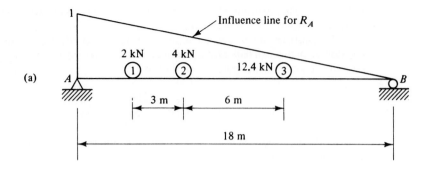

(a)

(b)

$$R_A = \frac{(2)(18) + (4)(15) + (12.4)(9)}{18} = 11.53 \text{ kN}$$

(c)

$$R_A = \frac{(4)(18) + (12.4)(12)}{18} = 12.27 \text{ kN}$$

(d)

$$R_A = 12.4 \text{ kN}$$

Figure 10-10

Since the influence ordinate increases toward the left, the system of wheel loads must not stay in an intermediate position on the beam, but should continue to move until wheel load 1 reaches support A. The first possible position for producing the maximum R_A therefore has wheel 1 directly over A as shown in Fig. 10-10(b). Next, with wheel 1 leaving the span, the second possible position has wheel 2 over A, as shown in Fig. 10-10(c). In each case, we obtain the value of R_A by multiplying each wheel load by the corresponding influence ordinate and adding, as indicated in Fig. 10-10(b) and (c), respectively. The final trial position has wheel 3 over A, as shown in Fig. 10-10(d).

By comparing the results, we conclude that the maximum reaction is 12.4 kN when wheel 3 is directly over support A.

Example 10-6

For the bridge truss subjected to the passage of the group of wheel loads in Fig. 10-11(a), find the maximum force in the member Bc.

To do this, we construct the influence line for the vertical component of the bar force in Bc as shown in Fig. 10-11(b).

The best approach is to try several loading positions and to compare the changes in the value of the function because of the movement. The increase or decrease in the value of the function caused by a moving load is determined by the multiplication of three quantities, that is, the load, the slope of the influence line, and the distance the load moves. Let us try the first loading position, shown in Fig. 10-11(c), with wheel 1 at the peak ordinate. Next, let the system move to the left until wheel 2 reaches the peak ordinate, as shown in Fig. 10-11(d). The computations to the right of Fig. 10-11(c) and (d) show that the movement results in an increase in the value of the function. Next, let this system move farther to the left until wheel 3 reaches the peak ordinate, as shown in Fig. 10-11(e). The computations to the right of Fig. 10-11(d) and (e) show that this causes a decrease in the value of the function. Thus, the second position of loading, shown in Fig. 10-11(d), produces the maximum tensile force in member Bc.

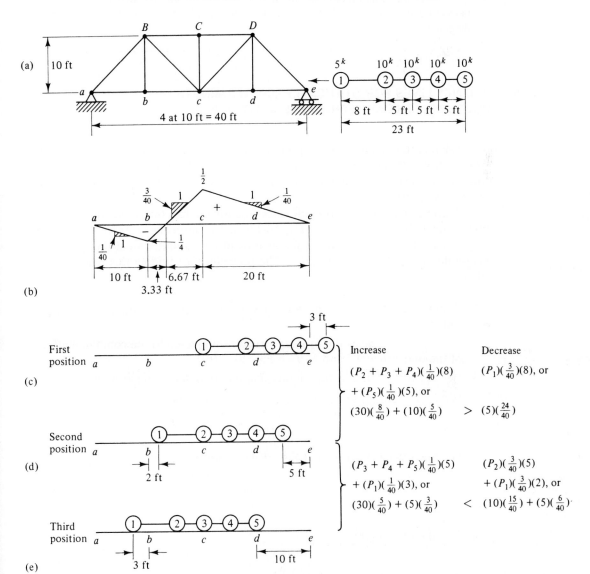

Figure 10-11

By using the influence diagram, we find the maximum value of V_{Bc} to be

$$V_{Bc} = (10)\left(\frac{20 + 15 + 10 + 5}{40}\right) - (5)\left(\frac{1}{4}\right)\left(\frac{3.33 - 2}{3.33}\right)$$

$$= 12.5 - 0.5 = +12 \text{ kips}$$

or

$$S_{Bc} = +12\sqrt{2} \text{ kips}$$

Note that this method of situating a load system for the maximum effect is perfectly general and may always be employed in cases with more complicated influence diagrams.

10-6 INFLUENCE LINES FOR STATICALLY INDETERMINATE STRUCTURES: THE MÜLLER–BRESLAU PRINCIPLE

We recall that the Müller–Breslau principle was used to construct the influence lines for statically determinate structures (see Sec. 10-3). We shall demonstrate that the principle is equally applicable to obtaining the influence lines for statically indeterminate linear structures.

Suppose that we want the influence line for the reaction at support b of the indeterminate beam abc shown in Fig. 10-12(a). The influence ordinate at any point i a distance x from the left end is obtained by placing a unit load at that point and computing the reaction at support b. The procedure for finding this reaction is as follows:

1. Remove the support at b and introduce in its place a redundant reaction called R_b.
2. Consider beam ac as the primary structure subjected to the combined effects of the unit force at i and R_b [see Fig. 10-12(b)].
3. Use the condition of compatibility that the total deflection at point b must be zero:

$$\Delta_b = R_b \, \delta_{bb} - \delta_{bi} = 0$$

See Fig. 10-12(c) for δ_{bi} and Fig. 10-12(d) for δ_{bb}.

$$R_b = \frac{\delta_{bi}}{\delta_{bb}}$$

4. Use the reciprocity

$$\delta_{bi} = \delta_{ib}$$

to obtain

$$R_b = \frac{\delta_{ib}}{\delta_{bb}}$$

Note that in the last equation the numerator δ_{ib} represents the ordinate of the deflection curve of the primary beam ac caused by applying a unit force at b. The denominator δ_{bb} is only a special case of δ_{ib} (i.e., $\delta_{bb} = \delta_{ib}$ if $i = b$), as shown in Fig. 10-12(d). Each ordinate of the curve of Fig. 10-12(d) divided by δ_{bb} will give the corresponding influence ordinate for R_b, as shown in Fig. 10-12(e).

Referring to Fig. 10-12(e), we note that at b, $\delta_{bb}/\delta_{bb} = 1$. Hence, the influence line for R_b is nothing more than the deflected structure resulting from removal of the support at b and introduction in its place of a unit deflection along the line of reaction.

We have hitherto used the reaction of a support as illustration. This, then, is the Müller–Breslau principle and may be stated as follows: *The ordinates of the influence line for any element* (reaction, axial force, shear, or moment) *of a structure equal those of the deflection curve obtained by removing the restraint corresponding*

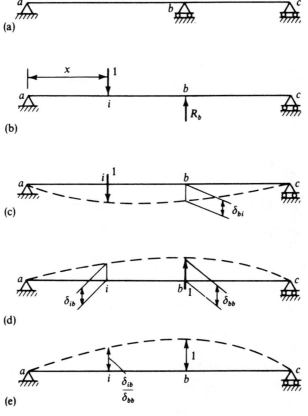

Figure 10-12

to that element from the structure and introducing in its place a unit load divided by the deflection at the point of application of the unit load.

This may be rephrased as *the deflected structure resulting from a unit displacement corresponding to the action for which the influence line is desired gives the influence line for that action.*

The Müller–Breslau principle provides a very convenient method for sketching qualitative influence lines for indeterminate structures and is the basis for certain experimental model analyses.

1. In the simplest case the influence line for a reaction component can be sketched by removing the restraint and allowing the reaction to move through a *unit displacement.* The deflected structure will then be the influence line for the reaction.

Thus, the dashed line in Fig. 10-13(a) shows the influence line for the vertical reaction at support *a* of the three-span continuous beam. In Fig. 10-13(b) the dashed line indicates the influence line for the fixed-end moment at support *a* of the fixed-end beam *ab*. The curve is obtained by replacing the fixed support at *a* with a hinge support and by introducing a unit rotation. Figure 10-13(c) shows the construction of the influence line for the horizontal reaction component at the fixed support *d* of a portal frame. Note that the fixed support at *d* is replaced by a roller and slide acted on by a horizontal force so as to produce a unit horizontal displacement.

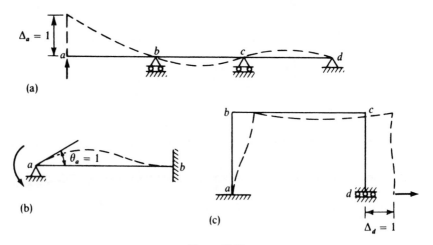

Figure 10-13

Note the following:

a. The vertical deflections of the structure will be influence line ordinates for the vertical loads on the structure.

b. The horizontal deflections of the structure will be influence line ordinates for the horizontal loads on the structure.

c. The rotation of the tangents of the structure will be influence line ordinates for the moment load on the structure.

2. The moment influence line for a section of a beam or rigid frame can be drawn by cutting the section and allowing a pair of equal and opposite moments to produce a *unit relative rotation* (but no relative translation) for the two sides of the section considered. The deflected structure will then be the influence line for the moment. Thus, the influence line for the moment at the midspan section of a three-span continuous beam is the dashed line in Fig. 10-14.

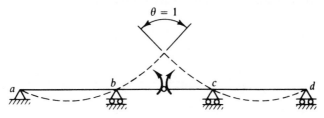

Figure 10-14

3. The shear influence line for a section of a beam or rigid frame can be drawn by cutting the section and applying a pair of equal and opposite shearing forces to produce a *unit relative transverse displacement* (but no relative rotation) for the two sides of the section considered. The deflected structure will then be the influence line for the shear. The influence line for the shear at the midspan section of the fixed-end beam *ab* is shown in Fig. 10-15 by the dashed lines.

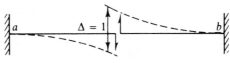

Figure 10-15

4. To obtain the influence line for the axial force in a bar, we cut the bar and apply a pair of equal and opposite axial forces so as to cause a *unit relative axial displacement* for the two cut ends. The deflected structure will give the desired influence line.

Figure 10-16 serves as a simple illustration of obtaining the influence line for the bar force in *bC* of the indeterminate truss. The vertical components of the panel point deflections are thus the influence ordinates for the vertical panel loads.

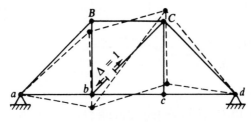

Figure 10-16

For highly indeterminate continuous beams or rigid frames, the technique of sketching qualitative influence lines, based on the Müller–Breslau principle, is extremely useful in determining the loading patterns for design. Figure 10-17 shows typical influence lines for a five-span continuous beam.

The sketches in Fig. 10-17 indicate that if a maximum R_a is desired then spans ab, cd, and ef should be loaded; if the maximum values of reaction, of shear, and of bending moment at b are desired, then spans ab, bc, and de should be loaded.

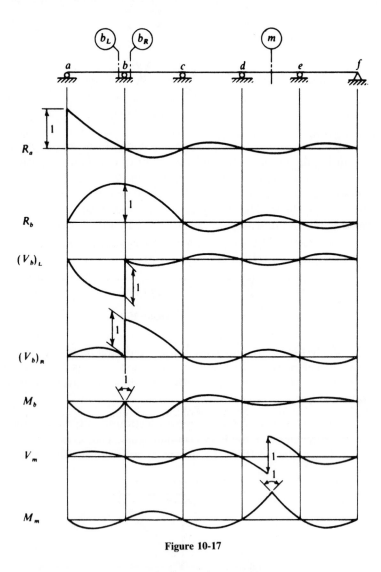

Figure 10-17

Figure 10-18(a) shows the influence line for the positive moment at the midspan section of $A3$–$B3$ of the frame shown. The uniform loading pattern for obtaining the maximum positive moment of this section is shown in Fig. 10-18(b).

Numerical examples for influence lines of statically indeterminate structures follow.

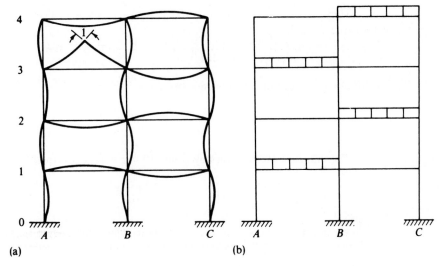

Figure 10-18

Example 10-7

Using the Müller–Breslau principle, construct the influence line for the reaction at support b of Fig. 10-19(a).

We begin by removing the support at b and placing a unit load along the line of reaction, as shown in Fig. 10-19(b). The ordinates of the resulting deflection curve, in Fig. 10-19(b), divided by δ_{bb} give the corresponding influence ordinates for the reaction at b, called R_b.

Probably the easiest method for computing the ordinate of the curve in Fig. 10-19(b) at any point i a distance x from the left end is the conjugate beam method, shown in Fig. 10-19(c).

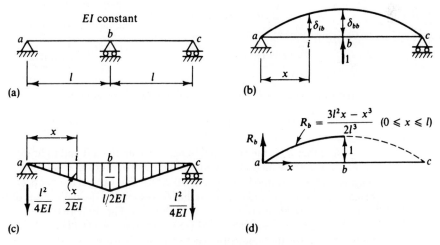

Figure 10-19

Thus,

$$\delta_{ib} = \left(\frac{l^2}{4EI}\right)(x) - \left(\frac{x}{2EI}\right)\left(\frac{x}{2}\right)\left(\frac{x}{3}\right) = \frac{3l^2x - x^3}{12EI}, \qquad 0 \leqslant x \leqslant l$$

Substituting $x = l$ in the expression above gives

$$\delta_{bb} = \frac{l^3}{6EI}$$

The influence ordinate for any point i $(0 \leqslant x \leqslant l)$ is governed by the equation

$$R_b = \frac{\delta_{ib}}{\delta_{bb}} = \frac{3l^2x - x^3}{2l^3}$$

as shown in Fig. 10-19(d). Because of symmetry about the middle support, we can accomplish the other half, as shown by the dashed line in Fig. 10-19(d).

Example 10-8

Compute the ordinates at 2-ft intervals of the influence line for the moment at the midspan section d of ab for the beam shown in Fig. 10-20(a).

The ability to resist moment at section d is first destroyed by inserting a pin. Unit couples are applied on each side of the pin to produce certain relative rotation, denoted by θ, between the two sides, as shown in Fig. 10-20(b). The conjugate beam and elastic load are then obtained, as shown in Fig. 10-20(c). Note that we assume $EI = 1$ (EI will be canceled out in the final stage of calculation); hence, the elastic load of Fig. 10-20(c) is the moment diagram based on Fig. 10-20(b).

Referring to Fig. 10-20(c), we may solve reactions R_a, R_c, and R_d by the equilibrium equations and the condition equation $M_b = 0$. Thus,

$$\sum M_a = 0, \qquad 20R_c + 5R_d - \frac{(2)(20)}{2}(10) = 0 \qquad (10\text{-}1)$$

$$\sum M_c = 0, \qquad 15R_d - 20R_a - \frac{(2)(20)}{2}(10) = 0 \qquad (10\text{-}2)$$

$$M_b = 0, \qquad 10R_c - \frac{(2)(10)}{2}\left(\frac{10}{3}\right) = 0 \qquad (10\text{-}3)$$

Solving Eqs. 10-1, 10-2, and 10-3 simultaneously, we obtain

$$R_a = 10, \qquad R_c = 3.33, \qquad R_d = 26.67$$

Note that R_d is the shear difference between the left and right sides at section d of the conjugate beam and thus equals the relative rotation θ between corresponding portions of the distorted beam in Fig. 10-20(b). The various moments of the conjugate beam at 2-ft intervals and at point d that correspond to the deflections of the distorted beam in Fig. 10-20(b) are computed as shown in Fig. 10-20(d).

These values divided by 26.67 (so as to make $\theta = 1$) will give the ordinates of the influence line for the moment at section d, as shown in Fig. 10-20(e).

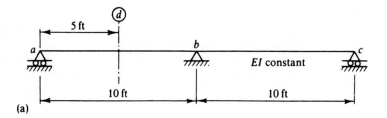

(a)

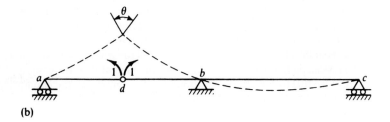

(b)

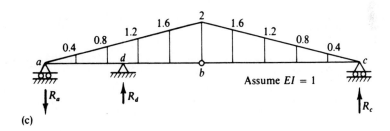

(c)

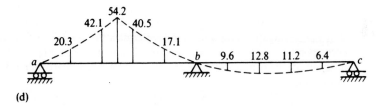

(d)

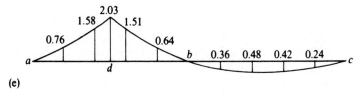

(e)

Figure 10-20

Example 10-9

Compute the influence ordinates at 2-ft intervals for the shear at the midspan section *d* of *ab* for the beam shown in Fig. 10-21(a).

We start by removing the shearing resistance at section *d* without impairing the capacity for resistance to moment. This can be accomplished by cutting the beam and inserting a slide device. Next, we apply a pair of equal and opposite unit forces to produce certain relative vertical displacement, denoted by *s*, between the two cut ends without causing relative rotation, as shown in Fig. 10-21(b). Also indicated in Fig. 10-21(b) are the induced reactions and moments at the cut ends required by equilibrium.

The conjugate beam together with the elastic loads is shown in Fig. 10-21(c). Attention should be paid to the elastic load M_d acting at *d*. This is necessary since the relative vertical displacement (without relative rotation) between the two cut ends at section *d* of the distorted beam in Fig. 10-21(b) requires a moment difference (without a shear difference) for the two sides at *d* of the conjugate beam shown in Fig. 10-21(c). This can be fulfilled only by applying a moment at *d* for the conjugate beam. Referring to Fig. 10-21(c), we solve reactions R_a, R_c, and M_d by the equilibrium equations and the condition equation $M_b = 0$. Thus,

$$\sum M_a = 0, \qquad 20R_c + M_d - \frac{(10)(20)}{2}(10) = 0 \qquad (10\text{-}4)$$

$$\sum M_c = 0, \qquad 20R_a - M_d - \frac{(10)(20)}{2}(10) = 0 \qquad (10\text{-}5)$$

$$M_b = 0, \qquad 10R_c - \frac{(10)(10)}{2}\left(\frac{10}{3}\right) = 0 \qquad (10\text{-}6)$$

Solving Eqs. 10-4, 10-5, and 10-6 simultaneously, we obtain

$$R_a = 83.33, \qquad R_c = 16.67, \qquad M_d = 666.67$$

Note that M_d is the moment difference between the left and right sides at section *d* of the conjugate beam and therefore equals the relative deflection *s* between the corresponding portions of the distorted beam shown in Fig. 10-21(b). The various moments of the conjugate beam at 2-ft intervals and at *d* are then computed, as shown in Fig. 10-21(d).

These values divided by $M_d = 666.67$ (so as to make $s = 1$) will give the ordinates of the shear influence line for section *d*, as shown in Fig. 10-21(e).

For highly indeterminate structures, the influence ordinates for various functions may be found by using a computer for a number of equations based on consistent deformations. Let us consider the four-span continuous beam shown in Fig. 10-22(a). Find the influence line for the reaction at support *b*, called R_b.

We start by removing support *b* and applying to it a force X_b along the line of reaction so as to produce a unit displacement at *b*. Then, by the Müller–Breslau principle, the elastic line of the distorted beam, shown by the dashed line in Fig.

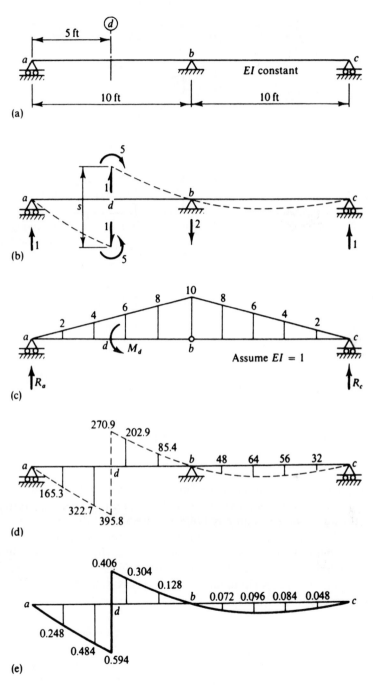

Figure 10-21

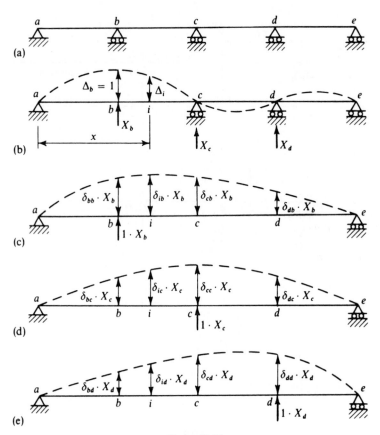

Figure 10-22

10-22(b), will be the influence line for R_b. Also indicated in Fig. 10-22(b) are the induced reactions at supports c and d, called X_c and X_d, respectively, and the ordinate of the curve at any point i, called Δ_i, at distance x from the left end.

To obtain the value of Δ_i by the method of consistent deformations, we regard the indeterminate beam in Fig. 10-22(b) as a simple beam ae (primary structure) subjected to forces X_b, X_c, and X_d, the effects of which can be separated by the principle of superposition into three basic cases, as shown in Fig. 10-22(c), (d), and (e), respectively. Thus,

$$\Delta_i = \delta_{ib} X_b + \delta_{ic} X_c + \delta_{id} X_d$$

in which the unknowns X_b, X_c, and X_d can be solved by the compatibility condition:

$$\begin{Bmatrix} \Delta_b \\ \Delta_c \\ \Delta_d \end{Bmatrix} = \begin{bmatrix} \delta_{bb} & \delta_{bc} & \delta_{bd} \\ \delta_{cb} & \delta_{cc} & \delta_{cd} \\ \delta_{db} & \delta_{dc} & \delta_{dd} \end{bmatrix} \begin{Bmatrix} X_b \\ X_c \\ X_d \end{Bmatrix} = \begin{Bmatrix} 1 \\ 0 \\ 0 \end{Bmatrix} \tag{10-7}$$

In a similar manner, we can find the influence line for the reaction at each of the other supports. This done, the influence lines for the moment and shear at various points can be deduced from them by simple statics.

PROBLEMS

10-1. Given a simple beam 24 ft long, construct the influence lines for the shear and bending moment at a section 8 ft from the left end, and obtain the maximum shear and bending moment for the section resulting from a moving uniform load of 3 kips/ft and a movable concentrated load of 50 kips.

10-2. A cantilever beam 20 ft long is fixed at the right end. Construct the shear and moment influence lines for sections 5 ft, 10 ft, and 20 ft from the free end. Using the same loadings given in Problem 10-1, compute maximum shears and moments at these sections.

10-3. Figure 10-23 shows a simple beam with an overhang. Draw the influence lines for R_B, R_C, V_D, M_B, and M_D.

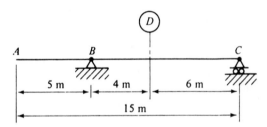

Figure 10-23

10-4. Given a compound beam such as that shown in Fig. 10-24, construct the influence lines for R_A, R_C, R_E, V_B, M_B, and M_C. Compute the maximum value for each of them due to a moving uniform load of 20 kN/m.

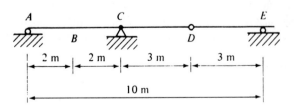

Figure 10-24

10-5. Solve Problem 10-3 by Müller–Breslau's principle.

10-6. Construct the influence lines for Problem 10-4 by Müller–Breslau's principle.

10-7. For the trusses shown in Fig. 10-25, construct the influence lines for the bar force (or component) in each of the lettered bars.

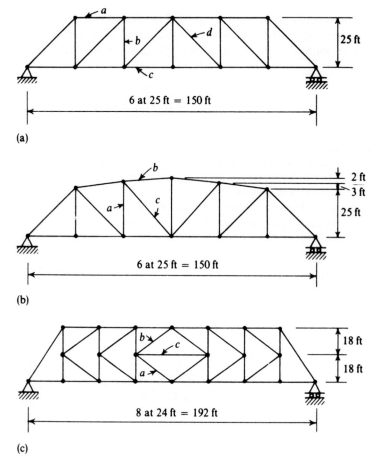

Figure 10-25

10-8. A simple beam 45 ft long carries moving loads of 5 kips, 10 kips, and 10 kips spaced 5 ft apart. Calculate (a) the maximum left reaction and (b) the maximum shear and bending moment at a section 15 ft from the left end.

10-9. For the truss and the loading shown in Fig. 10-26, compute the maximum forces in bars *a* and *b*. Consider both tension and compression in bar *a*.

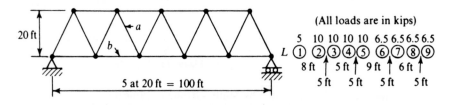

Figure 10-26

10-10. For the compound beam and loads shown in Fig. 10-27, find (a) the maximum reaction at *C* and (b) the maximum moment at *D*.

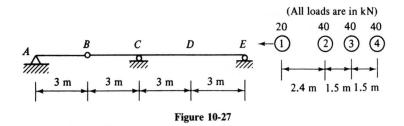

Figure 10-27

10-11. Refer to the frame and loads in Fig. 10-28. Find the maximum moment and vertical reaction at support E due to the passage of loads over the beam.

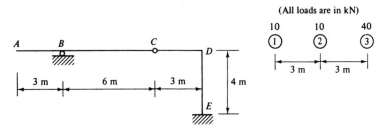

Figure 10-28

10-12. Compute the ordinates at 2-m intervals of the influence line for the reaction at a of the beam shown in Fig. 10-29.

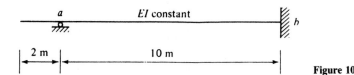

Figure 10-29

10-13. Compute the influence ordinates at 2-m intervals for the end moment at a of the beam shown in Fig. 10-30.

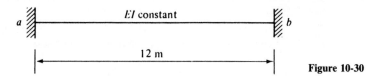

Figure 10-30

10-14. Refer to the beam in Fig. 10-31. Compute the influence ordinates at 2-m intervals for the following elements: (a) the reaction at support a, (b) the moment at b, and (c) the shear at the midspan section of ab.

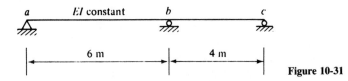

Figure 10-31

10-15. Sketch the influence lines for R_a, R_c, M_c, V_c (left), V_c (right), and M and V for the midspan section of bc of the beam shown in Fig. 10-32.

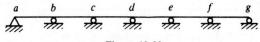

Figure 10-32

10-16. Sketch the influence lines for the shear and moment in the midspan section of member ab of the rigid frame shown in Fig. 10-33.

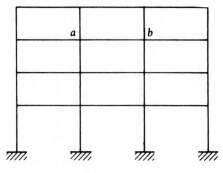

Figure 10-33

Chapter 11

Treatment of Nonprismatic Members

11-1 GENERAL

In the previous discussion of framed-structure analysis, we were concerned only with structures composed of uniform elements. In many instances, however, the members forming a structure are nonprismatic or, in the more general case, have variable rigidities such as those shown in Fig. 11-1. The fundamental concepts of analysis remain the same as if the structure were built up by prismatic members. However, the expression for member constants, including the fixed-end actions, the flexibility and stiffness coefficients, and the stiffness and carry-over factor necessary for a moment distribution, derived specifically for prismatic members, are no longer valid for nonprismatic members. These constants applied for nonprismatic members must be first determined so that the analysis of structure either by slope-deflection equations, moment distribution, or matrix procedure can be carried out in the usual manner.

In this chapter we develop various integral formulas expressing these constants and demonstrate how to employ a numerical approach to approximate an integration.

11-2 FIXED-END ACTIONS

Consider a member of varying flexural rigidity with both ends fixed and subjected to the bending action caused by member loads, as shown in Fig. 11-2. The general

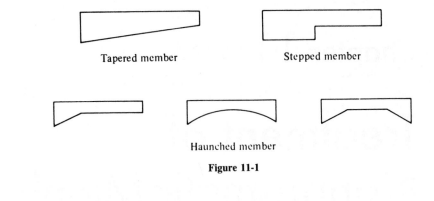

Tapered member   Stepped member

Haunched member

Figure 11-1

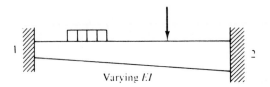

Varying *EI*   **Figure 11-2**

expression for the fixed-end moments may be found by the method of least work, using Eqs. 5-30 and 5-31:

$$\int_0^l \frac{M\,dx}{EI} = 0 \tag{11-1}$$

$$\int_0^l \frac{Mx\,dx}{EI} = 0 \tag{11-2}$$

If the member is made of the same material, we can assume that E is a constant. The preceding expressions thus become

$$\int_0^l \frac{M\,dx}{I} = 0 \tag{11-3}$$

$$\int_0^l \frac{Mx\,dx}{I} = 0 \tag{11-4}$$

where both M and I are functions of x.

As an illustration, let us find M_1 and V_1 for the fixed beam shown in Fig. 11-3 due to a uniform load over the entire span.

The moment at any section distance x from the left end is

$$M = M_1 + V_1 x - \frac{wx^2}{2}$$

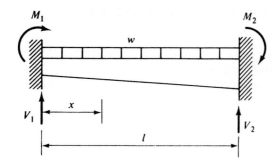

Figure 11-3

Substituting M in Eqs. 11-3 and 11-4 gives

$$M_1 \int_0^l \frac{dx}{I} + V_1 \int_0^l \frac{x\,dx}{I} - \frac{w}{2} \int_0^l \frac{x^2\,dx}{I} = 0 \qquad (11\text{-}5)$$

$$M_1 \int_0^l \frac{x\,dx}{I} + V_1 \int_0^l \frac{x^2\,dx}{I} - \frac{w}{2} \int_0^l \frac{x^3\,dx}{I} = 0 \qquad (11\text{-}6)$$

In matrix form,

$$\begin{bmatrix} \int_0^l \dfrac{dx}{I} & \int_0^l \dfrac{x\,dx}{I} \\ \int_0^l \dfrac{x\,dx}{I} & \int_0^l \dfrac{x^2\,dx}{I} \end{bmatrix} \begin{Bmatrix} M_1 \\ V_1 \end{Bmatrix} = \frac{w}{2} \begin{Bmatrix} \int_0^l \dfrac{x^2\,dx}{I} \\ \int_0^l \dfrac{x^3\,dx}{I} \end{Bmatrix} \qquad (11\text{-}7)$$

Eliminating V_1 from Eqs. 11-5 and 11-6 yields the fixed-end moment at 1:

$$M_1 = \left(\frac{w}{2}\right) \frac{\left(\int_0^l (x^2\,dx)/I\right)^2 - \int_0^l (x\,dx)/I \int_0^l (x^3\,dx)/I}{\int_0^l dx/I \int_0^l (x^2\,dx)/I - \left(\int_0^l (x\,dx)/I\right)^2} \qquad (11\text{-}8)$$

The fixed-end moment at 2 can also be obtained from Eq. 11-8 by taking the integral origin at 2 and using reverse sign. For a member of varying I, M_1 and M_2 are not equal except in a symmetrical system. For a member of uniform section, Eq. 11-8 reduces to

$$M_1 = -M_2 = \left(\frac{w}{2}\right) \frac{\left(\int_0^l x^2\,dx\right)^2 - \int_0^l x\,dx \int_0^l x^3\,dx}{\int_0^l dx \int_0^l x^2\,dx - \left(\int_0^l x\,dx\right)^2} = -\frac{wl^2}{12} \qquad (11\text{-}9)$$

With M_1 and M_2 obtained, we can find V_1 and V_2 by simple statics.

11-3 ROTATIONAL FLEXIBILITY MATRIX OF A BEAM ELEMENT

Consider the beam element with a variable cross section subjected to end moments R_1 and R_2 with the corresponding rotations r_1 and r_2, as in Fig. 11-4(a). To find flexibility coefficients, we must have the element properly supported. If we regard the element as a simple beam, as in Fig. 11-4(b), then the bending moment at any section distance x from the left end is

$$M = R_1 - \frac{(R_1 + R_2)x}{l} \tag{11-10}$$

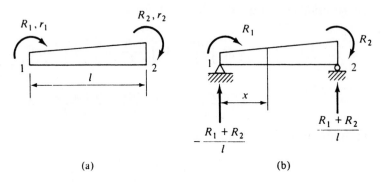

(a)   (b)

Figure 11-4

By the method of least work, we obtain the end rotations r_1 and r_2 as

$$r_1 = \frac{\partial W}{\partial R_1} = \int_0^l \frac{M(\partial M/\partial R_1)\,dx}{EI}$$

$$= \int_0^l \frac{[R_1 - (R_1 + R_2)(x/l)][1 - (x/l)]\,dx}{EI} \tag{11-11}$$

$$r_2 = \frac{\partial W}{\partial R_2} = \int_0^l \frac{M(\partial M/\partial R_2)\,dx}{EI}$$

$$= \int_0^l \frac{[R_1 - (R_1 + R_2)(x/l)][-x/l]\,dx}{EI} \tag{11-12}$$

Setting $R_1 = 1$ and $R_2 = 0$ in Eqs. 11-11 and 11-12, respectively, leads to the rotational flexibility coefficients f_{11} and f_{21}:

$$f_{11} = \int_0^l \frac{(l - x)^2\,dx}{EIl^2} \tag{11-13}$$

$$f_{21} = -\int_0^l \frac{(l - x)(x)\,dx}{EIl^2} \tag{11-14}$$

Similarly, setting $R_1 = 0$ and $R_2 = 1$ in Eqs. 11-11 and 11-12, respectively, yields

$$f_{12} = -\int_0^l \frac{(l - x)(x)\,dx}{EIl^2} \tag{11-15}$$

$$f_{22} = \int_0^l \frac{x^2\,dx}{EIl^2} \tag{11-16}$$

Collecting Eqs. 11-13 to 11-16 and assuming a constant E, we form the rotational flexibility matrix:

$$[f] = \begin{bmatrix} f_{11} & f_{12} \\ f_{21} & f_{22} \end{bmatrix}$$

$$= \frac{1}{EI^2} \begin{bmatrix} \displaystyle\int_0^l \frac{(l - x)^2\,dx}{I} & \displaystyle-\int_0^l \frac{(l - x)(x)\,dx}{I} \\ \displaystyle-\int_0^l \frac{(l - x)(x)\,dx}{I} & \displaystyle\int_0^l \frac{x^2\,dx}{I} \end{bmatrix} \tag{11-17}$$

For a member of uniform cross section, this expression reduces to

$$[f] = \frac{l}{6EI} \begin{bmatrix} 2 & -1 \\ -1 & 2 \end{bmatrix} \tag{11-18}$$

11-4 ROTATIONAL STIFFNESS MATRIX OF A BEAM ELEMENT

Consider the same beam element in Fig. 11-4(a). By definition, the rotational stiffness coefficients k_{11} and k_{21} are the respective moments at coordinates 1 and 2 due to a unit rotation of coordinate 1 ($r_1 = 1$). Similarly, the rotational stiffness coefficients k_{12} and k_{22} are the respective moments at coordinates 1 and 2 due to a unit rotation at coordinate 2 ($r_2 = 1$). They are illustrated in Fig. 11-5(a) and (b).

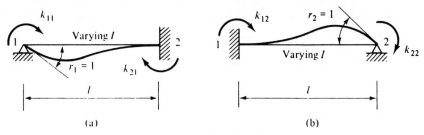

(a)   (b)

Figure 11-5

To find the integral expression for the rotational stiffness matrix, we need only perform the inversion for the rotational flexibility matrix given by Eq. 11-17. Thus,

$$[k] = \begin{bmatrix} k_{11} & k_{12} \\ k_{21} & k_{22} \end{bmatrix} = \begin{bmatrix} f_{11} & f_{12} \\ f_{21} & f_{22} \end{bmatrix}^{-1}$$

$$= \begin{bmatrix} \dfrac{1}{EI^2}\displaystyle\int_0^l \dfrac{(l-x)^2\,dx}{I} & -\dfrac{1}{EI^2}\displaystyle\int_0^l \dfrac{(l-x)(x)\,dx}{I} \\ -\dfrac{1}{EI^2}\displaystyle\int_0^l \dfrac{(l-x)(x)\,dx}{I} & \dfrac{1}{EI^2}\displaystyle\int_0^l \dfrac{x^2\,dx}{I} \end{bmatrix}^{-1} \quad (11\text{-}19)$$

$$= \dfrac{E}{\displaystyle\int_0^l \dfrac{dx}{I}\int_0^l \dfrac{x^2\,dx}{I} - \left(\int_0^l \dfrac{x\,dx}{I}\right)^2} \begin{bmatrix} \displaystyle\int_0^l \dfrac{x^2\,dx}{I} & \displaystyle\int_0^l \dfrac{(l-x)(x)\,dx}{I} \\ \displaystyle\int_0^l \dfrac{(l-x)(x)\,dx}{I} & \displaystyle\int_0^l \dfrac{(l-x)^2\,dx}{I} \end{bmatrix}$$

Equation 11-19 shows that the stiffness matrix is symmetrical (i.e., $k_{12} = k_{21}$). For a member of uniform cross section, Eq. 11-19 reduces to

$$[k] = \dfrac{2EI}{l}\begin{bmatrix} 2 & 1 \\ 1 & 2 \end{bmatrix} \quad (11\text{-}20)$$

11-5 GENERALIZED SLOPE-DEFLECTION EQUATIONS

The slope-deflection equations derived for a typical uniform member 1–2 (see Sec. 8-2) are

$$M_{12} = 2E\dfrac{I}{l}\left[2\theta_1 + \theta_2 - 3\left(\dfrac{\Delta}{l}\right)\right] + M_{12}^F \quad (11\text{-}21)$$

$$M_{21} = 2E\dfrac{I}{l}\left[2\theta_2 + \theta_1 - 3\left(\dfrac{\Delta}{l}\right)\right] + M_{21}^F \quad (11\text{-}22)$$

In cases involving a variable moment of inertia, these equations are not valid and some generalized slope-deflection equations must be formed. To do this, we recall that the basic slope-deflection equations are derived from the sum of four separate effects:

1. The rigid-body translation Δ between two ends. This is equivalent to a rigid-body rotation Δ/l or R of the whole member.
2. The rotation $(\theta_1 - \Delta/l)$ at end 1 only.
3. The rotation $(\theta_2 - \Delta/l)$ at end 2 only.
4. The application of member loads with end displacement prevented.

These steps are recaptured as in Fig. 11-6 and are also applicable to the instances of nonuniform member.

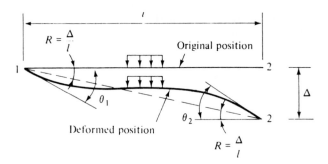

Figure 11-6

Now the rigid-body motion of step 1 causes no moments. Step 2 produces

$$M_{12} = k_{11}\left(\theta_1 - \frac{\Delta}{l}\right)$$ (11-23)

$$M_{21} = k_{21}\left(\theta_1 - \frac{\Delta}{l}\right)$$ (11-24)

Similarly, step 3 gives

$$M_{12} = k_{12}\left(\theta_2 - \frac{\Delta}{l}\right)$$ (11-25)

$$M_{21} = k_{22}\left(\theta_2 - \frac{\Delta}{l}\right)$$ (11-26)

Note that k_{11}, k_{12}, k_{21}, and k_{22} are the rotational stiffness coefficients defined in Eq. 11-19.

The end moments corresponding to step 4 are the fixed-end moments discussed in Sec. 11-2. They are usually denoted by M_{12}^F and M_{21}^F in slope-deflection equations.

Collecting these effects, we arrive at the generalized slope-deflection equations applicable to cases involving variable moment of inertia:

$$M_{12} = k_{11}\theta_1 + k_{12}\theta_2 - (k_{11} + k_{12})\frac{\Delta}{l} + M_{12}^F$$ (11-27)

$$M_{21} = k_{21}\theta_1 + k_{22}\theta_2 - (k_{21} + k_{22})\frac{\Delta}{l} + M_{21}^F$$ (11-28)

Assembling Eqs. 11-27 and 11-28 in a matrix and using $R = \Delta/l$, we have

$$\begin{Bmatrix} M_{12} - M_{12}^F \\ M_{21} - M_{21}^F \end{Bmatrix} = \begin{bmatrix} k_{11} & k_{12} \\ k_{21} & k_{22} \end{bmatrix} \begin{Bmatrix} \theta_1 - R \\ \theta_2 - R \end{Bmatrix}$$ (11-29)

which gives the relationship between member end forces and displacements. For a member of uniform section,

$$\begin{bmatrix} k_{11} & k_{12} \\ k_{21} & k_{22} \end{bmatrix} = \frac{2EI}{l} \begin{bmatrix} 2 & 1 \\ 1 & 2 \end{bmatrix} \tag{11-30}$$

and Eqs. 11-27 and 11-28 reduce to Eqs. 11-21 and 11-22.

With the fixed-end moments and rotational stiffness coefficients for each member determined, application of generalized slope-deflection equations 11-27 and 11-28 in analyzing frames composed of nonuniform members can be carried out by the procedure given in Chapter 8.

11-6 STIFFNESS AND CARRY-OVER FACTOR FOR MOMENT DISTRIBUTION

To develop an expression for stiffness and carry-over factor for a member of varying I in moment distribution, let us recall the definition of rotational stiffness for an end of a member as the end moment required to produce a unit rotation at this end (simple end) while the other end is fixed, and the definition of carry-over factor as the ratio of induced moment at the other end (fixed) to the applied moment at this end. See Fig. 11-7, in which we use the conventional notation S_{12} in moment distribution as the rotational stiffness of end 1 (this end) of member 1–2 and C_{12} as the carry over factor from end 1 to end 2. By definition, S_{12} is the same stiffness coefficient k_{11} given in Eq. 11-19. Thus,

$$S_{12} = \frac{E \int_0^l (x^2\,dx)/I}{\int_0^l dx/I \int_0^l (x^2\,dx)/I - \left(\int_0^l (x\,dx)/I \right)^2} \tag{11-31}$$

The rotational stiffness of end 2 of member 1–2, denoted by S_{21}, can similarly be explained and is equal to k_{22} given in Eq. 11-19. Thus,

$$S_{21} = \frac{E \int_0^l (l - x)^2\,dx/I}{\int_0^l dx/I \int_0^l (x^2\,dx)/I - \left(\int_0^l (x\,dx)/I \right)^2} \tag{11-32}$$

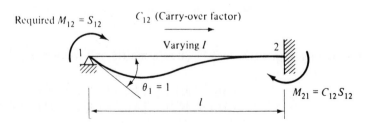

Figure 11-7

Note that, for a member of nonuniform cross section, S_{21} is usually not equal to S_{12}. For a member of constant cross section,

$$S_{12} = S_{21} = \frac{4EI}{l} \tag{11-33}$$

Again, refer to the setup in Fig. 11-7. The induced moment M_{21} at end 2 is the carry-over moment from end 1 and is therefore equal to $C_{12}S_{12}$ or $C_{12}k_{11}$. But it can also be interpreted as the moment restraint at end 2 due to a unit rotation only at end 1 and therefore is equal to the stiffness coefficient k_{21} in Eq. 11-19. Thus,

$$C_{12} = \frac{k_{21}}{k_{11}} \tag{11-34}$$

Using the expression of k_{11} and k_{21} in Eq. 11-19, we obtain

$$C_{12} = \frac{\displaystyle\int_0^l (l-x)(x\,dx)/I}{\displaystyle\int_0^l (x^2\,dx)/I} \tag{11-35}$$

By the same reasoning,

$$C_{21} = \frac{k_{12}}{k_{22}} \tag{11-36}$$

Using the expressions of k_{12} and k_{22} in Eq. 11-19 gives

$$C_{21} = \frac{\displaystyle\int_0^l (l-x)(x\,dx)/I}{\displaystyle\int_0^l (l-x)^2\,dx/I} \tag{11-37}$$

Note that for a member of nonuniform cross section, C_{12} and C_{21} are usually not equal. For a member of constant cross section,

$$C_{12} = C_{21} = \tfrac{1}{2} \tag{11-38}$$

Since $C_{12}S_{12} = k_{21}$, $C_{21}S_{21} = k_{12}$, and $k_{12} = k_{21}$, we reach

$$C_{12}S_{12} = C_{21}S_{21} \tag{11-39}$$

This relationship provides a check on separately computed value of the stiffness and carry-over factors.

The determination of fixed-end moments, stiffnesses, and carry-over factors prerequisite to a moment distribution procedure usually involves a large amount of computation. Fortunately, the values of a considerable number of these factors for the more common types of nonprismatic members have been published for the convenience of structural engineers. One such source is the *Handbook of Frame Constants* published by the Portland Cement Association. The member stiffness matrix and, therefore, the flexibility matrix required for a matrix analysis of frames can be deduced from these data by using the relationships

$$\begin{bmatrix} k_{11} & k_{12} \\ k_{21} & k_{22} \end{bmatrix} = \begin{bmatrix} S_{12} & C_{21}S_{21} \\ C_{12}S_{12} & S_{21} \end{bmatrix} = \begin{bmatrix} S_{12} & C_{12}S_{12} \\ C_{12}S_{12} & S_{21} \end{bmatrix} \qquad (11\text{-}40)$$

11-7 FIXED-END MOMENT DUE TO JOINT TRANSLATION

When frame sidesway is involved, it is necessary to determine the fixed-end moments due to joint translation for the relevant members before we can carry out a moment distribution. We recall that the fixed-end moment developed at either end of a prismatic member because of relative end displacement equals $-6EI\Delta/l^2$. This is no longer valid for a member of nonuniform cross section.

Consider member 1–2 having varying I subjected to a pure relative end translation Δ, as shown in Fig. 11-8. The moment restraints at end 1 and 2 can readily be obtained by setting $\theta_1 = \theta_2 = M_{12}^F = M_{21}^F = 0$ in the generalized slope-deflection equations 11-27 and 11-28. Thus,

$$M_{12} = -(k_{11} + k_{12})\frac{\Delta}{l} \qquad (11\text{-}41)$$

$$M_{21} = -(k_{21} + k_{22})\frac{\Delta}{l} \qquad (11\text{-}42)$$

in which k_{11}, k_{12}, k_{21}, and k_{22} are stiffness coefficients defined by Eq. 11-19. Equations 11-41 and 11-42 in terms of the conventional notation of moment distribution are given as

$$M_{12} = -(S_{12} + C_{21}S_{21})\frac{\Delta}{l}$$

$$\qquad (11\text{-}43)$$

$$= -S_{12}(1 + C_{12})\frac{\Delta}{l}$$

$$M_{21} = -(S_{21} + C_{12}S_{12})\frac{\Delta}{l}$$

$$\qquad (11\text{-}44)$$

$$= -S_{21}(1 + C_{21})\frac{\Delta}{l}$$

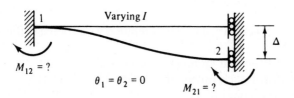

$M_{12} = ?$ $\theta_1 = \theta_2 = 0$ $M_{21} = ?$ Varying I **Figure 11-8**

by using the relationship $C_{12} S_{12} = C_{21} S_{21}$. For a member of uniform cross section, $S_{12} = S_{21} = 4EI/l$, $C_{12} = C_{21} = \frac{1}{2}$, and the expressions above reduce to

$$M_{12} = M_{21} = -\frac{6EI\Delta}{l^2} \tag{11-45}$$

If end 2 is hinged, the modified fixed-end moment at 1, called M'_{12}, resulting from the relative end translation Δ can be found by first assuming both ends fixed and subsequently restoring end 2 to its original hinged condition. Thus,

$$M'_{12} = M_{12} - C_{21} M_{21}$$

Using Eqs. 11-43 and 11-44, we obtain

$$M'_{12} = -S_{12}(1 - C_{12} C_{21})\frac{\Delta}{l} \tag{11-46}$$

For a member of uniform cross section, this expression reduces to

$$M'_{12} = -\frac{3EI\Delta}{l^2} \tag{11-47}$$

11-8 MODIFIED STIFFNESS FOR MOMENT DISTRIBUTION

The modified stiffness of this end of a member may be defined as the end moment required to produce a unit rotation at this end (simple end) while the other end remains in the actual condition other than being fixed.

Case 1   The modified stiffness for end 1 of member 1–2, if end 2 is simply supported, is given by

$$S'_{12} = S_{12}(1 - C_{12} C_{21}) \tag{11-48}$$

in which S'_{12} denotes the modified stiffness and S_{12} is the stiffness found by the usual manner. The equation above can be proved as follows.

By definition, the setup in Fig. 11-9(a) gives the configuration for finding the modified stiffness for end 1 of member 1–2, the other end being simply supported. To accomplish this, we may break member 1–2 down into two separate steps, as shown in Fig. 11-9(b) and (c). In Fig. 11-9(b) we temporarily lock end 2 against rotation ($\theta_2 = 0$). A moment S_{12} applied at end 1 will produce a unit rotation at 1 and induce a carry-over moment of $C_{12} S_{12}$ at 2. In Fig. 11-9(c) we release end 2 to its actual condition of zero moment and at the same time lock end 1 against further rotation. A moment of $-C_{12} S_{12}$ must be developed at end 2 and, consequently,

$-C_{21}C_{12}S_{12}$ will be carried over to end 1. The sum of the foregoing two steps for end 1 gives

$$S'_{12} = S_{12} - C_{21}C_{12}S_{12}$$

$$= S_{12}(1 - C_{12}C_{21})$$

as asserted.

For a prismatic member $C_{12} = C_{21} = \frac{1}{2}$; therefore,

$$S'_{12} = \tfrac{3}{4}S_{12} \tag{11-49}$$

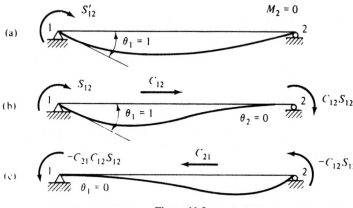

(a) S'_{12} $M_2 = 0$ $\theta_1 = 1$

(b) S_{12} C_{12} $\theta_1 = 1$ $\theta_2 = 0$ $C_{12}S_{12}$

(c) $-C_{21}C_{12}S_{12}$ C_{21} $-C_{12}S_{12}$ $\theta_1 = 0$

Figure 11-9

Case 2 The modified stiffness for end 1 of member 1–2, if end 2 rotates an equal but opposite angle to that of end 1 as in the case of symmetry, is given by

$$S'_{12} = S_{12}(1 - C_{12}) \tag{11-50}$$

To prove this, we refer to Fig. 11-10(a), which is postulated according to the definition of modified stiffness for the present case.

As before, we break this into two separate steps, as shown in Fig. 11-10(b) and (c). Figure 11-10(b) shows the usual way of determining S_{12}. In Fig. 11-10(c) a moment of $-S_{21}$ is applied at end 2 necessary to bring it back to its actual position. Consequently, a moment of $-C_{21}S_{21}$ is carried over to end 1. The sum of the results of these two steps for end 1 gives

$$S'_{12} = S_{12} - C_{21}S_{21}$$

On substituting $C_{12}S_{12}$ for $C_{21}S_{21}$ in the expression above, we obtain

$$S'_{12} = S_{12}(1 - C_{12})$$

as asserted.

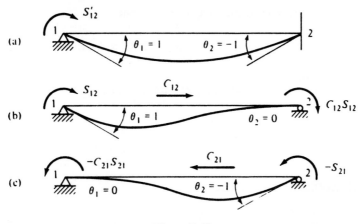

Figure 11-10

For a prismatic member $C_{12} = \frac{1}{2}$; therefore,

$$S'_{12} = \tfrac{1}{2} S_{12} \qquad\qquad (11\text{-}51)$$

Case 3   The modified stiffness of end 1 of member 1–2, if end 2 rotates an angle equal to that of end 1 as in the case of antisymmetry, is given by

$$S'_{12} = S_{12}(1 + C_{12}) \qquad\qquad (11\text{-}52)$$

To prove this, we refer to Fig. 11-11(a) for the setup of S'_{12}. As before, this may be considered as the superposition of two separate cases, as shown in Fig. 11-11(b) and (c). Consequently,

$$S'_{12} = S_{12} + C_{21} S_{21}$$

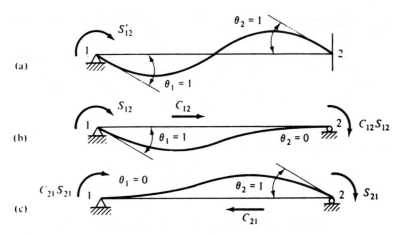

Figure 11-11

On substituting $C_{12} S_{12}$ for $C_{21} S_{21}$, we obtain

$$S'_{12} = S_{12}(1 + C_{12})$$

as asserted.

For a prismatic member $C_{12} = \frac{1}{2}$; therefore,

$$S'_{12} = \tfrac{3}{2} S_{12} \tag{11-53}$$

11-9 A NUMERICAL SOLUTION

One of the most frequently used methods of approximate integration is Simpson's one-third rule. Consider an integral $\int f(x)\, dx$ between the limit a and b. If the integral from $x = a$ to $x = b$ is divided into n equal parts, where n is an even number, and if $y_0, y_1, \ldots, y_{n-1}, y_n$ are the ordinates of the curve $y = f(x)$ at these points of subdivision (Fig. 11-12), then according to Simpson's one-third rule,

$$\int_a^b f(x)\, dx \approx \frac{\Delta}{3}(y_0 + 4y_1 + 2y_2 + 4y_3 + \cdots + 2y_{n-2} + 4y_{n-1} + y_n) \tag{11-54}$$

where $\Delta = (b - a)/n$. Simpson's rule gives an accurate result if $f(x)$ is a linear, quadratic, or cubic function.

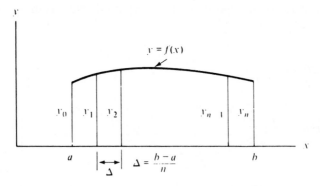

Figure 11-12

To illustrate, let us solve the rotational flexibility matrix of a beam element expressed in Eq. 11-17. Consider the coefficient f_{22}:

$$\frac{1}{EI^2} \int_0^l \frac{x^2\, dx}{I}, \quad I = I(x)$$

We divide the length l into 10 equal segments, each with $0.1l$. An application of Eq. 11-54 yields

$$f_{22} = \frac{1}{EI^2}\int_0^l \frac{x^2\,dx}{I}$$

$$= \frac{0.1l}{3E}\left[\frac{(1)(0)^2}{I_0} + \frac{(4)(0.1)^2}{I_1} + \frac{(2)(0.2)^2}{I_2} + \frac{(4)(0.3)^2}{I_3} + \frac{(2)(0.4)^2}{I_4}\right. \tag{11-55}$$

$$\left. + \frac{(4.0)(0.5)^2}{I_5} + \frac{(2)(0.6)^2}{I_6} + \frac{(4)(0.7)^2}{I_7} + \frac{(2)(0.8)^2}{I_8} + \frac{(4)(0.9)^2}{I_9} + \frac{(1)(1)^2}{I_{10}}\right]$$

with $I_0 = I(0)$, $I_1 = I(0.1l)$, $I_2 = I(0.2l)$, and so on. In matrix form,

$$f_{22} = \frac{0.1l}{3E}[I_0^{-1}\ \ I_1^{-1}\ \ I_2^{-1}\ \ I_3^{-1}\ \ I_4^{-1}\ \ I_5^{-1}\ \ I_6^{-1}\ \ I_7^{-1}\ \ I_8^{-1}\ \ I_9^{-1}\ \ I_{10}^{-1}]\begin{Bmatrix} 0 \\ 0.04 \\ 0.08 \\ 0.36 \\ 0.32 \\ 1 \\ 0.72 \\ 1.96 \\ 1.28 \\ 3.24 \\ 1 \end{Bmatrix} \tag{11-56}$$

In the same manner, we obtain

$$f_{11} = \frac{1}{EI^2}\int_0^l \frac{(l-x)^2\,dx}{I}$$

$$= \frac{0.1l}{3E}\left[\frac{(1)(1)^2}{I_0} + \frac{(4)(0.9)^2}{I_1} + \frac{(2)(0.8)^2}{I_2} + \frac{(4)(0.7)^2}{I_3} + \frac{(2)(0.6)^2}{I_4} + \frac{(4)(0.5)^2}{I_5}\right.$$

$$\left. + \frac{(2)(0.4)^2}{I_6} + \frac{(4)(0.3)^2}{I_7} + \frac{(2)(0.2)^2}{I_8} + \frac{(4)(0.1)^2}{I_9} + \frac{(1)(0)^2}{I_{10}}\right] \tag{11-57}$$

$$= \frac{0.1l}{3E}[I_0^{-1}\ \ I_1^{-1}\ \ I_2^{-1}\ \ I_3^{-1}\ \ I_4^{-1}\ \ I_5^{-1}\ \ I_6^{-1}\ \ I_7^{-1}\ \ I_8^{-1}\ \ I_9^{-1}\ \ I_{10}^{-1}]$$

$$\begin{Bmatrix} 1 \\ 3.24 \\ 1.28 \\ 1.96 \\ 0.72 \\ 1 \\ 0.32 \\ 0.36 \\ 0.08 \\ 0.04 \\ 0 \end{Bmatrix}$$

$$f_{12} = f_{21} = -\frac{1}{EI^2}\int_0^l \frac{(l-x)(x)\,dx}{I}$$

$$= -\frac{0.1l}{3E}\left[\frac{(1)(1)(0)}{I_0} + \frac{(4)(0.9)(0.1)}{I_1} + \frac{(2)(0.8)(0.2)}{I_2} + \frac{(4)(0.7)(0.3)}{I_3}\right.$$

$$+ \frac{(2)(0.6)(0.4)}{I_4} + \frac{(4)(0.5)^2}{I_5} + \frac{(2)(0.4)(0.6)}{I_6} + \frac{(4)(0.3)(0.7)}{I_7}$$

$$\left.+ \frac{(2)(0.2)(0.8)}{I_8} + \frac{(4)(0.1)(0.9)}{I_9} + \frac{(1)(0)(1)}{I_{10}}\right] \qquad (11\text{-}58)$$

$$= \frac{0.1l}{3E}[I_0^{-1}\quad I_1^{-1}\quad I_2^{-1}\quad I_3^{-1}\quad I_4^{-1}\quad I_5^{-1}\quad I_6^{-1}\quad I_7^{-1}\quad I_8^{-1}\quad I_9^{-1}\quad I_{10}^{-1}]$$

$$\cdot \begin{Bmatrix} 0 \\ -0.36 \\ -0.32 \\ -0.84 \\ -0.48 \\ -1 \\ -0.48 \\ -0.84 \\ -0.32 \\ -0.36 \\ 0 \end{Bmatrix}$$

If we let $c_{11} = f_{11}$, $c_{12} = f_{12}$, $c_{21} = f_{22}$, and $c_{22} = f_{21}$, we have

$$\begin{bmatrix} c_{11} & c_{12} \\ c_{21} & c_{22} \end{bmatrix}$$

$$= \frac{0.1l}{3E}\begin{bmatrix} I_0^{-1} & I_1^{-1} & I_2^{-1} & I_3^{-1} & I_4^{-1} & I_5^{-1} & I_6^{-1} & I_7^{-1} & I_8^{-1} & I_9^{-1} & I_{10}^{-1} \\ I_{10}^{-1} & I_9^{-1} & I_8^{-1} & I_7^{-1} & I_6^{-1} & I_5^{-1} & I_4^{-1} & I_3^{-1} & I_2^{-1} & I_1^{-1} & I_0^{-1} \end{bmatrix}$$

$$\cdot \begin{Bmatrix} 1 & 0 \\ 3.24 & -0.36 \\ 1.28 & -0.32 \\ 1.96 & -0.84 \\ 0.72 & -0.48 \\ 1 & -1 \\ 0.32 & -0.48 \\ 0.36 & -0.84 \\ 0.08 & -0.32 \\ 0.04 & -0.36 \\ 0 & 0 \end{Bmatrix} \qquad (11\text{-}59)$$

or simply

$$[C] = [A][B]$$

For a prismatic member, the I value for each segment is constant. Therefore,

$$\begin{bmatrix} c_{11} & c_{12} \\ c_{21} & c_{22} \end{bmatrix} = \frac{l}{6EI} \begin{bmatrix} 2 & -1 \\ 2 & -1 \end{bmatrix} \tag{11-60}$$

That is, the rotational flexibility matrix becomes

$$\begin{bmatrix} f_{11} & f_{12} \\ f_{21} & f_{22} \end{bmatrix} = \frac{l}{6EI} \begin{bmatrix} 2 & -1 \\ -1 & 2 \end{bmatrix}$$

as expected.

With element rotational flexibility coefficients determined, the element rotational stiffness coefficients as well as other constants can readily be derived.

PROBLEMS

11-1. Figure 11-13 shows a beam of varying cross section with both ends fixed and subjected to the bending action of a concentrated load P. Find the integral expressions for the fixed-end moments.

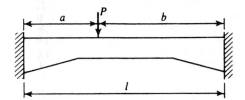

Figure 11-13

11-2. For the beam element of constant width shown in Fig. 11-14, find, by the numerical method, the rotational flexibility matrix. Assume that the element is simply supported.

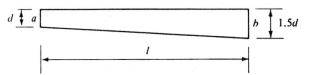

Figure 11-14

11-3. Use the result of Problem 11-2 to find the rotational stiffness matrix for the same element.

11-4. For the haunched member of constant width shown in Fig. 11-15, find the stiffnesses and carry-over factors by the numerical method or from the table of frame constants if available.

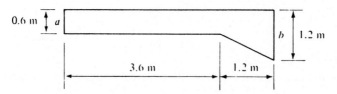

Figure 11-15

11-5. Using the result of Problem 11-4, give the rotational stiffness and flexibility matrices for the element shown in Fig. 11-15.

11-6. Use the numerical method or table of frame constants to determine the fixed-end moments for the haunched beam of Fig. 11-15 due to a uniform load of 5 kN/m over the entire span.

11-7. Use the relevant calculation from Problems 11-4 to 11-6 to find, by moment distribution, the end moments for the beam in Fig. 11-16 subjected to a uniform load of 5 kN/m over the entire span.

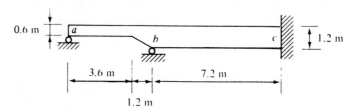

Figure 11-16

11-8. Repeat Problem 11-7 by the method of slope-deflection.

11-9. Repeat Problem 11-7 by the matrix force method.

11-10. Repeat Problem 11-7 by the matrix displacement method.

Appendix A

Gaussian Elimination and Matrix Inversion

A-1 GENERAL

Gaussian elimination is a well-known method for solving simultaneous linear algebraic equations and inverting a nonsingular matrix. The fundamental basis of the method is the fact that any linear combination of equations does not affect the solution. Thus, a sequence of linear combination of equations is executed until each equation contains only one unknown. In matrix presentation, this means the off-diagonal terms of the matrix A in the following matrix equation are all turned into zeros.

$$AQ = R \tag{A-1}$$

In the following sections a simple example is used to illustrate this process and the process for matrix inversion.

A-2 EQUATION SOLVING

Let us use the equilibrium equations of the truss problem in Fig. 3-20 as an example (Sec. 3-5). The matrix A, unknown force vector Q, and given applied load vector R are copied from Sec. 3-5 as follows:

$$
\begin{bmatrix}
-1.00 & 0 & 0 & 0 & -0.60 & 0 \\
0 & -1.00 & 0 & 0 & -0.80 & 0 \\
0 & 0 & -1.00 & 0 & 0 & 0.80 \\
0 & 0 & 0 & -1.00 & 0 & 0.60 \\
0 & 0 & 0 & 0 & 0.60 & -0.80 \\
0 & 0 & 0 & 0 & 0.80 & 0.60
\end{bmatrix}
\begin{Bmatrix}
H_A \\ V_A \\ H_B \\ V_B \\ S_a \\ S_b
\end{Bmatrix}
=
\begin{Bmatrix}
0 \\ 0 \\ 0 \\ 0 \\ 0 \\ -10.00
\end{Bmatrix}
\tag{A-2}
$$

The procedure is to reduce the off-diagonal terms to zero column by column starting from the first column. Since the first four columns are already in the desired form, after we normalize the diagonal terms to unity, we start at the fifth column. We will use the fifth row to reduce the nonzero off-diagonal elements in the fifth column to zero. After dividing the fifth row by 0.60 and using the resulting equation to eliminate the off-diagonal terms in the fifth column, we obtain

$$
\begin{bmatrix}
1.00 & 0 & 0 & 0 & 0 & 0.80 \\
0 & 1.00 & 0 & 0 & 0 & 1.06 \\
0 & 0 & 1.00 & 0 & 0 & -0.80 \\
0 & 0 & 0 & 1.00 & 0 & 0.60 \\
0 & 0 & 0 & 0 & 1.00 & -1.33 \\
0 & 0 & 0 & 0 & 0 & 1.66
\end{bmatrix}
\begin{Bmatrix}
H_A \\ V_A \\ H_B \\ V_B \\ S_a \\ S_b
\end{Bmatrix}
=
\begin{Bmatrix}
0 \\ 0 \\ 0 \\ 0 \\ 0 \\ -10.00
\end{Bmatrix}
\qquad \text{(A-3)}
$$

Note that the load vector is not changed. This is because the fifth element in the loading vector is zero to begin with. In general, each elimination step will change the load vector. Finally, after the sixth column is taken care of, the matrix A is completely diagonalized and the solution appears at the right-hand side (RHS), replacing the original applied load vector.

$$
\begin{bmatrix}
1.00 & 0 & 0 & 0 & 0 & 0 \\
0 & 1.00 & 0 & 0 & 0 & 0 \\
0 & 0 & 1.00 & 0 & 0 & 0 \\
0 & 0 & 0 & 1.00 & 0 & 0 \\
0 & 0 & 0 & 0 & 1.00 & 0 \\
0 & 0 & 0 & 0 & 0 & 1.00
\end{bmatrix}
\begin{Bmatrix}
H_A \\ V_A \\ H_B \\ V_B \\ S_a \\ S_b
\end{Bmatrix}
=
\begin{Bmatrix}
4.80 \\ 6.40 \\ -4.80 \\ 3.60 \\ -8.00 \\ -6.00
\end{Bmatrix}
\qquad \text{(A-4)}
$$

It is clear that if more than one loading condition is to be considered, we may simply lump one loading vector after another at the RHS and perform Gaussian elimination simultaneously. The solution vectors will replace the loading vectors.

A-3 MATRIX INVERSION

The inverse of the matrix A is defined in the following equation.

$$
A(A^{-1}) = I
\qquad \text{(A-5)}
$$

where I is the identity matrix containing unity on the diagonal and zeros elsewhere. Thus, we may obtain A^{-1} by simply solving Eq. A-5 using Gaussian elimination, treating the identity matrix as a set of loading vectors. The identity matrix will be turned into the inverse of A. We start by setting the RHS of Eq. A-5 to be the identity matrix

$$\begin{bmatrix} 1.00 & 0 & 0 & 0 & 0 & 0 \\ 0 & 1.00 & 0 & 0 & 0 & 0 \\ 0 & 0 & 1.00 & 0 & 0 & 0 \\ 0 & 0 & 0 & 1.00 & 0 & 0 \\ 0 & 0 & 0 & 0 & 1.00 & 0 \\ 0 & 0 & 0 & 0 & 0 & 1.00 \end{bmatrix}$$

After the treatment on column 5 of A in Eq. A-2, the identity matrix becomes

$$\begin{bmatrix} -1.00 & 0 & 0 & 0 & -1.00 & 0 \\ 0 & -1.00 & 0 & 0 & -1.33 & 0 \\ 0 & 0 & -1.00 & 0 & 0.00 & 0 \\ 0 & 0 & 0 & -1.00 & 0.00 & 0 \\ 0 & 0 & 0 & 0 & 1.66 & 0 \\ 0 & 0 & 0 & 0 & -1.33 & 1.00 \end{bmatrix}$$

After the treatment of column 6 of A in Eq. A-3, the above matrix is turned into the inverse of A.

$$\begin{bmatrix} -1.00 & 0 & 0 & 0 & -0.36 & -0.48 \\ 0 & -1.00 & 0 & 0 & -0.48 & -0.64 \\ 0 & 0 & -1.00 & 0 & -0.64 & 0.48 \\ 0 & 0 & 0 & -1.00 & 0.48 & -0.36 \\ 0 & 0 & 0 & 0 & 0.60 & 0.80 \\ 0 & 0 & 0 & 0 & -0.80 & 0.60 \end{bmatrix}$$

A-4 PIVOTING

In a more general application of the Gaussian elimination method, the diagonal term to be used may be too small or even zero. To avoid roundoff error or even numerical overflow, it is necessary to interchange rows so that the current operating diagonal has a maximum absolute value among all elements in the same column. This procedure is called *pivoting*. The computer programs used in the beam analysis and in the force method of truss and frame analysis described in Appendix B contain pivoting. For matrix displacement methods, the symmetrical stiffness matrix always has the largest stiffness coefficients on the diagonals; thus, no pivoting is needed.

Appendix B

Computer Programs

B-1 GENERAL

The computer programs included with this book are designed for the following purposes: (1) to check solutions obtained by conventional means, (2) to obtain solutions not easily obtainable otherwise, and (3) to demonstrate structural behavior by displaying internal member forces and structural deflection. The last purpose is especially important because a user may easily develop a *feel* for structural behavior through the repeated application of the programs to a class of similar problems. Such a feel is an integral part of an engineer's intuition and judgment in structural design.

The following five programs are given in the diskette:

beam: beam analysis
trussf: truss analysis by the matrix force method
trussd: truss analysis by the matrix displacement method
framef: frame/truss analysis by the matrix force method
framed: frame/truss analysis by the matrix displacement method

Since this book is limited to the analysis of two-dimensional structures, so are these programs. The programs are written for IBM-compatible personal computers (PCs). The inputs to these programs are interactive and self-evident, but users are encouraged to read the following descriptions first to familiarize themselves with the general methodology, program limitations, and parameter definitions. More detailed instructions and examples, as well as the required graphics capabilities of computers, are included with the programs in the diskette.

B-2 PROGRAM beam

The *beam* program is for the analysis of beams with or without intermediate supports and internal hinge connections between the two ends (Fig. B-1). At the intermediate supports, whose reactions are designated by r_i, $i = 1, 2, \ldots, R$, in Fig. B-1, zero or

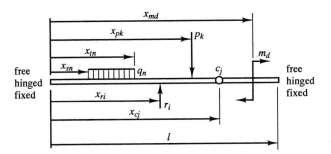

Figure B-1

nonzero vertical displacements are to be specified as input to the program. Alternatively, a spring with known spring flexibility may be specified. The locations of the intermediate supports and those of the internal connections $c_j, j = 1, 2, \ldots, C$, are defined by the distance from the left end. The beam may be composed of one or more segments. Each segment is of uniform cross section and constant EI.

Concentrated forces, p_k, $k = 1, 2, \ldots, P$, uniformly distributed forces of intensity q_n, $n = 1, 2, \ldots, Q$, each covering the region from x_{sn} (s for starting point) to x_{tn} (t for terminating point), and concentrated couples m_d may be applied.

The boundary conditions at the two ends are specified as free, hinged or fixed as shown in Fig. B-1. For a hinged end, zero or nonzero vertical displacement (w_0) may be specified. For a fixed end, zero or nonzero vertical displacement (w_0) and angular rotation (θ_0) may be specified. Alternatively, a hinged end may contain a spring with a known flexibility and a fixed end may contain a vertical spring and a rotational spring with known flexibility constants.

B-3 PROGRAM trussf

The *trussf* program is based on the matrix force method for truss analysis. As described in Section 4-8, it is convenient to treat the supports to a truss [Fig. B-2(a)] as reaction members [Fig. B-2(b)].

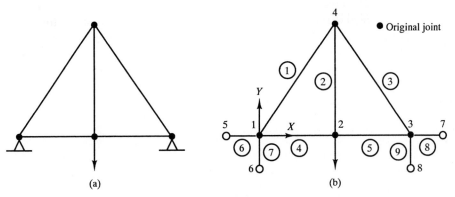

Figure B-2

The original joints are numbered consecutively first, followed by the additional joints of the reaction members, as shown in Fig. B-2(b). Similarly, the original members are numbered first, followed by the reaction members. This numbering scheme is convenient for programming considerations. A coordinate system, X–Y, is defined so that the X and Y coordinates of each joint may be input to the computer. The location and orientation of each member, including the reaction members, are defined by giving the joint numbers of the starting node (S node) and the terminating node (T node) of each member. The cross-sectional flexibility property of each member is defined by $1/EA$. Note that for reaction members representing rigid supports the cross-sectional flexibility should be set to zero. In case of spring supports, an appropriate value should be found for $1/EA$ so that the member flexibility L/EA is equal to the given spring flexibility. Note also that the length of a reaction member is relevant only in the case of a spring support.

For statically indeterminate trusses, the program will calculate the degree of indeterminacy and request the identification of redundant members. Users should be careful in selecting the redundant members so that the resulting primary truss is stable.

B-4 PROGRAM trussd

The *trussd* program is based on the matrix displacement method. The basic unknowns are the joint displacements (or degrees of freedom), two at each joint. The joints of the truss shown in Fig. B-3(a) may be numbered as shown in Fig. B-3(b). The members are also numbered.

The joint displacements are internally numbered in the program joint by joint with the X displacement first. The choice of the origin and orientation of the X–Y coordinate system is for the convenience of defining the joint locations and the support displacement constraints. In this program, specified displacements, zero or nonzero in value, must be in the X and/or Y direction. Thus, trusses with inclined roller supports may not be analyzed with this program. Such problems may be analyzed using the *framef* or *framed* programs, which treat trusses as special cases.

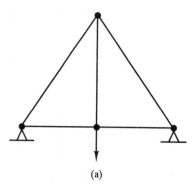

(a)   (b)

Figure B-3

The displacement unknowns are solved from joint equilibrium equations (two per joint), which are numbered internally in the program in the same way as the joint displacements. Thus, the single applied load shown in Fig. B-3 is associated with the fourth equation because it is applied in the second (Y) direction of the second joint, and its value should be negative.

The member cross-sectional stiffness is defined by the value of EA, which is input to the computer according to the member number. The length of each member is calculated internally in the program from joint coordinates and member geometry definition. The latter is achieved by inputting the joint numbers of the starting node (S node) and the terminating node (T node) of each member.

B-5 PROGRAM framef

The *framef* program may be used to analyze frames, trusses, and composite structures. It is based on the matrix force method. Each member (or element) is classified as one of four types, as shown in Fig. B-4. The circles at the end of the members represent hinges. Thus, a type 0 member is actually a truss member.

Each member is numbered consecutively, and its starting node (S node) and terminating node (T node) are associated with two structural (or global) nodes numbered for the entire structure. For the program input, the data for each member consist of (1) member type, (2) global node number of the S node, (3) global node number of the T node, (4) cross-sectional bending flexibility $1/EI$, and (5) cross-sectional extension flexibility $1/EA$.

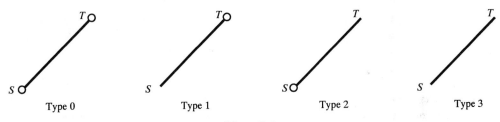

Type 0   Type 1   Type 2   Type 3

Figure B-4

At each structural node, three equilibrium equations may be assembled. They are ordered as (1) force equilibrium in the X direction, (2) force equilibrium in the Y direction, and (3) moment equilibrium in the clockwise direction, as shown in Fig. B-5(a). Note that the origin of the structural (or global) X–Y coordinate system may be placed at any convenient location. The X and Y coordinates of the structural nodes are then defined accordingly.

For this program, the applied loads are limited to nodal forces and moments only; that is, they must be applied at the nodes. They are identified by the node number and the sequence of equilibrium equations at the node. For example, an applied force of 10 kN in the Y direction at a node 5 is identified as being applied at node 5 in the second equation with a value of positive 10. Only nonzero forces need to be input.

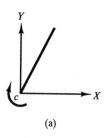

(a)

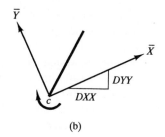

(b)

Figure B-5

The treatment of supports is quite general. A local coordinate system $\bar{X}-\bar{Y}$ is defined at each support [Fig. B-5(b)]. At each support, a fictitious "reaction element" is defined, which supplies three flexible springs: one force spring in the $\bar{X}$ direction, one force spring in the $\bar{Y}$ direction, and one rotational spring. The positive direction of the reaction force or moment is shown in Fig. B-5(b). As input to the program, we need to supply (1) the node number of the support, (2) the DXX and DYY values shown in Fig. B-5(b) to define the local $\bar{X}-\bar{Y}$ coordinate system, and (3) the three flexibility constants of the three springs. For rigid supports, the flexibility constants are zero. A greater-than-10^6 value of flexibility is taken to mean there is effectively no support in that particular direction.

For statically indeterminate structures, the program will give the statical indeterminacy and request user input on the selection of redundant member forces. Each member has three member forces recognized in the program in the following order: (1) member-end moment at the S node, (2) member-end moment at the T node, and (3) axial force. The member-end moments are positive in the clockwise direction, and the axial force is positive if in tension. Users should be careful not to select for redundant a member force that does not exist (i.e., the moment at a hinged end of a member). The program will reject such a selection and stop execution. More important, the selection of redundant forces must result in a stable primary structure.

B-6 PROGRAM framed

The *framed* program is a displacement-based program for the analysis of frames, trusses, and composite structures. Its members (or elements) are classified as one of four types (Fig. B-4). Each of the two nodes of a member is associated with a structural node, which is numbered sequentially for the entire structure and whose location is defined in a structural (or global) $X-Y$ coordinate system [Fig. B-5(a)]. For each member, the input data consist of (1) member type, (2) global node number of the S node, (3) global node number of the T node, (4) cross-sectional bending rigidity EI, and (5) cross-sectional extension rigidity EA.

Three displacement constraints may be specified at a support: translation in the local $\bar{X}$ direction, translation in the local $\bar{Y}$ direction, and rotation in the clockwise direction [Fig. B-5(b)]. The orientation of the local system is defined by DXX and DYY as shown in Fig. B-5(b). A specified zero value for a constrained displacement means the support is rigid for that displacement. A number greater than 10^6 is recognized to mean that there is no constraint for that displacement and the program will adjust for this. Any number in between represents a prescribed displacement amount.

The loads applied at nodal points are recognized by the program by the specified node number, the degree of freedom number (1 for force in the X direction, 2 for force in the Y direction, and 3 for moment in the direction of clockwise rotation), and the load value. Loads applied between nodes are limited to (1) concentrated loads transverse to a member, (2) uniformly distributed loads transverse to a member, and (3) concentrated couples, as shown in Fig. B-6.

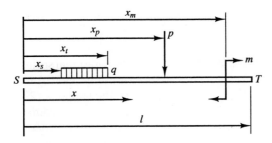

Figure B-6

Appendix C

Energy Theorems

<hr />

C-1 GENERAL

Energy theorems are used frequently in structural mechanics for the derivation of governing equations or the formulation of alternative ways of solving a problem. We have already used one of the energy theorems, the method of virtual force, for the solution of structural deflection, the derivation of which is given in Sec. 4-5. The method of virtual force is a force-based energy theorem. So is the Castigliano's second theorem detailed in Sec. 4-6. A force-based energy theorem is characterized by having an energy expression defined in terms of force quantities. The force-based energy theorems are mostly used in the realm of the force method of structural analysis.

It is expected, then, that there are displacement-based energy theorems that are used mostly in the realm of the displacement method of structural analysis. Three of the displacement-based energy theorems, the method of virtual displacement, the principle of minimum total potential energy, and Castigliano's first theorem, have been stated without derivation in Sec. 9-2. The derivation, in a limited way, is provided in this appendix for a one-dimensional elastic deformable body.

C-2 METHOD OF VIRTUAL DISPLACEMENT

The derivation of the method of virtual displacement, also called the principle of virtual displacement or principle of virtual work, for a three-dimensional deformable body requires knowledge of general elasticity and the mathematics on volume and surface integrals. If we limit ourselves to one-dimensional problems, only elementary mechanics and calculus are needed.

Consider an elastic bar loaded axially by a distributed force q, which may vary along the bar, and a concentrated force P at the right end, as shown in Fig. C-1(a). For simplicity, let us assume that EA is constant along the bar. The free-body

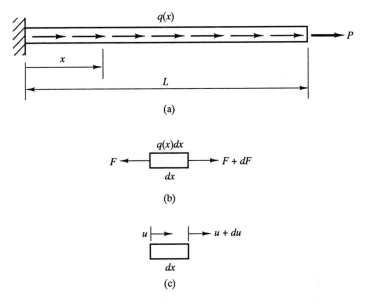

Figure C-1

diagram of a representative segment is shown in Fig. C-1(b). The condition of equilibrium in the axial direction results in the following differential equation in terms of the internal force F, which is designated positive if in tension.

$$q + \frac{dF}{dx} = 0 \qquad \text{(C-1)}$$

The internal force is the product of internal stress, σ, and cross-sectional area, A, and the stress is related to strain through $\sigma = E\epsilon$. Thus,

$$F = EA\epsilon \qquad \text{(C-2)}$$

The axial strain is by definition the relative elongation, and, by virtue of Fig. C-1(c), may be expressed in terms of the axial displacement $u(x)$ as

$$\epsilon = \frac{du}{dx} \qquad \text{(C-3)}$$

Combining Eqs. C-2 and C-3, we obtain

$$F = EA\frac{du}{dx} \qquad \text{(C-4)}$$

Substituting the expression in Eq. C-4 into Eq. C-1 results in the following differential equation in terms of the axial displacement u:

$$q + EA\frac{d^2u}{dx^2} = 0 \qquad \text{(C-5)}$$

The boundary conditions are

$$u = 0, \qquad \text{at } x = 0 \tag{C-6}$$

$$EA\frac{du}{dx} = P, \qquad \text{at } x = L \tag{C-7}$$

Equations C-5 through C-7 define the problem completely. The solution to the problem may be obtained by finding the displacement that satisfies the differential equation, Eq. C-5, and the boundary conditions, Eqs. C-6 and C-7.

We will now show that Eqs. C-5 through C-7 are equivalent to the statement of the method of virtual displacement: the virtual work of external forces is equal to the virtual work of internal forces (virtual strain energy). Multiplying both sides of Eq. C-5 by an assumed virtual displacement, δu, which satisfies the geometric boundary condition (Eq. C-6),

$$\delta u = 0, \qquad \text{at } x = 0 \tag{C-8}$$

and integrating over the length of the bar, we obtain

$$\int_0^L q(\delta u)\,dx + \int_0^L (\delta u)EA\frac{d^2u}{dx^2}\,dx = 0 \tag{C-9}$$

The second term is now recast into the following form through the use of integration by parts:

$$\int_0^L (\delta u)EA\frac{d^2u}{dx^2}\,dx = \left[(\delta u)EA\frac{du}{dx}\right]_{x=L} - \left[(\delta u)EA\frac{du}{dx}\right]_{x=0}$$

$$- \int_0^L EA\frac{du}{dx}\frac{d(\delta u)}{dx}\,dx \tag{C-10}$$

The first term on the right-hand side is equal to $P(\delta u)_{x=L}$ according to Eq. C-7, and the second term is zero because of Eq. C-8. Upon replacing the second term in Eq. C-9 by the expression in Eq. C-10, the following result is obtained:

$$P(\delta u)_{x=L} + \int_0^L q(\delta u)\,dx = \int_0^L EA\frac{du}{dx}\frac{d(\delta u)}{dx}\,dx \tag{C-11}$$

The left-hand side is the work done by the external forces P and q. The expression $[d(\delta u)]/dx$ in the right-hand side represents the virtual strain, and the expression $EA(du/dx)$ is the internal stress. Thus, the right-hand side is the work done by the internal stress, or the virtual strain energy. Equation C-11 may be stated as

$$\delta W = \delta U \tag{C-12}$$

This is the principle of virtual displacement for deformable bodies. We may reiterate that for a deformable body in equilibrium the virtual work done by the external forces and the virtual work done by the internal forces are equal. The only requirement on the assumed virtual displacement is that it satisfy the geometric boundary condition such as Eq. C-6 and be differentiable so that the virtual strain energy in Eq. C-11 can be computed.

C-3 PRINCIPLE OF MINIMUM TOTAL POTENTIAL ENERGY

The total potential energy contains two parts. The first part is the strain energy. For the linear elastic bar under consideration [Fig. C-1(a)], the strain energy expressed in terms of displacement is

$$U = \int_0^L \frac{1}{2} \sigma \epsilon (A\, dx)$$

$$= \int_0^L \frac{1}{2} \epsilon^2 (EA\, dx) \qquad \text{(C-13)}$$

$$= \int_0^L \frac{1}{2} EA \left(\frac{du}{dx}\right)^2 dx$$

The second part is the force potential, which is defined as the negative of the product of the force and the corresponding displacement. This force potential is only defined for the conservative forces, work by which does not depend on the path of force. Denoting the force potential by V, we obtain the following expression for the problem shown in Fig. C-1(a):

$$V = -P(u)_{x=L} - \int_0^L qu\, dx \qquad \text{(C-14)}$$

The total potential energy, Π_p, is then

$$\Pi_p = U + V = \int_0^L \frac{1}{2} EA \left(\frac{du}{dx}\right)^2 dx - P(u)_{x=L} - \int_0^L qu\, dx \qquad \text{(C-15)}$$

We will now show that if the displacement function $u(x)$ makes the total potential Π_p a minimum, the resulting equation is identical to that of the principle of virtual displacement.

Note that Π_p is a function of the function $u(x)$. If Π_p is a minimum for a displacement function $u(x)$, then any infinitesimal increment in Π_p caused by an infinitesimal increment in $u(x)$ should be zero. We use the symbol Δ to denote infinitesimal quantities. Thus,

$$\Delta \Pi_p = \Pi_p(u + \Delta u) - \Pi_p(u) = 0 \qquad \text{(C-16)}$$

where

$$\Pi_p(u + \Delta u) = \int_0^L \frac{1}{2} EA \left(\frac{du}{dx} + \frac{d \Delta u}{dx} \right)^2 dx$$

$$- P(u + \Delta u)_{x=L} - \int_0^L q(u + \Delta u) \, dx \qquad \text{(C-17)}$$

By substituting Eqs. C-17 and C-15 into Eq. C-16 and neglecting the higher-order infinitesimal terms, we arrive at

$$\int_0^L EA \left(\frac{du}{dx} \right) \left(\frac{d \Delta u}{dx} \right) dx - P(\Delta u)_{x=L} - \int_0^L q(\Delta u) \, dx = 0 \qquad \text{(C-18)}$$

Comparing Eq. C-18 to Eq. C-11, we conclude that they are equivalent because the virtual displacement δu, being arbitrary, may be made to equal the infinitesimal displacement Δu.

It is noted that the foregoing derivation is equally valid for maximum or stationary total potential energy. Within the scope of this book, however, the equilibrium of a deformable body always corresponds to the minimum of the total potential energy.

C-4 CASTIGLIANO'S FIRST THEOREM

We may use the principle of minimum total potential energy to derive Castigliano's first theorem. The derivation is general and there is no need to limit ourselves to the one-dimensional problem of Fig. C-1(a). Let us consider an elastic body loaded at n points by n concentrated forces $P_i, i = 1, 2, \ldots, n$. The strain energy of the body may be expressed in terms of the displacements, u_i, in the direction of the applied forces at these n points. The total potential energy is

$$\Pi_p = U(u_i, i = 1, 2, \ldots, n) - \sum P_i u_i \qquad \text{(C-19)}$$

According to the principle of minimum total potential energy, equilibrium is achieved if Π_p is a minimum with respect to the displacements $u_i, i = 1, 2, \ldots, n$. This means the partial differentiation of Π_p with respect to $u_i, i = 1, 2, \ldots, n$, is zero.

$$\frac{\partial U}{\partial u_i} = P_i, \qquad i = 1, 2, \ldots, n \qquad \text{(C-20)}$$

which is Castigliano's first theorem.

Appendix D
Useful Tables

D-1 GENERAL

Two tables are included for easy reference. The first is trivial but helpful in carrying out deformation computation involving the integration of the product of two linear functions. The second table is for the fixed-end moment of a beam under various loadings. Most of the entries in these tables may be derived through the principle of superposition from the more general cases in the same table but are included for fast reference.

D-2 INTEGRATION TABLE

TABLE D-1 SIMPLE FORMULA FOR $I = \int_0^L f_a f_b \, dx$

$$I = \left[\frac{a_1 b_2 + a_2 b_1}{2} + \frac{(a_2 - a_1)(b_2 - b_1)}{3} \right] L$$

$$I = \frac{abL}{2}$$

$$I = \frac{abL}{3}$$

$$I = \frac{abL}{6}$$

D-3 FIXED-END MOMENT

TABLE D-2   FIXED-END MOMENT

M_{ab}^F	Loading Case	M_{ba}^F
$-\dfrac{Pl}{8}$		$+\dfrac{Pl}{8}$
$-\alpha\beta^2\,Pl$		$+\alpha^2\beta Pl$
$-\alpha(1-\alpha)Pl$		$+\alpha(1-\alpha)Pl$
$-\dfrac{\alpha^2\,wl^2}{12}(6-8\alpha+3\alpha^2)$		$\dfrac{\alpha^3\,wl^2}{12}(4-3\alpha)$
$-\dfrac{11wl^2}{192}$		$+\dfrac{5wl^2}{192}$
$-\dfrac{wl^2}{12}$		$+\dfrac{wl^2}{12}$
$-\dfrac{wl^2}{20}$		$+\dfrac{wl^2}{30}$
$-\dfrac{5wl^2}{96}$		$+\dfrac{5wl^2}{96}$
$-\dfrac{wl^2}{15}$		$+\dfrac{wl^2}{15}$
$+M\beta(2\alpha-\beta)$		$+M\alpha(2\beta-\alpha)$

Note: Member-end moments are positive if acting clockwise and negative if acting counterclockwise.

Answers to Selected Problems

CHAPTER 2

2-1. (a) Stable and indeterminate to the fifth degree
    (b) Unstable
    (c) Stable and determinate
    (d) Stable and indeterminate to the second degree

2-2. (b) Stable and indeterminate to the third degree
    (c) Unstable externally
    (d) Unstable internally

2-3. (b) Stable and indeterminate to the fifth degree
    (e) Stable and indeterminate to the fourth degree
    (f) Unstable externally
    (g) Stable and indeterminate to the 102nd degree

CHAPTER 3

3-3. (b) $S_{ab} = S_{bc} = +14.6$ kN $S_{aB} = +9.1$ kN
        $S_{Bb} = +17.5$ kN $S_{Bc} = -18.6$ kN
    (d) $S_{bc} = S_{cd} = S_{de} = S_{ef} = 0$
        $S_{ag} = -S_{bg} = 26.9$ kN
    (e) $S_{ab} = S_{bc} = 0$ $S_{aB} = -11.3$ kN
        $S_{Bc} = -14.4$ kN

3-4. (a) $S_a = -32$ kips $V_b = +12$ kips $S_c = +24$ kips
    (b) $H_a = +18.75$ kips $V_b = -15$ kips $S_c = -6.25$ kips
    (c) $V_a = +11.6$ kips $H_b = +166.7$ kips $S_c = -20$ kips
    (d) $S_a = +20$ kips $V_b = +100$ kips $V_c = -45$ kips
    (e) $S_a = -50$ kips

3-5. $V_a = -20$ kips $V_b = +10$ kips $V_c = -20$ kips $S_d = 0$

3-6. $S_{AB} = S_{BC} = S_{CD} = S_{BF} = S_{CF} = 0$ $S_{AD} = +15.4$ kips
    $S_{AE} = +11.2$ kips $S_{DE} = -13.6$ kips $S_{EF} = -10$ kips

3-7. $S_{ad} = +7.85$ kN

3-8. (d) $M_c = +108$ ft-kips
    (e) $M_b = +31.25$ ft-kips
    (f) $M_b = -144$ ft-kips

3-9. (a) $M_c = +33.3$ kN $\cdot$ m

   (b) $M_b = +71.4$ kN $\cdot$ m

CHAPTER 4

4-1. $\Delta_c = 5wl^4/384EI$ (down) $\theta_a = wl^3/24EI$ (clockwise)

4-2. $\Delta_p = 0.0147Pl^3/EI$ (down) Δ (at midspan) $= 0.0236Pl^3/EI$ (down)

4-3. $\Delta = 0.54$ in. (down) $\theta = 0.006$ rad (counterclockwise)

4-4. $\theta_c = 0.003$ rad (counterclockwise, at the left side)

   $\theta_c = 0.0017$ rad (clockwise, at the right side)

   $\Delta_b = 0.267$ cm (down)

4-5. $\Delta_h = 0.43$ in. (right) $\Delta_v = 0.696$ in. (down)

   $\Delta_r = 0.006$ rad (counterclockwise)

4-6. $\theta_b = 0.0023$ rad (clockwise) $\Delta_b = 0.375$ cm (down)

   $\theta_c = 0.0038$ rad (clockwise) $\Delta_c = 1.35$ cm (down)

4-7. $\Delta_1 = 1.15$ cm (right) $\Delta_2 = 0.59$ cm (down)

   $\Delta_3 = 0.0039$ rad (counterclockwise)

4-8. $\Delta_1 = 0.1$ cm (right) $\Delta_2 = 0.12$ cm (down)

4-9. (a) $\Delta_B = 0.00746$ ft (down)

   (b) $\Delta_C = 0.00278$ ft (right)

   (c) $\Delta_{bC} = 0.0002$ ft (toward each other)

   (d) $\theta = 0.000434$ rad (clockwise)

CHAPTER 5

5-1. (a) $R_b = 50$ kips (up)

   (b) $M_b = -100$ ft-kips

5-2. $R_b = 10$ kips (up)

5-3. $R_b = 7.28$ kips (up)

5-4. $R_e = 0.916$ kN (up)

5-5. (b) $M_a = wm(m^4 + 4mn^3 + 3n^4)/8(m^3 + n^3)$

5-6. $H_c = 15.24$ kN (left)

5-7. $H_a = 1.25$ kips (right) $V_a = 5$ kips (up) $M_a = 4.16$ ft-kips (clockwise)

5-9. $S_{bc} = 5.25$ kN

5-10. (a) $S_{bC} = -0.75$ kip

   (b) $H_d = 30$ kips (left)

   (c) $S_{bC} = -5.4$ kips $H_d = 31.1$ kips (left)

5-11. $S_{Bc} = S_{bC} = +8.75$ kips

5-16. $S_{ac} = +4.25$ kips $M_a = -3.25$ ft-kips

   The effect of axial force in the beam is neglected.

5-17. 21.75 kips, 17.4 kips, and 13.05 kips

CHAPTER 6

6-1. $r_p = 5PL^3/6EI$ (down)

6-3. r (under 10 kips load) $= 0.01608$ ft (down)

   r (under 20 kips load) $= 0.00548$ ft (down)

6-4. $r_1 = (4L^3R_1 - L^2R_2)/6EI$ $\qquad$ $r_2 = (-L^2R_1 + 2LR_2)/6EI$

6-5. Deflection $= 5PL^3/6EI$ $\qquad$ Slope $= PL^2/EI$

6-6. $\begin{Bmatrix} Q^a \\ Q^b \\ Q^c \end{Bmatrix} = \begin{Bmatrix} 3.36 \\ 8.28 \\ 2.76 \end{Bmatrix}$ kips $\qquad$ $\begin{Bmatrix} r_1 \\ r_2 \end{Bmatrix} = \dfrac{1}{AE} \begin{Bmatrix} 83.2 \\ -15.72 \end{Bmatrix}$ ft

6-7. $S = -6.725$ kN

6-9. $Q_i^a = -44$ kN · m $\qquad$ $Q_j^a = -10$ kN · m $\qquad$ $Q_j^c = -23.3$ kN · m

6-10. slope $= \dfrac{1}{96EI}\left(wL^3 + \dfrac{51wL^3}{1 + L^3/3EIf_s}\right)$

$\qquad$ deflection $= \dfrac{17wL^4}{48EI(1 + L^3/3EIf_s)}$

6-11. $Q_i^a = 0.080LR_1 - 0.236LR_2 - 0.274R_3$
$Q_j^d = -0.094LR_1 - 0.392LR_2 + 0.030R_3$

CHAPTER 7

7-1. $M_{ab} = -22$ ft-kips $\qquad$ $M_{ba} = -M_{bc} = 28$ ft-kips $\qquad$ $M_{cb} = 31$ ft-kips

7-2. $M_{ab} = -23.55$ ft-kips $\qquad$ $M_{ba} = 16.89$ ft-kips
$M_{bd} = -8.89$ ft-kips $\qquad$ $M_{db} = -4.44$ ft-kips

7-3. $M_{ab} = -22.1$ ft-kips $\qquad$ $M_{ba} = -M_{bc} = 68.3$ ft-kips
$M_{cb} = 20$ ft-kips

7-5. End moment $= 14.6$ ft-kips

7-6. Moments at interior supports are 36.5 ft-kips and 27.3 ft-kips.

7-7. $M_{ba} = -M_{bc} = 11.4$ ft-kips $\qquad$ $M_{cb} = -M_{cd} = 0.6$ ft-kip

7-8. $R_c = 57.27$ kN

7-9. $K_{ab} = 3EIl_1^2/(l_1^3 + l_2^3)$

7-10. $M_{ba} = -M_{bc} = \dfrac{57wl^2}{816} - \dfrac{288EI\Delta}{17l^2}$

7-11. (a) $M_{bc} = 61.2$ kN · m
$\qquad$ (b) $M_{bc} = -33.8$ kN · m
$\qquad$ (c) $M_{bc} = -26.7$ kN · m

7-12. (a) $M_{ac} = 18.5$ kN · m $\qquad$ $M_{bc} = 14.2$ kN · m
$\qquad$ (b) $M_{ac} = -M_{bc} = -24$ kN · m

CHAPTER 8

8-1. $M_{ab} = -22$ ft-kips $\qquad$ $M_{ba} = -M_{bc} = 28$ ft-kips $\qquad$ $M_{cb} = 31$ ft-kips

8-2. $M_{ab} = -23.55$ ft-kips $\qquad$ $M_{ba} = 16.89$ ft-kips
$M_{bd} = -8.89$ ft-kips $\qquad$ $M_{db} = -4.44$ ft-kips

8-3. $M_{ab} = -22.1$ ft-kips $\qquad$ $M_{ba} = -M_{bc} = 68.3$ ft-kips
$M_{cb} = 20$ ft-kips

8-5. $M_{ab} = -44.8$ ft-kips $\qquad$ $M_{ba} = -M_{bc} = -34.4$ ft-kips

8-6. $M_{ab} = 4.9$ ft-kips $\qquad$ $M_{ba} = -M_{bc} = -0.9$ ft-kip
$M_{cb} = -M_{cd} = 2.24$ ft-kips $\qquad$ $M_{dc} = -1.76$ ft-kips

8-7. Spring force = 3.58 kN (compression)

8-8. R_c = 7.35 kN M_{ab} = −3.26 kN · m

8-9. M_{ab} = −0.63 kN · m M_{ba} = −M_{bc} = 2.49 kN · m
   M_{dc} = −1.87 kN · m

8-10. R_d = 3.03 kN

8-11. **(a)** M_{ab} = −14.9 ft-kips M_{ba} = −M_{bc} = 14.9 ft-kips
   M_{cb} = 39.4 ft-kips M_{ce} = −29.8 ft-kips
   (b) M_{ab} = −120.8 ft-kips M_{ba} = −M_{bc} = −112.6 ft-kips
   M_{cb} = −M_{cd} = 104 ft-kips M_{dc} = −103.6 ft-kips
   (c) M_{ab} = 8.52 ft-kips $M_{ba.}$ = −M_{bc} = 9.58 ft-kips
   M_{cb} = −M_{cd} = −1 ft-kip M_{dc} = 26.74 ft-kips
   (d) M_{ba} = M_{ef} = −150 ft-kips M_{be} = M_{eb} = 156.25 ft-kips
   M_{bc} = M_{ed} = −6.25 ft-kips M_{cb} = M_{de} = −43.75 ft-kips
   M_{cd} = M_{dc} = 43.75 ft-kips
   (e) M_{ab} = −118.1 ft-kips M_{ba} = −M_{bc} = −82 ft-kips
   M_{cb} = −M_{cd} = 11.5 ft-kips M_{dc} = −M_{de} = 25.8 ft-kips
   M_{ed} = −74.1 ft-kips

8-12. **(a)** M_{ac} = 18.5 kN · m M_{bc} = 14.2 kN · m
   (b) M_{ac} = −M_{bc} = −24 kN · m

8-15. M_{ab} = −41.25 kN · m M_{ba} = −M_{bc} = −6.75 kN · m

CHAPTER 9

9-8. Fixed-end moments are −8.4 kN · m (left) and 12.9 kN · m (right). The rotation at the interior support is 1.8/EI rad.

9-9. Q^a = 1.25P Q^b = −3.75P
   Displacements of the top joint are 5.208Pl/AE (right) and 1.953Pl/AE (down).

9-10. Q^a = −1.25P Q^b = −1.06P Q^c = −0.25P
   Displacements of the joint are 0.25Pl/AE (right) and 1.25Pl/AE (down).

9-11. End moments of the beam are 0.13wl^2 and 0.54wl^2. End moments of the column are 0.46wl^2 and 0.22wl^2.

9-12. Fixed-end moment is 0.08wl^2 including the axial effect.

CHAPTER 10

10-1. V = 49.33 kips M = 458.67 ft-kips

10-4. R_A = 45 kN R_C = 175 kN R_E = 30 kN
   V_B = −55 kN M_B = −90 kN · m M_C = − 180 kN · m

10-8. **(a)** R = 22.78 kips
   (b) V = 14.44 kips M = 216.67 ft-kips

10-9. V_a = +29.68 kips (maximum tension)
   V_a = −4.4 kips (maximum compression)
   S_b = +52.75 kips

10-10. R_C = 156 kN M_D = 111 kN · m

10-11. M_E = 135 kN · m R_E = 55 kN

10-12. The influence ordinates are 1.3, 1, 0.704, 0.432, 0.208, 0.056, 0.

10-13. The influence ordinates are 0, 1.39, 1.78, 1.50, 0.89, 0.28, 0.

10-14. (a) The influence ordinates are 1, 0.578, 0.222, 0, −0.05, 0.

(b) The influence ordinates are 0, −0.532, −0.668, 0, −0.30, 0.

(c) The influence ordinates are 0, −0.422, 0.222, 0, −0.05, 0.

CHAPTER 11

11-2. $f = \dfrac{l}{3EI}\begin{bmatrix} 0.73 & -0.27 \\ -0.27 & 0.40 \end{bmatrix}$

11-3. $k = \dfrac{EI}{l}\begin{bmatrix} 5.48 & 3.70 \\ 3.70 & 10 \end{bmatrix}$

11-4. $C_{ab} = 0.743 \qquad C_{ba} = 0.462$

$S_{ab} = 4.62EI_a/l \qquad S_{ba} = 7.43EI_a/l$

11-5. $k = \dfrac{EI_a}{l}\begin{bmatrix} 4.62 & 3.43 \\ 3.43 & 7.43 \end{bmatrix}$

$f = \dfrac{l}{EI_a}\begin{bmatrix} 0.329 & -0.152 \\ -0.152 & 0.205 \end{bmatrix}$

11-6. $M_{ab}^F = -7.5 \text{ kN} \cdot \text{m} \qquad M_{ba}^F = 14.4 \text{ kN} \cdot \text{m}$

11-7. $M_{ba} = 20.3 \text{ kN} \cdot \text{m} \qquad M_{cb} = 22.3 \text{ kN} \cdot \text{m}$

11-8. The moment at the fixed support = 12.85 kN · m

Index

Beam/Truss/Frame Analysis Modules
Elementary Theory of Structures, 4/e
Yuan-Yu Hsieh / S.T. Mau

YOU SHOULD CAREFULLY READ THE FOLLOWING TERMS AND CONDITIONS BEFORE OPENING THIS DISKETTE PACKAGE. OPENING THIS DISKETTE PACKAGE INDICATES YOUR ACCEPTANCE OF THESE TERMS AND CONDITIONS, IF YOU DO NOT AGREE WITH THEM, YOU SHOULD PROMPTLY RETURN THE PACKAGE UNOPENED, AND YOUR MONEY WILL BE REFUNDED.

IT IS A VIOLATION OF COPYRIGHT LAW TO MAKE A COPY OF THE ACCOMPANYING SOFTWARE EXCEPT FOR BACKUP PURPOSES TO GUARD AGAINST ACCIDENTAL LOSS OR DAMAGE.

Prentice-Hall, Inc. provides this program and licenses its use. You assume responsibility for the selection of the program to achieve your intended results, and for the installation, use, and results obtained from the program. This license extends only to use of the program in the United States or countries in which the program is marketed by duly authorized distributors.

LICENSE

You may:
a. use the program;
b. modify the program and/or merge it into another program in support of your use of the program.

LIMITED WARRANTY

THE PROGRAM IS PROVIDED "AS IS" WITHOUT WARRANTY OF ANY KIND, EITHER EXPRESSED OR IMPLIED, INCLUDING, BUT NOT LIMITED TO, THE IMPLIED WARRANTIES OF MERCHANTABILITY AND FITNESS FOR A PARTICULAR PURPOSE. THE ENTIRE RISK TO THE QUALITY AND PERFORMANCE OF THE PROGRAM IS WITH YOU. SHOULD THE PROGRAM PROVE DEFECTIVE, YOU (AND NOT PRENTICE-HALL, INC. OR ANY AUTHORIZED DISTRIBUTOR) ASSUME THE ENTIRE COST OF ALL NECESSARY SERVICING, REPAIR, OR CORRECTION.

SOME STATES DO NOT ALLOW THE EXCLUSION OF IMPLIED WARRANTIES, SO THE ABOVE EXCLUSION MAY NOT APPLY TO YOU. THIS WARRANTY GIVES YOU SPECIFIC LEGAL RIGHTS AND YOU MAY ALSO HAVE OTHER RIGHTS THAT VARY FROM STATE TO STATE.

Prentice-Hall, Inc. does not warrant that the functions contained in the program will meet your requirements or that the operation of the program will be uninterrupted or error free.

However, Prentice-Hall, Inc., warrants the diskette(s) on which the program is furnished to be free from defects in materials and workmanship under normal use for a period of ninety (90) days from the date of delivery to you as evidenced by a copy of your receipt.

LIMITATIONS OF REMEDIES

Prentice-Hall's entire liability and your exclusive remedy shall be:

1. the replacement of any diskette not meeting Prentice-Hall's "Limited Warranty" and that is returned to Prentice-Hall with a copy of your purchase order, or
2. if Prentice-Hall is unable to deliver a replacement diskette or cassette that is free of defects in materials or workmanship, you may terminate this Agreement by returning the program, and your money will be refunded.

IN NO EVENT WILL PRENTICE-HALL BE LIABLE TO YOU FOR ANY DAMAGES, INCLUDING ANY LOST PROFITS, LOST SAVINGS OR OTHER INCIDENTAL OR CONSEQUENTIAL DAMAGES ARISING OUT OF THE USE OR INABILITY TO USE SUCH PROGRAM EVEN IF PRENTICE-HALL OR AN AUTHORIZED DISTRIBUTOR HAS BEEN ADVISED OF THE POSSIBILITY OF SUCH DAMAGES, OR FOR ANY CLAIM BY AN OTHER PARTY.

SOME STATES DO NOT ALLOW THE LIMITATION OR EXCLUSION OF LIABILITY FOR INCIDENTAL OR CONSEQUENTIAL DAMAGES, SO THE ABOVE LIMITATION OR EXCLUSION MAY NOT APPLY TO YOU.

GENERAL

You may not sublicense, assign, or transfer the license or the program except as expressly provided in this Agreement. Any attempt otherwise to sublicense, assign, or transfer any of the rights, duties, or obligations hereunder is void.

This Agreement will be governed by the laws of the State of New York.

Should you have any question concerning this Agreement, you may contact Prentice-Hall, Inc., by writing to:

Prentice Hall
College Division
Englewood Cliffs, N.J. 07632

YOU ACKNOWLEDGE THAT YOU HAVE READ THIS AGREEMENT, UNDERSTAND IT, AND AGREE TO BE BOUND BY ITS TERMS AND CONDITIONS. YOU FURTHER AGREE THAT IT IS THE COMPLETE AND EXCLUSIVE STATEMENT OF THE AGREEMENT BETWEEN US THAT SUPERCEDES ANY PROPOSAL OR PRIOR AGREEMENT, ORAL OR WRITTEN, AND ANY OTHER COMMUNICATIONS BETWEEN US RELATING TO THE SUBJECT MATTER OF THIS AGREEMENT.

ISBN 0-13-301201-8